Harvard Economic Studies, Volume 138

Plate 1.

Écu d'or au porc-épic of Louis XII, coined in Paris (actual size 2.65 cm., enlarged photograph by the Bibliothèque Nationale, Paris).

The International Economy
and Monetary Movements
in France, 1493–1725

Frank C. Spooner

Harvard University Press   Cambridge, Massachusetts   1972

Contents

Graphs

Maps

Atlases

Tables

Illustrations

The International Economy
and Monetary Movements
in France, 1493–1725

Introduction

I originally intended to study the spread of Protestantism in sixteenth-century France, in the context as far as possible of the prevailing social conditions. With this in mind, I began to probe the archives of the city and the department in Rouen, a city prominent in the Civil Wars. In the early stages of these conflicts, it was a hotbed of revolt and then later, turning away from dissidence, emerged as one of the "eyes of the League." Such changes seemed to offer special advantages in surveying the society and its problems. Toward the end of 1949, however, as a result of finding a significant series of documents on coinage in the Archives Nationales in Paris, I decided to alter my line of research.[1] From studying beliefs and social structures in the sixteenth century, I turned my attention to the economic activity of the period. It was tempting enough to assemble and study this extensive series of data, readily available but largely unpublished. They allowed estimates to be made of the total coinage of the mints in France during the sixteenth and seventeenth centuries, as the operations of fifteen of these were recorded continuously in detail.

In their own particular way, the data reveal much about the aggregate and sectoral activity of the economy and set the general problem in the geography of foreign exchanges. The shifts in structure, which can be observed, appear to have been valid not only for France but also beyond its frontiers.

At the outset, naturally enough, there were difficulties. Because there were many studies in the history of precious metals, I felt that it was unnecessary and even presumptuous to reopen a well-aired subject.[2] After all, most of the salient features had been established. Earl J. Hamilton had gone to the heart of the matter, taking advantage of the dominant position of Spain in the sixteenth, seventeenth, and eighteenth centuries, to settle many of the questions relating to bullion and currency, or at least to outline the essentials of the

---

[1] The most valuable are the archives of the Cour des Monnaies, kept in the series Z¹B.

[2] In the extensive bibliography on the subject particular attention should be given to: Adolf Soetbeer, *Edelmetall-Produktion und Werthverhältniss zwischen Gold und Silber seit der Entdeckung Amerikas bis zur Gegenwart* (Gotha, 1879); Wilhelm Lexis, "Beiträge zur Statistik der Edelmetalle," *Jahrbücher für Nationalökonomie und Statistik*, XXXIV (1879); Werner Sombart, *Der moderne Kapitalismus* (2 vols., Munich, 1922); Clarence Haring, "American Gold and Silver Production in the First Half of the Sixteenth Century," *Quarterly Journal of Economics*, XXIX (1915); Earl J. Hamilton, *American Treasure and the Price Revolution in Spain, 1501–1650* (Cambridge, Mass., 1934); John U. Nef, "Silver Production in Central Europe, 1450–1618," *Journal of Political Economy*, XLIX (1914); Fernand Braudel, "Monnaies et civilisations: de l'or du Soudan à l'argent d'Amérique. Un drame méditerranéen," *Annales: Économies, Sociétés, Civilisations* [hereafter cited as *Annales*], I (1946), and *La Méditerranée et le monde méditerranéen à l'époque de Philippe II* (Paris, 1949; 2d ed., 2 vols., Paris, 1966).

problem.[3] Even so, an inquiry into coinage in France seemed to have possibilities worth further exploration.

At first, also, there seemed to be little reason to assume that the economy of France enjoyed the same experience as its great imperial neighbor, Spain. What was valid on one side of the Pyrenees did not necessarily prevail on the other, and the adage was just as relevant to the economies of the sixteenth century. Indeed, France found a place in the international economy of this period different from that of Spain; its performance had another complexion.

In keeping with this, I felt that the basic problems could be reviewed to take account of new information on the period and of the improved methods now available to economic history — in brief, of the changes in attitude. Historical inquiry inevitably implies renewed investigation; even in recent decades our views on the role of money have undergone considerable modification.

Until now there has been a tendency to consider the history of precious metals as a unilateral, continuous process. This has favored a "sectoral" approach and, as a result, has produced divergent conclusions. It is difficult to maintain that, for the period under study, there are specifically autonomous histories of the different forms of currency, that there are separate histories of gold, of silver, of copper, and, beyond these, of credit. Their functions were, in reality, closely linked one with another, within the aggregate stock of "money." The evidence seems to indicate that the expansion of economic activity in the sixteenth century produced an increasing demand for circulating medium and that this had to be satisfied. At first, a partial solution was found in the growing supplies of gold and silver. Later, for want of better, the different monetary systems turned to copper, with the supplementary aid of credit. These expedients, however, rarely met the full requirements of a growing volume of transactions. And under such circumstances, adjustments were necessary, above all in the price set on gold and silver, in general devaluations which altered the intrinsic values of the coins. A series of dislocations inevitably took place. A concerted movement such as this between the different metals must be considered in conjunction with the often unsuccessful efforts to expand credit facilities. These considerations create a problem which must be seen in its full dimensions.

In theory at least, the internal development of the monetary system was simple enough. If gold came in relative abundance (as happened in the first half of the sixteenth century), then silver, by reason of increased effective demand, began to appreciate in terms of gold; in turn, the relative price of copper also tended to rise. On the other hand, if silver abounded (as was the case in the second half of the sixteenth century), then the other two metals, gold and copper, became relatively scarce, copper following the general rise

[3] Hamilton, *American Treasure,* and *War* and *Prices in Spain, 1615–1800* (Cambridge, Mass., 1947).

of commodity prices expressed in terms of silver. These conditions in some measure explain the lucrative speculation in copper, the least valuable of the monetary metals; the history of Germany provides ample evidence of this in the particular case of the copper mines of Mansfeld in Saxony.[4]

Every increase in the volume of transactions raised the demand for precious metals, whether gold, silver, or copper. The flow of bullion, which could both stimulate and sustain economic activity, was always to a greater or lesser degree reinforced by credit. Here is another basic reality which must not be overlooked. The inelasticities in the supply of money — its "rarity" as contemporaries remarked — may seem at variance with the histories of the opulent mines of Mexico and Peru. In the long term there was a process of catching up. In the fluctuations of a shorter term, however, the pressure on available specie was pushed to the limit. In this lay the success and failure of credit. In some instances, the shortcomings of the credit system were the key to the situation. To grasp this aspect of the problem it is hardly necessary to enlarge on the theories of the "income expenditure period" or the "payment interval"[5] to establish that, in the international economy of the sixteenth and seventeenth centuries, the arrival and distribution of bullion — actual or even anticipated — was enough to set in motion a series of credit transactions under the virtual monopoly of the great fairs and commercial centers. And yet the opposite conditions could also occur: an unexpected delay in the arrivals of bullion could precipitate a sudden spate of bankruptcies, and the repercussions were felt through Europe and even beyond.[6]

All this is well known. It may be added, however, that a certain volume of credit was created by the interaction of the two metals. This was apparent in the short-term operation of the import and export "points" of the two metals; it emerged in the secular trend, during the change from a phase of gold to one of silver and again in the break in prices when secular inflation in bullion terms gave way to deflation. Credit found its role in coordinating the irregular shipments of bullion and in adjusting the inconsistencies in production and circulation of the different metals. Credit tended to act as a compensator in these shifts in level.

In this scheme, the plurality but basic unity of the history of metallic money

[4] Walter Möllenberg, *Die Eroberung des Weltmarkts durch das mansfeldische Kupfer* (Gotha, 1911).

[5] James W. Angell, "The Components of the Circular Velocity of Money," *Quarterly Journal of Economics,* LI (Feb. 1937); and Howard S. Ellis, "Some Fundamentals in the Theory of Velocity," *ibid.,* LII (May 1938).

[6] This uncertainty could explain the cry of joy from Charles V on receiving the news of the arrival of the treasure fleet. Calendar of State Papers [hereafter cited as C.S.P.], Spanish, letter from Brussels of Nov. 28, 1553, the Emperor to Simon Renard. On November 30, 1554, Thomas Gresham wrote from Seville of the difficulties and bankruptcies of the local merchants and that nothing could be done "to help this matter considering the ships be not come from the Indies which be looked for daily." Public Record Office, State Papers [hereafter cited as P.R.O., S.P.], 69/5.

has been sufficiently emphasized. This paradox in itself justifies a reconsideration of problems already debated, as well as an examination of the new data available.

A second aspect to consider, in contrast, is the discontinuity of these monetary processes, both in time and space. As the years passed, gold, silver, copper, and credit each in turn emerged to the forefront of economic affairs. By all appearances, these created phases, each of different character, in a sequence of something more than mere accidents or random occurrences. In reality, by and large, an adjustment took place between a high value, full-bodied money — gold and silver — and a fiduciary or quasi-fiduciary money — copper and credit. If the stocks of full-bodied currencies failed to grow in proportion to the volume of transactions, or, what amounted roughly to the same thing, the velocity of circulation fell, or if money was immobilized in hoards or was exported beyond the confines of the economy, then copper and credit were together called upon to play a supporting role.

This is of considerable significance: on the one hand, the simultaneous use of billon[7] or copper money; and, on the other hand, of instruments of credit in the form of debts, loans, bills of exchange, government bonds and *rentes,* and assignments of all sorts. This double monetary stock provided some compensation for insufficiencies in the "superior" metallic inflation. There was a process of substitution. At a time when gold and silver were indispensable, the extended use of copper, billon, and credit on any scale was inevitably an indicator of deeper movements. In this matter, as indeed in every movement of economic growth, the ruptures, adjustments, discontinuities, and even structural changes were significant.[8] These breaks, it must be added, interrupted economic activity more profoundly than has often been supposed. And the question of the interrelationship between a rise in the circulation of copper and a rise in the volume of credit must find its place in this field of inquiry.

With the discontinuity in time, mentioned above, there was also discontinuity or rather disparity in space. A brief comment on this will suffice. It is difficult to consider France in the sixteenth century (of immense size in terms of the speed of transport and contemporary techniques) as forming a homogeneous economic unit. The combination of monetary movements, when taken in their widest context, implied something more than a group of areas. The case of France raised the question of a series of economic zones. In effect, if France is considered as a unity, there is every likelihood of confusing the issues. Along the great routes across the country, which created a basic

---

[7] The French term billon has been adopted as the most convenient way of describing fractional currency made of an alloy of copper and silver, in which the proportion of copper predominates.

[8] See in this context the excellent discussion of the problems of sociological method and the need to qualify too much emphasis on social continuity: Fernand Braudel, "Georges Gurvitch ou la discontinuité du Social," *Annales,* VIII (1953).

framework and opened the way to modern France, everything traveled quickly and tended to converge. Alongside these vital lines of communication, however, life moved more slowly and the factors of retardation were more impressive. Over large areas given to quasi-subsistence farming, everything changed with measured step; there were zones of inertia which tended to resist the penetration and diffusion of a monetary economy. The study of Henri Hauser makes it apparent that Burgundy and Champagne in the late sixteenth century were flooded with billon from trade with neighboring Germany, at a time when the heavy silver coins, the *reals* from Spain, were pouring into the west of the country.[9] This experience of the eastern regions serves to illustrate one patch in the mosaic of France.

Another encounter with the mosaic comes when we consider the turning point in the "long" inflation of prices in the sixteenth century. For René Baehrel, taking his stand on the evidence of Provence, the downturn came in the 1590s.[10] Pierre Goubert, from the mandate of his studies of the region of Beauvais, dates the turning point between 1630 and 1650.[11] Yet it requires little extension of the limits of the problem to realize that such disparities belong to the larger history of Europe. Recent studies in the history of prices have shown that the inflation of the sixteenth century tended to culminate in the south of Europe in the 1590s, but in the northwest it continued to the second quarter, even to the middle, of the seventeenth century.[12] By all appearances, the differences in response in France to these huge movements serve to emphasize very real variations in structures, and they accentuate the mosaic of its regions.

In the context of this variegated France, there is, however, a central, unifying feature to be kept in mind: the role of the state. Any consideration of the monetary sector confronts an immense problem, still largely unanswered. How effective and widespread was "the market"? What part of "the national product" of France was sold beyond the village, was subject to pricing, and required the use of money? In the present state of our knowledge a precise answer to such questions is unlikely to be forthcoming. Some information can be obtained indirectly of government activity in France. If not wholly "absolute," as the historians of institutions so often remind us, the monarchy exercised an unrelenting drive to govern and to tax; the Venetian ambassador observed that Francis I governed his subjects "harshly." This leitmotiv emerged more clearly than ever under the great ministers of the seventeenth century — Richelieu, Mazarin, Colbert — all of whose policies were at vari-

[9] Henri Hauser, "La question des prix et des monnaies en Bourgogne," *Annales de Bourgogne,* IV (1932).

[10] René Baehrel. *Une croissance: La Basse-Provence rurale (fin du XVIᵉ siècle — 1789)* (Paris, 1961).

[11] Pierre Goubert, *Beauvais et le Beauvaisis de 1600 à 1730* (Paris, 1960).

[12] Fernand Braudel and Frank Spooner, "Prices in Europe from 1450 to 1750," in *The Cambridge Economic History of Europe,* IV, ed. E. E. Rich and C. H. Wilson (Cambridge, Eng., 1967).

ous times directly related to tax levies. The flow of tax remittances, perfectly or imperfectly achieved, implied also the sale of cash crops, the use of money in commercial transactions, and inevitably the development of monetary institutions. All this imparts a certain cohesion and relevance to a monetary history, which focuses on the abrupt changes and reversals from the sixteenth to the early eighteenth century.

In this study, I have tried to emphasize the spatial transformations of the mosaic of France. The difficulties, however, are huge and too imperfectly documented to allow me at present to arrive at all the necessary conclusions, but an outline of the problem is an advance in the right direction.

This study grew out of a thesis presented at Cambridge in 1953 and published in Paris in 1956 through the kindness of many friends and colleagues in the École Pratique des Hautes Études. The 1956 edition covered the period 1493–1680. This seemed at the time a satisfactory termination "date," and there were reasons for the choice. In the first place, as explained later, I considered that the revival of world gold production in about the 1680s, and especially during the early eighteenth century, opened a new phase in the monetary structure of Europe, comparable, *mutatis mutandis,* with the experience two centuries earlier. France could hardly have failed to respond to this change. In the closing decades of the seventeenth century, the proportion of gold in the coinage of France rose from about a third to three-quarters of the value issued.[13]

Secondly, in the seventeenth century, the documentation altered. On the one hand, it probably represented a complex change in royal administration. The *arrêt* of the Conseil d'État, particularly from the time of Richelieu, became a preferred instrument of royal monetary policy, and, as a result, the archives of the Cour des Monnaies provide progressively fewer of those spontaneous reports which earlier had outlined the contours of monetary affairs. On the other hand, a split occurred in the monetary administration. By the royal edict of June 1704 a second Cour des Monnaies was established in Lyons, to which the mints of Aix, Bayonne, Grenoble, Lyons, Montpellier, Pau, Riom, and Toulouse were assigned. The explanation of this can no doubt be found partly in the monetary "war" with Britain, explained later,[14] and partly in the fiscal pressures to sell offices. The net result, however, was that the reports of these particular mints went to the Cour in Lyons and not Paris. The survival of the États des Délivrances has suffered, leaving gaps to be fillled in the series.

These matters rightly find their place in the monetary history of the *ancien régime*. I have attempted where possible to take note of them in the present English edition, which extends the study to 1725. These years mark a prelude

[13] See Chap. 3, Section 4.
[14] *Ibid.*

to the great monetary reform and consolidation of France (1726) and offer a number of conclusions of special interest.

The publication of this English edition in the Harvard Economic Studies has required some editing in order to take account of the supplementary material to 1725. The series of data used in Chapters 2 and 4 have been extended. Chapters 5 and 6 now include the results of statistical tests by computer and a section dealing with estimates of the aggregate stock of money, income, and public revenue. The graphs have been revised and often redrawn.[15]

In compensation for these extensions, I have shortened the narrative in Chapters 3 and 4. The appendixes in turn have been severely reduced: from the statistical data of coinage, only the totals and percentages of gold coined in France have been retained. The footnotes have also been abbreviated, largely through the omission of quotations from the original documents (the full texts may be obtained from the first edition).[16]

My debts to many friends have been expressed already in the introduction to the first edition, and these are now gratefully renewed. On completing this English edition, I owe special thanks to Alexander Gerschenkron for his unfailing warmth and generosity. Thomas Schelling and Max Hall have devoted their valuable time to its publication. Miss Patricia Fox has shown unremitting care and kindness in guiding the manuscript through the press. My researches and studies have been materially advanced by St. Antony's College and All Souls College, Oxford; by the Economic Growth Center of Yale University, where I was invited as Irving Fisher Professor of Economics; and by the University of Durham. The book is inscribed to Fernand Braudel, through whose many tokens of kindness I came to know France.

[15] The graphs established in terms of value have been drawn on semilogarithmic scale.
[16] In this edition, quotations have in the majority of instances been given in modern spelling and in English.

Chapter 1

Precious Metals in the International Economy during the Sixteenth and Seventeenth Centuries

In the sixteenth and seventeenth centuries, France was an open country, open in many respects to the world as then known. It would be an exaggeration to assume that France did not enjoy its own distinctive culture, but the relatively more advanced and progressive sectors of its economy found their identity only within the much wider context of the world beyond its frontiers. Historians tend to interpret the basic characteristics of France in terms of their own individual preoccupations.[1] Some have focused on the strategy of large-scale trade and its dynamic effects, others on the agricultural sectors and the rural economy, with its largely subsistence farming reliant on its own devices and so to be studied from within. Such points of departure are generally valid. Yet, when one considers movements of bullion, it becomes apparent that the economy of France functioned, and indeed was obliged to function, to a rhythm which in the final analysis was not its own. France did not have the requisite monetary structures to endow it with protection, detachment, and so, implicitly, the necessary degrees of freedom.

These international "boundary limits" — in the mathematical sense — create a framework of problems and sectors more or less integrated to the activity of France, and yet they form part of the world economy. They require some additional explanation at the beginning of this book, which gives special attention to the history of precious metals in France. Such a framework is necessary, for it prepares the way for an analysis using quantitative data and graphs. At the beginning, however, the general background offers an opportunity to review the overall problem and to suggest some explanations and theories. Following this, the more special case studies require detailed attention.

The general features of movements of bullion are fairly easy to establish. At the end of the fifteenth century, roughly from about 1450, gold was the dominant metal; the first half of the sixteenth century also belongs to this

[1] In the extensive literature on the subject, see in particular, Marc Bloch, *Les caractères originaux de l'histoire rurale française* (Oslo, 1931, and Paris, 1952); Gaston Roupnel, *La ville et la campagne au XVIIe siècle* (Paris, 1922), and *Histoire de la campagne française* (Paris, 1932); Paul Raveau, *L'agriculture et les classes paysannes: La transformation de la propriété dans le Haut-Poitou au XVIe siècle* (Paris, 1926); Paul Masson, *Histoire des établissements et du commerce française dans l'Afrique Barbaresque 1560–1793* (Paris, 1903); Raymond Collier and Joseph Billioud, *Histoire du commerce de Marseille, III, 1480–1599* (Paris, 1951); Michel Mollat, *Le commerce maritime normand à la fin du Moyen Âge* (Paris, 1952); Philippe Wolff, *Commerces et marchands de Toulouse* (Paris, 1953). Since the publication of the first edition of this book, there have been many important additions to this bibliography, among which special attention should be given to René Baehrel, *Une croissance: La Basse-Provence rurale (fin du XVIe siècle — 1789)* (Paris, 1961); Pierre Goubert, *Beauvais et le Beauvaisis de 1600 à 1730* (Paris, 1960); Emmanuel Le Roy Ladurie, *Les payans de Languedoc* (2 vols., Paris, 1966).

period.[2] The revolutionary phase of silver followed during the second half of the sixteenth and the early seventeenth centuries. Then for more than half a century, silver, copper, gold, and credit joined in the task of satisfying the requirements of economic activity. The unstable and disturbed monetary conditions of the seventeenth century probably derived from a general retardation in the international economy. The first indications of an escape from these difficulties probably began to appear in the critical years of the 1680s, largely as a result of the alluvial gold from the interior of Brazil. Gold reappeared, at first on a small scale and then in relatively large quantities.[3] In general, from the late seventeenth century, there was something of a renewal of the monetary phases of the previous two centuries. The earlier sequence, however, emphasized the failure, or relative shortage, of gold in more than a century after 1550, during a sort of "Hundred Years' War" when silver and copper were the standard currencies struggling with a gold problem. This was slowly overcome, but only much later, in the nineteenth century, with the substantial aid from banking development.

1. From Gold to Silver: From the Fifteenth to the Middle of the Sixteenth Century

From about 1450 to 1550 the essential features of the bullion structures of the international economy changed little. Gold was relatively abundant. In effect, the trading system was inherited from the past, with its immemorial customs. Gold, which gave these years their special character, no doubt arrived in small quantities, parcel by parcel, but even though small, the flow of gold was nevertheless sufficient to stimulate the monetary exchanges of the time.

It came, in the first place, from the African interior — the Sudan, Ethiopia, and West Africa — and found its way to the old trading centers of the Mediterranean, either by customary routes via Egypt and North Africa, or, after about 1460, perhaps even a little earlier,[4] to the Atlantic and Gulf of Guinea, where for many years the Portuguese traders exercised a virtual monopoly. Some small amounts of gold also came from the meager resources

[2] Wolff, *Commerces et marchands,* p. 344, n. 170.

[3] The mint in Bayonne reported important issues of gold coin in 1668 and following years. This was one of the first signs of a change in trend apparent in the last two decades of the seventeenth century.

[4] Edgar Prestage, *Portuguese Pioneers* (London, 1933), p. 196; gold arrived in Porto Pisaro in 1466 worth 40,000 ducats; in 1448, gold from Tibico worth 10,000 ducats; Armand Grunzweig, "Le Fonds du Consulat de la Mer aux Archives de l'État à Florence," in *Bulletin de l'Institut Historique Belge de Rome,* X (1930), pp. 99–100. About 1475 on the coast of Mina, the presence was noted of Spaniards and Flemings, among them factors of merchants of Bruges. See Jean Denucé, *L'Afrique du XVIᵉ siècle et le commerce anversois* (Antwerp, 1937), p. 35, and "Privilèges commerciaux accordés par le roi de Portugal aux Flamands et aux Allemands (XVᵉ et XVIᵉ siècles)," *Archivo historico português, VII* (1909), cited by Fernand Braudel, *La Méditerranée et le monde méditerranéen à l'époque de Philippe II* (Paris, 1949), p. 372.

of Europe. Finally it arrived from the New World, and in more substantial quantities, in the wake of Spanish conquests and plunder. If there was an upsurge of gold, or rather a renewal of the gold cycle, it came during the first decade of the sixteenth century, about the years 1506–1507 when the Genoese merchants, as André Sayous has observed, set up the powerful organization at Seville, the first to develop the American continent.[5]

All this is well known, although it has not been usual to emphasize the relative abundance of gold. In due course this stimulated the monetary and economic movements of the last third of the fifteenth century, and, with a few rare exceptions, does not seem to have faltered in its leading role during much of the ensuing half century. I use the term "abundance" intentionally, without wishing in any way to deny that now and again there were monetary difficulties and even economic retardation. A clear distinction, however, must at once be drawn between movements of bullion and economic activity in general. There were certainly monetary difficulties — perhaps even gold shortages — on the eve of the Italian wars, which were the outcome of a period of economic dislocations and the protracted depression at the turn of the century.[6] In general, it is possible to speak of abundant gold and point to the evidence of the relative shortage of silver which accompanied it. This was the second great structural feature of the period 1450–1550. The demand for silver in these years accounted for the rush to expand mining production in Germany, which otherwise would be difficult to explain. German silver was dear silver, priced up by the relative abundance of gold. With these basic features established, it becomes a simple task to outline the trade in bullion during this period.

During the closing decades of the fifteenth century the focal point of the trade in gold moved from the Mediterranean to Lisbon, an Atlantic port linked to Africa; then, from the beginning of the sixteenth century, to Seville, an Atlantic city looking to America. The Portuguese age in effect turned out to be only a passing episode.

Portugal was strategically placed between the Mediterranean and the Atlantic and commandeered gold during the second half of the fifteenth century. Victories were dearly won in Africa, but were soon relentlessly turned to advantage. In 1415 the Portuguese took over Ceuta, a famous trading

---

[5] André Sayous, "Les débuts du commerce de l'Espagne avec l'Amérique (1503–1518)," *Revue historique,* CLXXIV (1934), p. 201 (1506, perhaps even 1512).

[6] Henri Hauser and Auguste Renaudet, *Les débuts de l'âge moderne* (Paris, 1956), p. 53; Albert Girard, "La guerre monétaire (XIVᵉ–XVᵉ siècles)," *Annales d'histoire sociale,* II (1940), particularly pp. 217–218. Although he does not give a precise definition of the monetary structures and secular movements, Girard presents considerable evidence on the monetary difficulties from 1320 to the middle of the fifteenth century, an interminable period, as he describes it, of "monetary confusion." At the end of this, a new phase of gold, and "epoch of calm," emerged as a result of a series of striking events: in September, 1447, in Genoa, all payments had to be made in gold; reforms and stabilization followed in 1470 in England, in 1472 in Venice, and in 1475 in France.

center used by the Genoese, at least since 1441[7]. They pushed further south-ward, along the Atlantic coast of the Sahara, to make contact with the caravans from the interior. By this route, the gold trade was tapped at the expense of the more or less established flow from the Sudan to the Mediterranean.[8] In 1443 the island of Arguin was discovered off the west coast and became the first Portuguese outpost in the trade in gold dust from Timbuktu.[9] With regard to these changes, some importance can be attached to the coinage in Lisbon in 1457 of the first gold *cruzado*.[10] Then, in 1470, the Portuguese

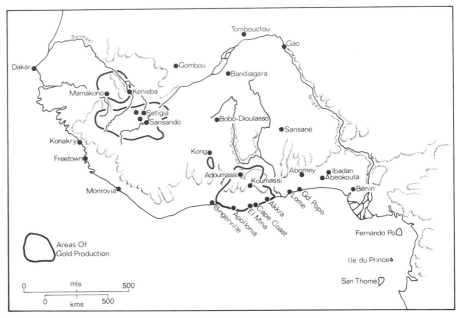

1. Zones of Gold Production on the Guinea Coast (Reference: H. Quiring)

reached the coast of Guinea, with, as Bodin later observed, "its riches and its gold mines." [11] Here, the long-established combination of maritime and land trade or barter with the Negroes of the interior assured the continuity of the gold traffic, which was effectively protected by the famous fort of São

[7] Robert Ricard, "Contribution à l'étude du commerce gênois au Maroc durant la période portugaise, 1415–1550," *Annales de l'Institut d'Études Orientales,* III (1937), and "Le commerce en Berbérie et l'empire portugais," *ibid.,* II (1936), both cited by Braudel, *Méditerranée,* p. 370.

[8] Braudel, *Méditerranée,* pp. 361–373; Vitorino Magalhães Godinho. "O comércio português, com a Africa Ocidental até 1520," *Mundo Literario,* XXI–XXIV (1946), and "Le Tournant de structure de l'empire portugais," typescript, pp. 151–153; J. Blake, *Europeans in West Africa, 1450–1560* (2 vols., London, 1942), p. 22.

[9] The island of Arguin, off the coast to the south of Cap Blanc.

[10] See n. 7, above.

[11] Jean Bodin, *Les Six livres de la république* (Paris, 1583), p. 873.

Jorge da Mina built in 1482.[12] Along with cargoes of ivory and melegueta pepper — the substitute pepper — gold arrived in Lisbon. The quantities were probably larger than the meager deliveries still reaching the Mediterranean from the Maghreb and the Nile Valley.[13]

All this can go far to explain the long-standing interest of the Portuguese merchants in the rich Gulf of Guinea. At the end of the century, this interest tended to fade, but was destined to revive again. About the year 1497, when Vasco da Gama successfully rounded the Cape of Good Hope, the opportunities of a sea route to the Indies meant in effect that merchants turned away from the Gulf of Guinea and the alluvial gold of Africa.[14]

Yet, more than the trade to the East Indies, there was America — the "Indies of Castile," recently discovered and rapidly taken over. This inflicted a decisive blow. The development of the Atlantic routes meant, without exaggeration, neglect and even crisis for the gold of Guinea. This preceded the general crisis of gold and economic activity which emerged later, and of which it is part. Silver, which flowed over Europe after the mid-sixteenth century, has often hidden the real onset of bullion from the New World. The first deliveries after 1503 were entirely in gold and came from the island that was later known as Cuba, from New Spain, and then from the Tierra Firme. Earl J. Hamilton has studied the shipments, using the official registers of the Casa de la Contratación in Seville. The evidence is clear: it is premature to speak of American silver in the early days of discovery; its heyday came later. The shipments of gold reached their maximum of 43,620,080 grams (that is, 43 metric tons) in the decade 1551–1560, declined to 9 metric tons in 1571–1580, rose again to 19 metric tons in 1591–1600, and fell once more to half a metric ton in 1651–1660. More important still, until 1519 gold arrived alone. The 1520s saw the first important appearance of American silver.[15] Again, the silver mines of Mexico were discovered in 1532, and the first shipment (gold and silver) came from Peru in 1533. Until about 1540, for all intents and purposes, gold was the only metal. The primacy of gold in the economic life of Europe was not threatened by the imperial conquests of Spain. There was, on the contrary, only one outstanding victim: the gold of Guinea. And with little difficulty, Seville assumed the place of Lisbon.

There are many signs of the primacy of gold in the first half of the sixteenth century. Up to, perhaps even after, the great peace of 1529, Charles V and Francis I fought their wars with gold coin. War meant mobilizing troops,

[12] Braudel, *Méditerranée*, p. 369; Damiâo Peres, *História de Portugal* (7 vols., Lisbon, 1928–1931), III, pp. 549–552, 630.

[13] Peres, *História de Portugal*; and n. 7, above. Could the wealth of the Niger be compared to the poverty of the Nile? Contemporaries often made such a contrast, but this should not be taken as conclusive; Gomes Eannes de Azurara called the Niger "the Nile of the Negroes," *Chroniques*, ed. V. de Castro e Almeida (Paris, 1943), p. 147.

[14] Edward W. Bovill, *Caravans of the Old Sahara* (London, 1933), p. 149.

[15] Earl J. Hamilton, *American Treasure and the Price Revolution in Spain, 1501–1650* (Cambridge, Mass., 1934), pp. 38–42.

storing provisions, and spying, but it also meant sending courier after courier with consignments of gold coin. By reason of its high value and small bulk gold was easy to hide, and the official or secret transfers were often made by hand. It is little wonder that historians, usually so alert to diplomatic encounters, have paid so little attention to these critical gold movements.

In this way, the gold from America pushed gold from Guinea into second place. It would perhaps be more exact to call it African gold, for even after the palmy days of Portuguese trade, gold continued to flow toward the Maghreb and Egypt.[16] At the beginning of the sixteenth century merchants from Marseilles or Montpellier went to North Africa in search of gold, but this met with increasing difficulties. As evidence of this, there is a telling report from the Montpellier merchants: "The trade to Barbary is as good as lost," they complained in 1518; and, again, "The gold nuggets from over there are being taken elsewhere."[17] At that time people were, naturally enough, not in a position to grasp the full dimensions of the situation; nor were they able to envisage the whole world scene. In 1526, again in Montpellier, local difficulties were attributed to a familiar cause: "From Barbary," it was said, "no more gold is being brought on account of the wars."[18] Leo Africanus, about this same time, also noted a preference for barter at Tefza, which was a long-established market for gold in the Sahara. It was an odd observation, but the implications of it should not be exaggerated.[19] A final piece of evidence takes us briefly to Guinea: during the first thirty years of the sixteenth century the French often plundered Portuguese ships returning from Guinea; they relieved them of goods and booty, but rarely managed to find any gold.[20]

This decline, almost eclipse, of gold from Africa can be explained no doubt by the fact that it was more expensive than that brought from America. Gold from Guinea came by way of the Atlantic, along the less frequented routes off the coast of Guinea, after long delays while the devious parleys and barter were being completed. During these delays, the seamen faced the dangers of terrible tropical disease on the African coast. All too often the ships returned home with crews decimated and sails flapping. All this added to the total cost, over and above the trinkets and goods sent in exchange, and trimmed the possible gains. In contrast, the gold of America, from the moment it left the goldfields until it reached Europe, followed in general the great transatlantic

---

[16] Braudel, *Méditerranée*, p. 371.

[17] Archives Nationales [hereafter cited as A.N.], Z¹B.363, a letter of July 31, 1518, from the mint in Montpellier to the Chambre des Monnaies.

[18] *Ibid.,* letter of Oct. 10, 1526, from the mint in Montpellier to the Chambre des Monnaies in Paris.

[19] Leo Africanus, *Description de l'Afrique*, trans. Jean Temporel, ed. Charles-Henri-Auguste Schefer (3 vols., Paris, 1896), I, p. 291, cited by Bovill, *Caravans of the Old Sahara*, p. 110.

[20] Godinho, "Tournant," p. 81. In East Africa, especially in Sofala, the trade was low at the beginning of the sixteenth century. See R. Coupland, *East Africa and Its Invaders* (Oxford, 1938), pp. 41–50 *passim*.

routes under the control of European merchants. It came more easily and in greater abundance than gold from Africa. At least this is how it appears to have happened. Europe's requirements were fairly well provided with gold, and its markets seemed unwilling to pay the extra costs of acquiring gold in Africa. And so the latter tended to fade from the picture, although it was not completely forgotten. In case of need, Europe had the African resources on hand. Such was the case in 1530 when an abrupt crisis paralyzed the markets and for a brief moment revived the interest of traders in the Gulf of Guinea. In 1534 the Portuguese sent an expedition under Peros Fernández to the King of Mali. In 1539 the Portuguese complained — this time successfully — and the merchants of Rouen found themselves forbidden to trade with the Portuguese colonies in Africa. Their consternation at this showed clearly the powerful interests either implied or actively concerned.[21]

Between 1450 and 1550, paradoxically enough, Europe searched for the less precious of the two metals: silver. In Venice, in July 1542, toward the end of this period, the Senate particularly noted in its deliberations that "the operation of our mint is in dire straits since it has nothing to work, silver being unavailable." [22] In Ragusa, a city accustomed to use silver in its trade with the Levant, the bimetallic ratio fell (a sign of increased demand for silver) from 1 : 11.269 in 1519 to 1 : 10.776 in 1525.[23] In Rome, where no doubt the situation was exceptional (everything was extraordinary in Rome), the ratio reached more or less the same figure as that in Ragusa. For 1526 it was 1 : 11.06 and fell to an average of 1 : 10.64 in 1551–1563.[24] Throughout most of Europe, it may be said that silver was a rather scarce commodity. And, as a result, there were constant efforts in France, England, Scandinavia, and, above all, in Germany and Central Europe to find new deposits or exploit old ones. The upswing in the production of the silver mines of Central Europe at the end of the fifteenth and the beginning of the sixteenth centuries has long been noted by German historians. There emerged what has been called "the second age of the mines," following an earlier spate of prosperity from the eleventh to the thirteenth century. Gustav Schmoller suggested that the beginnings were about 1480,[25] but, by all appearances, well-established

---

[21] Archives Municipales [hereafter cited as A.M.], Rouen, A.4., déliberation of Jan. 22, 1539; Bovill, *Caravans of the Old Sahara*, p. 149; Godinho, "Tournant," p. 78.

[22] Archivo di Stato [hereafter cited as A.S.], Venice, *Senato Zecca*, Filza 36, July 26, 1542, document communicated by Braudel.

[23] W. Anderssen, "Materialien zum ragusanischen Mass- und Geldwesen," *Vierteljahrschrift für Sozial- und Wirtschaftsgeschichte*, XXVIII (1935), p. 143.

[24] Jean Delumeau, *Vie économique et sociale de Rome dans la seconde moitié du XVI*e *siècle* (2 vols., Paris, 1959), II, pp. 665–676.

[25] Gustav Schmoller, "Die geschichtliche Entwicklung der Unternehmung," *Jahrbuch für Gesetzgebung, Verwaltung und Volkswirtschaft im deutschen Reich*, XV (1891); John U. Nef, "Silver Production in Central Europe, 1450–1618," *Journal of Political Economy*, XLIX (1941); H. Spannenberg, *Territorialwirtschaft und Stadtwirtschaft* (Munich, 1932), pp. 113 ff.; see also Michael M. Postan, in *The Cambridge Economic History of Europe*, II, ed. M. M. Postan and H. J. Habakkuk (Cambridge, Eng., 1952), pp. 211–212.

techniques helped to advance the huge development before this. In 1451, for example, the Duke of Saxony authorized a new lead process to facilitate the extraction of silver from copper ores.[26] It was, however, mainly a rising demand for silver that stimulated production from the German and Central European mines.

John U. Nef has established that, with the exception of the Tirol (at Schwaz), the production of these mines before 1450 was not important.[27] About the middle of the century, no center had an output in excess of 10,000 marks a year. Eighty years later, at least eight mines were each producing yearly 10,000 to 15,000 marks or more. After 1488, those astute dealers, the Fuggers, gained a monopoly of the production of silver from the Schwaz mines as security on a loan of 150,000 florins to the Emperor. The mining boom was then in full swing. According to Nef, the expansion reached its peak between 1526 and 1535.[28] This dating seems more convincing than that of 1545–1560, proposed earlier by Adolf Soetbeer.[29] If a slump did occur after 1535, silver from America was less to blame than the serious recession in the economy of Europe itself. A general slowing down of the interregional monetary transfers of money (both gold and silver) was apparent over the whole Continent. In reality, it was not until 1550, perhaps even 1552,[30] that silver from the New World became more prevalent than silver from Germany. Jakob Strieder was one of the few historians to have noted this fact.[31]

For all this, however, the relative shortage of silver during the first half of the sixteenth century underpinned the revolutionary fortune of Central Europe. Immense profits were derived from the strategic situation of the mines. The adjacent regions also shared in the benefits: Hungary, threatened constantly by the incursions of Turkish horsemen and marauders;[32] the Tirol, buttressing the financial ascendancy of Augsburg, so soon endowed with riches; Bohemia and its Erzebirge dotted with mining camps:[33] Silesia; Alsace; Saxony;

---

[26] Nef, "Silver Production in Central Europe," p. 576.

[27] *Ibid.*, pp. 585–586.

[28] *Ibid.*, p. 578.

[29] Adolf Soetbeer, *Edelmetall-Production und Werthverhältniss zwischen Gold und Silber seit der Entdeckung Amerikas bis zur Gegenwart* (Gotha, 1879), pp. 14–33.

[30] The first sizable import of American silver can be dated with precision: the discovery of Potosí in Peru coincided with the rebellion of the Spaniards against the *Leyes Nuevas* which freed the Indians. After the pacification in 1584, mining licenses were granted. In 1549 Pedro de Hinojosa arrived in Lima from Potosí with 3,813 bars, which were loaded at Callao, and arrived in Seville in 1552. They were used to repay the 76,000 ducats borrowed from the Fuggers at 12 percent (the loan of Villach). See Marie Helmer, "La Encomienda à Potosí en 1550," in *Proceedings of the Thirtieth Congress of Americanists,* held in Cambridge, England, 1952 (London, 1955), pp. 235–238.

[31] Jakob Strieder, *Aus Antwerpener Notariatsarchiven* (Stuttgart, 1930), preface.

[32] The Turks raised the siege of Vienna on October 15, 1529. See Maurice Smets, *Wien in und aus der Turken-Bedrängnis* (Vienna, 1883), pp. 23–25, cited by Roger Merriman, *Suleiman the Magnificent* (Cambridge, Mass., 1944), p. 108.

[33] Aloys Schulte, *Geschichte der grossen Ravensburger Gesellschaft* (3 vols., Berlin, 1923), I, p. 377; II, p. 194; III, pp. 209, 242.

and so forth. The point is emphasized by the rapid rise of so many mining towns, among them, Mansfeldt, Schneeberg, Annaberg, Marienberg, Schwaz, Joachimsthal, and Neuberg.[34] Just as at other times and in other countries, these mining camps rapidly gathered together motley collections of men. In the second decade of the sixteenth century, the owners of the Joachimsthal mines in Bohemia, the Schlick family, received the Emperor's permission to mint coins after the style of Saxony; this gave rise to the famous *Joachimstaler,* or *taler* for short. With other coins of the same sort, it was valuable enough to become a standard and soon conquered Europe. It made its debut at a time when silver was in demand.[35]

Far-reaching improvements in mining techniques were partially responsible for the rising productivity of the silver mines.[36] The process of refining by the lead process had already appeared officially in 1451, but the amalgamation process was even more decisive.

The latter method was further extended in the first half of the sixteenth century. The close coincidence between its apparent "discovery" and the massive arrival of silver from America led Spanish observers to suppose, with an almost excessive alacrity, that the new process emerged in America. Already in 1540 in Venice, however, Vannoccio Biringuccio, in his work *De la pirotechnia,* gave full details about such processes of extraction and indicated that mercury had been tried on gold ores in Central Europe (Bohemia and Hungary). He records that, at the cost of a diamond ring, he had obtained the information on how to separate precious metals, using mercury and common salt. Silver ore could be treated in the same way as gold: after being crushed by hammers in a sort of stamp, it was mixed with salt, vitriol, and mercury; it was then pressed through a leather pouch or a canvas bag, as was the practice in America.[37] The latter method, using the action of sun and air, became known as the *patio* process, introduced in 1557 under Viceroy Mendoza at Zacatecas. Some thirty mills were in operation there by 1562.[38] Berrio de Montalvo, in his treatise published in Mexico in 1643[39],

[34] Nef, "Silver Production in Central Europe," p. 586.

[35] The dates of the first coinage of silver *talers* mark the rise of mining in Germany and Central Europe: 1484 in the Tirol; 1500 in Saxony; 1518 in Bohemia (the *Joachimstaler*); 1524 in Austria. See Alfred F. Pribram, *Materialien zur Geschichte der Preise und Löhne in Österreich* (Vienna, 1938), I, p. 27.

[36] A careful description of the amalgamation and refining techniques is given by Marie Helmer, "Potosí au XVIIIᵉ siècle," in *Journal de la Société des Américanistes,* XL (1951), pp. 21–50.

[37] Vannoccio Biringuccio, *De la pirotechnia Libri X* (Venice, 1540), I, Chap. I, Pt. 9; Chap. XI; and John Percy, *Metallurgy: Gold and Silver* (2 vols., London, 1880), I, pp. 559–562, to which I am greatly indebted, especially for the information on technical procedures. The treatise of Georgius Agricola, *De Re Metallica,* begun about 1533, was published by Froben in Basle in 1556: see the introduction to the edition by Herbert and Lou Hoover (London, 1912).

[38] Walter Howe, *The Mining Guild of New Spain and Its Tribunal General, 1770–1821* (Cambridge, Mass., 1949), p. 6.

[39] See Percy, *Metallurgy: Gold and Silver,* p. 561.

later confirmed that the process had been acquired in Spain, which was likely since Spain possessed the important mercury mines of Almadén. The Fuggers had operated these mines from the beginning of the reign of Charles V.[40] But the origin of the process, aside from the German groups in Spain, was probably in Central Europe, since the Germans remained the undisputed masters of mining techniques throughout the world of the sixteenth century.[41] A rapid perusal of the historical literature indicates that their methods were not exported very far. Mining activity in the late fifteenth and early sixteenth centuries, as historians of technology have noted, was directed mainly to developing deep lodes, and in this German financiers and technicians held the lead. It meant digging adits, shoring up galleries, ventilating pits, and pumping out water. In the New World it was often possible to develop lodes near the surface. Under such conditions cheap native labor could substitute for many of the capital-intensive German methods. More hands were employed. Among the technical methods available, only amalgamation, with the extensive use of mercury (either European or American), won wide acceptance across the Atlantic.

In order to complete the picture of the primacy of gold, to confirm our statements, we must look beyond Germany to Hungary, Poland, and Russia, to those frontier lands where an older, traditional Europe merged into Asia. Germany, sophisticated and already urbanized, was clearly associated with Western Europe, as is shown in the prestige of Nuremberg, Augsburg, and Cologne, and was praised in the reports of travelers.[42] Controlling as it did supplies of silver, the metal in demand, Germany exercised no small influence over its neighbors. Because that area was rich in silver, it could, logically, attract a sufficiency of gold. Reissued as its own coins, for example, the Rhenish *Goldgulden* found their way to the east along with other gold coins from the west and the Mediterranean.

These gold coins, passing across Germany, apparently traveled far: through the lands of the Hanseatic traders, they reached Eastern Europe; or, by the valley of the Danube, in particular, they arrived, as Botero later said, "to the final destinations of Muscovy." [43] There was nothing new, no doubt, in the trading network of the Hanseatic League.[44] Beyond the Empire, the gold coins

[40] The process apparently was not employed in the silver mines at Guadalcanal in Spain. Cf. Richard Ehrenberg, *Das Zeitalter der Fugger* (2 vols., Jena, 1896), I, p. 114; Ernst Hering, *Die Fugger* (Leipzig, 1940), p. 270; Götz Freiherr von Pölnitz, *Jakob Fugger* (2 vols., Tübingen, 1939–1951), I, pp. 550–559; Ramón Carande, *Carlos V y sus banqueros* (2 vols., Madrid, 1943–1949), II, pp. 417–443.

[41] John U. Nef, "Industrial Europe at the Time of the Reformation," *Journal of Political Economy*, XLIX (1941), pp. 201–215; Hering, *Die Fugger*, pp. 270–279.

[42] Pölnitz, *Jakob Fugger*, I, p. 508; Baron Siegmund von Herberstein, *Rerum Moscoviticarum Commentarii* (2 vols., London, 1851), I, p. 110.

[43] Giovanni Botero, *Le Relationi Universale* (Venice, 1599), p. 72.

[44] See Michael M. Postan, "The Economic and Political Relations of England and the Hanse from 1400 to 1475," in *Studies in English Trade in the Fifteenth Century,* ed. E. Power and M. M. Postan (London, 1933).

from Western Europe — ducats, crowns, angels, nobles — were given new names. The English rose noble became in Muscovy the *korablenniki;* the Portuguese peso and the gold crowns received the general name of *iefimki.*[45] In his travels between 1516 and 1526 Herberstein declared that the Muscovites had no gold currency (that is, Muscovite gold), but used mainly Hungarian and sometimes Rhenish gold.[46] Elsewhere the silver coins, which in the fifteenth century had replaced the "squirrels heads and ears" in Novgorod in 1420 and in Pskov in 1424, followed the same movement of silver in Europe: they appreciated in relation to gold.[47] Herberstein noted that "The money of Moscow is pure and good silver although now also it is debased." [48]

In Poland, during the first half of the sixteenth century, the monetary situation remained confused. Many types of foreign coins — Lithuanian, Polish, Prussian, and, more particularly, Hungarian gold coins — circulated. After 1528 Poland had its own gold currency, ducats coined on the Hungarian pattern. In the same context, the silver currency was reformed in 1526–1528.[49]

From 1540 to 1560 a structural crisis occurred in which the gold phase tended to a limit. The approaching primacy of silver was foreshadowed by disturbances in these two decades, when, in spite of the increase in the absolute quantities of silver, the monetary circulation gave evident signs that it required further volume. The increases apparently came in ways different from those expected. In response to a series of crises and disruptions the various governments, for better or worse, attempted to adapt to these seemingly intractable circumstances. Already in 1537 Charles V accepted a slight devaluation in gold by issuing a new gold *escudo* which was lighter than the current *excelente* of Granada.[50] This fact alone indicated restrictions on gold in Spain. Similar measures marked the following years. In the Hanseatic towns, difficulties appeared about 1540. In France, after 1540, the important heavy silver *testons* were converted into fractional money by the addition of copper.[51] There was a copper inflation, severely felt about mid-century. More serious still was the runaway debasement in England, unleashed by the policies of Henry VIII and Edward VI. The standard fineness of gold coins fell to 22 carats in 1542 and to 20 in 1547; in silver coins this fineness fell to 9 ounces in the pound troy in 1544, to 5 in 1547, and then to 3 in 1551.[52] All

---

[45] Stanislav de Chaudoir, *Aperçu sur les monnaies russes* (2 vols., St. Petersburg, 1936), I, pp. 55–57, 77, 109.
[46] Herberstein, *Rerum Moscoviticarum Commentarii.*
[47] Chaudoir, *Aperçu sur les monnaies russes,* I, pp. 9, 29.
[48] Herberstein, *Rerum Moscoviticarum Commentarii.*
[49] Jan Rutkowski, *Historia gospodarcza Polski* (Poznan, 1947), I, pp. 209–213.
[50] The *excelente* of Granada of 23¾ K. fine and weighing 65 to the Castilian mark; the *escudo* of 22 K. fine and 68 to the mark. See Hamilton, *American Treasure,* pp. 51, 55.
[51] See Chap. 3.
[52] Sir Albert Feavearyear, *The Pound Sterling* (Oxford, 1921), pp. 47–66.

these measures no doubt were intended both to increase the monetary circulation and to swell governmental revenues. Changes were also noticeable in the geography of money, which was evident in the distribution of gold and silver (gold from the Spanish peninsula, silver from the German mines). The new Spanish control of both leading precious metals overturned everything. Apparently the imports of gold no longer met the requirements for money, and it is possible that the transactions of the European economy expanded to the point where it could absorb more easily the increasing arrivals of American silver. A silver inflation, a superior inflation, put an end to the devaluations and the increasing volume of copper in circulation, but the remedy was not without inconvenience. With silver in abundance, copper appreciated along with all the other commodities. This price mechanism, beyond the control and sanction of individuals or governments, checked the copper inflation at its very outset. A new era opened, and the whole structure of gold, as we shall soon see, was transformed.

2. The Ascendancy of Silver: From 1550 to 1610–1620

The productivity of the mines of New Spain[53] and of Peru, where the amalgamation process was widely employed after 1572,[54] radically transformed the monetary structures of Europe and, indeed, the world. Potosí became a byword: "rich Potosí, the treasure of the world, the King of the mountains, and the envy of Kings" as declared the coat of arms, given by Charles V to the city. The silver of America, "the admiration of the whole world," [55] restored the balance between the two metals in Europe and then proceeded to reverse the situation. It substituted another system, this time the primacy of silver, which lasted the century. The circulation of bullion remained focused on Seville, formerly the capital of gold and now the capital of silver.

According to the data of Earl J. Hamilton, the reversal apparently took place in the 1530s, but in appearance only, since it is a question of approach: the relative increases in the total values of imports of the two metals must also be taken into account. In the discussion, indeed, he prudently makes clear that he dates the success of silver from the years after 1545–1558.[56] From all the evidence, this conclusion is correct. Well before the final date of 1558, nevertheless, sufficient silver had already entered Spain to produce widespread effects on the monetary system of Europe.

It is also clear from the 1540s that, as a result of this concentration, a "ridge of high pressure" of silver — to use a convenient image — gradually established itself in Spain. The great difficulty, however, is to explain when

---

[53] Amalgamation was introduced there in 1554 and was effective after 1557.
[54] Percy, *Metallurgy: Gold and Silver*, p. 562.
[55] Alvaro Alonso Barba, *El arte de los metales* (Madrid, 1640), fol. 33.
[56] Hamilton, *American Treasure*, pp. 38–42.

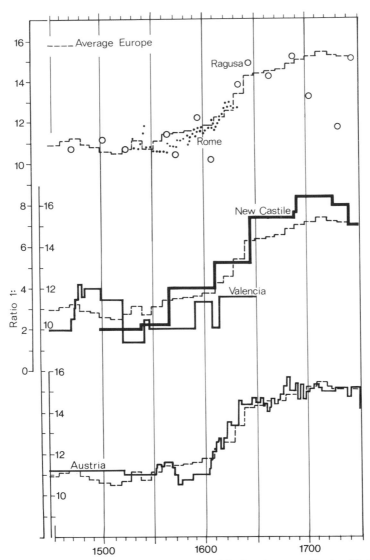

1. Bimetallic Ratios in Europe Compared with the Average Ratio (Reference: *Cambridge Economic History of Europe*, Vol. IV)

and how this American silver filtered from the peninsula into Europe.[57] A certain number of contracts in Bordeaux in the 1540s indicate that silver reached France from nearby Spain fairly soon, though on a small scale.[58]

[57] At first the Spanish *real* employed in commercial transactions was coined also in Antwerp. See Alphonse de Witte, *Histoire monétaire des Comtes de Louvain, Ducs de Brabant* (3 vols., Brussels, 1896–1899).

[58] See Chap. 3, Section 1, n. 65. Later, for example, the payment to Jehan de Malus

The geography of the movements of precious metals, which remained in force up to that time — gold from Portugal and Spain, silver from Germany and Central Europe — underwent radical transformation. The requirements for silver were as high as ever, but as we approach the mid-century (and so the reversal of the trend) the products of the German mines were not exported with customary ease to the west and south. The sphere of expansion became restricted by silver coming from that direction, and with the early 1550s Spain began to send increasing quantities of silver into Europe. Although the effects were felt immediately, the deep structural changes were realized more slowly; in all probability they were not finally confirmed until the crisis of 1575. Graph 1 shows something of the nature of this movement. Until the gold debasement of 1566, the bimetallic ratio in the key region of New Castile remained below the average; that is, silver was still relatively in demand.[59] Afterward the situation was reversed. In the case of Austria and the old silver-producing zones of Central Europe, however, the opposite was the case: after 1571–1572 the demand for silver was relatively higher than the average for Europe. These complex disturbances and shifts partly explain the monetary difficulties all over Europe after the middle of the century when the silver of America asserted itself, bursting through in full strength. One of the great monetary turning points of the century was passed.

The imperial policies of Charles V entailed a huge export of silver from Spain. By comparison with present-day experience and the mechanism of gold standards, this movement may appear insignificant. After 1551, perhaps even earlier, there is evidence of official deliveries of silver from Spain to Antwerp, in December 1551, for example, when it was sent under the control of Alonso de Castilla.[60] In the autumn of 1552 some large cargoes of silver arrived in Genoa and Antwerp, in particular on account for the Fuggers.[61] From December 1552 smuggling played its part, if we are to believe some minor pieces of evidence: some silver was found at Bilbao secretly towed in a ship of the wool fleet; some silver also was found later (in all, four quintals in bars) concealed in another ship loaded with wool, captured by the pirates of Saint-Jean-de-Luz.[62] The defeat of Charles V before Metz largely removed the

---

for the sale of land of 36 francs bordelais was made with 3 gold écus and "two testons of ten sols each, three English groats and reals." Archives Départmentales [hereafter cited as A.D.], Gironde, Ser. 3E, 4211, Jan. 18, 1544 (N.S.).

[59] For New Castle, see Hamilton, *American Treasure,* and for Austria, see Pribram, *Materialien.* This graph is republished from Fernand Braudel and Frank Spooner, "Prices in Europe from 1450 to 1750," in *The Cambridge Economic History of Europe,* IV, ed. E. E. Rich and C. H. Wilson (Cambridge, Eng., 1967).

[60] Archivo General de Simancas [hereafter cited as Simancas], *Estado* 504, Dec. 17, 1551, instructions to Alonso de Castilla, document communicated by Braudel.

[61] Ehrenberg, *Das Zeitalter der Fugger,* I, pp. 155, 158; Braudel, *Méditerranée,* p. 377; C.S.P., Spanish, letter of Jan. 29, 1554, Francisco de Aresti in Antwerp to Juan Vásquez de Molina.

[62] Simancas, *Guerra Antigua,* LII, 35, Bilbao, Dec. 2, 1552, document communicated by Braudel.

financial reasons for emptying Spain of its bullion. The summer of 1553 again saw large deliveries of silver northward, however, and the powerful effects soon made themselves felt on the Antwerp market. There, on November 10, 1553, Christopher Dawntesey wrote, "Here is great quantity of reals of Spain and all payments in the same." [63] The merchants of Antwerp, overwhelmed so it seemed and blinded by an unexpected situation, gave themselves over to speculation. "This Bourse of Antwerp," wrote Thomas Gresham on December 20, 1553, "is so strange that as any day you shall have money plenty and the next day none. The reason is that here are so many takers and deliverers so that if one will not another will." [64] In the middle of this ferment, the speculators themselves were no longer very clear about the situation. Some, dazzled by the abundance of a money so long in short supply, rushed for silver almost without reflection, while others, more wary and perspicacious, anticipated a change in trend and cornered gold which thus disappeared from the market. Indeed, Gresham added the same day: "Here is no kind of gold stirring which is the strangest matter that ever was seen upon the Bourse of Antwerp having no other payment but silver Spanish reals as for angels[65] and sovereigns[66] here is none to be gotten . . . for that the exchange is so high." [67] During the winter of 1553–1554 some merchants skillfully took advantage of silver on the market of Antwerp and managed to make profitable deals with countries where silver, still fairly rare, retained its value. There was, for example, the case of England, still shaken by recent debasements. At the beginning of 1554 Gresham eagerly accepted a contract for huge sums of silver, taking delivery in Spain.[68] This contract, it should be noted, was made with Genoese merchants, whose deft ability in sensing the right moment for financial speculation contributed in no small measure to their fortune. For this indeed was the dawn of that century, so aptly named the "century of the Genoese." The pattern of these profitable operations was maintained for some time. The countries of the eastern Mediterranean and beyond, of the Near and Far East, customarily set a high value on silver in terms of gold, which offered the chance for long-term speculation. In the midst of all this was the case of the Jewish merchants from Ancona who were denounced by the Portuguese ambassador in Rome in the spring of 1555.[69] They had been buying gold from Mina[70] in Lisbon "and sending it to Flanders where they made large profits on gold and remitted their money to

[63] P.R.O., S.P.69/2.
[64] *Ibid.*
[65] The new gold *angel* was coined in 1552 at 23 K, and 3½ gr. fine and weighed 80 gr. (Troy). Feavearyear, *Pound Sterling,* Appendix, III.
[66] The new gold sovereign of 1552 at 22 K. fine and weighed 174.5 gr. (Troy). *Ibid.*
[67] P.R.O., S.P.69/2.
[68] P.R.O., S.P.69/3, letter of Jan. 18, 1554, Gresham to the Council in London.
[69] *Corpo Diplomatico Português,* ed. Luis Augusto Rebello da Silva (10 vols., Lisbon, from 1862), VII, 379, Rome, Mar. 23, 1555, document communicated by Braudel.
[70] The exports of gold from Guinea tended to revive. See below, Chap. 3, Section 2.

Rome with profit." [71] The gold taken up in Lisbon was exchanged for silver in Antwerp, then sent to Rome, where, as noted above, silver had a favorable rate. This continued for a long time for reasons not particularly clear. For every speculation now revealed by historical research, there were no doubt ten, or even a hundred, more without trace. These transfers reduced a long-standing disequilibrium, adjusting the relative value between the two metals. Over the world, at large, it may be said, these differences between gold and silver affected international trade and relative costs. They particularly concerned the relations between Europe and the Far East, dealt with below.[72]

In the old silver-producing regions of Germany the effects inevitably were rapid and widespread. For the mining centers of Germany and Central Europe — the most developed were the most vulnerable — the new trend by the 1570s meant an inescapable, catastrophic decline.[73] In March 1576 the ambassadors from the Swiss cities of Berne, Fribourg, and Soleure declared that "until now, they have been unable to draw or have silver from the lands of the Empire and Germany because it was at a high and excessive price." [74] This relative dearness in itself underlines the falling productivity of the German mines. Some, such as Freiberg, Rammelsberg, and Kuttenberg, no doubt held out until the beginning of the seventeenth century, but little by little they became impoverished. Mining was increasingly depressed, and depression in mining meant that unrest grew among the miners. In December 1569 at Schwaz, not long before a flourishing center, there was the rumor that "the miners were on the point of rising on account of the religion." Was that the only reason? Thirty years later, in October 1599, two priests with six hundred troopers provided by Ferdinand of Austria, arrived in Eisenarz, "and the inhabitants and miners wanted to resist them with arms." [75] This incident could have been partly the natural reaction of unsettled subjects, and partly also the disorders that armed troopers provoke, but it also belongs to a series of minor incidents that show clearly that in the closing decades of the century any pretext was good enough for miners to vent their discontent, in the mining camps once so prosperous but degenerating into the ghost towns of the future.

The emigration of German miners and engineers became what may be called part of the diffusion of technology. Between 1527 and 1530 some eighty or ninety German miners crossed the Atlantic at the instigation of the

[71] See n. 69, above.

[72] See Chap. 5.

[73] Nef, "Silver Production in Central Europe," pp. 586–591.

[74] A.N., Z¹B. 376, Mar. 19, 1576, "Abscheyd et resolution des Ambassadeurs des Trois Villes, Assavoir de Berne, Frybourg et Solleure pour le faict de la monnoye de France et autres."

[75] Nef, "Silver Production in Central Europe," p. 589; *The Fugger News-Letters,* ed. Victor von Klarwill, 1st Ser. (London, 1924), letter from Augsburg of Dec. 20, 1569; letter from Steyr (Austria) of Oct. 30, 1599.

Welsers,[76] to further their great schemes in Venezuela.[77] Another example, in France, at the beginning of the sixteenth century, reveals German names in the lists of miners, and De Bras De Bourgeville speaks of German miners, although the shortage of ready capital and no doubt the wars with the Empire had obliged them to quit the country in 1537.[78]

These may be considered modest beginnings, but about the middle of the century this emigration became more impressive. In 1551 some four hundred German miners set off to open new mines in Ireland, which they later abandoned. When it came to refining the depreciated coinage in England, a German, Daniel Wolfstadt, was summoned by the Queen herself. On May 26, 1565, Thomas Thurland and Daniel Hochstetter explained to Elizabeth the difficulties of mining copper in Cumberland and asked for authority to bring over "from parts beyond the Seas III or IIII hundred arts men strangers." These were, no doubt, to be Germans because the following year she recommended "certain Almaynes" to the Justices of Westmoreland and Cumberland.[79] On another occasion, in 1556, "mineros alemanes" were dispatched to Spain to work in the silver mines of Guadalcanal.[80] At the end of the century, refiners from Nuremberg were working in Lyons.[81] It would be easy to repeat these examples, small in themselves, which at least give the impression that German miners were everywhere. They had been trained in the silver and other mines of their country and then released to travel the roads of the Old and New World alike.

The profound transformation of Germany was one of the great spectacles of history. Here were the end of a phase of prosperity, the twilight of the "century of the Fuggers," and the finale, for a time at least, of the outstanding achievements of its native merchants at home and overseas. After the middle of the sixteenth century, with the change in trend, Germany slumbered in the religious Peace of Augsburg (1555), which left its chroniclers few great events to retell. The conquest of Germany by merchants infiltrating from the north (the Calvinists of the Low Countries), from the east (the Jewish traders from Posen), and from the south (the Italians) was achieved with studied

[76] Carl Liesegang, *Deutsche Berg- und Hüttenleute in Süd- und Mittelamerika* (Hamburg, 1949), p. 9.

[77] Konrad Häbler, *Die überseeischen Unternehmungen der Welser und ihrer Gesellschaften* (Leipzig, 1923), pp. 60–70.

[78] Charles de Bourgeville, sieur de Bras, *Les recherches et antiquités de la ville de Caen* (Caen, 1588).

[79] C.S.P., Spanish, Jan. 1551; *ibid.,* Advices from Jehan Scheyfe, Apr. 28, 1553; C.S.P., Foreign, letter of July 7, 1560 from Gresham to Parry; *Tudor Economic Documents,* ed. R. H. Tawney and Eileen Power (3 vols., London, 1924), I, pp. 240–249; Henry Hamilton, *The English Brass and Copper Industries to 1800* (London, 1926), p. 12, for the subsequent difficulties of this undertaking, pp. 29–31.

[80] Simancas, *Estado Flandes,* 1556, Leg. 511–513, document communicated by Braudel; Hering, *Die Fugger,* p. 275.

[81] A.N., Z¹B.391, letter of June 7, 1601, from the mint master in Lyons to the Cour des Monnaies in Paris.

silence. Powerful commercial centers emerged, still new in many respects, such as Leipzig; or, restored, such as Frankfurt, after 1554, according to the studies of Alexander Dietz;[82] or, again, such as Hamburg, where powerful fortunes began to merge with those of the Netherlands and of Sweden, along the routes of the Baltic and the Atlantic.[83]

The silver-gold system, an important aspect of economic activity, even when neglected by history, is not the only one to be discussed. It would indeed be too much to claim that the reversal of the gold-silver system and its replacement by a silver-gold system determined everything in this complex and discordant past, even though it was passed over largely without comment by German historians in the second half of the sixteenth century. But the latter system could not have been possible without the former. This in itself indicates at once the scope of the phenomena developing over whole areas of the world, and it must be emphasized far beyond the France of the Valois. The basic features of the silver revolution must be kept in mind. A high-powered system dependent on gold was gradually replaced by a more clumsy mechanism, which was effective in a different way. It was more directly related to the inflation of retail prices, without which it would be difficult to explain the "price revolution" and the burst of activity in the later sixteenth century. The inflation coupled also with increasing aggregate demand, rising levels of production transactions,[84] swelling budgets, and population growth — a crop of new generations — without taking into account, finally, the spectacular procession of wars, colonial systems, and empires.

Silver was an essential part of all this and contributed in no small measure to the progressive convergence of structures in Europe. Without it, many changes perhaps would not have been possible, or at least would have been accomplished in a very different guise.

Gold was a silent factor, which often passed unnoticed by the historians of the Renaissance. It needed only a few men of determination, carrying it on their backs ("a costas" as the Spanish documents record) and crossing the frontiers of Spain and Portugal, those happy hunting grounds for smugglers.[85] An intrepid seaman with no less success could pass a pouch of doubloons from Irun to Hendaye, from Spain into one of those areas of France renowned for contraband in specie — escudos in the age of gold and pieces of eight reals in the century of silver.[86] If silver achieved much, it also had undoubted

---

[82] Alexander Dietz, *Frankfurter Handelgeschichte* (4 vols., Frankfort on the Main, 1910–1925), I, pp. 305–308, Ernst Kroker, *Handelgeschichte der Stadt Leipzig* (Leipzig, 1925), p. 105.

[83] Hermann Kellenbenz, *Unternehmerkräfte im Hamburger Portugal und Spanienhandel, 1590–1625* (Hamburg, 1954); Fernand Braudel, Report in *Annuaire du Collège de France* (1953).

[84] Huguette and Pierre Chaunu, *Séville et l'Atlantique* (8 vols., Paris, 1955–1959).

[85] Simancas, *Estado Portugal,* 171, Lisbon, Aug. 27, 1558, from Juan de Mendoza to Princess Juana, document communicated by Braudel.

[86] Simancas, *Guerra Antigua,* XXVI, 68, Feb. 16, 1543, "Información tornada por la

limitations, for it was more bulky, less subtle, and less mobile than gold. On the other hand, it escapes the historian's eye less than gold. Because of its bulk it had to be carried on mules or in wagon trains. When Philip II traveled to Barcelona in 1585, he left the ambassadors of his court behind in Saragossa. Although these notables no doubt had something better to do, they passed the time in their lodgings counting the lines of mules from Madrid on their way to Barcelona, laden with silver.[87] A mule could carry about 5,000 silver crowns, but in the palmy days of gold a man could carry 4,000 crowns (sometimes sewn into his clothing). More often, the sea route was used, and large cargoes of silver were shipped by galleon or galley, and later by man-of-war. The specie could be hidden in cargo, in bales of wool or bundles of hides or numerous other places. On arrival in Seville from the New World, the silver had then to be taken from Spain, and although at first sight that country seemed a veritable fortress almost surrounded by water, inevitably it became also the great distributor of bullion. When it is recalled that after 1552 (after the surprise of Innsbruck by Maurice of Saxony when Charles V was almost captured) all the official and secret sluice gates were open, it is easy to understand that silver from America did not stay long in the peninsula. It soon left by way of land and sea. For a long time the official carriers kept to the Atlantic when sailing for Antwerp from ports such as Bilbao.[88] The conflict between England, Spain, and Flanders in 1568–1569, however, dealt this route a serious blow, although it remained open for merchants and their ships from the north. When carriers to Spain brought wheat, they had permission to export silver free. By way of compensation, another route was developed after 1572 for the fleets of galleys plying between Barcelona and Genoa. Although its potential was not at first apparent, this route gradually expanded to make Genoa the financial capital of the century of silver, which assumed the role of Augsburg in the preceding phase.

All these details are well known. They are mentioned briefly because they give the attentive observer some measure of the revolution effected by silver. This silver, brought from America, traveled the world. It was aided by the financial difficulties of His Most Catholic King who was constantly under too many pressures to be able to exercise full control over his monetary affairs. There were pieces of eight reals everywhere in the Mediterranean, and they were the driving force in a wide complex of relationships.[89] They were in Marseilles, in Leghorn, in Naples, and, not least, in Venice, where the strict policies of the Provveditori alla Zecca kept them from influencing too deeply the economic life of the *Signoria*. From there, packed in casks, they were

justicia ordinaria dela villa de Fuenterrabia sobre cierta moneda que passa al Reyno de Francia," document communicated by Braudel. This report concerned 3,500 ducats in *doblones* sent to France.

[87] A.S., Venice, *Dispacci Spagna,* Saragossa, June 1, 1585, document communicated by Braudel.

[88] Braudel, *Méditerranée,* pp. 391–394.

[89] *Ibid.*

sent to the islands of the Levant, for Venice was a city not only of good but of excellent coin. There were reals in the ports of the Levant, Smyrna, Alexandria, and Tripoli in Syria, and from there they passed inland to Aleppo, Damascus, and the Persian Gulf. In no time at all, they were in the Indies, reaching China, the Philippines, and the Malay Peninsula. In other directions, too, they were just as avidly received: the silver of America penetrated France, the Low Countries, England (where later coins similar to reals, the "royalles" or "rialls of platte," for example, were minted for use in trade to India[90]), not to mention Germany, Poland, and Russia. Historians have found no other satisfactory explanation for the balance of trade between the Baltic and Western Europe (the Baltic exported grains, timber, textiles, and salt) other than large payments of silver shipped into the Baltic. Who can deny that the replacement of gold by silver favored not only the sea routes but also the ports and maritime states of the Atlantic seaboard? For some time to come, nevertheless, merchants found traditional reserves of gold in the interior of the Continent. After 1550 two English merchants, Thomas Chamberlain and Joachim Gondelfinger, received instructions to send kerseys to the German cities of Transylvania by way of Nuremberg, on condition of receiving payment in gold.[91] This is no doubt a marginal case, in view of the date. But, again, at the end of the century, there is the instance of the confiscation of the fortune of the opulent Jewish merchant of Prague, Meisel: his hoard was composed mostly of gold coin, a large number from England and Portugal, dating from the end of the fifteenth and the early sixteenth centuries.[92]

Whatever may have been the reality in these particular instances, it must be noted that in general the revolution of silver was almost universal. It knocked on all doors to demand entry. The wide diffusion of American silver to the Baltic and China found several routes from Seville and Lisbon to India and Malacca, from New Spain to the Philippines (by the yearly *Nao de China,* which went, year in year out, from Acapulco on the Pacific coast of Mexico to Manila). This diffusion was one of the comparative advantages that quickened and broadened the trade relationships between Europe and the Far East. At the same time it moderated the silver inflation in the western world by encouraging a continuous drain of silver bullion and specie minted "with the stamp of Spain." By the end of their travels the coins tended to disappear in the East for a time at least; the size of the populations and habits of hoarding there aided this disappearance. Marsden noticed during his travels in Sumatra at the beginning of the eighteenth century that "the Spanish dollars are everywhere current."[93] On this topic one can find ten, twenty more witnesses just as late. The most interesting aspect among these striking examples

---

[90] C.S.P., Colonial, East Indies, London, Oct. 10, 1600.

[91] C.S.P., Foreign, Oct. 16, 1550, "Extraict des Instructions de Syre Thomas Chamberlain et Joachim Gondelfinger, commiz vers Dennemarck et Scweden."

[92] *The Fugger News-Letters,* 1st Ser., letter from Prague of Apr. 5, 1601.

[93] William Marsden, *History of Sumatra* (London, 1784), p. 137.

was the tendency to unify the trading world by the pervasive presence of silver deriving from a universal demand. Whatever the final explanation, it must be said at once that the world of silver was vaster and better integrated than the world of gold. Largely owing to silver, the Atlantic was placed at the service of Europe, and then of the Far East, which was linked to the narrow but successful Europe by the routes of the Cape of Good Hope and the Levant, by the routes of Russia and Persia, and also by other dependent routes not so favored by attention in the *grande histoire:* the *Nao de China,* a regular feature in the Pacific after the 1580s, and the subsidiary line from Japan to Macao, provided by the *Nao do Trato.*[94] This world network of silver was quickly established and strengthened with strategic relay points: Nagasaki, Macao, Malacca, Goa, Aden, Seville, Lisbon.

As silver flowed into international markets, there was a reversal of what had been the accepted state of affairs: in place of the former abundance of gold was substituted a relative shortage, a progressive appreciation of this currency. This, it appears, was a logical consequence. The search for gold was made with the same avidity as for silver a few years before. Although gold continued to arrive from America (the deliveries of gold reached a first maximum in the decade 1551–1560), the old sources in Africa began once more to attract interest.[95] From Islam there was the expedition of Salah Reis to Ouargla in 1552;[96] perhaps it was only a foray, but it offered the possibility of reopening the route for gold from the Sudan northward to the Mediterranean coast. European traders seemed, in any case, to revive their interest in Guinea. A small but significant piece of news circulated: gold, so the report went, was discovered at Bambuk in 1550.[97] There was also a report of mines some fifty miles from Mina.[98] Others looked even further to the future. Jean Nicot, the alert French ambassador in Lisbon, wrote in a letter of August 17, 1561, about the plans of King John III of Portugal, who proposed to explore the Zambezi, thought at the time to have the same source as the Nile and the Congo, and provide the origin of Guinean gold.[99] This roused Nicot's anxiety: were the Portuguese, by gaining control of the estuary of the Zambezi, about to divert the whole trade in gold to the east coast of Africa, well out of reach

---

[94] Braudel, *Méditerranée,* p. 415; Pierre Chaunu, "Le galion de Manille," *Annales: Économies, Sociétés, Civilisations,* [hereafter cited as *Annales*] VI (1951); T'ien-Tsê Chang, *Sino-Portuguese Trade from 1544 to 1644* (Leiden, 1934), p. 99; De Hieronimo de Banuelos y Carillo, *Relation de Iles Philippines,* in De Thévenot, *Voyages* (3 vols., Paris, 1664–1684).

[95] Hamilton, *American Treasure,* p. 42.

[96] Braudel, *Méditerranée,* pp. 368, 748, citing Diego de Haedo, *Topographia e Historia, Epitome* (Valladolid, 1612), Chap. 7, Section I, p. 66ᵛᵒ.

[97] Bovill, *Caravans of the Old Sahara,* p. 150.

[98] Blake, *Europeans in West Africa,* p. 178, letter of Feb. 5, 1551, from John III to the Count of Castanheira.

[99] Jean Nicot, *Sa correspondance diplomatique,* ed. Edmund Falgairolle (Paris, 1897), pp. 69–72, letter of Aug. 17, 1561.

of competition from other Europeans, and so gain a virtual monopoly? The expedition of Francisco Barreto advanced up the Zambezi in 1572 in search of the goldfields of Manika, but in the end achieved only minor success. The Portuguese did not manage to find sizable quantities of gold in this area until the beginning of the seventeenth century.[100] But whatever the rebuffs or successes, all these episodes in search of gold began to emerge logically, once the trend in bullion movements had been reversed.

In the years after 1550, the Portuguese were not alone in showing interest in the gold of Africa. It was not by chance that Gian Battista Ramusio's *Navigationi,* the first and most important volume containing the *Descrizione dell'Africa* by Leo Africanus, began to appear in 1550. By 1553 it was in its third edition, with a French translation in 1556. In 1551 and 1552 the English organized voyages to Morocco of which Richard Hakluyt later published the account.[101] The following year they sailed further south on the first of a long series of expeditions to the coast of Guinea. Pepper (probably melegueta) and some 150 pounds of gold dust were the main result of the first venture, which benefited from the advice of a former Portuguese pilot, Anthony Anes Pinteado, formerly a coastguard in Brazil and Guinea. In 1553 three ships brought back spices and four hundred pounds of gold. William Towrson sailed with two ships from Newport for the same destination in 1550 and in 1556 returned from a second voyage with gold and ivory.[102]

In France, for similar reasons, the same search for gold began. By all accounts, the route was a regular one for French navigators; in 1552 a French ship, driven to seek safety in an English port, was found to be carrying, as luck would have it, forty-five *marcs* weight of gold from Mina. When in 1555 Towrson encountered an unknown ship, he prepared at once to defend himself, fearing "that it was some Portuguese or French ship." The following year, on his second expedition, he met the *Espoir* of Le Havre, the *Levriette* of Rouen, and another ship of some seventy tons coming from Honfleur, from whom he learned that the coast had already been visited by the *Roeberge* and the *Shandet* (240 tons), in addition to another vessel of eighty tons. If we add another French ship, also of about eighty tons, which Towrson passed on the return trip, seven French vessels at least had made the voyage to the coast of Guinea at the same time as he. The English naturally were not pleased about all this. They complained of the encounters they suffered with their determined competitors, just as with the Portuguese (who had first claim), but still it was about the French presence that they complained most. They had done "much hurt to our markets," ran the English account, and

[100] Coupland, *East Africa and Its Invaders,* p. 50; George McCall Theal, *The Portuguese in South Africa* (London, 1896), p. 129.
[101] Richard Hakluyt, *The Principal Navigations, Voyages, Traffiques and Discoveries of the English Nation* (8 vols., London, 1927; 2 supplementary vols., 1928), IV, pp. 32–33.
[102] *Ibid.,* pp. 66–94.

"filled them with cloth."[103] The French probably sought gold, more than anything else, on the African coast, in exchange for cloth or knickknacks. If additional proof is needed, it can be found in the famous ship *Salamandre* which was fitted out on the Normandy coast, in 1559, for the express purpose of going to Mina to find gold, then in great demand in France.[104] And Towrson, when he captured the *Mulet de Batville* on his third voyage to Guinea in 1577, found fifty pounds of gold on board and learned at the same time that the *La Foi* and the *Aventureuse,* from Honfleur, which had slipped past him, had carried back about 120 pounds and that another ship from Dieppe and a caravel had left earlier with seven hundred pounds.[105]

After the middle of the century, then, the gold trade with the coast of Guinea recovered some of its vigor.[106] But, even when added to the gold arriving from America, it did not match the requirements of economic activity. Nor did it restore the balance between the two precious metals. Prospectors did not hesitate to lay out new and costly investments. There were the searches carried out in Brazil, after 1560, unrewarding at first and indeed for many years, but finally producing substantial results later, toward the end of the seventeenth century. Gold also featured in the voyages of Sir Martin Frobisher: the first trip had the express purpose of discovering a Northwest Passage to the East Indies, but a sample of ore brought back set in motion two subsequent expeditions in 1577 and 1578. These expeditions, which included a hundred miners, returned laden with marcasite ore and gold-bearing rock, but proved a bitter disappointment for those who had financed the affair (Queen Elizabeth included). The ores were found to produce little. Later, in England in 1661, a new gold coin was minted from the gold brought from the coast of Guinea by the Africa Company, and it soon became famous as the "guinea."[107]

To round out the picture, mention must be made of the numerous, and indeed nameless, colonies of gold prospectors, found here and there in Europe plying their skills along the rivers in France, on the Rhine, or in Bohemia, Moldavia, and Transylvania.[108] These are scattered details. Even if gold oc-

---

[103] *Ibid.*, pp. 95–128.
[104] See Chap. 3, n. 119. C.S.P., Foreign, letters of Dec. 12, 19, 1559, from Francis Edwards to Cecil; A.N., Z¹B. 371, Feb. 10, Aug. 19, Sept. 15, Oct. 19, 1560, Jan. 18, Feb. 20, 1561, which give details on the voyages in search of African gold.
[105] Hakluyt, *Principal Navigations*; C.S.P., Foreign, May 27, 1562, declaration of Martin Frobisher.
[106] Duarte Gómez Solis, *Alegación en favor de la Compañia de la India Oriental y comercios ultra-marinos* (n.p., 1628), and in "Advice to the Reader," records the arrival of a ship "from Mina with much gold."
[107] C.S.P., Domestic, Apr. 22, Sept. 26, Nov. 26, 1577; C.S.P., Colonial, East Indies, Jan.–Feb. 1578, Feb. 18, 1579, Feb. 1581; Feavearyear, *Pound Sterling*, pp. 89–90.
[108] In the same way, along with the silver mines of Germany and Central Europe in the early sixteenth century should be noted those in France (such as in Lyonnais and Nivernais), in Scandinavia "fertile di miniere d'argento," and in England in the tin mining of Cornwall. The product was small, but the operations were significant since these small undertakings survived only at a time when there was excess demand for the metal,

casionally appeared in small quantities, the fact has some relevance, for in the sixteenth century, no privilege, no exclusive monopoly for gold could be maintained.

To complete this outline of the century of silver one final factor must be mentioned: the extraordinary price put on gold during the silver inflation. This should not pass unnoticed for the inflation lasted the century. There were, on occasion, signs that gold made some reappearances. Thus on November 29, 1597, in Venice, there was an abundance of gold for a brief moment in the hands of merchants.[109] It was natural that they all wanted to be paid in gold and did their utmost to demand this. As a result, the resources of some of the banks were overextended, and various possible remedies were tried to expand or supplement the circulation of gold. As the currency in demand, it was a better store of value. In Genoa in 1586, after the crisis of 1583, the "famosissima" Casa di San Giorgio opened a *cartulario d'oro* for current accounts in gold, repayable in gold.[110] This *cartulario d'oro* will be discussed later.

Many even smaller instances show the advantages of gold during the second half of the sixteenth century. In 1562–1563, after a series of poor harvests, Venice was alarmed, with good reason, about its food supplies. The Senate passed two decrees (November 6, 1562, and October 15, 1563) at the onset of winter allowing *zecchini,* the precious gold sequins, to be used only for the purchase of wheat. Contarini later records that it "was thought half sufficient" to bring "plenty" to Venice, for the peasants and landowners of Apulia had a special preference for sequins.[111] In Naples it was thought that, in order to acquire the better quality wheat from Apulia, the Venetians were prepared to use all sorts of devices, even fraud. They dealt through their subjects, the merchants of Bergamo, and their interested accomplices, the monks of the Tremiti Islands, who also traded in wheat.[112] But gold had its part to play. In the same way, it seems that in supplying wheat to the city of Lisbon the Breton seaman received payment in the "red gold" of Guinea.[113] Governments preferred to make their payments and mobilize their resources in gold, for it was far more negotiable and efficient than silver. Thus couriers

---

or as a by-product of other metal production. See Botero, *Relationi Universale, passim,* but especially pp. 84, 111; C.S.P., Foreign, letter of Jan. 8, 1551, from Gaeret Harman to Sir William Cecil; George Randall Lewis, *The Stannaries* (Cambridge, Mass., 1908), pp. 41–43.

[109] A.S., Venice, *Senato Zecca,* Filza, 5, Nov. 29, 1597, document communicated by Braudel.

[110] Giovanni Domenico Peri, *Il negotiante* (2 vols., Genoa, 1647), II, p. 95; Heinrich Sieveking, "Das Bankwesen in Genua und die Bank von S. Giorgio," in Johannes G. van Dillen, *A History of the Principal Public Banks* (The Hague, 1934).

[111] *Marciana,* VII–MCCXVIII, pp. 1–9, Contarini, *Scritture oro e argento,* Aug. 16, 1671, document communicated by Braudel.

[112] A.S., Naples, *Regina Camera, Consultationum,* II, p. 237–241, document communicated by Braudel.

[113] Nicot, *Correspondance diplomatique,* letter of Dec. 12, 1559, p. 45.

carried gold, the coins being sewn into their clothing, to the Low Countries in 1576, probably from Genoa.[114] The agents of Spain often tried to acquire gold on the markets of Paris and Lyons for the repeated payments that Spanish policy demanded in the Low Countries.[115] Again, in 1581, on the eve of the official truce between Spain and Turkey, Spain made secret payments in gold for political reasons "in crowns, of Spanish stamp," as a French correspondent described it.[116] A former Venetian ambassador returning from Spain wrote from Savona on September 27, 1586, that twenty galleys brought the Count da Miranda from the peninsula with 300,000 crowns in silver reals and 100,000 crowns in gold. "The whole affair passed under the name of private persons," he explained, "but in reality they are for a contract with the Genoese who are obliged to transfer them to Flanders." And so everything was in order. But he goes on to say, "What is of greatest consideration in this business is the 100,000 (crowns) in gold, because unless in greatest need the King (Philip II) would not grant permission to send gold from Spain, from which may be supposed great embarrassment in his affairs." [117]

In conclusion, one can infer that any transfer or any payment in gold appeared extraordinary and worth notice; nothing could better reveal its scarcity.

3. The Appreciation of Copper

Remembering the remarks in the Introduction, the reader might ask, "And what about copper?" The relative value of copper rose during the first period, but also in the second period, the century of silver. During these phases copper continued to improve in relative value, in the first place by comparison with gold and then with silver. In the royal mint in Aix-en-Provence, on January 30, 1592, under exceptional conditions, it was reported that the prices of "all other commodities have increased by half, even copper and charcoal." [118] On May 8, 1598, in Venice, the *Zecca* had stocks of copper worth about 30,000 ducats as a result of a purchase in 1590 at 127 ducats the *migliaro*. As this copper was unsuitable for coinage, it was decided that it should be sold since "copper has greatly risen in price, being worth about 130 ducats." [119] Even poor-grade copper had appreciated.

At an early stage governments used as an expedient the remelting and conversion of copper coins (in addition to billon, which contained a small proportion of silver). The classic book of Ludovico Bianchini shows this in

[114] Braudel, *Méditerranée*, p. 382, n. 45.
[115] Henri Lapeyre, *Simon Ruiz et les Asientos de Philippe II* (Paris, 1954), *passim*, and *Une famille de marchands: Les Ruiz* (Paris, 1955).
[116] Braudel, *Méditerranée*, pp. 993–995.
[117] A.S., Venice, *Senato Dispacci, Spagna*, Savona, Sept. 27, 1586, document communicated by Braudel.
[118] A.N., Z'B.383, letter of Jan. 30, 1592, from the gardes of the mint in Aix to the Cour des Monnaies in Paris.
[119] A.S., Venice, *Senato Zecca*, Filza 5, May 8, 1598, document communicated by Braudel.

Sicily during the viceroyalty of the Duke of Feria (1602–1606).[120] The reason was clear enough: the intrinsic value of the billon coins — the "black money" — had risen sufficiently far above the face value. And so there were conversions and issues of lighter coins, but these usually occupy only a small place in the general histories of the period. Eventually it became more practicable to use pure copper. These fractional coins, of course, were used largely in everyday transactions, by poorer people and in backward economies. There was the case of Aquileia ("Adler" in the German documents), a mountain canton largely supported by the intensive cultivation of saffron; this allowed it to enter international trade, mainly through buyers for the markets of Germany and the Low Countries, foremost among whom were the Welsers.[121] The German merchants, it should be noted, often settled their accounts in copper. At Aquileia the mint issued copper or largely copper coins and could be certain of putting them into circulation at favorable rates among the trusting peasants. Copper and peasants, copper and the poor, copper and semi-barter economies — these realities must be kept together. In any case, throughout the sixteenth century the prevailing structures of economic activity favored copper. It is, consequently, easier to understand the progress of the copper mines in Germany and Hungary, which, as is well known, were generally closely tied to the mining of silver. The latter faced difficulties; the former prospered. The copper of Mansfeld and Neusohl easily conquered the international markets during the gold phase.[122] Copper offered profitable business in the century of silver, as the authorities in Frankfurt on the Main revealed in 1554.[123] Under the same conditions the wealthy and daring merchants — or, rather, the authorities — of Leipzig were caught up in the dangerous and ultimately catastrophic operations of 1619.[124] Increasing arrivals of gold or silver improved the position of copper by making it relatively scarce, not only for particular industrial uses, but also for money. It is clear that these arrivals considerably facilitated the expansion of its role.

The monetary phase from the mid-sixteenth century was characterized by an inflow of silver, with its consequent progressive appreciation both of gold and copper. The conditions of disequilibrium owing to this state of affairs lasted for almost a century; the decline in silver imports, at first gradual, then rapid in the 1630s and 1640s, led to repercussions throughout the international economy.[125] There was, according to Earl J. Hamilton, a fall in the efficiency

---

[120] Ludovico Bianchini, *Della storia economico-civile di Sicilia* (2 vols., Naples and Palermo, 1841), I, p. 336.
[121] Karl O. Müller, *Welthandelsbräuche, 1480–1540, Deutsche Handelsakten des Mittelalters und der Neuzeit* (Stuttgart, 1934), pp. 241–246.
[122] Möllenberg, *Die Eroberung des Weltmarkts durch das mansfeldische Kupfer*; Günther von Probszt, *Die Stadt Wien* (Stuttgart, 1926).
[123] Dietz, *Frankfurter Handelsgeschichte*, II, pp. 185–186.
[124] *Ibid.*, pp. 187–188.
[125] Hamilton, *American Treasure*, pp. 40–42.

of silver.[126] Additions to the stocks of precious metals followed a declining trend, which was progressively accentuated. In 1601, or perhaps a little earlier, in Spain and the "advanced" economies of the western Mediterranean prices in terms of silver had reached a climax. Although the rise in prices continued in some of the economies of Northwestern Europe until the 1640s, in Holland and England, for example, the days of this great inflation were drawing to a close. By the outbreak of the Thirty Years' War and the commercial crisis of 1619–1620, the various economies seem to have escaped the more disturbing effects of silver. One monetary phase was ending, and one was beginning. The ensuing years were extremely complicated, and the monetary structures did not regain a state of order until the closing two decades of the seventeenth century. At that time, the Brazilian miners, among others, finally succeeded in introducing another phase of gold. Until about 1680 (the date is very approximate) a confused state of affairs generally prevailed. It was paradoxical since the decline in the primacy of silver did not remove completely demand for it from the markets of Europe and the world. The most curious feature of these years of economic difficulty was the double role of copper and credit. Pressures to expand the circulation of copper almost constituted, so to speak, a copper revolution.

In the waning inflation of precious metals, copper and, to some extent, credit could become substitutes; here, then, is a contrast between the failure of the circulations of gold and silver and the emergence of copper and credit. Such conditions raised problems of a more general kind, and the phases of gold and silver must be considered in this context. There is some advantage in returning in more detail to the earlier arguments.

During the years roughly from the 1590s to the 1610s, supply of silver to the international economy broke down; different regional economies experienced the problem in varying degrees.

Historians have tried to explain this situation in terms of conditions prevailing in America, the progressive exhaustion of mines of the New World being used as one possible explanation. The costs of extraction and production rose, and, perhaps, as Hamilton has suggested, the stream of silver was diverted across the Pacific to China.[127] Pierre Chaunu, in his careful assessment of the Pacific trade in the sixteenth and seventeenth centuries, discounts such an explanation. He considers that the movement of Spanish trade to China had essentially the same characteristics as that across the Atlantic to Seville; the declining production of the mines must be considered causal.[128] Similarly, the contraband trade in Peruvian silver by way of the Río de la Plata — Alice Piffer Canabrava dated its prosperity to the years 1590–1623

[126] *Ibid.,* Chap. IX.
[127] *Ibid.,* p. 37; Braudel, *Méditerranée,* p. 416; Chaunu, "Galion de Manille," p. 34.
[128] Chaunu, "Galion de Manille."

— lost its importance about the same time as the great official trade to Seville,[129] or may even have preceded it.

During the seventeenth century, as the deliveries of silver progressively diminished, the trading companies encountered increasing difficulties in acquiring sufficient reals for their transactions in the Levant and the East Indies. Such factors and incidents naturally produced a spate of reports. This copious literature, still largely unpublished, includes technical manuals, occasionally of some importance (for example, the treatise of Barba,[130] published in Peru in 1639 and in Madrid in 1640, and that of Montalvo,[131] published in 1643), which reveal the gravity of the problem. They show clearly the new conditions that troubled the mines in Spanish America.[132] In Mexico the mineral deposits were extremely varied; this was later confirmed in the voyages of Alexander von Humboldt at the turn of the eighteenth century. Some unpleasant surprises in mining resulted from this variety. The lodes of the Veta Madre at Guanajuato, usually about twelve to fifteen meters thick, could shrink to half a meter or branch out into veins often with low silver content. Also at Guanajuato, in the famous mine of Valenciana (as described by Humboldt), the operations depended on a lode seven meters thick without ramifications, going down some 170 meters, but this was most productive at a depth ranging from 100 to 340 meters from the surface. At Rajas the rich ore began at ground level.[133]

In the seventeenth century conditions for producing silver were persistently unfavorable, and this often meant unrewarding and uncertain operations. The final value of the metal produced no longer carried the same profits as before. The problem in this structural change is to determine whether the European — or, indeed, the international — economy had the strength and capacity to overcome the ensuing technical and material difficulties. It was in reality a huge problem. For the moment, some attention must be given to technical considerations, to the quasi failure of the methods that had up to that point proven so effective.

The amalgamation process had been introduced into Mexico about 1554–1557 and was further developed and applied in Peru in 1572 by Pedro Fernández de Velasco. It was widely used, owing to the abundant mercury deposits both at Challatiri near Potosí and in the neighborhood of Guarina and Moromoro. These were kept more or less in reserve, while the nearby produc-

---

[129] Alice Piffer Canabrava, *O comércio português no Rio da Prata (1580–1640)* (São Paulo, 1944).

[130] Barba, *Arte de los metales.*

[131] Luis Berrio de Montalvo, *Al Exmo Señor Don Garcia Sarmiento de Sotomayor y Luna . . . en informe del nuevo beneficio que se ha dado a los metaloz ordinarios de plata por azogue* (Mexico City, 1643), cited by Percy, *Metallurgy: Gold and Silver,* p. 562.

[132] Communicated by Mlle. Marie Helmer.

[133] Friedrich Heinrich Alexander von Humboldt, *Essai politique sur le royaume de la Nouvelle Espagne* (2 vols., Paris, 1811), II, pp. 1–50; Percy, *Metallurgy: Gold and Silver,* p. 579.

tive Guancavelica mine[134] remained in production, as it did until the cave-in of 1776. The combination of silver ore and mercury therefore operated in Peru. Rich deposits of salt, which was generally employed in the production process, were found both near the mines of San Cristóbal de Achocolla and in the springs of García Mendoza.[135] The amalgamation process, as a result, long continued to be employed in the mines of the Andes. As Barba records, however, the method was extremely wasteful: the silver ore, especially in Peru, came in various forms and required different processes. For example, in order to part the gold and silver in one particular ore called *machacado,* a special process had to be employed. Another source of wastage was the huge loss of mercury, driven off by heat and not recovered. Thus the costs of production in this sector tended to rise, as the silver content of the ore progressively declined. From 1590 to 1631, 345,827 quintals of mercury (official figures) were extracted from Guancavelica.[136] Although these observations do not exhaust the technicalities of the subject, they are sufficient to indicate the general scope of the problem.

In effect, this situation was similar in some respects to that in Germany in the mid-sixteenth-century. As the ore resources became more difficult of access, the operations inevitably became more capital intensive. The operators had to resolve certain technical problems in order to work the deep deposits at a profit. Georgius Agricola has admirably recorded some of these in his *De Re Metallica.*[137] The situations were essentially the same no doubt, but the outcomes were very different. The powerful movement of the international economy had given the German mines a second lease on life, but this was not true for the mines of the New World. The recovery of silver mining in the eighteenth century came in Mexico rather than in Peru. From this it would seem that the crisis in silver mining at the end of the sixteenth and the beginning of the seventeenth centuries especially concerned the latter area. The mines of Potosí had, apparently, passed the moment of their astonishing innovation, of their rising marginal productivity. Because of the state of the international markets, these mines were not to benefit from fresh technology and labor which would allow them immediately to recover their prosperity. Insufficient labor in Mexico prevented this recovery. There was, perhaps, a general labor shortage in New Spain, a decline in population that became unmistakable by the early seventeenth century.[138] A similar recession appeared in the mines of Potosí, a "degeneration" [139] in the working of the *mita* (con-

---

[134] *Ibid.,* p. 562; Barba, *Arte de los metales,* fols. 7, 33, 38, 55–56, Bk. II, Chaps. 3, 12, 21; Bk. III, Chaps. 1, 16; Bk. IV, Chaps. 8, 22. Guancavelica, according to Helmer, even supplied Mexico with mercury in 1591 because of the shortage of supplies from Almadén.

[135] See the photographs of Robert Gerstmann, *Bolivia* (Mulhouse, 1928).

[136] Communication by Helmer.

[137] See Agricola, *De Re Metallica,* n. 37, above.

[138] François Chevalier, *La formation des grandes domaines au Mexique* (Paris, 1952), p. 54.

[139] According to Helmer.

scripted Indian labor). Could the world economy overcome this labor problem? Outward appearances of events indicate that it could not. One can cite the downturn in the economy in America, its progressive lack of vitality as the seventeenth century advanced, the symptomatic rise in land values, and, above all, the establishment of the great aristocratic estates, the Mexican haciendas and their counterparts in Peru.[140] This period has been called by some Latin American historians by the new, though deceptive, term of "Middle Ages" [141] in America; the great "Renaissance" was to come later in the eighteenth century.

All these questions logically find their place alongside the history of precious metals and money and indeed go beyond the present purpose of description. It may be added perhaps that the explanations become more difficult after 1620–1640, that great turning point, as Hamilton has observed, which can be discussed at length. Was there, in effect, a decisive break in the European economy, as the official data of precious metal imports into Spain appear to indicate? After all, these figures do stress the abrupt decline in the deliveries of silver from America.[142] It would go beyond the limits of the subject to ask whether there were differences in phasing between the various economies of the world. It is even possible to assume that smuggling may have had some bearing on the overall validity of the official imports of bullion into Spain, which particularly affected the decline in silver. But this is a partial hypothesis. After summing up the total importations of silver, one would find, in all probability, a general decline. It is possible, by the same token, to set this reality in the context of a general economic recession, which some historians have been inclined to place around the 1620s. This is probably valid for the "advanced" economies of the Mediterranean area in the sixteenth century, which after 1600, and certainly after 1620, experienced retardation. In the wider context of Europe, it is likely that the downturn was spread over a much longer period. The smaller economies of northwestern Europe, Holland and Britain, for example, may have survived until the second quarter of the seventeenth century.[143] It was probably not until the mid-seventeenth century that the long recession was finally confirmed. Whether it came a little sooner or a little later is a matter of chronological detail, significant enough in itself, but this should not conceal the overall picture of a pause in the development of the international economy.

The international economy looked for ways to escape from its monetary difficulties. Some are fairly well known, but there is also a whole field, largely unstudied, concerning the different issues of inferior and counterfeit money

---

[140] See also n. 30, above.

[141] German Arciniegas, *Este pueblo de América* (Mexico City, 1945), p. 49.

[142] Hamilton, *American Treasure*, pp. 40–42.

[143] Frank Spooner, "The Economy of Europe, 1609–1650," in *The New Cambridge Modern History*, IV, ed. J. P. Cooper (Cambridge, Eng., 1970).

which were current in the seventeenth century. These signs of stress have some importance in showing what emerged from the increasing demand for gold. The search was carried from Western Europe eastward to Poland, Russia, and the Balkans.[144] These surreptitious movements are difficult to trace, for gold was a silent traveler, but some indications appear in the letters of Venetian merchants at the end of the sixteenth century.[145] In Venice, with gold at a premium, the main purpose appears to have been to obtain in trading operations return payments in gold sequins. At the end of the century Botero also observed that the gold of Ethiopia arrived in Egypt "a copia." Later still, in 1661, Jean-Baptiste Tavernier records in his travels that Ethiopian gold arrived by way of the valley of the Nile.[146] The long report put out by the "master" of the Zecca of Venice on the subject of gold deserves close attention.[147] After a long discussion of the advantages to the Venetian economy of coining gold and since "at present everything is running down," he proposed, in his memorial of August 16, 1671, to take advantage of the period of calm following the end of the Candian War (1669). At that time, there was a double problem of coining gold and silver in the Zecca. Concerning silver, the "master" wrote; "for the silver scudo and *ducatone* are at a high price, and so the coinage has stopped for lack of bullion and for being unable to obtain silver at a reasonable price." And there were even more severe difficulties over gold, for the *zecchini* continued to disappear through trade to the Levant. "As regards gold specie, there was formerly the coinage of the gold scudo, that is, the Venetian doppia; then there was afterward the noble and precious money, the zecchino, at the moment considered a scandalous thing, destructive of trade; in view of the value put on the zecchino in countries abroad and especially in the Levant, there is every year a demand to export zecchini rather than goods from the city." There was only one way to stop the drain of gold coin: a tax on its export, as Contarini proposed, so that at least the *Signoria* would have a share in the profits. Another possible answer was to raise the current rate for the sequin.

The same difficulties were apparently experienced in Amsterdam. In 1673 Johannes Phoonsen proposed in a memoir to transform the Wisselbank into a bank of current money. In Genoa, in the *Casa,* by then the Banco di San Giorgio, the same trend appeared in 1675 with the establishment of the Banco di moneta corrente, discussed later.[148]

---

[144] Was the return of Hungarian gold coins into circulation in the west a coincidence?

[145] Ugo Tucci, *Lettres d'un marchand venitien, Andrea Berengo (1533–1556)* (Paris, 1957).

[146] Botero, *Relationi Universale,* p. 163; Jean-Baptiste Tavernier, *Les six voyages* (2 pts, Paris, 1679), Pt. 2, p. 324, cited by Braudel, *Méditerranée,* p. 178.

[147] *Marciana,* VII–MCCXVIII, pp. 1–9, *Contarini, Scritture oro e argento,* Aug. 16, 1671, document communicated by Braudel.

[148] Johannes G. Van Dillen, *Bronnen tot de geschiedenis der Wisselbanken* (2 vols., The Hague, 1925), I, p. 166; Sieveking, *Bank von S. Giorgio,* p. 31. According to Adam Wiszniewski, *Histoire de la Banque de Saint-Georges de Gênes* (Paris, 1865), p. 128, the Casa became the Banco di San Giorgio in 1675.

But wide-ranging adjustments were out of the question; only minor expedients were possible. Contarini suggested that, in view of the lack of sequins, they should use *ongari* (the gold coins from Hungary), which would offer a way out of their difficulties, "and which is reason why the aforesaid goods remain here idle." [149] The gold ongari were used extensively in trade in the Balkans at that time.

A decade later everything became much clearer: gold was being coined for the first time in Mexico; Brazilian gold began to have an effect. The latter event is still largely overlooked. Werner Sombart was one of the first to note its immense importance.[150] Brazilian historians go so far as to attribute to the panning of gold and intensive exploitation of the goldfields of the Brazilian interior by imported colored labor[151] all the great achievements of Europe in the eighteenth century among them, the Industrial Revolution in England and even the French Revolution.[152]

From the New World, again, little by little, a new cycle of precious metals emerged. In spite of a number of well-entrenched misconceptions, it is clear that if the silver of America in the sixteenth century was successfully exploited by indigenous labor almost to the point of exhaustion, the gold of Brazil, on the other hand, relied on Negro slaves. No doubt because of climatic conditions, the silver mines remained largely unknown to them: the dry heat of northern Mexico and the intense cold of the mountains of Peru were not conducive to the systematic employment of Negro labor. The goldfields of Brazil combined natural resources in gold, a hot subtropical climate, and labor of African origin.

Thus, by different phases, we arrive at a point roughly about the 1680s, when the primacy of gold reemerged. It would be wrong, however, to imagine that before this date, or indeed afterward, there was a decline in the silver market. The situation was far from being so simple. Silver exercised economic pressures much longer than may at first be supposed. Doubtless, it did not have the same effects as formerly, but numerous documents show that in Genoa (probably still one of the richest cities of the time) silver continued to play a prominent role. It arrived from Spain, although not in such huge quantities as before. The *Negotiante* of Peri, published in Genoa in 1638, gave instructions on how to count, or rather weigh, the boxes of coin unloaded from ships or galleys onto the wharves of the city. In the last quarter of the sixteenth century the Spanish, Genoese, Neapolitan, and even Sicilian galleys, en route

---

[149] *Marciana*, VII–MCCXVIII, pp. 1–9, *Contarini, Scritture oro e argento*, Aug. 16, 1671, document communicated by Braudel.

[150] Werner Sombart, *Der moderne Kapitalismus* (2 vols., Munich, 1922), I, p. 533 *et passim;* see also Vitorino Magalhães Godinho, "Le Portugal, les flottes du sucre et les flottes de l'or," *Annales*, V (1950).

[151] On the wastage of this labor, see notably Liesegang, *Deutsche Berg- und Hütten-leute in Süd- und Mittelamerika.*

[152] This proposition is often formulated. See the numerous studies by Alfredo Ellis Junior, especially in *Revista de historia,* IV (1952).

from Barcelona or nearby ports, often carried millions of crowns worth in reals and bars of the still abundant silver. Thus in January 1597 eight galleys brought a cargo worth a million crowns.[153] During the following century they continued their activity in bullion and specie: in December 1616 five galleys shipped 400,000 crowns from Barcelona;[154] in March 1627 the galleys loaded more than three hundred boxes in Barcelona, in April two hundred boxes,[155] and in June six hundred boxes.[156] These examples, it should be remembered, came just after copper coinage was discontinued in 1626. One can find many similar details: in May 1648 there is mention of 150 boxes of *contanti* at Tarragona;[157] in August 1650 the convoys of mules (*condotte*) that transported silver to the ports of Catalonia were arrested and their precious cargoes confiscated.[158]

But the silver trade from Spain to Genoa went on, served as usual by the galleys. The Genoese would probably have preferred to transport by ship rather than by galley, for the latter had to go alongside the wharf to take on cargo and so came under the surveillance of the port authorities. A ship, on the other hand, could anchor in the Bay of Cádiz and load its cargo in the freeway, almost on the open sea, thus making Cádiz, or rather the Bay of Cádiz, the center for distributing silver from America to the Mediterranean and Europe.[159] The available correspondence of French consuls in Genoa provides a fairly clear picture, from 1670, of the shipments of silver, generally in English, Dutch, or Genoese men-of-war. Small merchants were also concerned, sending consignments in ships from St. Malo, for example, where the shipments figured along with cargoes of codfish. One news report indicates the arrival of an English vessel on April 16, 1670, with 600,000 crowns in bars and pieces of eight reals: "it gave no salute [on entering port] claiming that the salute should be returned salvo for salvo." [160] Such an altercation was of minor importance, but it emphasizes that Genoa continued to be a focal point of Europe, receiving regular deliveries of silver.

It was not possible, actually, for silver alone to meet the total monetary demand. As a result, copper achieved exceptional success, promoted almost to the status of a precious metal. Copper had, in reality, always played a part

[153] *Mediceo*, 4925, fol. 5ᵛᵒ, letter from Madrid of Jan. 12, 1597, from Francesco Guicciardini to the Grand Duke. This and the following documents communicated by Braudel.

[154] A.S., Genoa, *Lettere ministri, Spagna,* 23, 18. 2427, letter of Dec. 5, 1616.

[155] *Ibid.,* 23, 25. 2434, letters from Madrid, Mar. 31, Apr. 20, 1627, from Batista Serra to Genoa.

[156] *Ibid.,* letter of June 11, 1627, from Gio. Batista Salazzo and Luca Pallavicino to Genoa.

[157] *Ibid.,* 38, from Madrid, May 20, 1648.

[158] *Ibid.,* from Madrid, Aug. 24, Sept. 28, 1650.

[159] See Fernand Braudel, "Note sull'economia del Mediterraneo nel XVII secolo," *Economia e storia,* II (1955).

[160] A.N., Affaires Étrangères, B.1, 511, Genoa, Apr. 16, 1670, document communicated by Braudel.

in the stock of money, and, although admittedly a minor part, nevertheless it should not be underestimated.[161] It appeared generally at all levels of money since it was alloyed with the more precious metals. If the proportion increased, then the intrinsic value of the gold and silver coins fell. By such adjustments, therefore, copper became a means of debasement, which had some importance. Lower down the monetary scale, in fractional coinage, it became the principal component. There were technical difficulties of keeping small coins in circulation when they contained only a small quantity of silver, owing partly to their small size and the prevailing techniques of coinage and partly also to the persistent difficulty during inflation, when their intrinsic values rose above their fixed face values. This meant that copper was frequently used as an alternative solution. When the coins contained less silver than copper they were not known as billon, but were more familiarly called "black coins." As has already been noted, they were used by the poor, by backward areas, and by semiclosed quasi-autonomous economies, which were a frequent feature of the preindustrial world. The black coins were important: they gave cohesion to economic activity and facilitated transactions, but, following Gresham's law, there was a constant dialogue with the more valuable currency. There was even speculation in copper. The weight of the small silver coins was reduced until finally, by the seventeenth century, coins of pure copper largely filled the lower grades of monetary circulation. There was a temptation, and perhaps an obligation, to use this when bullion was relatively scarce.

In the production of metal, copper represented about a tenth of that of iron,[162] a ratio that has since been greatly altered by industrialization. It may even be said that in the seventeenth century copper had relatively more uses than today; besides its use as money, it served many prime industrial purposes. During the sixteenth century increasingly large quantities were made into utensils, basins, and bracelets that were shipped to America, North Africa, and Asia. The Portuguese settled their deficit trading balances by exporting precious metals and copper. Such exports were of capital importance, explaining to some extent the immense fortune of the Fuggers, who were able to sell both silver and copper, through their control of the German and Hungarian mines and their associated distribution outlets to such great cities as Danzig, Antwerp, and Venice. The abundance of gold and then silver improved the position of copper; the wider use of bronze artillery assured its fortune. There have been many studies of the way in which the copper of Mansfeld in Saxony conquered the markets in the early sixteenth century. Other studies have shown that later (roughly from 1550 to 1650) there followed the remarkable expansion of copper mining at Neusohl in Hungary, a development that was by no means mediocre.[163] There can be little doubt, on

---

[161] Hamilton, *American Treasure,* Chap. IV *passim;* Braudel, *Méditerranée,* p. 420.
[162] John U. Nef, *War and Human Progress* (Cambridge, Mass., 1950), p. 35.
[163] R. A. Peltzer, "Geschichte der Messingindustrie . . . in Aachen," *Zeitschrift des*

balance, that copper has assumed a prominent place in modern economic development. The seventeenth century gave it monetary significance.

After 1570, however copper faced a period of difficulty. In the mines of Germany, especially those of Mansfeld,[164] the lodes diminished and production declined, but these developments were not valid for the whole of Central Europe.[165]

The underlying difficulties made their presence felt in the Frankfort fairs, where copper was distributed to Aachen and the Netherlands. The situation deteriorated further, and the quotations of this German copper disappeared from the Prijscouranten of Amsterdam in 1609, the Coperdraet van Oostland in 1624, and the Oosters Latoen in 1638.[166] It should be noted, in compensation, that Swedish mines rose to prominence in the late sixteenth and the early seventeenth century. Swedish copper was developed, organized, and financed by the merchants of Lübeck, Hamburg, and Amsterdam.[167] As German copper disappeared from the great international markets, it was replaced by copper from Sweden and then from Neusohl. The Swedish product was sent to Spain, France, England, Russia, Persia, and other countries.[168] It was of better quality than that from Germany, more abundant, and cheaper. And soon, in further support of this industrial and monetary fortune, the excellent and cheap copper of Japan was developed by the Dutch and, following them, by the English. The main market for this was found in India, in name at least a Portuguese preserve.

Swedish and Danish historians are studying the history of the production and international trade in copper.[169] Without attempting to follow their studies

---

Aachener Geschichtsvereins, XXX (1908), cited by Josef Wolontis, *Kopparmyntningen i Sverige 1624–1714* (Helsingfors, 1936), p. 46, n. 1; Eli Heckscher, "Den europeiska kopparmarknaden under 1600-talet," *Scandia*, XI (1938), p. 275; Probszt, *Die Stadt Wien*; Dietz, *Frankfurter Handelsgeschichte*, II, pp. 180 ff.

[164] Heckscher, "Europeiska kopparmarknaden," pp. 226, 275, citing Walter Möllenberg, *Die Eroberung des Weltmarkts durch das mansfeldische Kupfer* (Gotha, 1911).

[165] Probszt, *Die Stadt Wien*, p. 311.

[166] Heckscher, "Europeiska kopparmarknaden," p. 275. In 1617 Emperor Mathias sent his agent to Frankfort to find out the reasons for the fall in demand for Hungarian copper. See Friedrich Bothe, *Gustav Adolfs und sein Kanzlers wirtschafts-politische Absichten auf Deutschland* (Frankfort on the Main, 1910), p. 207; Dietz, *Frankfurter Handelsgeschichte*, II, p. 187.

[167] Johannes G. van Dillen, "Amsterdamsche notarieele acten betreffende den kopperhandel en de uitoefening van mijnbouw en metaalindustrie in Zweden," *Bijdragen Mededeelingen van het Historisch Genootschap*, LVIII (1937), p. 214 *et passim;* Georg Wittrock, *Svenska Handelskompaniet och Kopparhandeln under Gustaf II Adolf* (Uppsala, 1919), p. 7.

[168] Heckscher, "Europeiska kopparmarknaden," p. 258; Wittrock, *Svenska Handelskompaniet och Kopparhandeln*, p. 160; Hamilton, *Brass and Copper Industries in England*, p. 57. See also Chap. 3.

[169] For the principal studies in this debate, see Eli Heckscher, "Gustav Vasas myntpolitik," *Svensk historisk tidskrift*, XLVI (1926), pp. 370–375; review of Tom Söderberg, *Stora Kopparberget under medeltiden och Gustav Vasa* (Stockholm, 1932), *ibid.*, LIII (1933), pp. 346–354; "Kopparen under Sveriges stormaktstid," reviews of Josef Wolontis, *Kopparmyntningen i Sverige, 1624–1714* (Helsingfors, 1936), and Albert Olsen,

in detail, one can present a general outline of the history of this third metal. The production in Sweden (Graph 2) rose from 1,393 metric tons in 1623 to 2,941 tons in 1650, which was a record year. After that there was a slump, and production leveled off at about 1,800 tons; the last outstanding year of

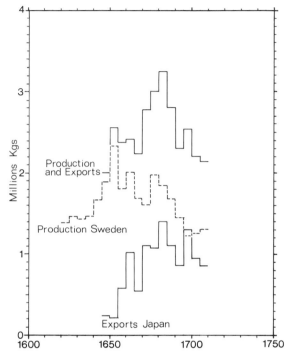

2. Copper: Production in Sweden; and Exports by the Dutch East India Company from Japan (Reference: F. Tegengren and K. Glamann)

the seventeenth century was 1682 with 2,147 tons.[170] The yearly production in Hungary, struggling to compete with Sweden, was reorganized after 1641,

Kobberpolitik i den svenske Stormagtstid (Lund, 1937), *ibid.,* LVII (1937), p. 257; "1600-tals-kopparen än en gång: Repliker till dr. Wolontis och professor Olsen," *ibid.,* LVIII (1938), p. 129; "Europeiska kopparmarknaden"; "Ett brev av Conradt von Falkenberch om japansk koppar," *Svensk historisk tidskrift,* LX (1940), pp. 43–48; Albert Olsen, "Kobberpolitik i den svenske Stormagtstid," *Scandia,* X (1937); "Kobberpolitik og Kritik (Eli Heckscher)," *ibid.;* "Kobberet og det 17. Aarhundredes Verdensmarked," *ibid.,* XI (1938); "Professor Eli Heckscher og det japanske Kobber," *ibid.;* Aksel Christensen, review of Eli Heckscher, *Sveriges economiska historia från Gustav Vasa: Första delen I Medeltidshushållningens organisering 1520–1600; II Hushållningen under internationell påverkan 1600–1720* (Stockholm, 1935–1936), *Dansk historisk tidsskrift,* X (1937–1938); Astrid Friis, "Forbindelsen mellem det europaeiske og asiatiske kobbermarked," *Scandia,* XII (1939), Kristof Glamann, "The Dutch East India Company's Trade in Japanese Copper, 1645–1736," *Scandinavian Economic History Review,* I (No. 1, 1953).

[170] Data from F. R. Tegengren given in Wolontis, *Kopparmyntningen i Sverige,* Appendix A.

but settled at a level of some 330 tons in 1650–1660 and fell in 1661–1680 to 280 tons.[171]

Precise information on Japanese production for the seventeenth century is still lacking, but the important Ashio mines then came into operation and remain active today. There are, on the other hand, data of the exports of copper from Japan, carried by the Dutch East India Company, the greatest if not the only operator in this field. The article by Kristof Glamann[172] clarifies the situation after the middle of the seventeenth century. The five-year averages of exports in metric tons are: 22 in 1650–1654; 1,393 in 1680–1684; 849 in 1705–1709 (see Graph 2).[173]

Copper was thus sought, developed, and delivered. It was not in short supply for the mints, and it was available as an instrument of inflation, when inflation became almost a necessity.

The copper inflation did not occur everywhere at the same time, nor necessarily in the same way. There were early symptoms in Spain but they were not the only examples. It is important to date and fix the various inflations, in the context of different periods of economic activity. About 1620 (experts in Italian history would say more precisely 1619), a serious crisis struck the European economy, at the outbreak of the Thirty Years' War. Then, about the 1680s, perhaps more precisely about 1686, the trend appeared to change. Even before these latter dates, however, there were clear signs of an improvement in conditions.

Within this economic activity, at least three general periods of copper inflation can be observed: a first period to about 1630; a second from 1630 to the middle of the century; a third from about 1650 to the eve of recovery set for convenience at about 1680. This is a first classification. In order to simplify the question, the copper of Transylvania and Japan will not be considered, for it is clear that the market was dominated by copper from Sweden. Its history is well known, from the movement of its market price, from the difficulties it faced in world markets, and finally from the way governments used copper as an instrument in power politics.

The policy of the Swedish monarchy at first met with great success, for the technical superiority of Swedish copper in industrial uses was acknowledged by buyers all over Europe. The industries of Aachen and Namur used it almost exclusively; in 1671 in England Jean-Baptiste Colbert, marquis de Seignelay, reported that Swedish copper was preferred for use by the Royal Navy.[174] This superiority was further confirmed by the prices quoted on the market of Amsterdam, where Swedish copper competed with imports from Japan. Sometimes Swedish copper was mixed with the latter in order to make a more

[171] Heckscher, "Europeiska kopparmarknaden," p. 224.
[172] Glamann, "Dutch East India Company's Trade."
[173] *Ibid.*
[174] Cited by Heckscher, "Europeiska kopparmarknaden," p. 260.

marketable product. It should be added that Sweden employed the most advanced technical processes in exploitation and refining.[175] Finally, the royal policy in Sweden encouraged production and supported the market. Extensive privileges had been granted to the copper company at Väsby on March 1, 1615. On July 24, 1619, the Kopparkompaniet, also called the Svenska Handelskompaniet, was founded; in the following decade it took the title of Societas mercatorum Sueciae. The King himself directed this monopoly.[176]

At the beginning, everything went smoothly. The company produced for a rising market, and this was considerably encouraged in the years 1617–1619 and especially 1621–1626 by the policy in Spain of minting *vellon* (or copper money). As a result there were large exports of copper to the peninsula.[177] A link was thus forged between Spain and Sweden; thus, any sign of a change in monetary policy in the former meant disaster for the latter. At the beginning of 1625 the price of Swedish copper reached its maximum. In Lübeck the *skeppund* (136 kg.) sold for 91 *riksdalers,* in Hamburg for 93, then, finally, 93 and 96, respectively.[178] Almost immediately afterward, these easy conditions ended. From the summer of 1625, in effect, the market in Spain declined. Johann Skytte wrote to Gustavus Adolphus on September 18 that the demand had considerably diminished because of the high price of the metal.[179] On April 29, 1626, Anders Svensson announced that the Spanish market was closed.[180] A month later (May 31) Philip IV stopped the coinage of copper. These unpleasant tidings arrived in Stockholm by way of Amsterdam, Hamburg, and Lübeck. It was thought, not without good reason, that with the fall in exports of copper to Spain the price of copper (*gårkoppar*) would go below 60 riksdalers the skeppund.[181] A period was, in fact, coming to a close. The abrupt fall in 1625 more or less marked a limit. The capital of the *Kopparkompaniet,* which had been 7,800 *daler* in 1620, settled in 1627 at 295,947 daler, but in the following year (April 1628) it was compelled to liquidate.[182]

From that time, the price of gårkoppar continued to fall. In 1652 (see Graph 3) the price in Amsterdam for 100 pounds (Dutch) hit its lowest point, 38.30 guilders (compared with 64.55 in 1624). The situation improved

---

[175] *Ibid.,* p. 251.

[176] Wittrock, *Svenska Handelskompaniet och Kopparhandeln,* pp. 16–20.

[177] These shipments were so large that they attracted the attention of English pirates, who in 1624 captured a vessel laden with copper, sailing south. *Ibid.,* pp. 60–62; Heckscher, "Europeiska kopparmarknaden," p. 267.

[178] Wolontis, *Kopparmyntiningen i Sverige,* pp. 32–34.

[179] Wittrock, *Svenska Handelskompaniet och Kopparhandeln,* pp. 66, n. 2.

[180] *Ibid.,* pp. 77, 78, n. 1.

[181] *Ibid.,* pp. 60–63; Wolontis, *Kopparmyntningen i Sverige,* p. 33; Hamilton, *American Treasure,* pp. 80–85; Wittrock, *Svenska Handelskompaniet och Kopparhandeln,* p. 103, citing a letter of May 30, 1626, from Eric Larsson to Didrik von Falkenberg, Stockholm; for an explanation of the Swedish skeppund, see note by Göran Ohlin, in his translation of Eli Heckscher, *An Economic History of Sweden* (Cambridge, Mass., 1954), p. 88.

[182] Wittrock, *Svenska Handelskompaniet och Kopparhandeln,* pp. 25–27, 77, 110, 118.

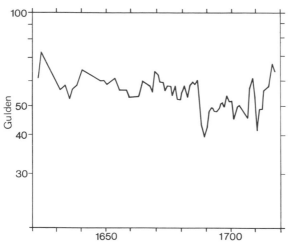

3. Prices of Copper in Amsterdam, in Gulden per 100 Dutch Pounds (Reference: N. Posthumus)

in 1655 when copper sold for 59.07 and reached 63.71 in 1672, but a new break in the market came in 1682 (52 guilders). Only at the beginning of the eighteenth century did the market recover.[183]

From these data four fairly distinct periods can be established for prices in Amsterdam: a rise to 1625; a fall from 1625 to 1652; a renewed rise from 1652 to 1672; a recession to 1682.

To complete this pattern of development, it should be noted that the key years 1625–1652 coincided with a period of exceptional difficulty. Its significance goes far beyond the bounds of the history of copper itself, but it helps to explain an improvement in its market. The first measures attempted to restrict sales in order to bolster up the sagging prices. Another method proposed to find new outlets; copper was thus sent to Russia and from there to Persia by way of Kazan and Astrakhan.[184] It was hoped that these outlets would compensate for the declining markets in the West. By a contract dated August 26, 1637, the Dutch merchants Baeck and Elias Trip agreed to deliver 500,000 pounds of copper in Moscow.[185] Another proposal entailed using political pressures to regulate the distribution of copper, since, as a royal monopoly, it affected public revenues. On March 14, 1631, Gustavus Adolphus complained of the unfavorable conditions offered by the market of Amsterdam

[183] Nicolaus W. Posthumus, *Inquiry into the History of Prices in Holland* (2 vols., Leiden, 1946–1964), I, Table 173.

[184] "Van Nicolaes Jacobsz, overschie, Gamroon, aan Gouverneur Generaal en Raden, Batavia," Mar. 25, 1636, in Hendrik Dunlop, *Bronnen tot de geschiedenis der Oostindische Compagnie in Perzië* (The Hague, 1930), I, p. 614; Arthur Attman, *Den ryska marknaden i 1500-talets baltiska politik, 1558–1595* (Lund, 1944), p. 111; Heckscher, "Conradt von Falkenberch om japansk koppar," p. 45.

[185] Dillen, "Amsterdamsche notarieele," pp. 280–284.

and proposed to sell copper directly to France.[186] The need to break out of the restricted market for the sale of copper, among other considerations, apparently influenced Gustavus Adolphus in deciding to intervene in Germany and attempt to impose his rule on Europe. Great schemes also include small expedients, such as the vote of the Riksradet on December 2, 1633, on the demand of the Chancellor, Count Axel Oxenstierna, to end the monopoly of copper.[187] Small measures produced small results. The balance of the copper market was not restored until well after the death of Gustavus Adolphus, about 1652, and then only partially. It thus lasted for some thirty years.

This development of copper is, however, only an introduction to its more general history. It sets forth the basic phases, which begin with the situation in Spain.

During the years 1598–1628 the crux of the problem lay in Spain. That country was like an entrenched fortress for precious metals during most of the sixteenth century, and in the end was the first to be affected seriously by the "scourge of copper" in the seventeenth century, almost as a direct consequence of being a prime distributor of bullion. From the time of his accession in 1598 Philip III was obliged to abandon the strict policy of Philip II in order to find a way out of his financial embarrassment: in 1599 he authorized the coinage of pure copper. According to the computations of Earl J. Hamilton, which take into account the devaluation of 1603 and a reduction of the weight of the coins by half, the issues from 1599 to 1606 amounted to 22,000,000 ducats. Disasters then followed, in particular the state bankruptcy of 1607.[188] On November 22, 1608, the Spanish government promised to abandon the minting of copper,[189] but this promise was kept for only a decade. With the formal permission of the Cortes the issues were started again in 1617–1619, when about 5,000,000 ducats were issued. Two years later 14,000,000 ducats were put in circulation and lasted until 1626; they had a favorable affect on the market for copper in Sweden and in other parts of the north, as has already been noted. A total of 41,000,000 ducats of copper currency was issued in a quarter of a century.[190]

This flood of vellon invited forgeries, of which the treatises of the time complained. There were, for example, in 1621, a report of the *Introducción en España de moneda de vellon fabricada en Holanda* and *Avisos de los baxeles holandeses que iban a conducir moneda falsa a España* . . . and, in 1624, *Rumores de que el Duque de Rennes fabricaba moneda falsa y la metia por S. Lucar en España, año 1624.* On October 14, 1624, these imports were officially stopped (although this meant very little), and on February 27, 1627,

---

[186] Wittrock, *Svenska Handelskompaniet och Kopparhandeln*, p. 162; see below, Chap. III.

[187] Wolontis, *Kopparmyntningen i Sverige*, pp. 88–100.

[188] Hamilton, *American Treasure*, pp. 74–77.

[189] *Ibid.*, p. 77.

[190] *Ibid.*

contraventions of the law were placed under the jurisdiction of the Inquisition.[191]

Contemporaries followed the inflation with interest. For example, two letters from the Genoese ambassador in Spain, Giovanni Battista Saluzzo, are revealing: he reported on April 12, 1628, the atrocious consequences of this policy that "no remedy is seen to the vellon money, and so the disorder increases daily exceeding the rates by 50 percent" (by comparison with other moneys); on April 30 he wrote that "the confusion from the disorder of money continues to such extremes that is difficult to find bread to eat . . . in all other regions of Spain it is said that matters are almost as bad." [192] In the face of all this vellon (or, more correctly, pure copper) and especially after the commercial recession of 1619–1620, silver appreciated rapidly. In the spring of 1628, if we follow the movement (see Graph 4), the premium on

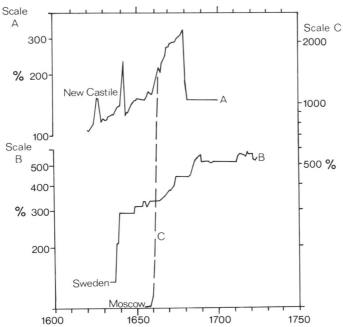

4. Premium on Silver in Terms of Copper in (A) New Castile, (B) Sweden, and (C) Moscow (Reference: E. J. Hamilton, J. Wolontis, and A. Brückner)

silver in terms of copper was 50 percent in New Castile, thus indicating that silver tended more and more to disappear from circulation.[193]

[191] *Ibid.,* p. 81; these reports in A.N., K.1456, K.1478, K.1479, have been communicated by Braudel.

[192] A.S., Genoa, *Lettere ministri, Spagna,* 25.2434, letters of Apr. 12, 30, 1628, from Gio. Batista Saluzzo in Madrid to Genoa, documents communicated by Braudel.

[193] Hamilton, *American Treasure,* pp. 94–97. It should be noted that, in spite of the

But Spain was not the only case. In France, after 1607, copper coinage, which until then had followed that of other money, was now made to meet growing shortages of precious metals.[194] It was, in fact, a leap in the dark. From 1607 to 1621 a new phase in coining copper opened in France. Politics also played a part, for there was a price to pay for the Swedish alliance. Indeed, as soon as France was committed to the war, which was waged openly from August 1636, the coinage of copper was suspended for a time.[195] Copper was also coined in Germany, around Hamburg, for example, where several mints issued copper coins, some no doubt for export to Spain. The danger of copper again became evident during the campaigns of Gustavus Adolphus, as is shown in the pamphlet *Vorschlag wegen einer kupfernen Münze* (1632), which noted "the great confusion the coinage of copper money provoked a very few years ago in Germany and Spain."[196] The same state of affairs existed in Sweden, naturally attached to copper more than any other country. Between 1624 and 1631, 4,583,891 copper daler were issued. It was advantageous for Sweden, from a monetary point of view, to convert part of its output into coinage. Gustavus Adolphus was aware of the perils of excessive copper production and tried to keep up the price by delivering the surplus metal to the Swedish mint. He also strove more strenuously still to unload copper on Germany, then occupied by his armies. Even before his death in 1632, however, this policy faced considerable opposition.[197] There were the inevitable economic consequences: as copper became more important, more decisive as an inflationary force, the relative prices in silver (see Graph 6) began to fall, or, in other words, the premium on silver began to rise. The riksdaler, quoted at 6½ marks in copper in 1626, passed for 10 in the autumn of 1628 and for 14 in 1630.[198] This was a complementary movement, a check on the economic success of copper.

During the years 1628–1630, and this is more or less valid, the history of copper entered its second general phase in the seventeenth century. In Spain from 1627 to 1641 the face value of copper vellon was raised three times and lowered four times. The most critical moment was at the time of the revolt of Catalonia and Portugal (1640). Copper coins were raised in face value on February 11 and again on October 27, 1641; the result was an astonishing increase in the premium on silver, which reached 120.62 percent in Andalusia and 132.25 percent in Old Castile. The pragmatic of August 31, 1642, then

---

heavy issues of copper currency between 1599 and 1606, the premium on silver rose rapidly only after the beginning of the Thirty Years' War.

[194] See Chap. 3.

[195] *Ibid.*

[196] Bothe, *Gustav Adolfs und sein Kanzlers wirtschafts-politische Absichten* pp. 240–250.

[197] Wittrock, *Svenska Handelskompaniet och Kopparhandeln,* pp. 72–73.

[198] Wolontis, *Kopparmyntningen i Sverige,* pp. 59–61, 320–321.

imposed a sharp deflation, the premium on silver being reduced to 42.29 percent, and then to 25.74 percent (see Graph 4). It recovered gradually, rising
to exceed 50 percent by December 1650.[199] Sweden witnessed a period of
stability. The rating for the silver riksdaler in terms of copper altered only
from 14 in 1630 to 16 in 1654 (see Graph 4).[200]

With the 1650s a new period of copper depreciation began and continued
until about 1680 or, perhaps, 1686. In Spain, according to Hamilton, the
monetary disorders reached their peak. After 1650 the inflationary movement
of copper began anew: on November 11, 1651, the face value of the two-
maravedi coins was increased four times, that is, to eight maravedis.[201] And
the indecisive policy of Philip IV made the situation worse. Copper was
everywhere. In settling accounts in 1651–1660 copper constituted 92 percent
of the currency used, and in the three following decades this probably rose
to 95 percent. The depreciation of copper was clear in the important period
1661–1664, both in the speculation on the Amsterdam market and in the
economic life of Europe generally. The premium on silver in terms of copper
(see Graph 4), according to Hamilton, rose rapidly after January 1657; it
fell to 50 percent in June–July 1659 and August 1660, however, but increased to 150 percent in August and September 1664. With a policy of deflation in mind, the Spanish government had silver billon coined in its five
mints for a total of about four million ducats. From that moment, a halt was
called. But the rise in the premium on silver soon began again: it reached
187.5 percent in 1669 and 275 percent in February 1680.[202]

Much the same situation existed in Sweden. From 1651 to 1680, 11,706,-
367 daler in copper were issued compared with 3,286,758 for 1632–1650.
The premium on the riksdaler in terms of copper (see Graph 4) rose more
rapidly than in the preceding period, the ratio passing from 1 to 16 in 1654,
to 21.2 in 1665, and then, after leveling off in 1665–1672, a renewed rise to
27.125 in 1680. It declined, however, to 24.9 after 1681 and to 25 at the
end of the century.[203]

In Poland 7,000,000 copper gulden were coined in the period 1659–1663
followed by a heavy issue from 1663 to 1666. The unit at the nominal rate of
30 *gros* was, in reality, worth only 12 *gros*.[204]

The coinage of copper money in Russia began in Novgorod and Pskov in
1655. In Moscow (see Graph 4) the premium on the silver ruble in terms of
copper rose to 30 percent in March 1660, to 200 percent in December 1661,

---

[199] Hamilton, *American Treasure,* pp. 84–86, 96–97, and *War and Prices in Spain,
1651–1800* (Cambridge, Mass., 1947), p. 13.
[200] Wolontis, *Kopparmyntningen i Sverige.*
[201] Hamilton, *War and Prices in Spain,* pp. 13, 35.
[202] *Ibid.,* pp. 9–10, 14–15.
[203] Wolontis, *Kopparmyntningen i Sverige,* Appendix N, pp. 320–321.
[204] Albert Despaux, *Les dévaluations monétaires dans l'histoire* (Paris, 1936), p. 453.

and then shot up to 1400 percent in June 1663 when the coinage was stopped.[205]

Apparently no economy was spared the rigors of copper money.

Around 1680 everything tended to move at a slower pace. Deflation carried the day in Spain. In 1680 the silver vellon of 1660, halved in face value in 1664, was finally reduced to a quarter of its original face value. A start was made by withdrawing copper from circulation in order to manufacture different objects and utensils. Another measure was also used: after May 22, 1680, the coinage of vellon was rigorously limited. The success of the operation was demonstrated by the stability of the premium on silver in terms of copper from 1686 to 1700. It was fixed at 50 percent in March 1680, and in October and November 1686 it was stabilized at this rate for the new silver reals; for the old reals it was set at 88.25 percent. Still another sign of the change in trend and of the appreciation of silver in the new phase of gold was the debasement by a fifth of silver coins on October 14, 1686. It was the first since Isabella the Catholic.[206] The same sort of symptoms can be found in Sweden, where after 1681 the ratio between silver and copper remained stable until the end of the century. Finally, the coinage of copper, which was concerned more and more since 1684 with smaller quantities, was interrupted from 1693 to 1706.[207] The plague of copper was halted, and for the moment, with more gold flowing into circulation, the monetary health of Europe seemed to be improving.

The Far East had its part to play both as a supplier and purchaser of copper; this part has been considered so far in the context of Europe. The question remains whether the role played by the Far East was at all significant. Was there, in other words, any comparison between Europe and that area during the successive periods that have been outlined — 1598–1630, 1630–1650, and 1650–1680? It must be noted that Japanese copper continued to be sold on the markets of India in the 1630s. And there were English merchants in 1635–1636 buying copper from the Dutch for resale to the Portuguese in Goa, and at favorable prices.[208] These exportations certainly had repercussions on the circulation of copper money in Japan. Because of this, apparently, the exports of copper were forbidden in 1636, and the shortage of metal even led to the melting down of the Great Buddha in the same year, when the copper mint (Zeni-Za) was set up in Edo and Sakamoto.[209] When the great

[205] Chaudoir, *Aperçu sur les monnaies russes,* I, p. 129; see also Alexander Brückner, *Finanzgeschichtliches Studien. Kupfergeldkrisen* (St. Petersburg, 1867), pp. 1–76.

[206] Hamilton, *War and Prices in Spain,* p. 22.

[207] Wolontis, *Kopparmyntningen i Sverige,* pp. 306–307.

[208] Sir William Foster, *The English Factories in India* (Series in 13 pts., Oxford, 1906–1927), *1624–1629* (1909), July 18, 1627, p. 181; *1634–1636* (1911), Feb. 24, 1635, p. 101; Dec. 7, 1635, p. 121; Jan. 2, 1636, p. 148.

[209] Takao Tsuchiya, "An Economic History of Japan," *Transactions of the Asiatic Society of Japan,* XII (1937), p. 214.

crisis of 1640 intervened, the Dutch (compelled to shift their center of trade to Nagasaki) continued to export copper; permission for this was granted from 1641. On December 22, 1646, the English factor in Persia wrote to his colleagues in Surat that there was no demand for copper at Gombroon.[210] A few months later, on February 22, 1647, the Dutch ship *Snuke* arrived in Swally Marine, bringing a mixed cargo including copper but no silver. It also brought the darkest news of the difficulties of the Dutch trade in Formosa and Japan, which was "much declined, the former by reason of wars in China." [211] And so there is reason to infer that the state of trade in the Far East bore some resemblance to that in Europe. It emphasized the role of copper in international trade. This was, in fact, at the very heart of the seventeenth century, apparently as unsound on one side of the world as on the other, and almost about to collapse. The adaptability of the Dutch merchants was not enough to overcome such adversities, though they persisted in drawing on copper from the islands of Japan. In 1659, at their request, copper coins were minted for export.[212] The market in India half opened again and allowed the English to emulate the Dutch. A report from Surat to London of April 13, 1660, noted that "copper at this time is exceeding dear, and a great quantity will vend. Considering, therefore, the loss that Your Honours have in silver, please you to send out a quantity of that sort as the sugar vessels are made of, 'twill sell at this time for 45 mahmudis per maund." [213] The same correspondents, on March 12, 1665, indicated: "Of the English copper in cakes you cannot send too much. We confess it raises you not much profit; yet it is better than reals of eight, besides the trouble and inconvenience in procuring them which you have often complained of." [214] This last letter happened to coincide with a steep fall, from 1664 to 1668, in the exports of copper from Japan.[215]

The history of development of the market in copper and the relationship between Europe and the Far East suggests that the problem extends across the trading world. The combination of international trade and the special conditions relating to copper, which will be more deeply considered later, must be kept in mind.

4. The Role of Credit

The history of precious metals, as already suggested, has a place in the general development of the world economy. It was also closely linked to the evolution of credit; the chronology of that problem will now be reviewed. Such an approach will simplify the sector of credit and set it in the context of the history of money and precious metals.

[210] Foster, *English Factories, 1640–1650* (1914), Dec. 22, 1646, pp. 65–66.
[211] *Ibid.,* Feb. 26, 1647, p. 106.
[212] Yosoburo Takekoshi, *The Economic Aspects of the History of Civilisation of Japan* (3 vols., London, 1930), II, 36.
[213] Foster, *English Factories, 1655–1660* (1921), Apr. 13, 1660, p. 306.
[214] *Ibid., 1665–1667* (1925), Mar. 12, 1665, p. 2.
[215] See Graph 2.

The most relevant point of comparison in the monetary stock is with billon. During the long period under consideration credit acted as a supplementary factor in much the same way as billon. This was especially apparent during the periods of metallic shortage and monetary tension, when sudden crises tended to deteriorate into a run of sensational bankruptcies. There was always, so it seems, an element of risk in the uncertain credit operations of that time; they were rarely far removed from settlements in specie. This element of uncertainty and risk promoted the great fortunes of the merchant bankers, of the financiers in those fairs which settled payments in transactions across Europe, of the great companies and corporations with their branches and associated firms, which built the splendid edifice of commercial capital already stretching around the world. Credit also appeared often in the difficult struggle to remedy the shortcomings of the monetary circulation, to act as a sort of replenisher, and it could, on occasion, be a substitute for precious metals as well as an aid to their circulation. Thus, credit drew its strength both from the expansion of the different components of the monetary circulation, since it did not exist without real currency, and from the considerable imperfections of the system.

The structure of credit was, in effect, supported by progressive increases in the stocks of precious metals; these tended to reduce the risks involved. Bullion and specie formed a basis for a whole series of speculations. It so happened that both governments and commercial organizations were bound to meet their current obligations by paying out sums of money that arrived in Europe at irregular intervals. Anyone who studies the history of Spain in the sixteenth and seventeenth centuries can appreciate the anxiety in waiting for the fleets from the New World. Were they going to arrive on time? Would they be as richly laden as expected? If there were delays, the merchant houses in Seville were threatened with collapse for want of hard cash to meet their agreements; high-risk credit became suspect. Under such circumstances, debts were harshly reclaimed, and the more distant obligations were not renewed. The whole structure of credit implied a certain time horizon, and, beyond that, should the fleets arrive late, came ruin. Royal creditors refused to make further advances in Flanders or Italy to meet the imperial needs of the Most Catholic King.

If these simple mechanisms are set in proper perspective, one can see the role of credit as a means for transforming irregular deliveries by treasure fleets into a more constant, manageable stream of international payments. It created the conditions of structural continuity in economic activity. Indeed, in one respect, the imperfections of the system of precious metals gave rise to the efficiency of credit. And there were more imperfections than those at first apparent on the wharves of Seville and in the great counting rooms of the Casa de la Contratación. Everywhere, to the circulation of gold and silver specie and, indeed, billon must be added the floating mass of bills of exchange between one market and another, an essential component of speculations and requirements of commercial transactions. Sixteenth-century bills of exchange have often been compared to ships, some stoutly built and seaworthy, others in poor shape, almost unfit to stand the buffets of a long voyage. There was a whole network of credit transfers and payments, sometimes risky, but generally supplementing the transfers of bullion and specie, paid in cash. The great international merchants at the time — the Welsers, Fuggers, Bonvisi, Capponi, Grimaldi, Spinola — performed this function. They played off the shifts in level between different regions of the international economy. They had before them a range of choices, taking advantage of the various circuits in gold or silver, of calculating transfers by bills of exchange, without mentioning other speculations, such as advancing money to governments, operations in the commodity markets, agios and arbitrages, the differential rates of inflation, and the recurring disequilibrium, however brief, between precious metals themselves. The volume of credit contributed in numerous ways to the monetary stock by means of speculations and real or fictive services. It was a question not only of the float to bridge the *payments interval* resulting from the irregular arrivals of the treasure fleets, but also of organizing — for profit, naturally — the distribution of bullion across Europe and the world. The merchant-financiers of Genoa, astute if not always honest, performed this outstanding role during the second half of the sixteenth and first half of the seventeenth century. They led the way, and their masterly acumen brought them substantial profits.

In these circumstances, a testing time for credit came, for example, with the abrupt decline in the arrivals of bullion, or with other monetary transformations. Could the structure of credit withstand sudden bankruptcies or the excessive expansion of loans by merchants? In the long as well as the short run these periods of tension and credit inflation indicated a lack of adjustment in the customary bullion ratio. Credit bears, in this respect, some resemblance to copper currency, since it represented an extension of the available monetary stock, and actually was a substitute for money. For this reason, it is a valuable indicator in the history of precious metals and money.

An interesting study could no doubt be made of the short-term crises of credit. In Lyons and Antwerp, in Venice and Naples, everywhere in fact where there is information, the short-run crisis surprised merchants who specialized in speculative banking. Their clients' investments were often tied up in slowly maturing commercial operations, and so these firms frequently had to face a sudden run on their reserves. The sharp crisis of 1570, caused by the outbreak of the war against Turkey, demolished the Dolphini bank in Venice. In 1584, the second Pisani-Tiepolo bank, shaken by the difficulties of 1583, seemed outwardly a marvel of strength, but crashed in its turn. Henri Lapeyre has shown that in the 1580s there were numerous bankruptcies in Italy, Antwerp, and Lyons.[216] Alphonso Silvestri, in his study of the bankers of Naples,

---

[216] Lapeyre, *Une famille de marchands: Les Ruiz,* pp. 453–454.

reached similar conclusions.[217] In effect, short-term crises destroyed many firms with extended resources. At the end of the sixteenth century, the intervention of the state, particularly through municipal authorities, was a direct way of regulating banking activity, of escaping even the longer crises by widening the base of activities and obligations. In their own particular way, the establishment of the Banco della piazza di Rialto and the renovation of the Banco di San Giorgio signified the beginning of years of difficulty, unfavorable to private activity. But this will be dealt with later.

The problem of these long crises naturally demands special attention. In the following discussion an attempt will be made to formulate some general considerations relevant to France.

The first long crisis — a structural crisis — came in the middle of the sixteenth century. It should not have risen, basically, from a real shortage of bullion, for the data published by Hamilton show that the deliveries from America continued to increase. It can be said, nevertheless, that these deliveries were hampered to some extent in their circulation by the interruption of the circuits of specie and bullion; they did not conform to the same customary movements of gold and silver (since logically any further expansion should have relied largely on Spanish gold and German silver). The interregional circulation had evidently been altered. Such statements are only hypotheses; in reality, two reasonably sound assumptions can be made: there ensued a period of economic stagnation or rather reorganization which slowly emerged.[218] Owing to the disruption of the customary patterns of exchanges, the monetary circulation finally slowed down. Formerly, the system had operated in a relative abundance of gold; now the conditions were moving toward an abundance of silver. As a result there was a reversal in trends. The fabric of economic activity in Europe was deeply shaken, but the situation was complicated, for it was a period when, from about 1540 to 1560 or perhaps more precisely from 1546 to 1554, almost every aspect of life seemed to be in question — politics, religion, cities, markets, and the economies in general. This was the time, moreover, of the great debasements of currencies and of the more extensive use of copper in the monetary systems. Can it be assumed that there were also attempts to expand the volume of credit to meet the financial requirements at this juncture?

By all appearances, public borrowing rose. Wherever data are available they show that the expansion was certainly spectacular: in Rome, according to the studies of Clemens Bauer,[219] in France, from the researches of Roger

---

[217] Alfonso Silvestri, "Sui banchieri pubblici napoletani dall'avvento di Filippo II al trono alla constituzione del monopolio," *Bollettino dell'Archivio Storico del Banco di Napoli,* I (No. 3, 1951).

[218] See my conclusion and Graph 32.

[219] Clemens Bauer, *Unternehmung und Unternehmungsformen in Spätmittelalter und in der beginnenden Neuzeit* (Jena, 1936).

Doucet, in the Empire of Charles V, so aptly revealed by Ramón Carande,[220] in the Low Countries, as shown by Fernand Braudel and Henri Lonchay,[221] and, indeed, in high finance all over Europe, revealed in the old but classic book by Richard Ehrenberg.[222] As the graphs show, all these developments are fairly easy to quantify. In Graph 5 the loans to the Spanish monarchy (in 1551–1555) reached a total of 11,546,249 ducats; the nearest approach to this had been 7,049,286 ducats in 1536–1540. The loans raised by the Emperor Charles V on the Antwerp market[223] increased sharply in the early 1550s. The total debt had fluctuated by about 1,000,000 Flemish pounds since the late 1520s and then from 1551 rose steeply, so that by the eve of the bankruptcy of 1557 this total had almost reached 7,000,000 Flemish pounds. For France, public borrowing went ahead in 1522 with the establishment of the first rentes sur l'Hôtel de Ville de Paris.[224] It reached a peak in the Grand Parti, which consolidated old debts with fresh borrowings in Lyons.[225] The situation grew progressively worse until the breaking point in the 1550s.[226] Thus the primacy of silver appears as a revolution. In the background were the repeated wars of Henry II and the Spanish bankruptcy of January 1, 1557,[227] which soon afterward entailed bankruptcies in the Low Countries,[228] Naples,[229] Milan,[230] and then the bankruptcy of the French monarchy itself.[231] These tribulations, however, were soon lost in the euphoria of peace on the signing of the Treaty of Cateau-Cambrésis (April 1, 3, 1559) and in the astonishing rise in prices, more rapid than in the preceding half century. All

[220] Carande, *Carlos V y sus banqueros,* and *El crédito de Castilla en el precio de la política imperial* (Madrid, 1949); Roger Doucet, *L'état des finances de 1523* (Paris, 1923), *L'état des finances de 1567* (Paris, 1929), *La Banque Capponi à Lyon en 1556* (Lyons, 1939), "La banque en France au XVI⁰ siècle," *Revue d'histoire économique et sociale,* XXIX (1951).

[221] Fernand Braudel, "Les emprunts de Charles-Quint sur la place d'Anvers," in *Charles-Quint et son temps* (Paris, 1959); Henri Lonchay, "Études sur les emprunts des souverains belges aux XVI⁰ et XVII⁰ siècles," *Académie royale de Belgique, Bulletin de la classe des lettres* (Pt. 12, 1907).

[222] Ehrenberg, *Das Zeitalter der Fugger.*

[223] Carande, *Crédito de Castilla,* pp. 57ff., Appendix II; Braudel, *"Emprunts de Charles-Quint."*

[224] Paul Cauwès, "Les commencements du crédit public en France," *Revue d'économie politique,* IX (1895); X (1896).

[225] Roger Doucet, "Le Grand Parti de Lyon au XVI⁰ siècle," *Revue historique,* CLXXI–CLXXII (1933).

[226] Henri Hauser, "The European Financial Crisis of 1559," *Journal of Economic and Business History,* II (1929–1930), expressed the opinion that "the credit inflation which became general indicated that the mechanism of credit had outstripped its development."

[227] Braudel, *Méditerranée,* p. 765.

[228] *Ibid.;* Lonchay, *"Études sur les emprunts des souverains belges,"* pp. 923–1013.

[229] Alfonso Silvestri, "Sui banchieri pubblici napoletani nella prima metà del Cinquecento," in *Bollettino dell'Archivo Storico del Banco di Napoli,* I (No. 2, 1951), pp. 22–34; and see n. 217, above.

[230] There are numerous references, notably Roger Doucet, *Finances municipales et crédit public à Lyon au XVI⁰ siècle* (Paris, 1937), pp. 53–63.

[231] Doucet, "Grand Parti"; Hauser, "European Financial Crisis."

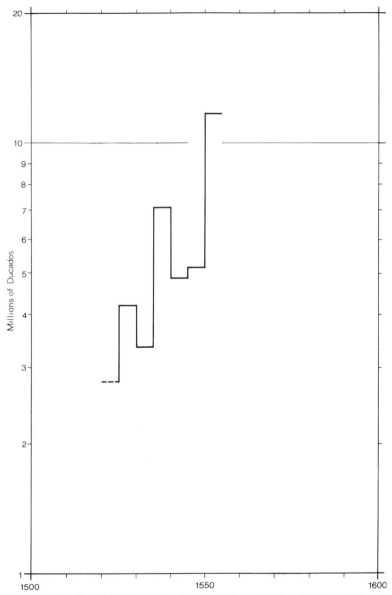

5. Loans to the Spanish Monarchy by Spanish and Alien Bankers, Five-Year Totals (Reference: R. Carande)

these setbacks were soon absorbed in the expansion of production and transactions, of which Huguette and Pierre Chaunu have shown one aspect in the case of Seville, one of the great centers of transatlantic shipping and international trade.[232]

[232] Chaunu, *Séville et l'Atlantique.*

The mid-sixteenth century was, indeed, one of the turning points of the century. From the Empire of Charles V to the Spain of Philip II, from the France of Francis I to the disruption of civil conflict after the death of Henry II, and from the supremacy of the merchants of Augsburg to the arrival of the Genoese to the peak of power and influence, there were signs of profound, though often silent, changes. It would scarcely be convincing to explain the recession of southern Germany without referring to the passage (unfavorable as it was in its consequences) from gold to silver, the cheaper silver of the New World.

The fortune of the Genoese, nevertheless, was a huge achievement, a fortune created out of paper and exchanges, of *scontratatione,* above all in the fairs of Besançon. Later, the Fuggers remarked that "to deal with the Genoese is to deal not in cash, as we do, but in paper." [233] Dealings in paper offered a way out of the mid-century difficulties, and they created the successful credit operations of the Genoese, those new men with new methods.

A second crisis, much longer and different from the first, began to emerge in the closing years of the sixteenth century. It was, above all, reflected in the unseating of the dominant economy, Spain, from its place of eminence. The currency systems of Spain, Genoa, and Poland, interdependent to some extent in the age of silver, suffered notable depreciations in the early seventeenth century (see Graph 6).[234] This signified profound changes in the international economy, sometimes for convenience called the "crisis" of the seventeenth century. The smaller, more robust economies of Northwestern Europe, notably Holland and Britain, resisted longer. For them, the crisis was a pause in their progress to economic ascendancy in Europe.

These structural changes also roughly coincided with the first sizable issues of copper coins and the evolution, or more extensive use, of new forms of banking and credit. In reality, this state of affairs lasted through a large part of the seventeenth century. This was not so much a question of an abrupt change in monetary structures as a retardation in the supply of bullion to Europe, of perhaps a fall in the current ratios and reserves that its economic structures required or had become accustomed to require. The bullionist theories of Thomas Mun and Gerard Malynes and the policies of Cardinal Richelieu, Conde-Duque de Olivares, and Count Axel Oxenstierna formed one composite facet of this mercantilist problem, deeply rooted in the economic life of Europe.

One aspect of the difficulties of the "advanced" economies was the appearance of differential exchange rates. In Spain the escudo (valued at 400 maravedis in 1566) and in France the *écu d'or au soleil* (set at 60 *sols* in 1575 and used as an accounting unit from 1578) were both real coins and standards of

---

[233] See n. 226, above.
[234] This graph is republished from Braudel and Spooner, "Prices in Europe from 1450 to 1750."

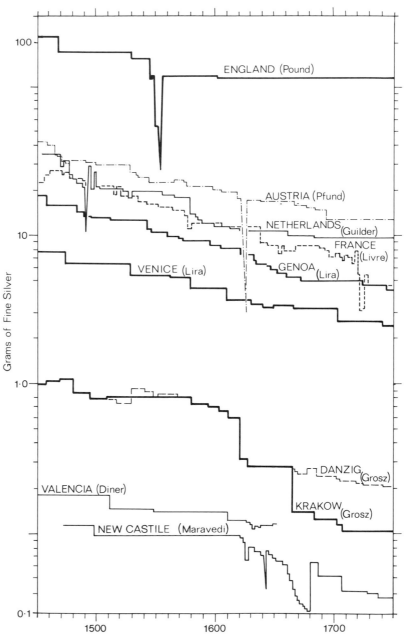

6. Moneys of Account According to Their Equivalents in Silver (Reference: *Cambridge Economic History of Europe*, Vol. IV)

value for bills of exchange. The devaluations in France in 1602 raised the écu (in coin) to 65 sols and in Spain in 1609 raised the escudo (in coin) to 440 maravedis, but the values of these units in bills of exchange remained at their old levels, 60 sols and 400 maravedis, respectively. Did this indicate that the volume of international obligations had become so complex that the financial markets could not follow the radical alterations made in domestic economies? Or did it mean that the financial circuits of Europe had become international, almost detached from the component countries?

The volume of credit and bills of exchange probably expanded in the first two decades of the seventeenth century in the big financial centers of Europe. There is some evidence that in the 1600s and 1610s the number of bills of exchange rose considerably. After the outbreak of the Thirty Years' War (1618) monetary questions increased in seriousness. Bullionist theories were more in evidence. The problem of silver was often acutely felt in the great markets, even in the more distant areas of trade. In Danzig, basically on a silver standard, the devaluation of 1619–1623 was the beginning of a period when

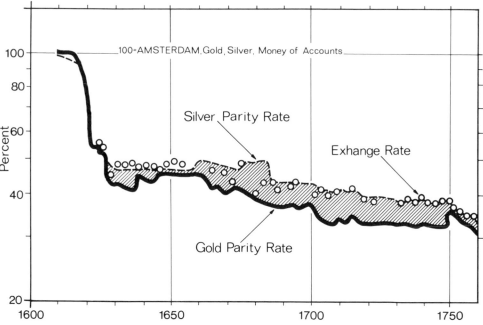

7. Index of Exchange Rates of the Danzig grosz on Amsterdam, Base Period 1609–1760 = 100 (Reference: N. Posthumus)

silver tended to be at a premium (see Graph 7) and lasted until the great devaluation of 1661–1663, when that city apparently detached its monetary system from the rest of Poland.[235] The incident serves to demonstrate the short-

[235] *Ibid.* I hope soon to complete this particular study of exchange rates.

age of silver and the pressure exerted by a combination of economic expansion and the accumulating debts of societies and states in a period of metallic deflation. The latter was shown in the attempts to extend banking and financial services, and in more subtle ways than in the preceding century.

Every period may be said to have its own special credit instruments and techniques. In the opinion of Raymond de Roover,[236] the exchange contract was the rule from about 1275 to 1350. Then the simple bill of exchange was introduced. It was not generally until the close of the sixteenth century that the endorsed bill of exchange became easily negotiable, passing from hand to hand more frequently than in the past. In the same way the *patto di ricorsa,* carefully made out to avoid the charge of usury, was not unknown in the sixteenth century. As is usual with technical inventions, however, a distinction must be drawn between the appearance and the innovation on a large scale. In the seventeenth century, according to Giulio Mandich,[237] the use of the patto di ricorsa spread from the Italian exchange centers. Of significance was its relatively brief existence; it did not, in general, survive the seventeenth century. One might say that it characterizes the long crisis under discussion. In order to complete this picture and to take account of further developments in endorsement and the ricorsa, note must also be taken of the slow spread of discounting. It appeared, for example, in England in the seventeenth century. The spread of all these different techniques of credit represented a certain advance, and their significance must not be overlooked. The credit sector was attempting to alleviate the stagnation of monetary circulation.

The appearance of public banks is more revealing. Even the name "public" indicates a change in the substance of economic affairs. In the sixteenth century there were the massive merchant dynasties, with their powerful personalities, palaces, and huge estates. In the seventeenth century there were the associations, corporations, and public banks, which tended to be impersonal institutions. It seems at first sight that the purpose of the latter was to manage national debts and to facilitate the administration of swelling governmental budgets. But, beyond this, they often allowed transfers from account to account, and so attenuated some of the monetary difficulties.

From the end of the sixteenth century the operations of *giro di banco* (simple transfers from one bank account to another) assumed a new importance. These operations on paper also helped to combat both inelasticities in the supply of bullion and the cumbrous and often ineffective remedies imposed by the ubiquitous copper money. The total volume of these bank settlements tended to widen — within very restricted limits — the scope of bills of ex-

---

[236] Raymond de Roover, *La lettre de change* (Paris, 1953), pp. 17–18; see also Michael M. Postan, "Private Financial Instruments in Medieval England," *Vierteljahrschrift für Sozial- und Wirtschaftsgeschichte,* XXIII (1930), pp. 26–75.
[237] Giulio Mandich, *Le Pacte de Ricorsa et le marché italien des changes au XVIIe siècle* (Paris, 1953), pp. 166–170.

change, at a time when, as so many documents indicate, the confusion of money in circulation became increasingly oppressive.

In Venice the Banco della piazza di Rialto, founded by a decree of the Senate on April 11, 1587, lasted until 1638 (January 2, 1637, *more veneto,* that is 1638), when it merged with the Banco Giro. It dealt in deposits and payments by transfer and on bills of exchange.[238] The nature of its operations was clearly described later in a disapproving Senate decree, dated December 14, 1593: "the transfer, which has for some time been introduced, in place of making payments in bank money or cash, reduces private credits to paper, and passes it in various hands from one to another." [239] In 1605 and 1607, significant years in monetary history, the Senate decided, curiously enough, to limit the activity of the bank, declaring that it made too much profit from the fluctuations of the *Partite.* The bank was accused of opening accounts and allowing balances to increase, all of which were illegal. These accusations suggest that it was moving in the direction of providing credit (in principle, but in principle only, for the benefit of the state). Again, this may be considered typical of the conditions in the early seventeenth century. In 1619, moreover, the Banco del Giro was established in Venice, with the purpose of managing public debts and of satisfying merchants, creditors of the state, who wished "that in the said same bank they should be given prompt and immediate satisfaction of their credits from divers markets, bills of exchange and other dues, who go daily to contract with our *Signoria,* in order thus to escape the delays and obstacles which in cash payments and transfers which they are agreed are very frequently the case." [240] It was particularly revealing: in Venice, with support by the state, the public banks were protecting and extending the facilities of credit.

The old Casa di San Giorgio in Genoa also made attempts to alleviate the scarcity of bullion. In order to ease the circulation of gold the bank opened the *cartulario del banco dell'oro* (or, *cartulario d'oro*) in 1586; these payments and settlements in gold were entered and accounted for separately.[241] In 1606, with the beginnings of the difficulties over silver, the bank set up for three years the *cartulario d'argento* or *cartulario di scudi di cambi;*[242] in 1625 it

[238] Gino Luzzatto, "Les banques publiques de Venise (XVIᵉ, XVIIᵉ, siècles)," in Dillen, *History of the Principal Public Banks,* p. 45.

[239] *Ibid.,* p. 49.

[240] "In cartulario monetae aureae creatur etiam partita, de contanti et in scutis aureis ad rationem solidorum 68 pro quolibet scuto, et illi scuti aurei intelliguntur illi de quinque stampis quare creditori in isto cartulario debentur scuti aurei in auro quinque stamparum; et non cogitur accipere solutionem in alia moneta." Sigismondo Scaccia, *Tractatus de commerciis et cambiis* (Genoa, 1664), p. 457.

[241] Sieveking, "Bank von S. Giorgio," pp. 28–29.

[242] "Quod fuit institutum de anno 1606 die 29 decembris, duraturum per annos tres et postea de anno 1609 29 decembrio fuit prorogatum. In cartulario de numerato scutorum cambiorum creantur etiam partitae de contanti in scutis argenteis, unde creditori in hoc cartulario solutio fieri debet in scutis argenteis et non in alia moneta." Scaccia, *Tractatus de commerciis et cambiis,* p. 457.

opened the *cartulario de numerato* or *di moneta di reali,*[243] dealing with, as the title indicates, the circulation of Spanish silver reals. These cartularii in some measure may have created a system of deposits on call and under guarantee and offered a further aspect of servicing debts and perhaps also of freeing the monetary circulation. At least this complicated problem may permit such an explanation.

Important changes also occurred in Amsterdam. On May 10, 1606, a committee was set up to found the Wisselbank, finally realized in 1609;[244] its first phase of activity lasted until 1683. It was, above all, a deposit bank, with 100 percent reserves, allowing transfers from account to account and the settlement of bills of exchange. In this instance the establishment of credit was expressly forbidden, but restricted credits were granted to the East India Company in 1615 and to the city of Amsterdam in 1624.[245] At the outset the accounts in *florin banco* were intended to solve, among other problems, the variety of moneys presented,[246] the penalty, as Adam Smith observed, of being a small state with large commercial interests. In 1641, during a period of difficulties over silver and on the eve of monetary reforms in Spain, the silver ducaton was recognized as banco money in Amsterdam.[247] Similar conditions existed in other banks. In Valladolid the pragmatic of 1603 set up a public exchange bureau.[248] On December 20, 1608, the Sieur de Fontenu proposed to the Conseil d'État that a Banque de France be established.[249] In 1619 the Hamburg Giro-Bank was founded, in close liaison with the Wisselbank of Amsterdam.[250] A public bank was established in 1621 in Nuremberg.

The Bank of Sweden was established under similar conditions. It was begun in 1656 and was formally organized in 1668.[251] More than any other banking institution, it faced the problem of copper money, and these coins became so large and cumbersome that they were virtually metal plates. Little wonder, therefore, that a solution was sought in the issue of bank notes — the first in Europe — in 1661 (before the "official" existence of the bank). These "copper" notes were given to the miners. As a result, the public increasingly rejected the copper coins.[252] The success of the bank notes was clear, but by 1664 the situation became uncontrollable, and the issue of bank notes was stopped. The flight from copper benefited more susceptible countries to the

---

[243] *Ibid.;* cf. Peri, *Il negotiante,* II, 101.

[244] Dillen, *Bronnen tot de geschiedenis der Wisselbanken* I, pp. 5–7; Ludwig von Mises, *The Theory of Money and Credit* (London, 1953), p. 324.

[245] Dillen, "The Bank of Amsterdam," in *History of the Principal Public Banks,* p. 94.

[246] *Ibid.,* p. 87.

[247] *Ibid.,* p. 89.

[248] Sánchez Sarto, "Les banques publiques en Espagne jusqu'en 1815," in Dillen, *History of the Principal Public Banks,* p. 10.

[249] Gustave Fagniez, *L'économie sociale de la France sous Henri IV* (Paris, 1897), p. 234.

[250] Heinrich Sieveking, "Die Hamburger Bank," in Dillen, *History of the Principal Public Banks,* p. 125.

[251] Eli Heckscher, "The Bank of Sweden," *ibid.,* pp. 161–162.

[252] *Ibid.*

east. Can this have added, at least in part, to the famous copper riots in Moscow in 1663? [253]

In brief, the public banks, although not entirely new, were perhaps symptoms of the disturbances arising from the scarcity of bullion and the level of economic activity in the early seventeenth century. They provided a means of easing the transfer of balances. In Venice, Genoa, Amsterdam, Hamburg, and Nuremberg, although deposits were made in specie and strict limitations on loans were imposed, the banks eventually became in some limited measure sources of credit. Such moves were, clearly, still within the framework of gold and silver money. Yet, the banks and associated institutions sometimes underwritten by the state tended to respond to a crisis which required easier credit conditions and facilities.

Available statistics provide information on the structures and operations of public banks. Explanations must, wherever possible, be susceptible to measurement. However imperfect the data may be, such checks offer both confirmation and further insight into the complexity of economic movements at the time.

One possible indicator would be the total volume of exchange dealings cleared in the fairs. Though these are not available, in their absence the deposit rates for the quarterly fairs can be used as a test; Lyons is the first fair I will consider. In their own particular way these rates reveal successive phases of such activity. The movement[254] shows four periods: a rise to 1574; a fall to 1590; a further rise to 1602; and a fall, which was particularly marked from 1610 until 1622, the last year of this series. These divisions require some explanation. In general the first period corresponds to the reconstruction after the rupture of the mid-century; the decline coincides with the full effects of the bullion from the New World and the period of boom in France; the second rise accompanies the beginnings of the scarcity of bullion; and the last phase, notably after 1610, may have been associated with the changing monetary structures, perhaps even with a fall in the demand for the deposits from fair to fair in Lyons. It is even more plausible that raising loans on the European market was dominated increasingly by the powerful Bourse of Amsterdam. I will discuss later in the book the important problem of deposit rates in Lyons.

For Naples, we have the study by Carlo di Somma on the Banco dello Spirito Santo.[255] Founded in 1558, this bank grew steadily to the end of the sixteenth century. Then followed two remarkable decades of expansion of the credits allowed by the bank; they rose from 46,210 *ducats* in 1600 to 841,285 on June 10, 1622 (see Graph 8). The great crisis of 1619–1620 brought this movement to a close.

---

[253] Vasily Kluchevsky, *History of Russia* (4 vols., London, 1911–1913), III, p. 231.
[254] The data run from 1536, 1557, and continuously from 1565; see Chap. 5.
[255] Carlo di Somma, *Il Banco dello Spirito Santo dalle origini al 1664* (Naples, 1960), pp. 21–29.

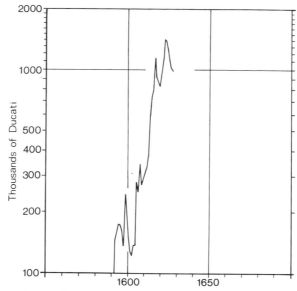

8. Expansion of the Debito Apodissario in the Banco dello Spirito Santo, Naples (Reference: C. di Somma)

For Genoa, an outstanding center for credit and finance, and, no doubt, the organizer of the wealth of the western world as far as "paper" transactions were concerned, some information can be found in the rates of return on *luoghi* (bonds)[256] issued by the Casa di San Giorgio. Published by Carlo Cipolla, they complete the gaps between 1509 and 1558 found in the earlier publication of Carlo Cuneo.[257] The first series gives samples of the number of luoghi.[258] It is obviously difficult to estimate from six or seven figures the ex-

Table 1. Luoghi in Genoa

Year	Number of luoghi
1509	193,185
1531	397,624
1540	416,487
1544	477,112
c. 1560	c. 500,000
1597	437,708
1681	476,706

[256] Carlo Cipolla, "Note sulla storia del saggio d'interesse, corse, dividendi e sconti dei dividendi del Banco di S. Giorgio nel sec. XVI," *Economia Internazionale,* V (1952).
[257] Carlo Cuneo, *Memorie sopra l'antico Debito Pubblico, Mutui, Compere e Banco di S. Giorgio in Genova* (Genoa, 1844), pp. 307–311.
[258] Cipolla, "Note sulla storia," p. 5.

pansion and contraction of credit during two centuries. These few figures do, however, appear to show a rapid increase in the number of luoghi between 1509 and 1531, followed by a period of calm from 1531 to 1560, and probably a decline toward the end of the century. This is a general impression and can be accepted only with prudence, but at least it is not contradicted by the general statements above. From 1540 to 1560, the time of the first structural crisis, the alterations in credit were probably not extensive. At the end of the seventeenth century there came stability, with a slight tendency to advance. In the periods of crisis Genoa did not give the impression of needing instruments of credit. This impression is partly confirmed by the general movement of the *corso* and the *reddito,* which responded to the movement of trade. The number of luoghi apparently rose during commercial recession, which may have accompanied a preference for public funds. These features make Genoa something of a special case, difficult to interpret in the general scheme of affairs. What was true for Genoa did not necessarily prevail beyond its geographical limits. In 1616–1618, years of speculation, when the interest on the luoghi was 1.4 percent, in the Wisselbank in Amsterdam there was an agio of 6¼ percent on converting currency into bank money.[259] In Lyons, during the same years, the deposit rate for a loan carried from one fair to the next was a little more than 2 percent (that is, more than 8 percent for the year).[260]

It is remarkable that a comparison of the movement of the corso and the establishment of the different cartularii in the Casa di San Giorgio shows that a fall in the corso coincided with the opening of a new cartulario. In 1586, at the time of the cartulario d'oro, the high rate of 2,580 *soldi* was followed by a fall and was exceeded again only in 1597. The cartulario d'argento of 1606 was followed by a fall from 4,660 soldi in 1605 to 4,395 in 1606; the cartulario de numerato of 1625 coincided with a fall from 5,080 soldi in 1624 to 3,965 in 1625.[261] In addition to the fact that 1606 and 1625 were not normal years but rather years of economic difficulties, the establishment of the cartularii coincided with a contraction in the value of the luoghi.

A fourth example of banking operations is provided by the Wisselbank, founded in Amsterdam in 1609. It played an important role there; as a result, the movement of its deposits gives some indication of institutional development in Northern Europe.[262] First of all (as is shown in Graph 9), the balances in the bank during the seventeenth century, established in *florins,* tended on the whole to rise, although there were fluctuations. An important recession after 1645 reflects a profound transformation of Dutch affairs, the increasing difficulties in the third quarter of the seventeenth century, and the

---

[259] Dillen, *Bronnen tot de geschiedenis der Wisselbanken,* II, pp. 949–950.
[260] See Chap. 5.
[261] Cipolla, "Note sulla storia."
[262] Dillen, *Bronnen tot de geschiedenis der Wisselbanken,* II, pp. 962–967 and "Een boek van Phoonsen over de Amsterdamsche Wisselbank," *Economisch-Historisch Jaarboeck,* VII (1921). I am particularly indebted to the late Professor Van Dillen for his careful explanations.

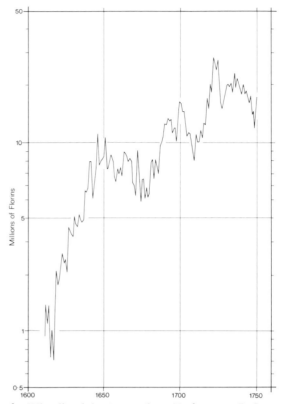

9. Deposits in the Wisselbank in Amsterdam (Reference: J. G. van Dillen)

cycle of wars in which Holland was involved — against England in 1652–1654 and 1665–1667; against Sweden in 1657–1660; against Portugal in 1657–1661; and, not least, against France.

Bank balances also responded to such changes: there was a long rising trend from 1609 to 1645, and, as the bank required 100 percent coverage at least in principle, this trend was followed closely by the metallic reserves (balances amounted to 11,288,142, and reserves, 11,841,183). Then ensued a long recession from 1646 to 1673, when the balances reached 4,933,701 and to 1678 when the metallic reserves fell to 4,396,395. By 1699, however, both movements had risen (balances to 16,750,540 and metallic reserves to 13,-716,236). In the history of balances and metallic reserves, two periods claim attention: from 1610–1618, and 1641–1649. For these two periods the metallic reserves exceeded the balances, particularly in the second period. The first followed the founding of the bank and no doubt reflects the advantages of the florin banco. At that time there were some difficulties over the gold currency, for the *rijder,* a gold coin, was raised from 10 florins 2 *stuivers* in 1606 to 10 florins 12 stuivers in 1610, and the gold ducat from 3 florins 16 stuivers to 4 florins. In the second period the metallic reserves passed the level of the balances, during the sequel to the silver troubles in Spain, where the first devaluation of silver occurred in 1642. The silver *ducatoon* was accepted as money banco in 1641.[263]

During the years 1616–1618 the agio on converting into bank money of 6¼ percent marked the fall from 1610 to 1616. In the rise which followed, the agio was at a rate of 5 percent from 1621 to 1623. The agio fluctuated about 4 percent in the long recession after the mid-seventeenth century. During the years 1662–1665 it fell to 3½ percent and then climbed to 4 percent in 1665. In the ratio between the movements of balances and metallic reserves, an inflationary gap developed in the years 1662–1667 when the balances rose without being followed in the same degree by the metallic reserves.[264]

In Venice the deposits in the Banco Giro rose to 2,622,171 ducats in June 1630, declined to less than 9,000 in 1643, and rose again to 1,651,119 in 1650, followed by a decline.[265] A simple demonstration makes clear the outstanding position of Venice in the early seventeenth century (see Map 2). In 1609 the metallic reserves in the Deposito Grande were equivalent to 204,290 kilograms of silver. In Amsterdam the average deposits in the Wisselbank for 1650–1654 were equal to 89,770 kilograms of silver.[266] Although this compares the positions of Venice and Amsterdam at two different periods, it serves to show the advance which Amsterdam still had to make at the institutional level. It is also clear that there was a difference between the credit situation at the end of the sixteenth century and that in the mid-seventeenth. Genoa established the cartulario d'oro in 1586 and that of silver in 1606; in Amsterdam the corresponding dates would be 1609 and 1641.[267] Was the economic downturn in the Mediterranean after the crisis of 1597–1599 followed by hoarding of gold in Italy, with a tendency in Northern Europe to use silver in the early seventeenth century? In any case, after 1630, the deposits in the Banco del Giro declined. Following the great crisis of 1628–1630 in Italy — a crisis in which famine, plague, epidemics, and economic difficulties all combined — gold coins appeared in France, mainly escudos and Italian *scudi*. They contributed, no doubt, to the attitudes taken in foreign affairs by France, which apparently entered a phase of absorbing gold. This was used in financial operations, to subsidize military allies, especially Sweden, formerly paid in bills of exchange negotiated on the market of Amsterdam. There were disturbances, losses and compensations, shifts between one country and another. These disparities further indicated the long

---

[263] Willem F. Schimmel, *Geschiedkundig overzicht van het Muntwesen in Nederland* (Amsterdam, 1882), pp. 18–31.

[264] Dillen, *Bronnen tot de geschiedenis der Wisselbanken*, II, pp. 949–950.

[265] Luzzatto, "Banques publiques," pp. 55–64.

[266] Frank C. Spooner, *Venice and the Levant: An Aspect of Monetary History, 1610–1614*, in *Studi in onore di Amintore Fanfani*, ed. Gino Barbieri (6 vols., Milan 1962), V, p. 646.

[267] Dillen, "Bank of Amsterdam," pp. 87–89.

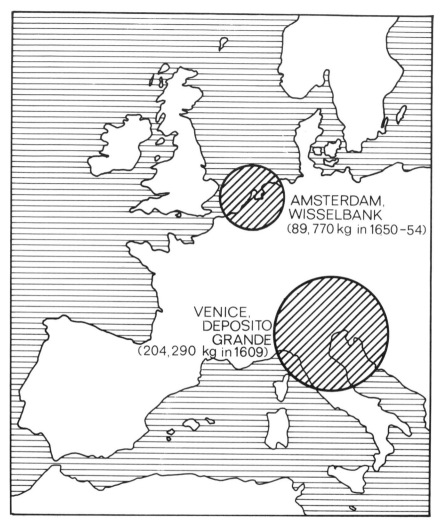

2. Comparison between the Reserves in the Deposito Grande in Venice (1609), with the Deposits in the Wisselbank in Amsterdam (1650–1654) (The bullion in the reserves has been converted into kilograms of fine silver.)

crisis of the seventeenth century, when the regional economies were thrown more and more on their own resources. Such differences direct attention to the years 1630, 1640, and 1650, almost a series of steps in the evolution of monetary circulations.

Yet the seventeenth century does not allow easy explanations. Among the many contingencies, the price recessions apparently were often accompanied in different countries by reductions in the legal rates of interest. In the 1670s there were other monetary reforms. In Amsterdam Johannes Phoonsen made a proposal, in a booklet on the Wisselbank published in 1676, to set up *een courant bank,* which was not accepted. His plans in the same study to allow advances in bank money on specie deposited in the bank were realized, however, in 1683. In the second half of the seventeenth century the rate of interest was about 4 percent which lasted until 1723 when it fell to 2½ percent. The agio on converting into bank money fell after 1683 from 4 to 3½ percent. This situation continued until the first quarter of the eighteenth century[268] and was not limited to the Low Countries. In Genoa, in 1675, the Banco di moneta corrente was established.[269] The difficulty, crisis, and readjustment for Genoa in these years were demonstrated by a report of August 15, 1674, from the consul of France that "one of the principal bankers of this town told me yesterday that for fifty years there have not been so many bills of exchange protested in Novi as in this year." [270]

5. Some Conclusions and Possible Explanations

To conclude, some general explanations are necessary; they inevitably lead the way to theories, and even to economic models. Can the successive phases in the circulation of precious metals, or the attempts to alter the structures of credit, be set in a framework of economic development? At once the insuperable difficulty arises that there is not enough precise information about the international economy, or rather the economic structures of the sixteenth and seventeenth centuries, to assign weights to the different factors. My aim is to reconstitute that past, and to put it into perspective, but the task carries its own risks.

There is a second and perhaps more difficult problem. The history of precious metals or, more precisely, monetary history in the wider sense has usually been set in the context of Europe and Latin America, since these areas are more easily known to western observers. But the international economy was far more than Europe and America. It remains to be seen whether beyond Europe — in Persia and the Far East, in India, China, and Southeast Asia — there were similarities which can be assimilated into the general explanation.

There is, in the first place, the complex problem of international trade. In this, the various movements found their place. The problem of comparative advantage was of critical importance, and the relative price structures of the sixteenth and seventeenth centuries were in progressive evolution. For a bulky (and so transport-intensive) commodity such as wheat in terms of an international standard such as silver, there were considerable price differentials across Europe (see Graph 10).[271] In Spain, Italy, and the "advanced" western

[268] *Ibid.,* pp. 95–101, and *Bronnen tot de geschiedenis der Wisselbanken,* I, 166.
[269] Sieveking, "Bank von S. Giorgio," p. 31.
[270] A. N., Affaires Étrangères, Gênes, B.1.512, Compans, Genoa, Aug. 15, 1674, document communicated by Braudel.
[271] Braudel and Spooner, "Prices in Europe from 1450 to 1750."

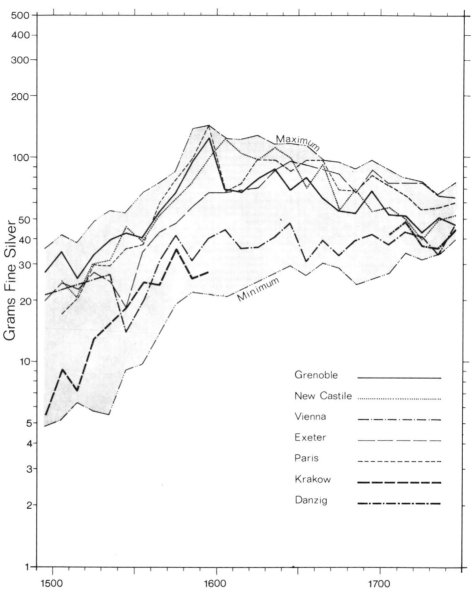

10. Range of Wheat Prices in Europe (1500–1750), One Hectoliter of Wheat in Grams of Fine Silver (Reference: *Cambridge Economic History of Europe,* Vol. IV)

Mediterranean the level of prices in the late fifteenth century was six or seven times that in "backward" Poland. By the end of the seventeenth century, however, with falling grain prices in Southern Europe and continued inflation in Poland, the gap was progressively narrowed so that by the 1730s and 1740s

— years of agricultural "depression" — the ratio had fallen to about 1 : 2. One can infer a considerable fall in the marginal efficiency of bullion in international trade in Europe. Although there were many compensating factors, interregional trade on the eve of the Industrial Revolution faced a problem of exchange different from that two centuries earlier. It is even possible to consider, among the range of explanations, that the expansion of trade in the Far East during the eighteenth century and indeed the emergence of new technological processes in Europe, particularly in Britain, were in one respect part of a vast system of relative costs. Only by expanding further afield, so it seemed, could Europe enjoy wide price differentials. The seventeenth century witnessed, in effect, a considerable measure of convergence in price structures in Europe.

One approach to the problem would be to reconstruct, starting from movements of bullion, the international economy of the sixteenth and seventeenth centuries, indicating the general trends of development. This is not, at first sight, a very convincing possibility. At least, in the present state of our knowledge, it cannot be denied that economic activity in the sixteenth and seventeenth centuries was diverse, but it is not yet certain what weights can be assigned to the monetary factor, by comparison with resources and population, also to be adjusted into a system of prices and market values. Gold, silver, copper, and credit comprised the money stock at different levels. Although the credit sector had before it a huge, revolutionary future, at this time it still occupied a relatively modest position. As has already been observed, the four different sorts of money were interrelated: they were complementary in a total stock of money, with the two dominant components, gold and silver, alone capable of acting on a large scale both as means of payment and as units for hoarding. The latter were controlling factors in monetary operations. In order that the system retain a certain stability, copper and paper were not able to pass certain restricted limits of confidence. They were managed so as to aid the functioning of a monetary system, but were not perfect substitutes for the principal components. There was nothing remarkable, finally, in Gresham's law which stated that the more abundant, and therefore relatively depreciated, money drove out the "better" types of money. The new shifts in levels and the revolutionary changes must be measured in terms of inflationary money. In the final analysis, the four different types of money were a composite function of economic activity. The imperfections of the system and the fortuitous discovery of gold and silver, as has been seen, often caused maladjustment and disturbances, sometimes catastrophes. But with returns to scale, everything depended, or appeared to depend, on the basic economic movement. Whatever the circumstances of their initial production, precious metals eventually became a function of economic activity, and their evolution was not entirely of their own making.

Merchants and governments had, then, four types of money at their disposal. These moneys had different volumes, different relative proportions, and, indeed, different spheres of diffusion. This diffusion was not immediate and direct because there were in the sixteenth and seventeenth centuries geographical differences, not only in the international economy, which was only natural, but also, in the particular case of this study, within the restricted area of France. Thus, for a large part of the sixteenth century, almost on a permanent basis, the Turkish Empire tended to be a zone of abundant gold;[272] Persia, Western Europe, India, and China were largely empires of silver.[273] These statements are valid only in general terms and must allow for exceptions. Another striking example, in the seventeenth century, was that on occasion the English merchants sent out gold to the Indian peninsula, while the Dutch merchants were largely concerned with silver.

The different categories of money, moreover, had velocities of circulation and functions which were rarely the same: silver had a range and circulation different from gold; copper had a role and potential different from silver; paper, limited as it was, had its own particular characteristics. Indeed, the velocity of circulation of the last two elements was considered to be their greatest defect. There was, as a result, repeated competition among the various elements of the monetary system; the abundance or superabundance of one of them imparted special features, even modified the structures of economic activity. The shift from one type of money to another was usually effected suddenly and was accompanied by a series of disruptions, with the consequent loss of continuity of revenue. These shifts never completely restored the former equilibrium. Only the moneys of account, and by implications the different types of credit instruments, seemed to have the necessary unity and continuity, doubtless on account of their polyvalent, or rather neutral, relationship to the other three real moneys which they constantly readjusted. Their alterations, in effect, represented adjustments between the different economies, but, underlying the movement, gold and silver remained the stable force.

It may also be possible to talk of a sociology of money. Every increase in the circulation of gold perhaps would tend to affect the more wealthy, powerful groups and encourage the accumulation of liquid capital. It was not remarkable that the first half of the sixteenth century offered an easy time for merchants, undisturbed in activity and indeed untroubled by conscience.[274] A progressive, and relative, rarification of silver may also have had the effect of restraining upward tendencies in retail prices. An abundance of silver, on the other hand, by setting a premium on gold, made it a "protected," appreciating sector, and susceptible to hoarding. Finally, an abundance of billon inflated retail prices and profoundly modified the structure of values.

---

[272] Braudel, *Méditerranée, passim;* Fernand Braudel and Frank Spooner, "Les métaux monétaires et l'économie du XVIᵉ siècle," in *X Congresso Internazionale di Scienze Storiche, Rome,* ed. Aldo Ferrabino (8 vols., Florence, 1955–1957), IV, pp. 233–264.

[273] Braudel, *Méditerranée, passim,* and especially pp. 1015–1016.

[274] Jakob Fugger, the Rich (der Reiche), is a good example; see in particular, Paul Joachimsen, *Die Reformation* (Leipzig, 1951), p. 46.

The premiums on gold and silver made them both more acceptable to hoard. Copper (with or without silver), by its very profusion, aggravated the problem and confused the function of precious metals themselves.

At the international level, there were, moreover, unavoidable lags implied in the shifts in social structure between different countries. It is possible to consider the transfers of bullion between one economy and another as responses to the movements of trade and the financial policies of governments. These transfers, however, in the hands of entrepreneurs or in public reserves acquired their greatest effects only when absorbed directly into the movement of the economy, through social mobilities, and adjustments in the distribution of incomes and price levels in terms of bullion.[275] Such a long process of returns to scale was not of the least importance in the analysis of monetary and economic movements and of those complex social movements in changing societies during the sixteenth and seventeenth centuries.

The validity of this simplified scheme may lie in its explanation of some of the abrupt changes in the bullion economy. Even with their many limitations precious metals served in a variety of ways. They were in a state of imperfect equilibrium one with another, not only because of their very nature but also because of the different functions and pressures from the international economy. Behind gold, silver, copper, and paper were forces of which the different economies had not yet acquired full control. Yet, if the monetary equilibrium faltered, the economic climate was transformed. Thus, between 1540 and 1560 the dislocation in the circulation of gold and silver was a classic instance of possible disturbances. These form the counterpart to the rigidities from which the metallic economy repeatedly attempted to escape, but, in the absence of an effective substitute, was obliged to accept. At the first shock, the system crumbled. The experience in Europe presupposes that the gold phase lasted perhaps as much as a century (1450–1550), that of silver for another fifty years or more, and that of copper until perhaps about 1680. These phases were, however, far from simple and were combined in a context of credit development.

A second problem is the part played by the "drain" to the Far East. This has been referred to several times already and must now be considered at greater length. I shall place the discussion in a wider setting with the aim of finding clearer definitions.

Here again it is possible to suggest the three metallic phases: gold, silver,

[275] For examples of lags in the movement of real wages, see Charles Verlinden, Jan Craeybeckx, and E. Scholliers, "Movements des prix et des salaires en Belgique au XVIe siècle," *Annales, X* (1955); E. H. Phelps Brown and Sheila V. Hopkins, "Seven Centuries of Building Wages," *Economica,* XXII (1955), Seven Centuries of the Prices of Consumables compared with Builders' Wage-rates," *ibid.,* XXIII (1956), "Wage-rates and Prices: Evidence of Population Pressure in the Sixteenth Century," *ibid.,* XXIV (1957), "Builders' Wage-rates, Prices and Population: Some Further Evidence," *ibid.,* XXVI (1959), "Seven Centuries of Wages and Prices: Some Earlier Estimates," *ibid.,* XXVIII (1961).

and copper. With gold the closer integration of world trade was still beginning, hesitant at first and lacking the clear incentives in comparative advantage and levels of activity. Gold, indeed, appears to have played an internal rather than an external role in European affairs. With silver, however, Europe was able to penetrate the economies of Asia. As a result, the imperfections and lags in the system played an important role. Merchants were able to gain extraordinary profits since the price differentials in terms of bullion between east and west were not immediately closed. These differentials explain some of the success of financiers and speculators in the early sixteenth century; at times they were able to earn profits of more than 100 percent, but these were not so easily won in subsequent years.

From the viewpoint of the Far East, the flow of silver both from America and from Europe meant greater bargaining strength for European entrepreneurs. At first silver found its way to Asia along the customary routes, from Russia, from Turkey by the routes from Trebizond to Tabriz as well as by the equally classic routes across Syria and Egypt. Silver flowed through Persia —the last outpost of Europe en route to Asia[276] — where it appeared in abundance in the markets and was no doubt of western origin. This can be seen from the travel accounts of the English merchants Geoffrey Duckett (1568) and Thomas Bannister (1568–1574).[277] The silver coins of Persia (*larins*) were accepted for their high degree of fineness, appearing in transactions in India, Southeast Asia, and China. Spanish silver reals were brought by the case to Goa and Malacca by Portuguese vessels.[278] Finally, after 1580, the Spaniards established themselves in Manila and organized a regular trading service between Acapulco and the Philippines. In this way American silver was transhipped by Chinese junks in return for gold, raw and manufactured silk, porcelains, and other products.[279] A glowing report of 1590 declared that "the trade of New Spain with China has become a common affair. The ships arrived there daily." [280] In 1610–1614 the official exports of silver from Venice alone to its colonies on the Dalmatian coast and in its trade to the Levant amounted to almost 6 percent of the silver imported at that time into Seville from the New World (see Graph 11).[281] Could more precise and extensive details have left a less impressive picture?

Europe, eager for pepper, spices, and silks, broadcast silver coins and bullion over the vast continent and islands of Asia. It made a buyer's market and represented an infinite propensity for luxury consumption. In the person

---

[276] Henri Berr, *En marge de l'histoire universelle* (Paris, 1953).

[277] "Voyage of Geoffrey Duckett and Thomas Bannister (1568–1574)," in *Early voyages and travels to Russia and Persia by Anthony Jenkinson and other Englishmen*, ed. Edward Morgan and Charles H. Coote (London, 1886), cited in Attman, *Den ryska Marknaden i 1500–talets baltiska politik*, p. 116.

[278] Communicated by Vitorino Magalhães Godinho.

[279] Braudel, *Méditerranée*, p. 415; Chaunu, "Galion de Manille," p. 456.

[280] *The Fugger News-Letters*, 1st Ser., letter of Jan. 13, 1590.

[281] Spooner, *Venice and the Levant*, p. 653.

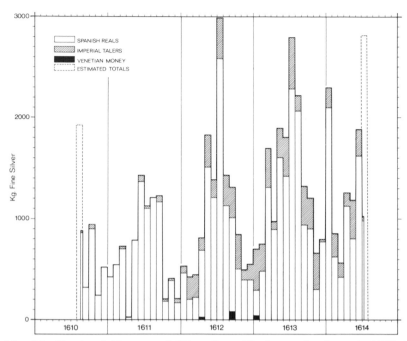

SPANISH REALS
IMPERIAL TALERS
VENETIAN MONEY
ESTIMATED TOTALS

11. Monthly Totals of Exports of Silver from Venice to the Levant, 1610–1614
(Reference: F. C. Spooner)

of Filippo Sassetti (1586), the Florentine, friend of Bernando Davanzati, all Europe was spellbound by the possibilities of the Chinese market;[282] with Gasparo Balbi (1588), it marveled at the splendors of Malacca, the gate to China, Japan, and the Moluccas.[283] The avidity of the Chinese for silver established a commercial epoch for the international economy. Without this avidity, wrote Sassetti on January 20, 1586, "the reals would not have risen so much in value as they are now. The Chinese, among all the peoples of Asia, are wild about silver as everywhere else are men about gold." [284] From Goa in 1588 the Portuguese Duarte Gómez also reported that China kept silver "at a higher price than all the powers of the world" and that "in the adjustment of silver to gold they make such a great difference that as the Catholics were seeking to continue the right value of these two metals, it was allowed that gold should be worth ten times more than silver; now, the Chinese value it at five times, more or less, as I can demonstrate." [285] In brief, at the monetary level there were conditions of relative advantage which stim-

[282] Filippo Sassetti, *Lettere* (Milan, n.d.), letter of Jan. 20, 1586.
[283] Gasparo Balbi, *Viaggio dell'Indie Orientali* (Venice, 1590), pp. 69, 131; Godinho, "Tournant," pp. 135–136.
[284] Sassetti, *Lettere*, letter of Jan. 20, 1586.
[285] Duarte Gómez Solis, *Discursos sobre los comercios de las dos Indias (1622)* (Lisbon, 1943), pp. 51–52.

ulated international trade; the unloading of silver in the Far East was only the more intense because of these conditions.

In principle, however, these sales of bullion were bound to have defined limits. The decline in the deliveries to Seville and in the output of mined silver in general was one, although very early the Portuguese had endeavored to send copper to the Indies.[286] Another limiting factor was the rise in the prices of commodities exported from the east to Europe. Because of the costs of transportation and the element of risk, conditions of equilibrium were, eventually, approached, and the east was no longer an open buyer's market for European traders. Furthermore, here and there, in the heyday of silver at the opening of the seventeenth century, some eastern markets were satiated with silver; sometimes even gold was found to be a better medium of exchange between east and west.

It is not easy to collate all these different pieces of evidence. The arrival of the Dutch and English traders in the Far East coincided paradoxically enough with the culmination of the silver imports from America into Seville. The English East India Company, an offshoot from the Levant Company, was founded by royal charter on December 31, 1600; the Dutch East India Company was officially established soon afterward in 1602 although earlier expeditions had already been made in 1595. These new arrivals confirmed the apparent difficulties in the operations of the Portuguese and Spanish: on January 11, 1593, edicts limiting the trade of Manila were issued.[287] The established veterans of European trade with the Far East reacted unfavorably against the newcomers and tried every means, as was revealed in the diplomatic maneuvers on the eve of the Twelve Years' Truce (1609), to dissuade them from venturing further.[288] As the incidents of 1624 revealed, they made a brave but ineffective show of force.[289] They were more successful, however, in their attempt to defeat the proposal, about 1610, to set up a French East India company.[290] In spite of all this, nothing could stop the shift in the center of gravity in the Far East's relations with Europe, from Manila to Bantam, and then about 1619 to Batavia, the new focus of Dutch power in the area. The English surrendered, scarcely without a word, to the success of the Dutch. In 1618 their agents recognized Batavia as the center for the East Indian trade.[291] Everything seemed to favor the Dutch; even their hostilities with Spain were suspended by truce from 1609 to 1621. Did not, after all, the Dutch merchants victual the enemy armies of the Most Catholic King as they threatened the very frontiers of Holland? War was associated not only with Spain but

---

[286] Communicated by Godinho.

[287] Chaunu, "Galion de Manille," p. 458.

[288] Henri Lonchay and Joseph Cuvelier, *Correspondance de la Cour d'Espagne sur les affaires des Pays-Bas au XVIIe siècle* (6 vols., Brussels, 1923–1937), I, p. 360.

[289] *Ibid.,* II, 188, letter from Madrid, Nov. 8, 1624, Philip IV to Isabella.

[290] *Ibid.,* I, 352, letter of May 24, 1610, Philip III to his ambassadors.

[291] C.S.P., Colonial, East Indies, letter of Jan. 19, 1618, George Ball, Thomas Spurway, and John Byndon to the East India Company.

also, more important still, with silver, then flowing from the New World in smaller quantities. Through smuggling and illicit trade the Dutch kept their entrée into the Spanish peninsula.[292] While Batavia was embarking upon its reign in the Far East, Amsterdam was taking over the powerful functions of Antwerp and Seville in Europe. The market of Amsterdam supplied the English East India Company with silver on more than one occasion. In 1615 there was further striking evidence of the dependence of the English traders on the Dutch. In India, the simple threat of the Dutch to enter the trade of Surat, the base of English trade, was enough to keep them quiet.[293] The merger of English and Dutch activity in 1619 ended with the bitter "massacre" of the English at Amboina in 1623. Dutch seamen, sailing under the flag of France, as in 1618, participated in French ventures to the east.[294]

Thus in the Far East, by the time of copper and the successful establishment of the Dutch, the easy conditions offered by silver seemed to have passed their prime. Prices were rising everywhere, and payments in silver from Europe did not meet altogether favorable conditions. Jan Pietersz. Coen, writing from Bantam on March 11, 1618, about the arrival of the Chinese junks, declared "the cassia has become so dear that one cannot now get more than 8,000 for a real, that formerly were worth 30,000 a real and of even better quality than are now marketed." [295]

A report by the English merchants from Surat in January 1618 also commented on the depreciation of the silver real of eight.[296] And Beaulieu, commanding the French expedition of 1621, found the Dutch and English desperately offering 48 reals for a *bahar* of pepper, but the King of Achim "did not want to give it to them for less than 64 reals, which is excessively dear." [297]

It seems that in the early seventeenth century European merchants were obliged to be astute and always ready to bring off small successes, to specu-

---

[292] Lonchay and Cuvelier, *Correspondance de la Cour d'Espagne,* I, p. 16, letter of Nov. 22, 1589, from Henry IV of France to the Archduke Albert; p. 92, letter of Jan. 16, 1602, from Pedro Franqueza to Andrea de Prada. On August 30, 1624, the municipal authorities of Nantes were proposing to write to the governor of San Sebastian to buy back a vessel belonging to the "Flemish merchants of this town" captured by the Spaniards near St. Nazaire. A. M., Nantes, Ser. BB. 30, fol. 255[vo].

[293] C.S.P., Colonial, East Indies, Apr. 24, 1627; Court Minutes of the East India Company, Jan. 12, April 4, 1615, Jan. 5, 1626, Apr. 13, 1627, Mar. 2, 1629; Violet Barbour, *Capitalism in Amsterdam in the 17th Century* (Baltimore, 1950), pp. 49–54, 95–96.

[294] C.S.P., Colonial, East Indies, letter of Nov. 10, 1617, from Thomas Keridge, and Thomas Rastell to the East India Company; letter of Jan. 19, 1618, from Ball, Spurway, and Byndon to the East India Company; letter of Jan. 31, 1618, from William Nicolls to Keridge and colleagues in Surat.

[295] Jan Pietersz. Coen, *Bescheiden omtrent zijn bedrijf in Indië,* ed. H. T. Colenbrander (6 vols., The Hague, 1919–1934), I, p. 332, letter from Bantam of Mar. 11, 1618.

[296] C.S.P., Colonial, East Indies, letter of Jan. 31, 1618, from Nicolls to Keridge and colleagues in Surat.

[297] Augustin Beaulieu, *Mémoires du voyage aux Indes Orientales du Général Beaulieu,* ed. Melchisedech Thévenot (4 pts., Paris, 1663–1672), Pt. II, p. 51.

late at short range, to trade between the different countries of the Indies. One indication of the demand for means of payment in these markets was the rising, systematic attempts to develop resources of precious metals in Asia. In the second half of the sixteenth century the Portuguese encouraged the development of the mines of Japan through the *Nao do Trato* which sailed from their treaty port of Macao. Japan had rich mines at Sado, Iwami, and in the south of Mutsu. Those of Sado, "a treasure island composed entirely of gold and silver," [298] had been worked for the first time in 1541 and then during the second half of the sixteenth century. Afterward, further deposits of gold and silver were discovered at Karnisawa, Imagashima, Tada (in 1540–1550), Swamurayama and Hotatouzan (in 1583), Daiya and Kamioka (in 1589), and Shirana and Komaki (in 1598). [299] The output from the mines of Sado during the years 1613–1647 reached 173 *kwam* 496 *momme* of gold in bars, 36 kwam 513 momme in placer gold, 158,704 *ryo* of *kobans,* and 55,735 kwam 513 momme of silver. [300] From the mines in Sado, Satsuma, Idzu, Buzin, Bungo, Suruga, and Tajima during the years 1624–1631 the annual production was 48,000 ryo of gold. From about 1592 to 1615 the production of the mines reached a peak. [301] At that time the use of silver slowly permeated the markets and transactions of the half-closed economy of Japan. When the Tokugawa dynasty, [302] began to reign, a third of the taxes on agricultural products, according to one estimate, was collected in silver. [303] As a result of its mineral resources, Japan succeeded in playing an important role at the end of the sixteenth century. This was emphasized when in 1600–1601 the Goto family took over the farm of the mine (the *kin-za* for gold, and the *gin-za* for silver). [304] Is it mere coincidence that the great street of Tokyo today is called the Ginza?)

From the second decade of the seventeenth century, at least, the Dutch documents refer frequently to exports of silver from Japan. The same hunger for silver drove the Dutch to develop the mines in Amboina (Moluccas) with Japanese miners in 1620, and they fought brutally with the English for control in 1623. Japanese silver assumed substantial importance in the Dutch network of trade in the second decade of the seventeenth century. Coen wrote on November 10, 1614, that "a good return of silver is coming from Japan

[298] Sawada Shō, *Financial Difficulties of the Edo Bakufu,* trans. Hugh Borton, in *Harvard Journal of Asiatic Studies,* I (1936), p. 312. See also A. Kobata, "The Production and Uses of Gold and Silver in Sixteenth- and Seventeenth-Century Japan," *Economic History Review,* xviii (1965).

[299] Takekoshi, *Economic Aspects,* I, pp. 545–546.

[300] *Ibid.,* I, p. 551. A ryo was a gold coin of fixed weight but variable fineness. A momme was about 3.75 grams; 1000 momme = 1 kwam; a koku has been estimated at 1.804 hectoliters.

[301] *Ibid.:* Shō, *Financial Difficulties of the Edo Bakufu.*

[302] The Tokugawa (or Edo) period covered the years 1600–1868.

[303] M. Takizawa, *The Penetration of Money Economy in Japan* (New York, 1927), p. 35.

[304] Takao, "Economic History of Japan," p. 213.

which here, as everywhere in the Indies, is completely deprived of specie. He wrote again from Bantam on January 5, 1616, "Here have arrived merchants, who with only 30 to 40,000 reals each have brought a very fine return and have long traded in Macao"; on August 5, 1619, "on the first of April . . . arrived the yacht Tiger . . . laden with pepper, 69,000 reals in Japanese silver and a few diamonds"; on January 22, 1620, he reported the arrival of ships "with 144,000 reals, as much in specie as in Japanese silver." [305] The Dutch trade actually kept silver specie for the purchase of spices, but consigned the silver bullion for the payments in China "even more than reals for the pepper trade and silver for the trade of China, but the demand is such that some must be sent from the Netherlands." The English merchants also joined in these transactions. [306] In 1613 their agent in Japan, William Adams, announced that there was "gold and silver in plenty" although he asserted that gold was so expensive that it offered little profit. [307] On April 10, 1615, Coen wrote to Jacques Specx in Japan: "in these 4 ships have been shipped by the English Company about 70,000 reals in cash." [308] And on January 13, 1618, Richard Cocks, the English factor in Japan, had silver melted down "to send to Bantam for a trial." [309]

Thus, Japan, grafted onto the Dutch network of trade, naturally responded to these monetary movements, which were more typical of Europe. Japan's effectiveness as a free source of silver, however, was progressively reduced by the rise in prices. Here was something of a repetition on a small scale of the European experience. Some scattered data for the price of rice in terms of silver appear to show a sharp rise during the second quarter followed by a period of relative stability in the last four decades of the century. [310]

This movement of the price of rice in Japan becomes even more significant when compared with that of Milanese rice sold on the Amsterdam market (see Graph 12). [311] It would be only prudent to accept a considerable margin of

[305] Coen, *Bescheiden,* III, p. 581, letter from Jakarta of Jan. 17, 1620; II, p. 650, letter of Feb. 28, 1620, from J.P.C. to Cornelis de Houtman and governors of the Moluccas; I, p. 84, letter from Bantam of Nov. 10, 1614, p. 167, letter from Bantam of Jan. 5, 1616, p. 453, letter from Bantam of Aug. 5, 1619, p. 512, letter from Bantam of Jan. 22, 1620, p. 485, letter from Bantam of Aug. 5, 1619.

[306] *Ibid.,* I, p. 485, letter from Bantam of Aug. 5, 1619.

[307] C.S.P., Colonial, East Indies, letter of Jan. 12, 1613, from William Adams to Augustin Spalding in Bantam.

[308] Coen, *Bescheiden,* II, p. 3, letter from Bantam of Apr. 10, 1615, from Coen to Specx in Japan.

[309] Richard Cocks, *Diary 1615–1622,* ed. Edward M. Thompson (2 vols., London, 1883), Jan. 13, 1618, Dec. 14, 1620.

[310] E. Honjō, *Tokugawa Bakufu no Beika Chōsetsu* (Kyoto, 1924), pp. 407–415, in Hugh Borton, "Peasant Uprisings in Japan of the Tokugawa Period," *Transactions of the Asiatic Society of Japan,* 2d Ser., XV (1938), pp. 208–209.

[311] Posthumus, *Inquiry into the History of Prices in Holland,* I. It should be stressed that the Amsterdam prices are given in fine silver and the Japanese prices in *Keichō* silver. There is little precise information about the degree of fineness of the latter except that it was a type of coin and considered of high quality. The comparison here is made to give an approximate order of magnitude.

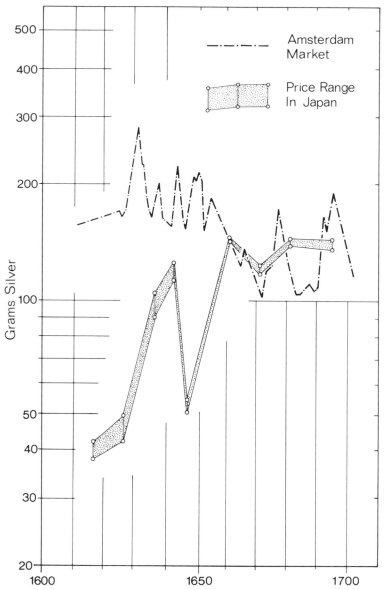

12. Rice Prices in Amsterdam and Japan, One Hectoliter of Rice in Grams of Silver
(Reference: N. Posthumus and E. Honjō)

error in the comparison of these estimates, but the comparison is nevertheless
of interest. The proximity of the two series is closer than is usually supposed,
even when it is remembered that rice in Amsterdam was something of a luxury
cereal and that Keichō silver was not fine silver but rather a type of high-grade
silver coin. The rise of these prices of rice in Japan, however, carried them more

or less into the range of the Amsterdam prices and brings up a number of questions: about the closing price differentials between Europe and the east; about
the relative ease with which the Dutch traders fastened their hold on the silver
of Japan; and, in a much more fundamental sense, about the potential "sympathy" which the economy of Japan even in these early contacts expressed for
western ideas and methods, and which may even have persisted through long
years of closure and bursts of xenophobia. Later studies will no doubt reveal
more of this relationship.

The full force of these changes in the early seventeenth century also brought
small-scale expedients. The directors of the great Dutch companies began to
pay attention to the route by which silver crossed the Pacific from Acapulco
to Manila. On March 5, 1616, the news reached Amsterdam from Seville and
New Spain that Joris van Spilbergen had arrived with five ships off the coast
of Acapulco.[312] After the crisis of 1619–1620 and the renewal of hostilities
in Europe of 1621, the Dutch beset this route. As early as May 11, 1620,
Coen wrote from Bantam: "the ships Nieuwe Maen, Swaen and Hondt should
sail to Cabo de Spirito Santo, there take the Spanish silver-ships sailing from
Acapulco to Manila." [313] In June and July 1622 his letters referred again to
the importance of the Spanish route across the Pacific.[314] The Dutch lay in
wait for plunder.

A further indication of the depth of the crisis and the progressive inability
of the Far East to satisfy the demands of Europe was the preference for gold
rather than silver in parts of the Indian peninsula and Southeast Asia. This
was not necessarily new, for gold had played a significant role in the monetary
history of southern India, but these changes and alternating tastes were perhaps important symptoms. In 1621, Beaulieu, in command of the expedition

Table 2. Rice Prices in Japan

Year	Per koku in momme of silver	Per hectoliter in grams of Keichō silver
1616	18.2–20.0	37.83–41.57
1626	20.0–23.6	41.57–49.06
1636	43.0–50.0	89.38–103.94
1642	54.0–60.0	112.25–124.72
1647	24.0–26.0	48.89–54.05
1660	69.0–70.0	143.43–145.51
1670	56.0–59.0	116.41–122.64
1680	67.0–70.0	139.27–145.51
1694	65.0–69.0	135.12–143.43

[312] Coen, *Bescheiden,* IV, p. 343, letter from Amsterdam of Mar. 5, 1616, to Coen.
[313] *Ibid.,* I, p. 541, letter from Bantam of May 11, 1620.
[314] *Ibid.,* III, pp. 201, 207, letters from Batavia of June 19, July 2, 1622, from Coen
to Commander Cornelis Reyersz.

from France, observed that in Achim gold was more in demand than silver and that the English merchants had "a large amount of gold," which resulted, in his opinion, from sales in Surat.[315] By 1615 John Jordain had noted that gold was freely accepted in the Moluccas;[316] this was again reported in 1624. The English East India Company was even accused at home in 1620, and with good reason, of having exported gold in bars.[317] Was the reappearance of gold in the discussions a sign of the times? During a period when there were no substitutes to take the place of silver, transactions turned to barter. These instances were indicative of other similar experiences. On November 1, 1624, the Amsterdam Chamber of the Dutch East India Company sent to Batavia 600,000 florins in gold and silver, of which 40 percent were in Hungarian gold ducats; they were destined for the markets of Persia and Surat.[318] The 1620s were, in general, marked by a favorable reception to gold in India and Persia. Surat, which had been so willing to accept the silver dollar in 1615, in 1626 was also receiving gold specie, principally Hungarian ducats, Turkish *sultanins,* and Venetian zecchini. John Kerridge, an English merchant, wrote home to the East India Company in the same year that gold brought 6 percent more profit than the silver real.[319] Masulipatam in 1626 and 1629 evinced the same preference for gold. It was observed also that the cloth of Coromandel which sold easily in India and Burma could be obtained on better terms in Siam for payments of gold.[320] Under these conditions, the East India Company in 1626 exported gold to the value of £30,000; the letters patent of February 1627 authorized the export that year of a similar sum. According to the report of John Benthall (January 1629), gold either in bars or in Venetian zecchini was ready for export to Persia. Finally, the letters patent of October 1629 gave the English East India Company permission to export £120,000 in silver and £40,000 in gold, in place of the £100,000, which had been authorized previously.[321] In 1638 the company once more requested permission to export gold.[322]

---

[315] Beaulieu, *Mémoires,* p. 51.

[316] C.S.P. Colonial, East Indies, letter from Bantam of Feb. 10, 1615, from Jordain to the East India Company.

[317] *Ibid.,* 1622 (?): "Reasons to prove that it is not the East India trade which doth consume the gold, silver coin, and other treasure of this Kingdom, but rather the said trade is an excellent means greatly to increase the same."

[318] Dunlop, *Bronnen . . . Perzië,* p. 122, letter from Amsterdam of Nov. 1, 1624, from Bewindhebbers to the governor-general en Raden, Batavia.

[319] C.S.P., Colonial, East Indies, consultation, Oct. 7, 1616 (Swally Roads); Court minutes of the East India Company, Mar. 28, 1626; letter of Nov. 29, 1626, from Kerridge and Council (in Surat) to the East India Company.

[320] *Ibid.,* letter from Batavia of July 18, 1627, from Hawley, Bix, Muschamp, and Steele to the East India Company; letter of Oct. 28, 1629, from Muschamp, William Hoare, and Anthony Kernworthy to the East India Company; letter of Dec. 20, 1617, from William Eaton to Sir Thomas Smythe.

[321] *Ibid.,* Court minutes of the East India Company, Feb. 15, 1626; Patent to the East India Company, Feb. 13, 1627; Petition of the East India Company to the King, Oct. 5, 1629; letter from Ispahan of June 14, 1626, from Thomas Barker, John Purifey, Robert Loftus, and George Smith to the East India Company.

[322] David Macpherson, *Annals of Commerce* (4 vols., London, 1805), II, p. 404.

The situation between the European merchants and the various Far Eastern markets was, in reality, far from stable. In 1630 the profits on gold in Persia appear to have been slim. In Surat in 1629 and at the beginning of 1630 there were difficulties in converting gold and putting it into circulation.[323] Twelve thousand pounds of gold brought in the English ship *Swan* was not easily disposed of in Masulipatam in 1632. On the other hand, in 1634, the cargo of gold brought in the *Jewel* went without difficulty.[324] It may be inferred, in general, that the lands which remained strictly under the control of the Dutch — the famous Spice Islands, the west coast of Sumatra, Java, and Djambi — retained conditions where silver was largely preferred, in spite of the presence of some gold mined in the islands.[325]

Japan probably played its part in this revival of gold. In 1601 the ratio between gold and silver in Osaka and Kyoto was of the order of little less than 1 : 12, while in Nagasaki, an important center of foreign trade, the ratio was 1 : 13. This great port, one of the principal outlets of Japan, may indeed have enjoyed a considerable trade in bullion. In any case, the ratio was fixed at 1 : 15 in 1627, in contrast to the ratios of 1 : 7 or 1 : 10 in the Indies and Burma and 1 : 10 or 1 : 13 in India, depending on the coast. These monetary problems became more complex when the Portuguese and Spaniards were expelled from Japan in 1636 and the subjects of the Emperor were forbidden to accept any foreign coins marked with a cross.[326]

Later, the export of gold from Japan may have increased, particularly after 1660, when there was a decisive decline in the export of copper. In 1668, 2,990,000 florins of gold and silver were exported by the Dutch from Japan, of which 74.72 percent was in gold; in 1669, 2,550,000 florins were exported, 77.68 percent in gold. In 1670 the nominal rate of the koban, a gold coin in the form of an oval plate, was between 56 and 58 *maas,* but increased to 68 *maas* in 1672. Shortly afterwards the exports of gold were stopped (1685–1686). But from this time onward it appears that the trend was in the

[323] C.S.P., Colonial, East Indies, letter from Ispahan of Feb. 27, 1630, from William Burt to the East India Company; Court minutes of the East India Company, Jan. 14, 1629; letter of Apr. 27, 1629, from President Richard Wylde, John Skibbowe, and George Page (in Surat) to the East India Company.

[324] C.S.P., Colonial, East Indies and Persia, Court minutes of the East India Company, Aug. 1, 1632; letter of Oct. 25, 1634, from Thomas Joyce and Nathaniel Wyche (Masulipatam) to the East India Company.

[325] *Ibid.,* letter from Swally Marine of Apr. 13, 1630, from Wylde and Council to the East India Company; letter from Surat of Dec. 31, 1630, from President Thomas Rastell, Joseph Hopkinson, James Bickford, and Arthur Suffeylde to the East India Company; letter from Surat of Apr. 24, 1632, from Hopkinson, Nathaniel Moutey, Nathaniel Wick, and Joyce to the East India Company; letter from Djambi of Feb. 11, 1616, from John Tucker to Smythe; Court minutes of the East India Company, Sept. 30, 1617, Aug. 20, 1634; letter from Batavia of July 18, 1627, from Hawley, Bix, Muschamp, and Steele to the East India Company.

[326] Takekoshi, *Economic Aspects,* II, p. 32; C.S.P., Colonial, East Indies, letter from Batavia of July 8, 1627, from Hawley, Bix, Muschamp, and Steele to the East India Company; Engelbert Kaempfer, *The History of Japan* (2 vols., London, 1727), I, p. 313.

direction of appreciating silver;[327] and this coincided with the beginning of a new phase for gold in Europe. It is possible that the conditions in Japan followed this trend. The *Genroku* period (1688–1704) and above all the year 1699 saw debasement, particularly of silver coins. The valuable silver coins of the Keichō period issued at the beginning of the seventeenth century soon disappeared. In 1696 an office was opened to regulate the use of gold and silver, especially gold leaf used in decoration.[328] When the Japanese economist Arai Hakuseki published his treatise in 1713, the gold coins did not weigh more than half of what they had in the past, and those of silver contained a much higher proportion of alloy than formerly.[329]

Only by continuing the discussion over many more pages would it be feasible to exhaust the possible explanations of the case of Japan. It would be necessary, above all, to find the basic reasons why, after 1636, when the Spanish and Portuguese were expelled, the Dutch were able to carry on their affairs with profit, at least until 1672.[330]

One must see the whole panorama of the countries of Asia, from Persia to Malaya and from India to China. After the easy conditions promoted by the affluence of silver, the seventeenth century, with all its disorders, did not offer the same relative advantages. Beyond the problems of economic activity were other troubles, such as in the pepper groves of the Indies (about 1620) and the growing attacks against the China of the Mings by the Manchus, who were soon to break through the barriers with the capture of Peking in 1644.[331]

It is difficult to escape the impression of a decline, if not collapse, of some of the relationships between Europe and the Far East in the seventeenth century. This was not a permanent state of affairs as can be seen from the export of bullion and the price inflation in China in the eighteenth century and from the export of silver to the east in the nineteenth century. The fact remains, however, that in the seventeenth century there was debility, troubled by copper, when everything seemed to relinquish something of the earlier vigor and richness of life. The Far East, perhaps even the whole world, half escaped the outcome.

[327] Glamann, "Dutch East India Company's Trade," pp. 72 ff.

[328] Arai Hakuseki, *Kengi*, in N. S. Smith, "An Introduction to Some Japanese Economic Writings of the 18th Century," *Transactions of the Asiatic Society of Japan*, 2d Ser., XI (1934), pp. 47, 53–54; Takizawa, *Penetration of Money Economy in Japan*, p. 37.

[329] Hakuseki, *Kengi*, pp. 51–57. He proposed (p. 62) that a sufficient reserve of gold should be kept to ensure payments to the Dutch merchants in the following twenty years.

[330] The Dutch entered the third phase of their trade. See Kaempfer, *History of Japan*, I, p. 359.

[331] Henri Hauser, *La prépondérance espagnole* (Paris, 1948) p. 410; Charles P. Fitzgerald, *China* (London, 1950), pp. 471–472.

Chapter 2

Monetary Theories and Institutions in France

The brief survey of the movements of precious metals in the world makes it easier to study the conditions in France. Though the basic conditions may become clearer in the light of this earlier discussion, it must not be assumed that the problem is simple. It is fundamentally complex, involving many factors, particularly those concerning the mentality of men in the sixteenth century. These people had their own particular preoccupations, some of which were monetary.

Money, said Malestroit, was "a mystery understood by very few people." [1] Private individuals and governments found themselves involved in monetary matters and groped their way toward solutions. Expedients were all too often blindly accepted in the light of precepts which modern experience would consider ill judged or even dangerous. It is important to realize that the motives for such decisions must be measured against a certain level of knowledge. Lucien Febvre's classic study on the religion of Rabelais sets out to estimate the mental capacity of men in the sixteenth century.[2] This is a timely reminder of the importance of a basic historical relativity, a concept which can be applied profitably within the framework of economic history. The problems, ideas, and realities observed in monetary development impute not only the decisions and activities of men but also their powers of comprehension, their intelligence, and their ability to observe and reason. Even their moral attitudes carry weight in the two centuries under discussion, especially in the seventeenth century, when the scientific "revolution" discovered so much about the natural world and brought marked changes in life and thought.

It is difficult to draw fine distinctions among the deeply ingrained traditions of those times, the propensity to adapt to change, and the intelligence to grasp the future significance of slowly emerging structures. A dichotomy exists between actuality and its interpretation. One way of measuring that difference is to examine how men explained contemporary problems. In the sixteenth century even the sharpest intellects could not range far beyond the established boundaries of accumulated experience. There were inevitable blind spots, serving all the more to define the understanding of the period and its evolution, but efforts were made to sort out the subtle definitions of the money of account and all that was flexible in the diverse monetary institutions and economic activity under the Valois and the Bourbons. The hesitations and shortcomings of these men provide valuable insights into the monetary conditions of France in the sixteenth and seventeenth centuries.

[1] Sieur de Malestroit, *Mémoires sur le faict des Monnoyes proposéz et leus par le maistre des comptes de Malestroit au Privé Conseil du Roy tenu à Sainct-Maur-des-Fosséz, le 16 jour de May 1567,* in *Paradoxes inédits,* ed. Luigi Einaudi (Turin, 1937), p. 105.
[2] Lucien Febvre, *Le problème de l'incroyance au XVIe siècle* (Paris, 1942).

1. Monetary Theories and Conditions

I have chosen a few representative speakers to give their views on monetary theories and conditions during this period.[3] Politicians, theorists, and officials endlessly pursued the polemics. All too often they were excessively wordy and limited in outlook. There is, on the other hand, almost no opportunity to reconstruct the thought of the merchants and traders, even if it ever existed in coherent form; they were too occupied in the daily task of forecasting future gains and considering the risks of their operations. And even they may have hesitated to voice opinions before the scholars and the experts.

The third quarter of the sixteenth century is the most fruitful period for an investigation of the subject, the need to reform and reorganize was pressing, and discussions abounded on monetary problems. The great controversy between Bodin and Malestroit was notable. Their dispute in print won international renown for the monetary problems of France at a time when so many of its difficulties were shared by other countries also facing far-reaching changes in price structures and monetary conditions. Malestroit first published his *Paradoxes* in 1566; he wrote his *Mémoires sur la monnaie* in 1567.[4] Bodin set his *Réponse* before the public in 1568.[5] At the same time, Alexandre de la Tourette, who was closely acquainted with the practical side of monetary problems in France because of his position as Second President of the Cour des Monnaies (September 18, 1553),[6] entered the discussion in 1567 with his *Réponse*.[7] These three were certainly not alone, for they lived in an age when even mathematics was a subject for public debate, but their positions are better known because of their public standing and the diffusion of their writings. Taken together, they review the difficult, elusive monetary problems of their time.

The Malestroit-Bodin controversy (1566–1568) sprang, above all, from the rise in prices and the massive arrival of silver after the 1550s, which occurred later in France than in Spain.[8] Bodin and his contemporaries clearly

---

[3] See, for example, the study of Paul Harsin, *Les doctrines monétaires et financières en France du XVIᵉ au XVIIIᵉ siècle* (Paris, 1928).

[4] Sieur de Malestroit, *Les Paradoxes du Seigneur de Malestroit, conseiller du Roi et Maistre ordinaire de ses comptes, sur le faict des Monnoyes presentez à Sa Majesté au mois de Mars MDLXVI* (Paris, 1566), in *Écrits notables sur la monnaie*, ed. Jean-Yves Le Branchu (2 vols., Paris, 1934).

[5] Jean Bodin, *La Response de Maistre Iean Bodin, advocat en la Cour, au Paradoxe de Monsieur de Malestroit touchant l'encherissement de toutes choses et le moyen d'y remedier* (Paris, 1568), in *Écrits notables*, ed. Le Branchu [hereafter cited as *Réponse*].

[6] In the course of his official duties he was a commissioner in the famous inquiry of 1556 and investigated the southwest of France and northern Italy. See Chap. 3.

[7] Alexandre de la Tourette, *La Réponse de la Sieur de la Tourette aux Paradoxes du Sieur de Malestroit touchant les Monnoyes, 1567*, in *Paradoxes inédits*, ed. Einaudi.

[8] The contemporary reactions in Spain to the state of monetary affairs can be seen in a study by Diego de Covarrubias y Leiva, *Veterum numismatum collatio*, published in 1550. A later edition appeared in Salamanca in 1565. Another important commentator, Martín de Azpilcueta Navarro, in his *Commentario resolutorio de usuras* (Salamanca, 1556), considered precious metals to be responsible for the inflation of prices. See an

appreciated current problems, but they did not have all the information now available to scholars.

Bodin's conclusions had the persuasive force of novelty: they explicitly declared the bullion from the New World to be responsible for inflation. They drew attention to differences in regional and international price levels, noting that prices were higher in Spain and Italy than in France.[9] The crude quantitative theory emerged from a mass of observations spread over a number of years. The reports by the Commissioners of Inquiry to the Cour des Monnaies were based upon tours of France in 1556 and emphasized the abundance of Spanish silver reals in their reports on monetary disorders.[10] Experts in Spain observed at the same time that silver in bars was exported to France and that the inflation of bullion was more advanced in Spain than in other countries of Europe, for example, in France and Flanders.[11] These instances should not negate the fact that Bodin arrived at his conclusions by original methods of analysis.

The inflationary trend was not simple and smooth; there was a series of fluctuations, composed of sharp rises and falls. In addition, the interplay of factors concerning gold and silver (about which Bodin was less clear) may have led to inflationary pressures on retail prices; the rise accelerated from the 1550s. The polemics on the rise in prices returned repeatedly to the same sorts of argument. Malestroit suggested the effects of civil unrest and the loss of labor after famines; he also insisted on the effects of the exports of bullion (passing in transit through France) which put a premium on money. High prices closely followed, moreover, the failures in harvests as in 1565.[12] Bodin asserted that the imports of bullion from the New World were largely responsible, but also attributed some importance both to the financial activities in the Lyons market and the failures in harvests which suddenly created excess demand.[13] Supply and demand were confused in all this.

It must be remembered that the controversy occurred during the first or at least early effects of the change in trend in the mid-century: the reversal in the circulation of gold and silver. And it coincided also with the growing, revolutionary pressure of rising prices. The timing of the arguments is therefore important. Both Bodin and Malestroit had consulted archives — the registers of the Cour des Monnaies and the Chambre des Comptes[14] — for a period of some four centuries.[15] The effect of this historical inquiry is by no

interesting study by Marjorie Grice-Hutchinson, *The School of Salamanca* (Oxford, 1952), pp. 51–52, 89–91; and also Jaime Carrera Pujal, *Historia de la economía española* (6 vols., Barcelona, 1943–1947), I, pp. 271–277.

[9] Bodin, *Réponse*, p. 94.

[10] See Chap. 3.

[11] This was the observation of Navarro, *Commentario*, p. 275.

[12] Malestroit, *Mémoires*, pp. 101, 104, 110.

[13] Bodin, *Réponse*, pp. 93, 117.

[14] They examined, for example, the *Livre Noir* of the *Châtelet*. *Ibid.*, pp. 83–84.

[15] Malestroit, *Mémoires;* Henri Hauser, edition of *La Response de Jean Bodin* (Paris,

means fully revealed in their opposing arguments, but it cannot be denied
that the method inevitably obliged both of them to find explanations which
were valid over the longer period. This put their problems in the context of
secular movements.

By general acclaim Bodin emerged the winner in the dispute. He was more
concise, more brilliant, and indeed more resourceful in his thinking. His victory, virtually a manifesto for the quantitative theory, must not obscure, however, some of the subtleties in Malestroit's argument.[16] More than Bodin,
Malestroit was aware of two fundamental issues: the problem of the *livre
tournois* (the money of account in France); and the appreciation of gold
in terms of silver. As already noted, these underwent significant changes in
the late sixteenth and early seventeenth centuries.

The depreciation of the livre tournois clearly indicated how the French
economy responded to changes in the ratio of expenditures to income by comparison with other countries. The function of the livre tournois, and indeed
of all moneys of account, was to produce a homogeneous system from a variety
of currency in circulation — gold, silver, and copper, both domestic and foreign — for the purposes of transactions and accounting.[17] As is well known,
the livre tournois was an imaginary money, a fiction, and the real circulation
was composed of gold, silver, and billon coins, together with some credit instruments, such as tokens or, at a higher level, bills of exchange. As the livre
coordinated this diverse system, it assumed in consequence the characteristics
of a supermoney. By adjusting the different types of money, on which it was
constantly remodeled, this money of account represented the relationship between France and the economies of other countries. This was the rate of exchange at which the livre tournois was converted into foreign currencies. It
could be measured against the stronger monetary systems of the dominant
economies — the currency of Spain in the sixteenth century or of Holland in
the seventeenth — and this was a measure of basic stability. Any signs of persistent depreciation reflected, in effect, more fundamental, structural changes
in the economy of France.

This function of the livre tournois in adjusting the variations between real
currencies presented practical difficulties, but it is not easy to assess these
difficulties as a whole. Fiat money actually became a monetary reality only
much later, with the bank note.[18] After 1803 the livre tournois became known
by its other name, the *franc,* which was also formerly a real coin. It is true

---

1932), pp. xxiv–xl; *Paradoxes inédits,* ed. Einaudi, p. 21; see also Harsin, *Doctrines
monétaires,* p. 31.

[16] Natalis de Wailly, *Mémoire sur la livre tournois* (Paris, 1856); Luigi Einaudi,
"Teoria della moneta immaginaria nel tempo da Carlomagno alla rivoluzione francese,"
Rivista di storia economica, I (1936), pp. 1–35.

[17] The same remarks are valid for other moneys of account such as the maravedi, the
guilder, the grosz, and the pound sterling.

[18] Einaudi, "Teoria della moneta," *passim.* The Bank of Sweden claims to have issued
the first bank note in 1656.

that, among the currency in circulation, the livre tournois was closest to billon, in which the intrinsic value was lower than the face value. Yet while, in
principle, bank notes remained in circulation until retired, billon disappeared
into the melting pot as soon as, with the depreciation of the money of account, its intrinsic value rose to equal and exceed its face value. This frequently occurred in the sixteenth century. Only with the extended use of the
bank note and the expansion of bank deposits was it possible to gain some
measure of control over the fluctuations between the various components of
the monetary circulation. In the sixteenth century the nature of changing marginal values was less clearly understood. The pressing need of people at that
time was to establish a fixed order to conserve value. Monetary units were,
indeed, considered as a stable standard against which values of goods and
services could be measured; they were placed in the same category as measures
of length and weight.[19] Under such circumstances, it was not expected that
governments and theorists should alter the money of account. This occurred
only when no other solution could be found and meant that the money of account constantly faced unstable conditions.

The money of account (except perhaps from 1578 to 1602)[20] underwent
a long series of devaluations in the sixteenth and seventeenth centuries, which
were part of the complex movement related to foreign exchanges, and, as it
were, the "balance of payments." (This aspect will be discussed later in more
detail.) The purpose for the moment is to consider the thought of Malestroit;
in this it is preferable to go further than his conclusions. At that time France
had a special position, more so than Malestroit apparently was prepared to
accept. Lacking clearly defined monetary structures, its economy was open,
almost without protection. In its own way, over the long run, the money of account showed a basic weakness compared with the currencies of neighboring
economies, which were, if anything, more compact[21] and able to depend on
more substantial metallic reserves.

In the middle of the sixteenth century the shift from a system weighted
with gold to one with silver apparently imposed a heavy cost on France, then
involved in war. There was a severe devaluation of its livre tournois, the lighter
gold écu, issued in 1561,[22] being official recognition of the change. With our
information, I find it difficult to accept such a conclusion without some doubts.
The whole matter is confused by the fact that gold was relatively cheap in the
first half of the sixteenth century and then appreciated fairly rapidly in the

[19] This concept was expressed, for example, by Thomas Turquaim before the Parlement of Dijon on September 10, 1573. Archives Nationales [hereafter cited as A.N.],
Z¹B.69, Sept. 10, 1573, "Remonstrances faictes au Parlement de Dijon"; see also the
opinion of Antoine de Montchrétien ("the essential value of goods is unchanging, not
the accidental price"), in *Traicté de l'œconomie politique* (Paris, n.d.), p. 257.

[20] In the years following the edict of 1577, accounts were kept in écus d'or au soleil.
See Chap. 3.

[21] See Chap. 5.

[22] The écu d'or au soleil was issued at 23 K. fine and 72½ to the marc and was
valued at 50 sols in 1561. See Chap. 3.

following years. The consequences for France in the critical years 1550–1575 were complex; probably, because the country was extremely sensitive to this crisis, it suffered more than can at first be estimated from the fall in the value of its money of account on the international markets.

In this situation, the *Paradoxes* of Malestroit, which was revised and enlarged in his *Mémoires,* appears more penetrating than has so far been assumed. There was not only a devaluation of the livre tournois; there was, at the same time, an appreciation of gold in terms of silver. In addition to Bodin's thesis concerning the effects of the discoveries of precious metals and the rise of prices in terms of bullion, Malestroit observed the important phenomenon of the long-term weakness of the livre tournois, especially in periods of reversal of the monetary trend. All the important devaluations of the money of account — at the beginning of the reign of Francis I; during the early years of the monarchy of Henry III; under Henry IV; during the ministry of Richelieu; in the last half of the reign of Louis XIV; during the decades in the mid-sixteenth century — occurred during what appear to be periods of instability in France's foreign exchange position, an instability regularly confirmed by monetary reforms. Luigi Einandi, in his introduction to the essay of Malestroit,[23] has made a rough estimate of the factors of nominal inflation (the Malestroit proposition) and metallic inflation (the Bodin theory). The price index used is approximate, but the results are well worth noting:

Table 3. Price Index in France Illustrating the Malestroit-Bodin Controversy

Period	Index of prices of goods and services, 1471–1472 = 100	Index of depreciation of livre tournois in terms of gold and silver, 1471–1472 = 100	Percentage of changes in price level of goods and services due to:	
			Depreciation of money of accounts (Malestroit's theory)	Other causes, including depreciation of precious metals (Bodin's theory)
1471–1472	100	100	—	—
1473–1486	111.5	91.0	86.73	13.27
1487–1514	106.6	78.8	—	—
1515–1554	161.6	65.5	90.09	9.91
1555–1575	265.2	51.4	72.27	27.73
1590–1598	627.5	47.7	35.47	64.53

Thus in the controversy Bodin has the reputation of being the winner, but this is not completely valid. Malestroit had a greater sensitivity for some complex and important aspects of the problem, beyond purely quantitative monetary theories.

---

[23] These questions are considered again in Chaps. 3, 5. See also Einaudi, *Paradoxes inédits,* "Introduzione."

It is not possible, however, to abandon this debate, for the conclusions stated above do not close the issue. The crux of the matter was not so much the behavior and individual merits of the adversaries, but rather the timing of their dispute. The phase of gold was drawing to a close; that of silver was unfolding. After 1560, among the difficulties over religion, politics, and society, the problems of gold currency emerged before the very eyes of the theorists. How did they manage to explain the question of bullion and the elusive realities of the money of account?

The inability of these theorists to break with the past was not the least of their weaknesses; it was difficult for them to abandon the concept that a naturally fixed proportion existed between the precious metals, that the bimetallic ratio of 1 : 12 was always valid. The notion had long been questioned: Nicolas Oremus, bishop of Lisieux, asserted about 1375 that this basic relationship ought to follow "the natural course and rate between gold and silver according to their value." [24] This did not, however, prevent the idea of a stable ratio from remaining firmly entrenched. Copernicus himself, in his treatise of 1526, set out some precepts on the subject: a pound of fine gold ought, as a general rule, to pass for the value of twelve pounds of pure silver, although inevitably there would be regional variations according to different countries.[25] Malestroit, in the *Mémoires sur le faict des Monnaies,* presented to the Conseil on May 16, 1567, maintained the basic concept of a ratio of 1 : 12 and rested his case on classical authors, Pliny and particularly Plato: "From this divine opinion of Plato we must gather two things, not only useful but absolutely necessary in the matter of money. The first is that the proportion of twelve ought to be kept without alteration." To this he added another principle of a more practical nature. In establishing the relative rates for coin, it was of paramount importance, in his opinion, to set an optimum ratio; he recognized that gold was rightly valued in terms of silver: "The proportion must always be put before the price of gold and silver, as the foundations must be made before the building. And on these two points our predecessors have always fallen short." He continued: "It has always been seen in past experience that whenever we maintained in France a ratio lower than twelve, foreign countries drew gold from France, and when we set it higher than twelve, they drew silver." [26] The statement was clear enough.

Bodin's ideas, on the other hand, derived not so much from the wish to arrange these matters in neat order as from historical observation. Gold had a persistent tendency, he declared, to depreciate: "gold was always at a high price and since has always fallen." [27] In the final analysis this proved to be a

---

[24] Nicolas Oremus, *Tractus de origine, natura, jure et mutationibus monetarum,* ed. M.-L. Wołowski (Paris, 1864), p. xxx (text). He died in 1382, but apparently completed this treatise before 1373. *Ibid.,* introduction, p. xxxiv.

[25] Nicolas Copernicus, *De monetae cudendae ratione* (Thorn, 1526), ed. Wołowski, *ibid.,* p. 73.

[26] Malestroit, *Mémoires,* pp. 109–110, 112.

[27] Bodin, *Réponse,* p. 143.

naïve conclusion and caused him to abandon his favorite theories of numbers and the harmony of equations.

For he also approached the matter with preconceived notions, one of which presupposed that the whole range of human activity could be subsumed in a system of numerical rhythms, in other words, "harmonic justice." Almost by transubstantiation, the figures seemed to acquire an importance and existence of their own, and, by dextrous manipulation, the problems of men could be reduced to certain simple relationships, represented by either masculine numbers or feminine numbers. The critical age for man, for example, was sixty-five; the duration and destiny of states could also be determined; the procedures of justice could conform to a symmetrical pyramid of 4.6.8.12. "The harmonic justice should follow it and join these four points together, that is to say, law, equity, execution of the law and the duty of the Magistrate either in the distribution of justice or in the government of the State for, just as in these four numbers 4.6.8.12, there is found the same difference between 4 and 6 as between 8 and 12 and as there is between the execution of the law and the duty of the Magistrate; and the same difference between equity and the duty of the Magistrate as there is between the law and its execution . . . and if you place the quantities in geometric order, the Harmony will be lost, as can be seen in these four numbers 2.4.8.12."

The four "perfect" numbers below 10,000 were, for him, 6, 28, 249, and 8,128. Among these, the number 6, at once divisible by 1, 2, and 3 also equal to the sum of these divisors, was *the* "perfect" number. And the number 6, doubled, became 12, the key figure in establishing a ratio between gold and silver. The reasoning, however illusory, was typical of his time. It explained the desire to set the ratio of gold to silver (in France and its neighbors) at about 1 : 12: "The right proportion of gold to silver, existing all over Europe and in neighboring regions is twelve to one or thereabouts." [28]

Almost as if to support his reasoning, the ratio between gold and silver at the time of the controversy was approaching one to twelve. Bodin's preconceived ideas were thus confirmed to some degree.[29] But his thinking was still representative of the first half of the sixteenth century, when silver tended to be the metal more in demand: "At the moment, the price is twelve to one, and a little less," he wrote. "It is true that formerly, the marc of fine gold was estimated . . . at eleven marcs, five ounces, eleven deniers, five grains argent-le-roi in bullion" (which was equivalent to a ratio of 1 : 11.68). Bodin did not neglect the possibility of regional differences between countries, in the north, for example, or in the Far East. "The price of one for twelve . . . is almost common in the whole of Europe, Asia and Africa: apart from the fact that toward the countries of the North, where mines abound and there is very little gold, the price of gold is a little higher: and on the other hand, toward the countries of the south and the Indies, where there is more gold, the price

[28] Jean Bodin, *Les Six livres de la république de I. Bodin, Angevin* (Paris, 1583) [hereafter cited as *République*], IV, pp. 564–567; VI, pp. 916–917, 1020.

[29] See Chap. 3.

of silver is higher than in the temperate countries. But the proportion ordinarily does not ever exceed a twenty-fourth more or less, which is a necessary arrangement and convenient for all peoples." [30]

The *Réponse* of Alexandre de la Tourette, less well known than the arguments of Malestroit and Bodin, appeared in the interval between the *Paradoxes* and the *Mémoires* and the *Réponse* of Bodin. He was a practical man, more prepared to accept the fluctuations between gold and silver, and, as a result, the fact that a generalized ratio could not be established once and for all; it was, rather, constantly subject to modification. "It must thus be concluded that the said proportion of twelve must not be kept as a general and everlasting rule; since it is subject to variation according to the change in time, as when gold is found to be scarcer than silver . . . and conversely when gold is abundant in the country." [31] The statement was clear. When the Cour des Monnaies later addressed an avis — that is, a report or recommendation — to the Conseil in April 1575, nevertheless, they still drew attention to the "proportion of 11¾ marcs, commonly followed by this realm with its neighbors." [32]

The ratio of 1 : 12 long remained engrained in the reasoning on the adjustment of precious metals. At almost every shock, every crisis, when a brusque change in the relative values of gold and silver occurred, the fixed principle was evoked. Thus, later in 1609, following the bankruptcy of the Spanish monarchy, a memoir of Nicolas Coquerel (dated May 14) proposed once more a ratio of 1 : 12. In their reply the Cour des Monnaies asserted that France in times of greatest prosperity had had a ratio of 1 : 11¾ but that the history of Rome and France revealed fluctuations around this level. They cited the cases of England, Germany, and Spain in the time of Philip II, and they referred to the differences between Flanders and France noted during the payment of the ransom for the sons of Francis I in 1530.[33] In another memorandum to the King and Conseil at Fontainebleau it was proposed not only to make new issues of coin to conform to the necessary accounting in livre tournois, "to make accounting in the livre tournois solid and unchangeable," but also to continue the old ratio between gold and silver.[34]

What conclusions can be drawn from all this? It is possible — and the prosperity of the period 1576–1588 would tend to support this — that the movement of the rate of exchange was favorable to France, with a potential bimetallic ratio which was probably lower than 12. But it was an old illusion. The idea died slowly: in 1641, at the time of further dislocation between the two metals, the Cour des Monnaies declared that "all that proportion is only imagination" and that a stable ratio between the two metals had never existed. "It has never been said that there was a real proportion between gold and silver; it has always been different at all times and places, now higher, now

[30] Bodin, *République*, VI, p. 92, and *Réponse*, pp. 143, 149 (variant of 1578).
[31] De la Tourette, *Réponse*, p. 133.
[32] A. N., Z¹B.70, Apr. 8–24, 1575, "Avis de la Cour des Monnaies au Conseil."
[33] A.N., Z¹B.76, June 16, 1609, "Avis de la Cour des Monnaies."
[34] A.N., Z¹B.397, June 28, 1609, "Avis de la Cour des Monnaies."

lower according to the scarcity or greater affluence of one or another of these two metals, or according to the needs of trade, or of the affairs of state or of the public." [35] Wisdom and sagacity were not at fault, but it was already 1641.

Copernicus felt that gold and silver ought to have the same ratio in bullion as in specie, "provided that they have the same proportion of alloy and equal weight." [36] Jacques Colas, the *Contrôleur de la Monnoye des Étuves* in Paris, made the same proposal to the Conseil Privé on October 6, 1560, but the Cour declared that it had never been allowed.[37] Malestroit correctly pointed out that one metal was always cheaper when coined than in bullion and supported, as a result, the ratio of 1 : 12 for coins: "Gold which is the most precious metal has always been cheaper in specie than in bullion," and "in the end we shall be left with neither gold nor silver . . . all for having failed to keep the proportion of twelve not only in bullion but also in specie." [38]

In contrast, he unhesitatingly claimed that the ratio of bullion between the two metals adjusted the rates of the currency: "The proportion of gold to silver in bullion is the model for the production of our moneys." The examples to support this theory were, not unreasonably, taken from the years of change in the mid-century. Thus, in 1549, the gold écu, when undervalued, began to disappear from circulation ("when écus were exported"), but in 1561, when overvalued, began to cause difficulties in the circulation of silver, "which is reason for finding hardly any of the said money of *douzains* and testons." These examples, it will be noticed, fit in fairly well with the notion of a ratio of 1 : 12, to which the preambles to the ordinances of 1541 and 1550 referred. The ratios between the two metals were, thus, set, so that France should not be deprived, alternatively, of its currency.[39]

Although Bodin had little difficulty in disposing of the confused arguments of Malestroit on the basic stability of prices, he did not, however, get far enough to define specific values. He proposed to issue both types of coinage at the same fineness, 23/24ths (or 23 karats), and also the same weight. It is possible that the ratio of 1 : 12 had been suggested to him by the rate of twelve Spanish silver reals to one écu. "As can be seen," he wrote, "in the case of the single reals of Spain which only weigh as much as an écu soleil as set by the ordinance of the year fifteen hundred and forty, that is to say, two deniers and sixteen grains, and that twelve single reals are valued at exactly an écu." [40] A small matter escaped his notice — the specific weights on the one hand of silver and copper and on the other of gold and copper were not exactly equivalent — and so destroyed much of his argument.

Tourette, speaking from experience, declared that the equivalence of weights

---

[35] A.N., Z¹B.408, Oct. 30, 1641, "Remonstrance de la Cour des Monnaies."
[36] Copernicus, *Monetae cudendae ratione*, p. 73.
[37] A.N., Z¹B.371, Oct. 24, 1560, "Requête et Avis."
[38] Malestroit, *Mémoires*, p. 114.
[39] *Ibid.*, pp. 107, 113–114.
[40] Bodin, *Republique*, VI, pp. 916–917.

and fineness "cannot and ought not to be made." [41] In reality, the royal government continually attempted to control the fluctuations between gold and silver and to check the devaluation of the livre tournois. It goes almost without saying that in the first half of the sixteenth century the authorities hesitated to overvalue silver. In the reform of 1519, for example, the rate for testons and bars of silver (at the fineness of *argent-le-roi* or 23/24ths) remained unaltered; the adjustment came two years later in 1521. Again, in 1541, the rate for the teston was raised from 10 sols 8 *deniers* to 11 sols, but the mint price for silver bullion remained unchanged until 1543, while the rate for gold coins stayed at the old rate established in 1533. A final example, in 1569, shows that while the rates for gold coins were altered, those of silver remained at the earlier rates fixed in 1561. The authorities apparently feared that a simultaneous devaluation of both types of currency would in fact make the alteration irrevocable.

Stability was constantly sought, but was it always possible to achieve? It depended, after all, on many considerations, not least on the heavy war levies and taxation and on the need to organize the collection of taxes to pay the armies, who were always hungry for payments in hard cash. The money in demand — silver in the first half of the sixteenth century, gold thereafter — tended to be undervalued at the mints in time of peace. The outbreak of war compelled the monarchy to reshape its policy in this respect: the price of silver was raised in 1521 and again in 1543; gold prices were raised in 1636.[42]

2. Government and the Price Rise

The policies of the monarchy require closer examination. Everything concerning adjustments of precious metals, coinage, and setting values depended in the final analysis on the price level. The price rise, and implicitly the devaluation of the livre tournois, although giving entrepreneurs the opportunity for profit, naturally had serious repercussions on the real value of incomes fixed in monetary terms. In 1517 the "worthy towns" raised the problem of this fall in income for the crown, the Church, and the nobility, "in which the King is greatly interested for the interest on payments which he has had to make . . . also the Church and gentry of this realm for their rents." [43] The changes brought reactions, expressed in the decisions of the different Parlements on the question of the payments of rents. Decisions were made that contracts should be settled in the equivalent number of coins originally paid. Those established in terms of money of account, the livre tournois, were, however, to be reimbursed in livres tournois.[44] This decision reveals a significant compromise.

[41] De la Tourette, *Réponse*, p. 136.
[42] See Chap. 3.
[43] The Assemblée des bonnes villes — virtually a meeting of the Third Estate — in March 1517, in Jean Barrillon, *Journal 1515–1521,* ed. Pierre de Vaissière (2 vols., Paris, 1897–1899), I, p. 281.
[44] Émile Szlechter, "La monnaie en France au XVIe siècle, droit public et droit privé," *Revue historique de droit français et étranger,* XXVIII (1951).

During the whole century there were repeated attempts to contain the general inflation. In contracts, exact lists were made of the currency offered in payment, even when the government issued strict orders to the contrary, that accounts should be kept in livres tournois. There was a difference, however, between the first half of the sixteenth century, the phase of gold, and second half of the century, the phase of silver. In the first half the demand for silver had a tendency to restrain retail prices, but after the 1550s, with a basic change in structures, a more rapid rise in prices occurred. Gold, not being so susceptible to inflation, became the store of value and so subject to hoarding. In this way the commercial sector developed a hedge against monetary depreciation. In France in 1549 (as in Flanders in 1542) the government gave strict instructions that all contracts should be drawn up in livres tournois without specifying the currency employed in the transactions. But it made an exception for the great market of Lyons. The merchants of Lyons insisted in 1551 that two-thirds of every payment (in particular for bills of exchange) should be made in gold specie.[45] The merchants clearly knew what they were doing, and this line of action soon found support in the monarchy itself.

The upward spiral of prices, more noticeable in the second half of the sixteenth century, imposed a significant drop in the real value of royal revenues fixed in monetary terms, although this, as will be shown in a later chapter, did not prevent it from increasing substantially its gross income during the century. In 1556 the commissioners of inquiry drew attention to the large quantities of billon finding their way into the royal coffers from tax levies. The apparent loss in real revenue which the King suffered was emphasized in the "Remonstrance" of November 20, 1576.[46] With the ingenuity of necessity, the crown found itself following the commercial expedients against the progressive depreciation of assets. It converted its credits and income into gold values, which, as the money in demand at that particular moment, tended to offer better protection against inflation. In this course of action, it did nothing more than follow the example set by the merchants of Lyons. Henri Lapeyre has recently revealed this obvious collusion.[47]

The structure of monetary affairs had arrived at a moment of difficulty and confusion. By the edict of Poitiers (September 1577) all accounts were to be kept in the écu d'or au soleil fixed at 60 sols. In 1575 it had shown signs of going even higher and then in 1577 was firmly reestablished at the rate of 60 sols.[48] The livre tournois was given a silver equivalent in the *franc d'argent,* which thus was equaled a third of an écu — a *tiers d'écu,* also used as an accounting term. The *quart d'écu,* valued at 15 sols, completed this reform

[45] Federico Chabod, *Note e documenti per la storia economico-finanziera dell'Impero di Carlo V* (Padua, 1937); Marc Brésard, *Les foires de Lyon aux XVe et XVIe siècles* (Paris, 1914), *pièce justificative* 18.
[46] A.N., J. 971–972, Nov. 20, 1576, "Remonstrance de la Cour des Monnaies au Roi."
[47] Henri Lapeyre, *Une famille de marchands: Les Ruiz* (Paris, 1955), p. 30, n. 4.
[48] For the edict of September 1577, see Chap. 3.

which provided combined accounting and currency units. The other billon coins naturally found their place in this system, being issued in units of the livre tournois. This reform opened what has been called a period of mono-metalism. Such a label, however, exaggerates the situation. The stabilization measure proved effective and fixed, at least officially, the exchange value of the livre tournois for a quarter of a century. If this structure remained largely valid until the upheaval of the League and survived until the subsequent re-form of September 1602, the success was due to the economic position of France, set between Spain and its enemies of the north, the United Provinces and England. Merchants' letters from Antwerp and many other documents re-count the advantages of the maritime sectors of France, which a neutral posi-tion conferred.[49] The traditional explanations for France at this point do not, perhaps, reveal the entire scope of the problem.

At the beginning of the seventeenth century, with the climax of the use of silver in Europe, the accounting in écus was abandoned. Henry IV ordered the return to accounting in livres tournois in 1602. A new period of general stabil-ity thus opened for a time, which, as has been noted, was concerned with the growing problems of copper. This was not so much innovation as the govern-ment's resignation to the inevitable. Well before 1602 the currency rates no longer conformed to those of 1575–1577 (when an écu was revalued at three livres tournois or three francs d'argent).[50] Sully declared that he had reestab-lished accounting in livres tournois since the character of transactions had not been altered in any way whether they were in écus or in livres.[51] His statement, however, was not entirely correct, for in the reform of 1602 the structures of the monetary system were modified. The gold écu was set at 65 sols, and the silver franc d'argent and quart d'écu at 21 sols 4 deniers and 16 sols, re-spectively. It is not so much a question of the government of Henry IV, nor, indeed, of the reputation of Sully. Bodin had already declared, "only he who has power to make law can give law to money." [52] Beyond the implication of the "law" were the inevitable pressures of economic activity. It may almost be said that the movements of the planets were less mysterious to the contempo-raries of Kepler than currency fluctuations.

The progressive change in price levels did not destroy all hope that the in-flation would reach an upper limit and then give way to stability and even a return to former positions. This hope was shown in the way the authorities

[49] See Chap. 5. The correspondence of the factors in Antwerp of the firm of Ruiz are published in Valentín Vázquez de Prada, *Lettres marchandes d'Anvers* (4 vols., Paris, 1960–1961).

[50] "The double *pistollets* are exposed at six livres eight sols, one must use this expres-sion since I cannot say two écus and eight sols." A.N. Z¹B.392, letter of Apr. 13, 1602, from the Procureur-Général to the Cour des Monnaies.

[51] Maximilien de Béthune, duc de Sully, *Économies royales,* IV, pp. 185–189, cited by Gustave Fagniez, *Documents relatifs à l'histoire de l'industrie et du commerce en France* (2 vols., Paris, 1898), II, pp. 54–55.

[52] Bodin, *République,* I, p. 342.

dealt with the situation. The rise in the different currency rates, that is, the increases in the market rates for coins expressed in livres tournois, was usually accompanied by royal orders which attempted to keep the basic monetary system in line with the earlier official rates. The orders of 1492, 1496, 1506, 1518, 1526, and so on were a few early instances. Even when the rise in currency rates was most rapid and difficult to contain, the ordinances which allowed higher rates often published also a graduated scale which would bring currency rates eventually back to the earlier levels. There was always the hope that the change was only an abrupt crisis, after which the disrupted system would return to its former position. This happened, for example, in 1569, 1572, and 1574, or later in 1629, 1631, and 1633, when the rise in the price of gold was clear. The desired deflation did not, however, occur, and with the passage of time the monarchy was finally obliged to accept officially a complete revision of currency rates. Thus the close of the two above-mentioned periods saw the important reforms of 1575 and 1636.[53]

Another solution did not commit the future irrevocably: the recognition of changes by toleration. An example of this occurred in 1533, when a higher rate of 45 *sols tournois* for the gold écu was allowed by "tolérance"; this was officially accepted in the reform of 1541.[54] Another procedure was to allow the official nominal rates to remain at the old levels, but reduce the weight or debase the fineness of bullion in coin. In 1516, although the écu was raised to 40 sols, the price of the former weight of silver in bars remained the same, but the fineness of this bullion was set at a minimum of 10 deniers instead of 12 deniers argent-le-roi.[55]

The hopes of deflation were also revealed in the issue of a new series of coins, of which the *sol parisis* was important. In the normal course of events, the coins of billon had a direct relationship with the livre tournois. It must be remembered that the sol and the sol parisis were the most important of the different types of billon.[56] The monarchy long hoped that in the event of deflation the nominal value of the sol parisis (at 15 *deniers tournois*) could be reduced by a fifth; thus the same coin would pass as a sol (or 12 deniers tournois). A new sol parisis was issued in 1564, different from that of 1550. At the time the Cour des Monnaies drew attention to the royal policy that the issue was made "in the hope of reducing them to tournois in order to return to sound money." [57] The attempt, however, did not succeed, and the inflation continued. The intrinsic value of these coins soon exceeded their face value, and they disappeared from circulation.

It must not be forgotten, nevertheless, that the repeated reforms of the monetary structure responded to economic activity. Thus the écu d'or of 1519

---

[53] See Chap. 3.

[54] For the ordonnance of Mar. 5, 1553, see Chap. 3.

[55] *Ibid.*

[56] The *livre parisis* was more valuable by a quarter: one livre parisis was worth 25 *sols tournois*.

[57] A.N., Z¹B. 65, May 17, 1564, "Remonstrance de la Cour des Monnaies au Roi."

and the silver teston of 1514 and 1521 were typical of the gold phase of the first half of the sixteenth century. In the same way, the écu d'or of 1561, the silver franc of 1575, and the quart d'écu of 1576 were the characteristic coins of the silver phase in France. The reform of 1640 and the subsequent issues of the gold *louis* and the silver écu were tardy developments of the French currency system, but they typified the seventeenth century. These changes in themselves expressed many aspects of the royal monetary policy, for the monarchy, faced with inflationary tendencies, had the choice of two remedies: to keep the existing coins in circulation and raise their rates or to keep the existing nominal rate and debase the currency. Sometimes both methods were applied. In 1519, the rate, weight, and fineness of the currency were modified, and, in 1640, as has already been noted, a new list of coins was adopted.[58]

For silver the system was essentially the same. The teston was issued in 1514 at 10 sols, but was reduced in fineness in 1521, without changing the nominal rate for the coin. But in subsequent devaluations the nominal rate of the teston was changed. It remained a standard coin until the reform of 1575 when it was replaced by the franc d'argent and the quart d'écu. These were both heavier coins, the latter introduced to meet a need to convert silver reals from Spain.

The same preoccupation to stabilize and bring matters to order still existed, and so attempts were made to keep the relationship between the livre tournois and the different coins in round figures. This was ostensibly to facilitate the system of accounting. The failure to retain the currency in distinct multiples of the money of accounts was itself, however, an indication of inflation. In this, the gold écu rated at 40 sols in 1519 passed to 45 sols in 1533; the gold *henri* was set at 50 sols in 1549; the gold écu started at 50 sols in 1561, was set at 60 sols in the reform of 1575, and reached 65 sols in 1602 and 75 sols in 1615. The silver coins, wherever possible, were kept closer to unity or a round fraction of the livre tournois; thus the testons of 1514 and 1521 were rated at 10 sols. This equivalence soon disappeared, and after a series of devaluations the coin was abandoned in the reforms of the 1570s, with the issue of silver franc and quart d'écu. The history of these new issues only repeated that of the teston. They too succumbed to progressive inflation: in the reform of 1602 when they were rated at 21 sols, 4 deniers, and 16 sols, respectively. Not long afterward, toward the end of the reign of Henry IV, there was talk of bringing out a new coin as a unit of the livre tournois, but this was abandoned in the civil disturbances which followed the abrupt end of his life. It was not implemented until 1640, with the issue of the silver écu, rated at three livres tournois.

The adaptation of billon presented other problems. More than the valuable currencies, it was closely tied to the livre tournois. Since these coins had a low intrinsic content and at the same time a fixed nominal value — such as the denier, the *double* (two deniers), the *liard* (three deniers) — they were

[58] See Chap. 3.

in part fiduciary money. Their circulation was in the long run irrevocably compromised by inflation. As a rule the nominal rates of the coins remained stable, but with the devaluation of the livre tournois the intrinsic value gradually exceeded the face value. They then fell victim to coin clippers or the melting pot and so disappeared from circulation. A currency devaluation was, consequently, accompanied not by raising the rates for billon but by the issue of a new series of billon coins, but the changes were not always clear cut. Although the *dixain* of Louis XII (a piece of 10 deniers) reappeared in the reform of 1519 as a *douzain* (12 deniers), the authorities apparently did not attempt to retire the old dixains. The great reforms of billon in 1550 and 1551 aimed to replace douzains taken from circulation with new issues, which were lighter and of lower fineness. This reform characterized the period of the midsixteenth century, which was almost a classic example of the role of billon during a period of difficulties in the circulation of gold and silver.

For technical reasons, for example, the fabrication of metal sheets of uniform thickness, it was difficult to make coins smaller than a certain size. Thus, more often than not, copper was used to dilute the silver in order to produce a coin of manageable proportions. With the advent of inflation, the silver content became progressively smaller. The higher proportion of copper gave them the well-merited title of "black money." In the smallest denominations, the denier and the double, the proportion of copper was high and the silver content infinitely small. The final step in this development was taken in 1578 when billon of pure copper was issued, although, it should be noted, France was not the first to move in this direction.

At that time, the devaluation of the livre tournois made it difficult to keep coins with low silver content in circulation. Billon, as Bodin observed, was particularly important to the poor — *le menu peuple* — and changes in this money affected them most of all.[59] Once the smaller units of billon were completely deprived of silver content, moreover, pure copper coins were accepted in circulation only with the greatest reluctance. Numerous edicts and orders were passed to convince people and to ensure that the coins gained public acceptance. Refusal to accept billon, however, tended to put a premium on the more valuable gold and silver coins. The issues of copper currency indeed caused ill-concealed dissatisfaction; as a result, the regulations concerning it were strict. The Cour des Monnaies attempted on several occasions, even in opposition to the King and Conseil, to protect the monetary system from a flood of copper similar to that which had caused so much upheaval in Spain during the reigns of Philip III and Philip IV. In order to do so, the ever vigilant Cour des Monnaies sometimes limited the quantity authorized, giving strict instructions to the different mints; at other times it drew up remonstrances or even refused to register the ordinances which gave them force of law. All this, naturally enough, met with varying success. At the beginning of the seventeenth century, as the heyday of silver from the New World waned,

[59] Bodin, *Réponse*, p. 140, and *République*, VI, p. 919.

Henry IV planned more extensive issues of copper. But the project was thoroughly modified.[60] Later, during the ministry of Richelieu, when France was in the throes of war in Germany, the powerful opposition of the Cour des Monnaies again made itself felt. In 1637 the monarchy had assigned to Isaac Texier and Company the right to mint copper coins to the value of 1,800,000 livres tournois. By the time the letters patent had been sent to the Cour des Monnaies for registration, the coining machines had already been set up and the issues begun.[61] Though the Cour succeeded in stopping the affair at this time, the project was resumed successfully six years later.

Monetary policy occupied an important place in the sessions of the Estates General. At Blois in 1576 the deputies gave some priority to monetary matters in their debates on general grievances. Opinions were aired on theory and practice, not least on the subject of the issues of gold, silver, and billon coins. Bodin, in his *Réponse* of 1568 and again in his *Six livres de la république,* proposed that currency should consist of gold, silver, and copper, all of as high a degree of fineness as possible. He recognized that it would be impossible to confine monetary circulation to gold and silver alone.[62] In 1576, at the sessions in Blois, Bodin was present as the deputy for Vermandois and was among the deputies named to investigate monetary affairs and formulate a plan of reform. The consensus of opinion held that his views — on the coinage of gold, silver, and copper, on the use of presses for coinage, on the setting up of a national mint — offered undeniable advantages, but that the state of the country made it unlikely that they could be implemented. The use of machines entailed a large capital investment and also, so it was asserted, a considerable margin of waste. Coinage at a high degree of fineness required, in addition, refining processes which greatly increased the costs of production. Thus, contemporary technology could not accommodate the plans of the theorist. It was also contended that the circulation of the heavy gold and silver coins which he proposed would create difficulties.[63] As a result, the plan was not put into effect, but some measure of success was attained later, in 1578, with the issue of pure copper doubles and deniers. The result, as in the case of many political expedients, was a compromise of possible solutions. On this occasion, only the recommendations concerning pure copper were finally accepted.

The disorders in the wake of inflation demanded constant readjustments; like many other governments in Europe, the French monarchy reluctantly gave way. War, civil unrest, and all sorts of pressing commitments repeatedly required governmental intervention. From this point of view, some of the critical years were 1526, 1533, 1548, 1550, 1557, 1561, 1564, 1569, 1597, 1602, 1607, and 1614. On such occasions, the government was obliged sooner

[60] See Chap. 3.
[61] *Ibid.*
[62] Bodin, *Réponse,* pp. 129–130, and *République,* VI, pp. 915, 920, 928.
[63] Bodin, *République,* VI, p. 936.

or later to take actions, as is shown by a partial list of ordinances; in 1504, 1519, 1521, 1533, 1541, 1543, 1549, 1551, 1554, 1555, and 1558.

There were, on the one hand, compelling problems, and, on the other hand, partial and tardy solutions. One cannot fully understand this double development without appreciating the government's preoccupation to stop the inflation and maintain stable conditions. In this there was not so much an understanding of long-term developments as an instinctive moral reaction, deriving from everyday attitudes to establish a just price. It opposed such abuses as the activities of tricksters and dishonest exchange dealers, who, under cover of their agio, sidestepped governmental orders. This did not take into account the goldsmiths who managed to raise prices by increasing the fees for fabrication to compensate for the low official rates for bullion. Nor did it consider the *billoneur,* the personal agent of Gresham's law, who culled out the coins of true weight and put the light into circulation.[64] All these were commentary on the economic and social structures of France and, beyond, the whole range of human attitudes — the indignation, the sense of public responsibility, the reactions against new conditions. The outcries and explanations were inevitably a running criticism of current developments, not least of the huge intellectual upheaval through which the sixteenth and seventeenth centuries advanced in the conquest of the natural world. Montaigne had declared, "there must be condemnation of every type of gain; the merchant only promotes his business by depraving youth." [65] The Huguenot songbook included this:

> Si le monde vous vient tenter,
> De richesse, honneur et plaisir
> Et les vous vient tous présenter,
> N'y mettez ny coeur ny désir[66]

It would be unjust to imagine that governments and subjects were insensitive to the changing fortunes of the world. Prosperity and depression were part of the everyday life of men in the sixteenth century, who were ready, so it seemed, for the alternations in economic activity. Even at the end of the fifteenth century the master of the mint at Bordeaux reported that they must wait for the return of prosperity "whenever the good times come." [67] In pleading the natural wealth of France (in wine and wheat), Bodin himself noted that the abundance of gold and silver ought in some measure to compensate for the rise in prices and its accompanying inconveniences. The Cour des Monnaies, in estimating the values of moneys in 1584, declared: "such wealth is more or less imaginary . . . as the example of Midas clearly shows

---

[64] For example in the payment of the ransom of Francis I in 1530, in the reforms of 1555, and in the edict of December 1614; see *ibid.,* p. 843.

[65] Michel de Montaigne, *Essais,* ed. Maurice Rat (3 bks., Paris, 1941), Bk. I, Chap. 22.

[66] H. Bordier, *Le Chansonnier Huguenot au XVIᵉ siècle* (Paris, 1871), p. 31.

[67] A.N., Z¹B.362, June 5, 1493, letter from the gardes of the mint in Bordeaux to the Généraux des Monnaies in Paris.

. . . the chief and true wealth is that which always brings the commodities of life." [68]

3. Money and Institutions

In the sixteenth century problems relating to money, prices, coinage, and the movements of bullion often made heavy demands on institutions. The place these problems occupied in the general monetary context should also be noted.

At the end of the fifteenth century, France was still largely traditional, agricultural, and aristocratic. A seigneur had the right to coinage and to take a part of the profits as seigniorage. Seigniorage was also a token of loyalty; the penalty for counterfeiting was death. This was an old code of rules, and changes were slow, but the time gradually approached when coinage came to be considered not so much a rent as an essential function of government and a political responsibility. This latter idea — essentially a modern notion — was experienced by France only in the seventeenth century and then for only a brief period.[69] In 1697, according to François Véron de Forbonnais, coinage brought two million livres in revenue to the crown.

At the beginning of the period of this study the crown had almost a monopoly on coinage, but, here and there, earlier privileges lingered on. Some cathedral chapters had claims to a part of the seigniorage, as, for example, in Angers and Bordeaux.[70] In the first half of the sixteenth century, Provence, Dauphiné, and Brittany continued to claim their ancient rights and resisted administrative centralization until the edict of Villers-Cotterêts in 1539. These rights were reasserted during the disturbances of the wars of the League. A society, an economy, still largely lacking articulate centralization both in the short and the long run was obliged to tolerate a decentralized system composed of numerous provincial mints. In some cases the mints were placed in towns at a distance from royal centers of tax collection. The chance effects of politics set up mints in Chambéry and Turin (when these cities were under French control). It may be said, in brief, that France had in monetary matters, just as in other respects, a varied experience. The policy of the crown was, wherever possible, to unify and integrate either by exercising patience and allowing events to run their course or by direct intervention, as was found in the general drive to uniformity. Circumstances, indeed, soon imposed a wide-ranging solution.

In the implementation of this solution the wars against the Emperor Charles

---

[68] Bodin, *Réponse*, p. 117; A.N., Z¹B.72, Jan. 28, 1584, "Remonstrance de la Cour des Monnaies au Conseil d'État."

[69] This responsibility was accepted by the déclaration of March 28, 1679, but seigniorage was restored by the edict of 1689 (registered December 15).

[70] A.N., Z¹B.369, Mar. 29, 1554, Saint-Lô-lès-Angers; A.N., Z¹B.76, Dec. 9, 1610, Bordeaux. On June 27, 1530, the monks of the Saint Croix de Bordeaux were found to be coining billon. A.N., Z¹B.364, letter from the gardes of the mint in Bordeaux to the Généraux des Monnaies in Paris.

V were critical in their own particular way. They necessitated a constant and strict control of monetary affairs to confront the great financial potential of the Spanish Empire. The raising of funds to pay the royal ransom in 1530 was an important stage in this movement. By the ordinance of March 19, 1541, monetary coordination was taken a step further: the officials of the mints in Burgundy, Dauphiné, and Provence were forbidden to contravene the jurisdiction of the Chambre des Monnaies and, in particular, to meddle in matters concerning coinage. In 1543 sixteen *recettes générales des finances* were set up, and in 1552 seventeen *trésoriers généraux* were established to organize taxation and administer the royal estates; in 1557 these two departments were merged. At the same time the monetary system was streamlined. The mints were moved to those cities in which trésoriers and *receveurs* were stationed, but there were some short-lived exceptions, such as in Châlons and Agen, and some shifts of old mints to new centers such as to Riom and to Caen.[71]

At the same time, questions relating to currency were assigned to the jurisdiction of the Cour des Monnaies; the *conseillers* exercised considerable influence not only in directing and controlling monetary affairs but also in reviewing royal policy by delaying the execution of orders considered to be badly timed, at least until peremptory *lettres de jussion,* which were direct orders issued by the King, obliged them to give way. The Cour des Monnaies also set up commissions of inquiry to bring to justice instances of illegal activities or malversations and issued recommendations (avis or *advis*) by which they proposed remedies for monetary difficulties. In addition, these conseillers assiduously managed to increase the competence of their jurisdiction at the expense of other rival courts. After the ordinance of March 1541 (Article 17), the officers were personally liable to one court alone, the Chambre des Monnaies. By Article 10 of the ordinance of January 14, 1550, the judges of the different Parlements were forbidden to interfere in matters relating to the *boîtes des monnaies* or to question the decisions of the Chambre on purely monetary matters. From 1552 it exercised sovereign jurisdiction on all matters concerning metals and became the Cour des Monnaies.[72] It was a power in the land; at the state banquet after the funeral of Louis XIV, the Cour, to its evident satisfaction, was given precedence over the university, the *châtelet,* and the City of Paris.

During the intervening years, however, the supreme authority of the Cour

---

[71] A. Fontanon, *Les édicts et ordonnances des Roys de France* (2 vols., Paris, 1585), II, p. 625; J. Vannier, *Essai sur le bureau des finances de la Généralité de Rouen* (Rouen, 1927); and see below, Section 2.

[72] The edict of January 1552 was verified on April 12. Spain recognized its importance in 1556, when consideration was given to having a "monetary council as there is in France." Archivo General de Simancas [hereafter cited as Simancas], *Diversos de Castilla,* libro 48, reference communicated by Fernand Braudel; see also the articles of Jean Bailhache, "Chambre et Cour des Monnaies," *Revue numismatique,* 4th Ser. XXXVII–XXXIX (1934–1936).

in Paris did not go unchallenged. In 1594 Henry IV created courts in Lyons, Toulouse, and Poitiers, but they were soon abolished. In March 1645 Louis XIV established Cours des Monnaies in Lyons and Libourne, but this edict was immediately revoked. On the third serious attempt, Lyons succeeded: by the edict of June 1704 a sovereign Cour des Monnaies, similar to that in Paris, was set up there. The official purpose of this Cour was to correct the abuses in monetary affairs in the region, which the orders and judgments from Paris "until now have been unable to stop." The court in Lyons was given jurisdiction over the provinces of Lyons, Dauphiné, Provence, Auvergne, Toulouse, Montpellier, Montauban, and Bayonne; these included the mints in Lyons, Grenoble, Aix, Riom, Bayonne, Toulouse, and Montpellier. The division of the monetary administration of France was thus almost a return to the conditions of the early sixteenth century when France had virtually two capitals: Paris and Lyons. The large northern area looked toward the Low Countries, Holland, and England; the southern group found links with Spain and the Mediterranean. But in evaluating the division such a simplification must not be given too much weight.

In the sixteenth century, however, the organization of the mints was a heritage of the past. According to custom, the mints were farmed out by auction to private contractors who undertook to coin a minimum quantity of currency or, on occasion, to a group working together, as in the instance of Pierre Assezat and his partners in 1564 (from whom the farm was withdrawn two years later). In some instances the crown took over the operations on its own account, and the mint would then function *sous la main du roi*. On other occasions several mints could be grouped under the same entrepreneur, as in the case of the Bedeau frères who operated the mints of Angers and Rennes. Normally the contract was given to a substantial merchant who could put up sufficient caution money as collateral for good conduct. At times a mint could not attract an operator, as in the case of Bayonne in 1522 when there was "no suitable merchant or changer" prepared to undertake the coinage. At Limoges in 1570 the mint was closed "because no one was found who wanted to take the farm." [73] The form of negotiated contract with the crown was also explicit: on the occasion of the melting down and conversion of the silver plate received from tax levies in September 1521, Nicholas Le Cointe, master of the Paris mint, traveled to Troyes to find the King "to bargain with him as much for the *brassage* . . . as for parting the silver gilt." [74]

The system of farming out the mints by auction lasted until 1645, when a long period began that was implicitly entwined with the history of the sale of offices and the swelling bureaucracy in France. In 1662 a general lease to Denis Genisseau was given for the mints in Paris, Rouen, Rennes, Bayonne, Lyons, and Aix. In 1666, Colbert gave the management to the Sieur Claude

[73] A.N., Z¹B.310, état de 1552 and état de 1570.
[74] A.N., Z¹B.326, état de 1521.

Thomas as Directeur Général des Monnaies de France with the right to appoint directors of the individual mints. There followed a line of successive officeholders: Sieur Vincent Fortier in 1672; Sieur Levot in 1674; Sieur de Live in 1677; Sieur Rousseau in 1683. The year 1696 brought a far-reaching reform: the edict of June created the central office of *Directeur et Trésorier Général des Monnaies*. The function of Treasurer General was suppressed in 1705; that of Director was converted in 1717 into the office of *Conseiller Directeur Général des Monnaies du Royaume*. The same edict also created the offices of *Directeurs et Trésoriers Particuliers des Monnaies* which assumed the duties of the individual mint masters suppressed fifty years before. They were assigned annual stipends which give a rough indication of the ranking of the different mints:

Annual stipend in livres tournois	Mints
3,000	Paris (the stipend was raised to 3300 in 1719); Lyons
2,400	Aix; Rennes; Rouen
1,800	Bayonne; Bordeux; Dijon; Lille; Montpellier; Rheims; Toulouse; Tours
1,200	Amiens; Besançon; Bourges; Caen; Limoges; Metz; Nantes; Pau; Poitiers; Riom; La Rochelle; Troyes

All this happened during the war when there were the inevitable financial pressures. The classification has, therefore, only a relatively approximate value as a measure of the regional administration.

The conversion of bullion or foreign specie into French coin was greatly facilitated by changers who, in principle, were obliged to pass to the nearest mint all precious metals and coin which were not current. Their operations, as is well known, were extremely diverse and often included banking transactions. There were also other important operators such as alien merchant-financiers against whom the Estates General complained: "they are to be seen daily entering the realm with only pen and paper in hand and in no time acquiring riches." [75] Against the changers there was always popular mistrust. In 1550, at the time of the great conversion of billon, the city councillors of Rouen appointed representatives to inspect the changers' dealings.[76] They did not, obviously, inspire confidence. The changers also roused government suspicions. By the ordinance of March 3, 1555, they were sworn in as royal officials, and their numbers in the various towns were limited. A royal pro-

[75] Georges Picot, *Histoire des États Généraux considérés au point de vue de leur influence sur le gouvernement de la France de 1355–1614* (4 vols., Paris, 1872), II, p. 255.

[76] Archives Municipales [hereafter cited as A.M.], Rouen, A.16, fol. 70, délibération of Feb. 7, 1550.

cureur and two sergeants were, furthermore, appointed in each mint, and the officials of the mints no longer received their salaries from the local receveurs out of royal taxes.[77] Henry IV took another step in removing monetary difficulties in 1602 when he abolished their offices and transferred the duties to the masters of the mints: they were "nationalized." But this was only a temporary move, and the changers were reestablished in 1607.[78] The truth is the government was not sufficiently competent to take over, even to supervise, all the operations. In the sector of gold and silver currency fraudulent activities were more frequent. Even when mints such as Villefranche-de-Rouergue and Saint Pourçain were established near silver mines, there was no certainty that the silver produced would find its way to the mint, other than at an acceptable official price, and this was one small example among many.

In each mint a *contre-garde* controlled the purchase of bullion and specie of all sorts. The bullion was made ready for coining, in the form of *brèves,* and these were passed by the gardes to the coiners to be beaten into sheets, cut into discs, struck, and then returned to the gardes for assay. Twelve coins were taken at random by the assayer and cut into quarters. The assays were made on twelve of these quarters, and the remainder were kept until the Cour des Monnaies had passed the accounts. They were then given to the mint master without charge in the case of gold and silver, but with the possibility of repurchase in the case of douzains. The profits contributed to the fees of the officials, half to the assayer and half to the gardes.[79]

During the greater part of the period the coins from the mints were hammered into thin discs of metal with a clear ring, since heavy coins gave more scope to the counterfeiter. In the mills there were difficulties of a technical nature, including a tendency to wastage. The mint of Paris, which was more efficient than the others, had an outstanding reputation for quality production.[80] There the mill was employed, at least after 1552, although in some years of exceptional activity the old mint for hammering coins was reopened (as in 1562) to convert silver plate into testons. The mill indeed offered great advantages. Bodin, as has already been noted, supported its use in 1576, but his proposal was not accepted, by reason, over and beyond those of a general nature already cited, of the technicalities involved: the ringing sound was not the same as those hammered, and the weights often varied "because the metal sheets were made thinner in some places than in others." [81] The success of the mill was assured only when the difficulties in producing metal sheets of uniform thickness were solved. The deniers and doubles were coined by milling, but, because the uneven quality of production was easily visible, they were often rejected in circulation.

[77] Fontanon, *Édicts et ordonnances,* II, p. 129.
[78] See Chap. 3.
[79] Fontanon, *Édicts et ordonnances,* II, p. 29.
[80] Étienne Pasquier, *Les Recherches de la France* (Paris, 1641). To be marked with an "A" (the mark of Paris) was, in everyday talk, the sign of honesty. See *ibid.,* p. 719.
[81] Bodin, *République,* CI, pp. 917, 936; A.N., Z¹B.64, lettres patentes of Mar. 27, 1551.

The machines of Nicholas Briot brought a considerable improvement. In effect, they made possible the great reform of 1640. From 1645, by the letters patent of March 8, the hammer mints were finally suppressed: all coins were, thereafter, issued from mills. The milled edge ended the opportunities for the coin-clipper, but the mill required heavy expenditures for dies. Under normal circumstances, the model, the pattern for the series, was cut in Paris under the watchful eye of the Cour des Monnaies. In 1547 this task was confided to a *tailleur-général,* which opened the way for Marc Béchot and his assistant, Pierre Milan, two brilliant engravers, to introduce new types of French coins. The life of both parts of the dies was relatively short, through the loss of temper from constant usage. This alone could hold up the issue of coin. In March 1710 the gardes in Montpellier found that the tailleur had not included the differentiating mark of the mint master in the dies; as a result 1,035 gold *louis* were returned to the melting pot, and the tailleur was charged with the costs.[82]

The activities of these mints should not, however, be viewed with the presuppositions about firms of the present day; nor should they be judged always by the consistent quality of work done in Paris or in the great Zecca of Venice. Often they were small undertakings with only a few workmen. The master of the mint in charge of the operations was perhaps a merchant with sufficient capital to carry the expenses of coinage. The lease of the mint was given out by auction, for a stipulated number of years, with the obligation of issuing certain amounts of coin. This agreed minimum was the contract on which the mint farmer had to pay the seigniorage, even if he did not produce that minimum. He could, however, fulfill his obligation, when necessary, by making up the required amount with other coin, following the rule, as his contract stipulated, "l'or portant l'argent et l'argent l'or." [83]

Agents of the crown supervised, moreover, the small undertakings. The purchase of bullion, the coining, the issues of coin for circulation — all were stages of operation in the context of commercial and industrial activity; they were part of a system for fixing official prices, and special tariffs were established for bullion. These requirements held a system in check which otherwise had considerable freedom; the whole organization was filled with risks and uncertainties. In time of economic crisis, when the market rates rose above those officially allowed at the mints, a merchant often could not fulfill his obligation, or, indeed, in the face of such uncertainty, he would be unwilling to undertake a further term.

Apart from its administrative functions, the Cour des Monnaies, was concerned with the technical operation of the mints. The samples of coin were

---

[82] A.N., Z¹B.63, letters patent of Aug. 1547, verified June 26, 1548; Archives Départementales [hereafter cited as A.D.], Hérault, Ser. B., 471.

[83] In Lyons, for example, in the contract of 1585, the form was "l'un portant l'autre"; in La Rochelle, in 1584, the mint master was authorized to complete his contract "l'or portant l'argent et billon." A.N., Z¹B.310, 888.

sent by the mints to Paris for assay and were then paid into the revenues of the Cour. This was another reason why it kept such meticulous accounts. These samples, sent in *boîtes des monnaies,* were made up of coins taken at random ("prinses dans la masse") from among the coin issued. The samples were taken in fixed proportions: in the sixteenth century, 1 gold coin out of 200; 1 silver coin out of 18 marcs weight for those of high fineness; and 1 out of 720 for silver and copper billon (that is, the sol parisis and below). In 1682 the sampling was altered to 1 gold coin in 400 and 1 silver coin in 72 marcs weight. This system lasted until a further adjustment in August 1750. The boxes were locked with three keys (according to the ordinance of 1554), sealed, and sent to Paris by the gardes of the mint for verification in the presence of the Procureur Général of the Cour and the respective mint master.[84] The samples were tested for weight and fineness and used to estimate the amount of coin issued in order to check whether the mint master had lived up to his contract.

Until the middle of the sixteenth century the accounts kept with the masters of the different mints were reconstructed from the coins in the boxes sent to Paris. From these coins, according to the fixed proportions, the total issues were known. And during the first half of the sixteenth century, in the accounts for the different towns, separate sections were set aside for gold, for silver, and for billon. This accounting system lasted until the reform of 1555, which aimed to set the confused monetary situation in order and to ascertain the exact amounts of the coin issued.[85] From that time individual accounts were compiled from the lists of issues (*états des délivrances*).[86] Each box represented a period of issues, sometimes lasting months, and sometimes covering several years. Because of the inconvenient irregularity of these variable periods, the gardes were instructed by the ordinance of January 14, 1550, to close the boxes each year on December 31. This order was repeated in the letters patent of March 3, 1555.[87] The receipt of the boxes and their contents was recorded by an official, the *receveur des boîtes,* who kept a separate series of registers.

[84] Fontanon, *Édicts et ordonnances,* II, p. 129.

[85] These data are used in the early section of the graphs and estimates in this book. In order to keep the administration of the Cour des Monnaies in perspective, one should note the following budget in livres tournois for 1583: 21,870 livres 2 sols 4 deniers for the stipends of officers (4 *présidents,* 19 *conseillers-généraux,* the *avocat et procureur du Roi,* the *greffier,* the *essayeur et tailleur général,* and 6 *huissiers*); 800 livres for the expenditure of the Cour; 800 livres for the "menues necessitez" of the Cour; 660 livres given by the king every January 1, for stationery; 27 livres 15 sols the expense of entry of each newly appointed officer.

There were, in addition, the upkeep of buildings, traveling expenses for commissioners, and so forth. A.N., Z¹B.381, Mar. 29, 1583. The total budget above was minute by comparison with the gross royal revenues: 27,895,653 livres tournois in 1588. Jean-Jules Clamageran, *Histoire de l'impôt en France* (3 vols., Paris, 1867–1876), II, p. 244.

[86] See Chap. 4.

[87] A.N., Z¹B.64, ordonance of Jan. 14, 1550; Fontanon, *Édicts et ordonnances,* II, p. 131.

In this study, I have used principally the series of the états des délivrances and the contrôle des boîtes.[88] It should be noted that the years begin with January 1, and the coinages of gold, silver, and billon have been arranged by annual totals; these small details have a certain importance in the calculations. For the first half of the sixteenth century the dates have been established from the delivery of the boîtes in Paris, although from time to time the exact dates of the coinage have also been included in the registers for the arrival of the boîtes. For the period after 1550, following the orders to close the boxes on December 31, it has become relatively easy to fix the dates of the issues and eliminate a margin of error.

Until the ordinance of March 19, 1541,[89] the monetary administration was arranged by provinces — Brittany, Burgundy, Dauphiné, Provence — and, finally, for France. The verification of the boxes at the outset was not entirely within the competence of Paris. The issues in Rennes and Nantes, until 1540–1550, for example, remained under the control of the Général des Monnaies de Bretagne. Another problem concerning the calculations was the conditions during the military operations in Italy: French coins were issued in various cities in the peninsula, for example, in Genoa and Milan in 1494, in Naples in 1502, and, more generally, "in Italy" in 1515. The case of Turin has been recorded as an example of these "extraterritorial" issues.

All these relate to significant difficulties; there were also minor problems. Thus the mint settled in Riom had arrived by way of Saint-Pourçain (until 1549) and Moulins (from 1550 to 1555). The operations of the mint were finally transferred to Riom in 1556. Such problems will be noted later; for the moment it is sufficient to indicate the essentials.

What uncertainties affected the activities of the mints? There were many factors: regional and accidental or general and relating to the level of economic activity. In the first place, a mint was part of a city and hinterland, and was the result of a complex of economic relationships already decided. It must be emphasized that the activities of the cities were by no means certain, and this absence of certainty had a place in the context of monetary history, more often than at first imagined. There was, for example, the well-known instance of plague, always a feature of urban life. The documents frequently reported that "the plague has flared up." Little more than that was required to stop operations. In 1554 the mint of Poitiers reported that "some of us have withdrawn to the fields, to wait until the danger has passed." No reports were sent to Paris from Limoges in 1584 and 1585 "on account of the sickness of contagion which is in the said town." [90]

Civil unrest was another uncertainty. The towns offered doubtful safety. In Lyons in 1508 the municipal authorities allowed soldiers returning from

[88] See Chap. 4.
[89] *Ibid.*
[90] A.N., Z¹B.369, letter of Sept. 21, 1554, from the gardes of the mint in Poitiers to the Cour des Monnaies; A.N., Z¹B.301 (1584–1585).

the war in Italy to pass through the town only in small groups.[91] The documents reveal many aspects of the vicissitudes of life, notably in the civil wars in the second half of the sixteenth century, when endless sieges and battles marked the marching and countermarching of armies.

Again, it is not the small detail which is of interest but rather the overall movement, and one must determine whether it was continuous or sporadic. Graph 13 shows the chronology of the activity of the mints from 1493 to 1725. The graph is clear enough, but the explanation is difficult. Only one mint — Paris — operated without interruption. Next in order came the almost continuous issues of Bayonne, although its mint was often inactive in the years 1620–1640. Lyons had intermittent activity about 1600; Rouen suffered many interruptions. In general, the first question to ask is: did the stoppages reflect changes in economic activity? The second question is: did the operations of the mints represent changes in royal policy and administrative convenience? This latter consideration clearly became more important as the period advanced, especially from the early seventeenth century. In order to examine these matters more closely, the period has been divided into phases: to the mid-sixteenth century; 1550–1610; 1611–1680; 1681–1725. In each of these phases, particular groups of mints were active at different times.

During the first period the following mints were active: in the west, in addition to Paris and Bayonne, Angers, Bordeaux, Rouen, Toulouse, Limoges, Poitiers, Tours; in the southern Mediterranean area, Montpellier and Villeneuve-lès-Avignon; in eastern, or rather in continental, France, Bourges, Lyons, and Grenoble.

In the period 1550–1610 the mints of secondary importance — Crémieu, Romans, Montélimar, Villefranche-de-Rouergue — collapsed. Other mints, by contrast, improved their performance: Rennes and Nantes, about which information is lacking for the previous period; La Rochelle; Saint-Lô; Aix-en-Provence; Dijon; and Troyes. Bourges, Grenoble, and Montpellier, however, encountered increasing difficulties at this time.

From 1611 to 1680 the most active mints were Aix, Bayonne, Lyons, Paris, Rennes, and Toulouse. The mints in the maritime towns of the west, particularly in the 1620s and 1630s, faced growing difficulties. Others survived as best they could in the difficult years 1620–1640, for example, Grenoble, Riom, and Villeneuve-lès-Avignon, which showed spasmodic activity.

The period 1681–1725 was dominated by two great developments: the wars of 1689–1697 and 1701–1713; and the reforms and movements under John Law. The mint in Paris worked continuously, as did that in Rennes. Aix and Bayonne are assumed to have done the same. Lyons missed a year in 1720, being heavily occupied with restamping coins, and Bordeaux was inactive only in 1689. Apart from these, few mints were in operation during the 1680s. With the outbreak of war, however, almost all worked at some time

[91] A.M., Lyons, Ser. BB.28, fol. 13ᵛᵒ.

13. Annual Activity of the Mints under French Control

during the 1690s. The years of the early seventeenth century opened with another period of uncertainty, no doubt affected by the treaties between England and Portugal in 1703. (This will be discussed later, but suffice it to say that beginning in 1709 the mints throughout France entered a period of prolonged activity.) The only interruptions were in Lyons (1720), Strasbourg (1711–1713), and Lille (1709–1712), the last being lost after the Battle of Oudenarde, but restored to the French crown by the Treaty of Utrecht. It is therefore worth remarking that when John Law came to power almost all the mints had been in continuous operation for several years. During his period of office only Orléans joined the list, and that in 1718.

In general, this outline of the operations of the different mints focuses attention on the role of national and regional centers: on the capital, Paris, above all; for a time at least, on the great market of Lyons, in spite of the many interruptions between 1611 and 1680; on the great provincial centers of administration; and on towns forming the network of land and sea routes such as Aix, Bayonne, Rennes, Rouen, Saint-Lô, and Toulouse. This commentary on Graph 13 is, however, only a preliminary review of the operations of the mints. It is not so much the continuity of their activities as the volume and changing character of their outputs through the years which are significant. Among the relevant factors, three merit particular attention: the export sector, for France lacked large mineral deposits of gold and silver and derived its supplies of bullion from trade and services; the dominant role of government; and the degree to which money functioned in the market system of France. These questions will be considered in more detail later in the book.

Chapter 3

Economic Activity and Monetary Periods

This chapter takes the theme of the book a stage further and is concerned not so much with the setting of monetary problems as the chronology of monetary developments, the influence of governmental "policy decisions," and the reactions of the regions of France. These must necessarily be detailed. The day-to-day monetary problems reflected many aspects of life in France, which, like the country itself, was far from integrated and, relatively, not a single entity. France was situated at the crossroads of Europe and thus became a channel through which flowed many kinds of money. Recurring crises and readjustments constantly underline the fundamental disparity of the country. It was obliged to countenance the affairs of its neighbors and adjacent economic centers, in Antwerp, Germany, England, Spain, and even the New World. These external influences, these international movements, repeatedly left their mark on events in France. Because of this, I have divided the narrative into the same three great phases outlined in the first chapter: the phase of gold, the phase of silver, and the seventeenth century. A closing section has been added to cover the years 1681–1725, opening a new period and taking the review to the eve of the great monetary reform in 1726. What were the successive reactions of France during these various phases?

1. The Gold Phase in France

The gold phase occurred during the first half of the sixteenth century and coincided with the long fight for the hegemony of Europe. The wars of Italy, the great Hapsburg-Valois rivalry, was an aggressive struggle which flared into open war in 1521 and drew to a close only with the settlement of Cateau-Cambrésis in 1559. This treaty ended the more or less glorious sequence of wars waged abroad by France and almost at once unleashed the civil and religious struggles which disrupted the country for nearly half a century. These domestic conflicts will be considered later.

First came the wars abroad, the pursuit of glory in Italy and then after, 1519–1521, the conflict with the ruling House of Austria to break the territorial encirclement by the astute Charles V. Did gold play a part in this drama? We could assume it had a greater influence if there had been a progressively wider circulation of gold currency. France for long held an intermediary position in Europe, between the south and the north, between the gold of Spain and the silver of Germany. The country had only meager resources of precious metals, and bullion came directly or indirectly from its neighbors. This had some importance when the Emperor Charles V could command both silver from Germany and gold from Spain after the famous election of 1519. His French rival would have been largely deprived of these means of payment had the governments of the time been able to exercise complete control over mining. In reality the movements of trade and financial settlements adjusted the flows of bullion. The governments were often able to make spectacular payments in bullion or specie, and these are the first to impress the observer. At first they were simple and direct but, with the passing years, they became more complicated. Without stretching the evidence; it is possible to consider: first, the situation at the end of the fifteenth century; next, the period of relative stagnation from 1499 to 1519–1521; then, the rising tension from 1521 to 1541; and, finally, after 1541 to 1542, when the silver from the New World increasingly made its presence felt.

The point of departure for the first period is, arbitrarily, 1493. This date has no special economic importance but the series of surviving account books of the Chambre des Monnaies begins at this date. The documents decide the matter. It suits the analysis fairly well, however, and the course of events shows that it had some importance from a monetary point of view. It came close to the first successful voyage of Christopher Columbus (1492) and to the decisive opening of a sea route to the East Indies by way of the Cape of Good Hope (1497–1498). Both of these events were important in the transformation of the international economy. In the following year, 1494, the armies of France invaded Italy. It is, then, in general, a convenient starting point.

France in that year apparently encountered difficulties, some political, others economic, many already long apparent. The calling of the Estates General in 1484 had been in itself a sign of difficulties, both political and financial. A monetary devaluation followed on January 29, 1488, another unfavorable sign; this raised gold prices by comparison with the rates of 1475. In December of the same year the mint master of Montpellier reported difficulties of another kind — this time of silver currency — but a little later, in November 1491, he complained of the disappearance of gold, especially in the direction of Lyons.[1] Again, in 1498, the money changers were ordered to keep strict account of all the coins they bought of a face value of more than sixty sols; they were also forbidden to keep coins which had not received official currency unless broken.[2] These troubled years (the revolt of the future Louis XII from 1488 to 1491; the marriage of Charles VIII and Anne de Bretagne in 1491) did not pass easily.

There were inflationary pressures at the end of the century, resulting no doubt from the foreign policy of Charles VIII. By 1943 he was ready to invade Italy. In order to protect his interests, he arranged treaties of alliance with the Kings of Spain and England and with the Emperor Maxmillian. There were large issues of gold coin in France in 1494 and 1495, more so than in 1493 and 1496, doubtless from taxation to pay the promised subsidies and to finance the French armies in the Italian peninsula. The successes were, however, brief:

---

[1] Archives Nationales [hereafter cited at A.N.], Z¹B.362, letters of Dec. 26, 1488, Nov. 28, 1491, from the gardes of the mint in Montpellier to the Généraux des Monnaies in Paris.

[2] A.N., Z¹B.62, ordonnance of July 4, 1498.

the mints had a spurt of activity, but toward the end of the century the appreciation of gold was apparent. The difficulties over gold currency accompanied the failure of the French in Italy — "beyond the mountains" — and the situation was marked again by heavy tax levies, monetary instability and shortages of currency, clipped coins, and exports of bullion.

France seems to be a particular case, at least by comparison with its northern neighbors. In Flanders the conditions were different from those in France, although the end of the century there also proved to be critical. After the Treaty of Frankfurt with France (July 19, 1489), an ordinance was issued there (December 14). By this, gold florins maintained their present rate (thus, there was not a gold devaluation as in France), but, by contrast, "the big silver real was raised in price because it was a means of payment and was to have currency at four and a half *patards*." [3] Although the rate of silver currency tended to fluctuate, the monetary system of Flanders aimed to favor silver. At that time the French system was adjusted to attract gold. This difference did not last long, apparently only until 1499 when both monetary systems faced difficulties. This change in trend coincided with an economic crisis in the Low Countries. It was particularly severe in the old textile industries and was aggravated by serious cyclic fluctuations in grain prices during the 1490s. [4] Were these fluctuations influenced by developments in the New World? Did the new conditions bring France to peace with its northern neighbors?

At the opening of the sixteenth century there were signs of a growing pressure of gold in Spain and along lines of communication from Spain to Europe. From 1503 the deliveries from America were registered in the famous Casa de la Contratación in Seville. After 1504 the French economy apparently felt the effects at a time of rapidly changing events, for Naples fell from French control. Issues of money from mints other than the one in Paris had been at a low level, but after 1504 the coinage of gold in Bayonne showed a marked increase, and the mint in Lyons suddenly reported operations greater than those in Paris. The growing activities in these two key cities — Bayonne and Lyons — both responsive to the movements in the Spanish peninsula, revealed a new trend in monetary affairs. The pressure from the south was further underlined in the debates in the Estates General in 1506; among the complaints about economic conditions and about pepper brought from Portugal (the Fuggers had underwritten substantial deliveries in 1505), were those concerning new monetary difficulties. [5]

The involved situation showed moderating signs soon afterward, and it became clear that it was not so much a passing disturbance as the progressive

[3] Alphonse de Witte, *Histoire monétaire des comtes de Louvain, ducs de Brabant et Marquis du Saint Empire Romain* (4 vols., Antwerp, 1894–1899), II, pp. 77, 84–86, 112.
[4] Émile Coornaert, *La draperie-sayetterie d'Hondschoote* (Paris, 1930), pp. 17–21.
[5] A.N., Z¹B.62, ordonnances of Mar. 23, 1504, Nov. 22, 1506; see also Archives Municipales [hereafter cited as A.M.], Lyons, Ser. BB.23, fol. 86ʳᵒ; A.M., Rouen, A.10, Nov. 10, 1506.

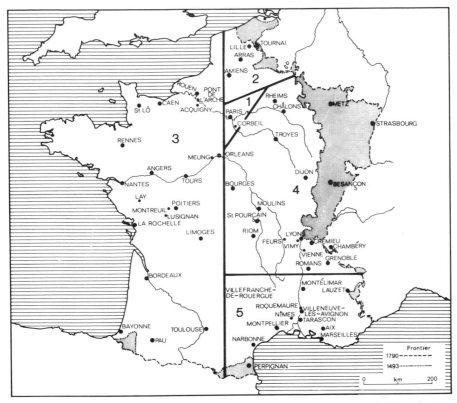

3. Mints in France, 1493–1725, divided into five zones (not including the independent mints during the League)

imposition of Spanish power. The increasing diffusion of gold currency in France brought at the same time a relative appreciation of silver. The ordinance of March 1504 attempted somewhat blindly to restrain the increase in the market rates of currency, but the main attention was soon directed to silver. An order of August 17, 1504, dealing with goldsmiths, money changers, and merchants in Paris, mentioned that silver plate was being sold at between 11 livres 5 sols and 11 livres 12 sols 6 deniers the marc. The official price of the marc of silver was then only 11 livres. An order was promulgated a little later that the costs of both of the silver used and of its fabrication should be stated separately, in the hope that this would prevent a hidden increase in the market price.[6]

The government aimed at all costs to achieve stability, and until 1519 the official mint prices remained those of 1488: the marc of gold at 130 livres 3 sols 4 deniers and the marc of silver 11 livres.[7] But the inflationary movement

[6] A.N., Z¹B.62, mandement of Aug. 17, 1504.
[7] The silver was argent-le-roi at a fineness of 23/24. See A. Dieudonné, "Note sur les origines de l'argent-le-roi," *Revue numismatique,* 4th Ser., XXXIV (1931).

continued: in April 1514, for the coinage of silver testons, the marc of silver fluctuated between 13 livres and 13 livres 10 sols, "and sometimes more." [8] Well before 1519 the retention of the official rates of 1488 had become a vain hope.

The foreign policy of the French monarchy, in such a situation, was an added burden. The consequences of the expeditions in Italy of Louis XII and then of Francis I inevitably had monetary repercussions. Military operations destroyed sound finance and simple monetary policies. On November 19, 1507, the government complained that its monetary regulations were "very badly kept" and blamed the mints.[9] The currency rates of 1488 were reissued, but how long could this last? Already in the previous year, to meet its requirements, the mint in Lyons had received the order of January 24, 1506, to confine itself to the coinage of écus d'or and douzains — the famous *grands blancs* — and to go above the mint prices of 130 livres 3 sols 4 deniers and 11 livres "no matter what inactivity." [10] Abroad the Holy League suddenly declared war on France, and the royal ordinances of December 1511 and February 1512 again confirmed the rates of 1488.[11]

The capture of Milan in 1512 and the salvage defeat of Novara in 1513 were the background to the issue of the silver testons, which has already been mentioned. The silver teston, it should be noted, was the French version of the Italian *testone*. The widening gap between the market and official bullion prices was partly overcome by acquiring bullion from the conversion of large quantities of silver plate raised in loans and taxes. At first the testons weighed 26 to the marc at a fineness of 11 deniers and 12 grains (or 23/24ths). In the discussions in the *Conseil* on February 11, 1514, however, the Chambre des Monnaies raised a number of objections; as a result, the weight of these coins was raised to 25½ to the marc and at a fineness of 11 deniers 18 grains argent-le-roi, that is, at 11 deniers 12 grains fine silver. Under these conditions, the teston, with its high intrinsic value and fineness, could be converted once more into plate should the occasion arise.[12] At the high face value of 10 sols, the marc of silver was worth about 12 livres 10 sols. Even in Lyons, the leading market for German silver, an order of June 6, 1514, allowed the mint master to pay a supplement "up to 17 sols 6 deniers tournois" above the legal price of 11 livres, in order to allow him to purchase 2,500 marcs of silver from merchants and money changers.[13]

---

[8] A.N., Z¹B.363, Apr. 6, 1514.

[9] A.N., Z¹B.62, ordonnance of Nov. 19, 1507, which limited the number of mints to Paris, Rouen, Amiens, Bourges, Bordeaux, Angers, La Rochelle, Tours, Toulouse, Montpellier, Limoges, Lyons, Dijon, Troyes, Grenoble, Aix, Nantes, and Rennes.

[10] A.N., Z¹B.363, letter of Jan. 24, 1508, from the Généraux des Monnaies to the gardes of the mint in Lyons.

[11] A.N., Z¹B.62, ordonnances of Dec. 5, 1511, Feb. 3, 1512.

[12] A.N. Z¹B.363, Apr. 6, 1514. The operations were intended to pay military and naval expenditures. See A.N. Z¹B.62, délibération of the Conseil d'État of Jan. 28, 1514, and avis of the Chambre des Monnaies of Feb. 15, 1514.

[13] *Ibid.*, mandement to the mint master in Lyons of June 6, 1514.

The triumphs of Francis I in Italy and his victory at Marignano (September 13, 1515) put further strains on the royal finances. The Queen Regent appealed in his absence to the Chambre des Monnaies. Their recommendation of October 23 proposed to raise gold prices to 147 livres the marc and silver to 12 livres 10 sols, at a fineness of 10 deniers argent-le-roi and above (instead of at the alloy of 12 deniers). This move obviously favored the existing ratio between gold and silver.[14]

In this period of French success the price of gold also tended to rise. The Chambre des Monnaies, in a letter to the *Chancelier* of May 31, 1516, on the subject of a proposed rate for the écu of 40 sols, noted that in the market it had already reached 41 sols and even more. Representatives of the guilds and money changers of Paris were summoned and ordered not to exceed the legal rates. Two months later (July 26, 1516) the Chambre explained to the *Grand Maistre de France* that there had been a delay in publishing the ordinance on the circulation of gold because no official tariff had yet been settled for the marcs of gold and silver bullion. Three days later a similar letter was addressed to the *Chancelier*.[15] There were several attempts to find a solution. In the autumn of 1516 the deputies from the bonnes villes assembled in Paris to discuss a list of problems, including money. On October 22, 1516, a number of proposals were submitted to the Chancelier, in general expressing the view that the weight of the écu should be reduced. The Chancelier, in opposition to the Chambre des Monnaies, suggested that the écu should have a reduced fineness of 22½ karats and that the weight of the coins should be reduced to 71½ to the marc. On November 27 the new rates were fixed provisionally "as a makeshift arrangement for a short period": the rate for the écu was raised to 40 sols, and a number of foreign gold and silver coins were given currency, such as the angel from England, the double ducats from Spain, and some coins from Flanders. The teston was kept at 10 sols, and some silver coins from Italy, Switzerland, and Germany were also given currency.[16]

Except for Paris, the issues of coins from the mints rose in 1516. Although the currency rates were raised, the mint prices for the gold and silver marc remained unchanged. The number of mints allowed to operate was changed in 1517, but the additional ones encountered increasing difficulties in meeting their obligations.[17] In order to coin the largest possible amount of bullion (including the silver produced from mines in France), a further order of March 6, 1517, instructed the mineowners to deliver their silver to the nearest mint at the rate of 12 livres the marc.[18]

[14] A.N. Z^{1}B.61, avis of the Généraux des Monnaies of Oct. 23, 1515.

[15] *Ibid.*, letter of May 31, 1516, from the Généraux des Monnaies to the Chancelier; remonstrance of the Généraux des Monnaies of July 26, 1516; and letter of July 29, 1516, to the Chancelier.

[16] *Ibid.*, délibérations of Oct. 21–22, 1516, and ordonnance of Nov. 27, 1516.

[17] The principal mints were Paris, Rouen, Lyons, and Bayonne; to these were added Tours, Angers, Poitiers, La Rochelle, Montpellier, Toulouse, Bordeaux, Limoges, and Bourges.

[18] A.N., Z^{1}B.62, lettres patentes of Mar. 6, 1517.

Again, on March 15, 1517, the deputies of the bonnes villes assembled in Paris and discussed monetary difficulties which the wars in Italy had imposed. They demanded an adjustment in the currency rates. From Bayonne and from Provence, came reports that the écu passed for 41 sols.[19] When, later, *lettres missives* again asked for the opinions of the cities, Rouen replied on January 20, 1518, against any attempt to change the monetary standards. From Dauphiné it was reported on January 22, 1518, that the price of gold had risen, and the opinion was expressed that in commercial transactions gold was a more convenient means of payment than silver.[20] Yet was that responsible for the rise?

Up to this point it has not been sufficiently stressed, perhaps, that Europe was passing through a period of truce, of monetary entente. This situation did not, however, exclude the fact that in the case of silver considerable regional differences existed. Thus in southwestern France, near the Spanish peninsula, gold was easier to acquire but this did not always mean that the same was true of silver, even through the simple operation of bimetallism. At Bayonne on July 16, 1508, the mint master was directed to buy the placer gold produced in the rivers of the region; otherwise it would escape to Mauléon and Pamplona "together with the gold and silver specie which usually found its way to the said Bayonne." [21] The importance of this city as both port and frontier town is shown clearly in the fact that full-bodied silver coins were minted there only much later, in 1553. In Bayonne and the surrounding region the disappearance of silver in the direction of Spain apparently was part of the growing pressure of gold in the peninsula. A letter from Bordeaux to Paris dated June 12, 1511, shows all too clearly that there was "no high grade silver to be found here on account of its being worth more in Spain.[22] In contrast to being allowed to coin full-bodied silver Bordeaux received permission on June 26, 1514, to coin billon — 300 marcs of silver liards — for local circulation.[23] A further report from Bordeaux on June 15, 1515, explained the inactivity of the mint because "the white metal cannot be found at the price set in the ordinance," that is, at 11 livres the marc.[24]

---

[19] Jean Barrillon, *Journal de Jean Barrillon, secrétaire du chancelier Duprat, 1515–1521,* ed. Pierre de Vaissière (2 vols., Paris, 1897–1899), I, pp. 27–28.

[20] Bibliothèque Nationale [hereafter cited as B.N.], Nouvelles Acquisitions Françaises, 7144, with the replies of Bourges, Dauphiné, and Provence; A.M., Rouen, A.38, Assemblée Communale, délibérations of Mar. 13, 1517, Jan. 20, 1518; and délibération of Jan. 22, 1518; see also Émile Coornaert, "La politique économique de la France au début du règne de François I," *Annales de l'Université de Paris* (1933); and M. Guitard, *Consultation demandée par François 1 en 1517 aux Échevins de Rouen touchant la politique économique du Royaume* (Rouen, 1939).

[21] A.N., Z¹B.76, Sept. 5, 1507; A.N., Z¹B.62, mandement of July 14, 1508.

[22] A.N., Z¹B.363, letter of June 12, 1511, from the gardes of the mint in Bordeaux to the Généraux des Monnaies in Paris.

[23] A.N., Z¹B.61, lettres missives of June 26, 1514, from the Généraux des Monnaies in Paris to the gardes of the mint in Bordeaux.

[24] *Ibid.,* Jan. 23, 1515, giving permission to mints in Paris, Lyons, Bordeaux, Bourges,

Similar geographic considerations, operating in the opposite direction, came into play during the coinage of 50,000 marcs of testons in 1514. The cities chosen for this were Paris, Rouen, Lyons, and Tours, towns in northern France which were able to procure the necessary silver without apparently too much trouble. They were also in closer contact with Germany and, with the exception perhaps of Lyons, were removed from the immediate influence of Spain.

On his accession to the throne in 1515, Francis I attempted to restore monetary order and to reform "the many abuses, faults, and malversations." But what was the value of this official declaration, with its faint promise of redress? There was some action on June 19, 1515, when he closed the majority of the mints and set up a commission of inquiry into those of Champagne and Burgundy. Four mints — Paris, Lyons, Rouen, Bayonne — were left in operation; they were key points that were essential to the monetary circulation of France.[25] The substitution in this "big four" of Bayonne for Tours (which had been authorized in 1514 to coin testons) underlined the growing importance of Spain. This importance also appeared clearly in the avis of the Chambre des Monnaies of October 23, 1515, which provides an excellent review of the monetary geography of France: Lyons held pride of place, as center of the silver-producing zone of France and also commanding "large quantities of silver bullion" (apparently of German origin); Bourges controlled the silver mines of Citry and some other centers in the province of Nivernais; Paris, Rouen, and Tours had supplies of silver plate and ornaments and some "cast" silver bullion.[26] The accent was on silver. On May 28, 1516, the order was given in Paris to coin testons from the large quantities of silver plate raised in taxes from the citizens; while on May 13, 1517, in contrast, Bayonne petitioned for permission to issue the low-alloy silver deniers and liards.[27]

The period of monetary entente soon drew to a close. In January 1519 the Emperor Maximilian died, and the imperial crown was virtually put up for auction. Francis I of France and Charles I of Spain both began to canvass the electors, creating tensions which rapidly deteriorated into the Valois-Hapsburg rivalry. Subsidies, specious promises of money, concessions, optimistic assurances were offered; in fact, no chance was lost to influence the imperial college. Yet, in reality, were the contenders well matched? Charles had behind him Spain, the treasure of the New World, and the financial support of the Fuggers, those interested partisans of the Hapsburgs.[28] To face this array of financial

---

Limoges, La Rochelle, Rouen, Châlons, Saint-Lô, Montpellier, Tours, and Poitiers; A.N., Z¹B.363, letter of June 12, 1515, from the gardes of the mint in Bordeaux to the Généraux des Monnaies in Paris.

[25] A.N., Z¹B.61, ordonnance of June 19, 1515.

[26] *Ibid.*, avis of the Chambre des Monnaies of Oct. 23, 1515.

[27] *Ibid.*, lettres patentes of May 28, 1516; A.N., Z¹B.362, letter of May 13, 1517, from the gardes of the mint in Bayonne to the Généraux des Monnaies in Paris.

[28] Richard Ehrenberg, *Das Zeitalter der Fugger* (2 vols., Jena, 1896), I, pp. 100–110; Götz Freiherr von Pölnitz, *Jakob Fugger* (2 vols., Tübingen, 1949–1951), I, pp. 410–

strength, Francis I could muster only meager resources. The mint at Lyons had been exceptionally busy with currency issues in 1517 and 1518. In 1519, however, the French crown attempted to extend its resources by a secret devaluation. On May 18 a royal ordinance "which was to be effective for only a short period" ordered the mints in Paris and Lyons during June and July to coin écus of lower intrinsic value (of 22⅞ karats fine and 71½ to the marc). The coinage of testons and douzains was also authorized. The unit prices for bullion were raised to 147 livres for the marc of gold and to 12 livres 15 sols for the marc of silver when used for coining testons and to 12 livres for douzains.[29]

The imperial election was finally decided on June 28, 1519. It coincided with these monetary maneuvers, which seems to indicate that the debased gold coin was destined for payments in Germany during the electoral campaign — in a Germany, it must be remembered, which was a large producer of silver in the first half of the sixteenth century. Gold was relatively more valuable there. The efforts of France, however, were too late.

The issues of gold coin of lower fineness lasted only two months and were restricted to the mints of Paris and Lyons. The Chambre des Monnaies protested;[30] according to its members, this state of affairs would end in driving the better gold écus and silver douzains out of circulation. Another memorial of the Chambre des Monnaies advised the King to withdraw permission for the lightweight écus to circulate as legal tender and stabilize the money by issuing new coins, at 23 karats and weighing 71 1/6th to the marc. These, at a face value of 40 sols, would put gold bullion at 147 livres the marc and silver bullion for the coinage of douzains and dixains at 12 livres 10 sols the marc. At the same time a number of foreign coins were forbidden to circulate, and the manufacture of large silver plate was stopped. On July 19, 1519, the prices of 147 livres for gold and 12 livres 10 sols for silver were officially allowed. After "several meetings of good and worthy persons," it was finally decided, on July 21, to issue écus of 23 karats and 71 1/6th to the marc, together with lighter douzains. The coinage of testons was abandoned, and they were not issued during the rest of 1519. At the mint price of 12 livres 10 sols the marc, it was, in reality, impossible to buy silver on the market for conversion into testons. Apart from this, the new system stimulated the activity of the mints, and the number in operation increased.[31]

A most pressing problem facing France, and Europe generally, during the

---

434; Karl Brandi, *Charles-Quint* (Paris, 1939), pp. 100–113; A. Spont, *Semblançay, la bourgeoisie financière au début du XVIᵉ siècle* (Paris, 1895), p. 159; Barillon, *Journal,* p. 142.

[29] The gold écu at the beginning of the reign weighed 70 to the marc at a fineness of 23⅛ karats. See also for the royal financial arrangements in Lyons. A.N., Z¹B.61, lettres patentes of Dec. 14, 1516, Aug. 8, 1517, Dec. 8, 18, 1518, Jan. 10, 22, 1519; A.N., Z¹B.364, déclaration of Francis I to the mint in Lyons of Feb. 21, 1522.

[30] A.N., J. 971–972, mémoire to the King. This document can be dated to May–July 1519 from the mention of the coinage of the new écus in Paris and Lyons.

[31] A.N., Z¹B.61, 536, ordonnance of July 21, 1519.

first twenty years of the sixteenth century was the distribution of gold arriving through Spain. One result was the relative demand for silver. France not having extensive mines of its own, attracted gold from Spain; on May 31, 1520, the deputies of the Cortes of Castile protested, with good reason, that there was a substantial loss of gold to France, where, they declared, the ducat was worth 50 maravedis more than in Spain.[32] There were, on the other hand, claims in France that silver was being lost to Spain, probably in compensation. The studies of Earl J. Hamilton show that in this period commodity prices in north-western Spain had a tendency to advance by comparison with those of Andalusia;[33] at the same time central and northern Castile experienced the bitter struggles of the *Comuneros*. The situation in Spain and France concerning silver may be considered in this context.

From many points of view, 1519 was a significant moment in this history. Charles V's success in the imperial election united under one authority the great resources of gold in Spain and of silver in Germany and Central Europe. From a monetary point of view, France was encircled, drawn both to the north and to the south, as the dictates of its economic activity or politics required. The struggle, implicit after 1519, broke out openly in 1521. In this year, for example, the operations of the mints of Paris and Antwerp were reversed: Antwerp tended to be occupied with gold, while Paris favored silver for almost a decade.[34] Because of the absence of precise details only tentative explanations are possible. Could France have suffered from unfavorable terms of trade with the neighboring economies?

The pursuit of silver, in effect, led to a reversal of monetary policy. On September 21, 1521, the government at last raised the price of silver to 13 livres 5 sols the marc, leaving the price of gold unchanged. These new rates encouraged the release of hoarded silver. The imposition of taxes and levies — often made in silver — also played their part. In Paris, in September, silver plate was requisitioned from house to house. In addition, silversmiths were ordered to stop making silverware for a period of six months.[35] Foreign merchants and financiers experienced even more restrictions. In July 1521 the houses of the "bankers of Paris" were searched and their papers seized, in order, it was explained, to prevent their aiding the imperial cause. On Christmas eve, letters patent were issued in Lyons ordering the great merchants Thomas Guadagni, Guillaume Nazi, and Robert Albisse to refuse payment to

[32] Anselmo Salvá, *Burgos en las communidades de Castilla* (Burgos, 1895), p. 64.

[33] Earl J. Hamilton, *American Treasure and the Price Revolution in Spain, 1501–1650* (Cambridge, Mass., 1934), pp. 108, 191; for Flanders and the ordinance of Feb. 4, 1521, see Witte, *Histoire monétaire*, II, pp. 165–185.

[34] See Chap. 5.

[35] A.N., Z¹B.62, mandement of Sept. 10, 1521. In Tours the great silver trellis around the reliquary of Saint Martin, worth about 80,000 livres tournois, was melted down and accounted for the heavy coinage of testons in that mint in 1523. See *Le Journal d'un bourgeois de Paris sous le règne de François Iᵉʳ, 1515–1536*, ed. V.-L. Bourilly (Paris, 1910), p. 112. In Laon the cathedral sold gold ware. *Ibid.*, pp. 135–136.

their counterparts in Milan, Florence, and Lucca on bills of exchange falling due during the next fair.[36]

The new price of silver by contrast with that of 1519 (12 livres 10 sols "to coin douzains") had been set with the express purpose of issuing testons. These were kept at the same weight as in 1514, but the fineness was lowered to 11 deniers 6 grains argent-le-roi.[37] The price of gold remained at the same level as in 1519; thus the ratio between the two metals in France was officially the lowest of the century. Permission to coin testons was granted only to Paris, Rouen, Lyons, Tours, Troyes, and Bourges. From a geographic point of view this arrangement underlined the more favorable conditions for silver in central and northern France. The permission to coin heavy silver coins was, however, soon extended to cities in the south, such as Toulouse and Bordeaux. It was stipulated that such issues should not be considered part of the *fait-fort* (the minimum required of the mint master). This distinction probably indicated, at this juncture, the importance of taxes raised in silver plate.[38] The financial situation deteriorated further, and gradually more cities received the right to coin testons.[39] Results were not, on the whole, encouraging, and a commission of inquiry appointed on June 1, 1522, toured the towns to see if the money changers were delivering bullion and specie to the mints.[40]

Actually, the country was more open to silver. Gold tended to take a secondary place in French policy, although it remained important in Spain and Germany (where it enjoyed a premium), but these were enemy camps for France. Among the many witnesses to this state of affairs, the mint of Bordeaux reported on November 9, 1520, that "all the gold which comes from Spain stays in Bayonne." Information came from Bordeaux on April 27, 1521, showing that the situation had not altered: there was hardly any profit in converting Spanish gold ducats. What was even more significant, the mint of Bayonne in May 1523 remarked on "the placer gold which used to come to this mint in large quantities." [41] Similar conditions prevailed in Languedoc: on October 10, 1526, the mint of Montpellier reported that "there was little coinage issued, especially in gold." [42] A comparison of the mints of Bayonne, Lyons, and Paris during these critical years shows the same delay in delivery of gold to the mints, and it is noticeable that, after the increase in the official mint price in 1521,

---

[36] *Journal d'un bourgeois de Paris,* ed. Bourrilly, p. 88; A. M. Lyons, Ser. FF.2, pièce 15, the reading of the lettres missives of Dec. 24, 1521.

[37] A.N., Z^{1}B.61, mandement of Sept. 10, 1521.

[38] *Ibid.*

[39] *Ibid.,* Mar. 8, Sept. 12, 1522, Mar. 7, 21, May 16, 25, 1523.

[40] *Ibid.,* June 1, 1522. The financial difficulties of Francis I and his anxiety to raise further loans and convert his silver plate in Lyons are shown in his letters A.N., KK. 104 of Apr. 20, 1524, to the prévôt of Paris and of Aug. 1, 13, 1524, to M. de Fresnes.

[41] A.N., Z^{1}B.363 letter of Nov. 9, 1520, from the gardes of the mint in Bordeaux to the Généraux des Monnaies in Paris; also A.N., Z^{1}B.364, letter of Apr. 27, 1521, from the gardes of the mint in Bordeaux to the Généraux des Monnaies in Paris.

[42] A.N., Z^{1}B.364, letters of Nov. 6, 1523, Oct. 10, 1526, from the gardes of the mint in Montpellier to the Généraux des Monnaies in Paris.

Plate 2.

Silver teston of Francis I, coined in Lyons about 1521 (actual size 2.95 cm., enlarged photograph by the Bibliothèque Nationale, Paris).

the activity of the mint in Bayonne declined. To all this must be added a difficult political situation: the Battle of Pavia in 1525, the capture of Francis I,
the League of Protestant Princes at Torgau (1526), the war against the Turks
(1526–1533), and the second war between Charles V and Francis I (1527–
1529).

Up to the time of the Ladies' Peace (1529), France, by trying to attract
silver, had tended to loosen its monetary dependence on Spain. This movement,
if indeed it existed, took place in the general difficulties of the European economy after 1525–1530,[43] difficulties which were accompanied by an advance in
gold prices. The ordinance of September 29, 1526, aimed to check the rise in
the market rates for gold coins, especially the *écu au soleil* and the *écu à la
couronne*. On October 27, a more detailed government order again set the rates
for gold currency and warned merchants not to set gold prices above those
officially announced.[44]

In attempting to detach itself from gold and from Spain, France also tended
to detach itself from Italy. Spanish influence was particularly strong in Genoa;
in 1529 this key city under Andrea Doria dramatically left France to join
Spain. After the break Genoese merchants were at a disadvantage in France,
especially in Lyons, and were finally accommodated by Charles V in the famous fairs of Besançon.[45] All this was part of France's experience: from the
defeat of Pavia and the Treaty of Madrid (January 14, 1526) to the execution
of the royal financier Jacques de Beaune, baron de Semblançay (1527); from
the attacks of the Spaniards on the coast of Brittany to the arrest of Albizzi in
Lyons and the flight of Thomas Guadagni to Avignon; from the Treaty of
Madrid (1526) to the Peace of Cambrai (1529).

These years deserve closer attention. Although the monetary rates were not
altered in 1526, there was a change in the relations between France and the
Empire. Merchants in Flanders had a strong position in the silver market;
while France, in difficulties after Pavia, was moving toward a policy favoring
gold. Politics soon reinforced this situation. The first phase of the struggle came
to an end with the Treaty of Cambrai, the so-called Ladies' Peace, of August
3, 1529, which ransomed the two sons of Francis I for 2,000,000 gold écus,
of which 1,200,000 were to be paid immediately.[46] This was a heavy burden for
French finances, especially because the payments were stipulated in gold. The
negotiations reviewed the position between the two countries: the inflation was
apparently more advanced in France than in Flanders. In August 1529 it was

---

[43] Fernand Braudel, *La Méditerranée et le monde méditerranéen à l'époque de Philippe
II* (Paris, 1949), p. 423 *et passim*.

[44] A.N., Z¹B.61, ordonnances of Sept. 28, 1526, Feb. 27, 1527; A.N., Z¹B.62, Oct. 27,
1526.

[45] A.M., Lyons, Ser. BB.47, fol. 190ᵛᵒ, Jan. 19, 1529; Ehrenberg, *Das Zeitalter der
Fugger*, I, p. 113.

[46] Émile Levasseur, "Mémoire sur les monnaies du règne de François Iᵉʳ," in *Académie
des Sciences Morales et Politiques, Ordonnances des Rois de France* (*nouvelle série*),
Règne de François Iᵉʳ, I, *1515–1516* (Paris, 1902), CXLIV, p. 272, cited by Michel
François, *Le Cardinal de Tournon* (Paris, 1951), p. 80.

estimated that the prices of the marcs of gold and silver in Antwerp, converted into livres tournois, were, respectively, 139 livres and 12 livres 12 sols, while the rates in France after 1521 were 147 livres and 13 livres 15 sols. France seemed to enjoy a privileged position, although this did not prevent Thomas Grammaye, the Général des Monnaies in Antwerp, from complaining to the Cour des Monnaies in Paris of the "great unsupportable faults, deceptions and abuses which have long been and are at present committed . . . in the kingdom of France." [47]

The ransom was paid in gold; by the Treaty of Cambrai it was stipulated that the payments should be made in écus of 71½ to the marc and of a fineness of 22¾ karats. Merchants delivered gold to collection offices set up by the government; they were forbidden to export it. By April 9, 1530, Francis I was informed that "all the écus that could be refined here have been sent and . . . no more are to be found." Was France emptied of its disposable gold? [48]

Some of the mint masters had profited despite the situation: in Dauphiné for example, they had issued coins without sending samples to Paris for assay. Commissioners were appointed on December 29, 1530, to inquire into these practices and to investigate the loss of gold and the difficulties in coining it. Were the official rates, unchanged since 1519 and 1521, too low? Perhaps the financial policies of Francis I and his ministers were responsible? The commercial rates, at least, were out of line with the official rates. In Lyons the merchants, who brought gold and silver to the fairs, found it possible, according to a report of 1529, to obtain prices ranging between 151 and 162 livres for the marc of gold and between 13 livres 10 sols and 13 livres 15 sols for the marc of silver.[49] These showed a relative appreciation of gold. In southwestern France there was similar evidence. In Bordeaux in March 1531 the mint was ready to convert large quantities of bullion and specie, but at the current legal rates, the prices of these precious metals put them out of reach of the mint. On March 22, 1530, the mint master of Bordeaux reported to the Général des Monnaies in charge of the inquiry that the merchants of Béarn preferred to sell gold locally.[50] Under these circumstances, the monetary circulation of France became progressively loaded with foreign currency, often below the

[47] Jaime Carrera Pujal, *Historia de la economía española* (6 vols., Barcelona, 1943–1947), I, p. 272; Marjorie Grice-Hutchinson, *The School of Salamanca* (Oxford, 1952), p. 36; A.N., Z¹B.61, Aug. 10, 1529, avis of the Généraux des Monnaies and letter of Aug. 10, 1529, of the Cardinal de Sens; Witte, *Histoire monétaire*, II, pp. 152–154, Rapport de Thomas Grammaye.

[48] The levies were authorized by the Assembly of Notables of December 1527 and by the Councils of Sens and Bourges for the Church. See François, *Cardinal de Tournon*, pp. 74–87. Commissions of control were set up in Paris, Rouen, Toulouse, Lyons, Tours, Bordeaux, and Bourges by the lettres patentes of Dec. 10, 1529. A.N., Z¹B.364. See also *Journal d'un bourgeois de Paris*, ed. Bourilly, p. 315.

[49] A.N., Z¹B.61, "Avis des Généraux des Monnaies baillé aux gens de l'"Empereur," in 1529; A.N., J. 971–972, "Mémoire . . . à Monseigneur le Révérendissime Légat Chancellier de France."

[50] A.N., Z¹B.364, letter of Oct. 22, 1530, from the mint master in Bordeaux to Gabriel Chicot.

official standards. An ordinance of July 6, 1531, prohibited these "defective" foreign coins and although mentioning silver testons "such as *marabais,*" the order was mostly concerned with gold coin: *écus à l'aigle,* écus from Avignon, Venice, Florence, and Genoa, as well as ducats *à la Mirandolle.*[51]

The gold was lost through the payment of the ransom, but the process of trade and the general inflation in Europe brought about a rapid recovery.[52] The market and official rates were adjusted by the important ordinance of March 5, 1533, which authorized (as a provisional measure) the raising of the rates for a series of coins.[53] The price of gold and silver at the mints remained unchanged in the hope, as ever, that there would eventually be a return to the former levels. The écu d'or au soleil was set at 45 sols and the teston d'argent at 10 sols and 6 deniers. In addition, the circulation of numerous coins from all over Europe was authorized: gold from Spain, Portugal, Italy, Flanders, England, and Hungary; silver testons from a number of countries. The latter were increased on April 2, by the silver *carolus* of Flanders, the *maille* of Hoorn, and the testoon of England.

French monetary policy reflected, in general, a demand for gold. Interest in the coast of Guinea revived, as Portuguese recriminations against French seamen showed.[54] And as the situation improved, the monetary system of France began to show the same symptoms of a quarter of a century before: a progressive disappearance of full-bodied silver, with an increase in billon from the small states on the frontiers of France. Thus in 1533 Bordeaux reported that silver money was difficult to find since the coins were disappearing in the direction of Navarre and Béarn. In return, other small coins, inferior to those of France, appeared in Aquitaine: the *vaches* of Béarn, for example, remained for some time in circulation. Coin-clippers, who added to the confusion, were denounced and threatened with the same penalties as counterfeiters in July 1536.[55] Yet official acts did not remedy the confusion. New sanctions were published against inferior currency coming from Béarn and Lausanne.[56] Counterfeit doubles from Flanders found currency in Bordeaux. In Lyons, even, these counterfeit coins appeared through the operations of a Toulouse

[51] A.N., Z¹B.61, ordonnance of July 6, 1531.

[52] The attraction of gold to France coincided with a gold devaluation in 1537 in Spain during the third war between Francis I and Charles V: the new escudo was coined at 22 karats. Hamilton, *American Treasure,* pp. 54–55. In Flanders *couronnes d'or au soleil* were ordered on October 29, 1540. Witte, *Histoire monétaire,* I, pp. 179–181; *Recueil des ordonnances des Pays Bas, 1536–1543,* ed. Jules Lameere (Brussels, 1914), in *Recueil des ordonnances des Pays Bas,* 2d Ser., *1506–1700,* ed. Charles Laurent, Jules Lameere, et al. (6 vols., Brussels, 1893–1922), IV.

[53] A.N., Z¹B.62, ordonnance of Mar. 5, 1533; A. Fontanon, *Les édicts et ordonnances des Roys de France* (2 vols., Paris, 1585), II, p. 92.

[54] A.M., Rouen, A.4., Jan. 22, 1539.

[55] A.N., Z¹B.364, commission of inquiry in Bordeaux, Aug. 8, 1533; letter of Mar. 24, 1534, from the gardes of the mint in Bordeaux to the Généraux des Monnaies in Paris; A.N., Z¹B.62, ordonnance of July 14, 1536.

[56] A.N., Z¹B.62, lettres patentes of Nov. 29, 1538.

merchant. Other defective money was reported from Piedmont; it was refused currency in August 16, 1532.[57]

Official prices, however, systematically disfavored coinage. The volume of issues for this period shows that the mints in Bayonne, Lyons, and Paris maintained a fair level of activity, but the others were generally in decline. Political policy had its effects, since fighting between Charles V and Francis I resumed again over the question of Milan. To finance this war (1536–1538) silver plate was converted into coin in Paris, Lyons, and Limoges, but this was of short duration. With the exception of Bayonne, which was more easily plied with gold, by 1538 coinage was at a low level. A letter from Bordeaux of November 5, 1538, drew attention to the flight of currency to Béarn and Navarre; foreign currency was also observed in Tours. In Paris the jewelers and goldsmiths pushed up the market price of silver, so it was said, to as much as 28 livres the marc.[58] Lyons reported In May 1540 that the silver testons were going abroad, attracted by prices well above the French levels. Another report showed that in November 1540 merchants brought testons to the fairs of Pézenas and Béziers, to pass them at rates above those officially allowed.[59]

The monetary system of France was once more out of line. From all sides came urgent requests for the monarchy to intervene, particularly from the mint in Lyons.[60] At first there were minor remedies: on January 14, 1540, the mints were given individually marked dies so that frauds could be more easily traced; on September 17, special rules were issued concerning mint masters; a few days earlier (September 11) measures were taken to check the outflow of bullion; a month later, the government ordered all goods in transit to be searched for the same purpose.[61]

Silver next began to have difficulties. The progressive disappearance of the high alloy testons led to a substitution of billon. On September 24, 1540, the general coinage of testons was stopped, and, although they continued to circulate as legal currency, the mints were authorized to melt them down for conversion into douzains. The mint master in Montpellier asked for a higher bullion price of 12 livres 10 sols the marc so that he could buy silver to make douzains.[62]

[57] *Ibid.*, Aug. 16, 1532; A.N., Z¹B.326, letter of Mar. 26, 1539, from the gardes in the mint in Bordeaux to the Généraux des Monnaies in Paris, which report in the city and neighborhood big and small alike were dealing in money changing.

[58] A.N. Z¹B.365, letter of July 12, 1539, from the gardes of the mint in Tours to the Généraux des Monnaies in Paris; A.N. Z¹B.62, fol. 81, avis from the Chambre des Monnaies to the King, 1538.

[59] A.M., Lyons, Ser. BB.58, fol. 72; A.N. Z¹B.365, letters of May 15, Aug. 5, 1540, and report of Nov. 13, 1540.

[60] A.M., Lyons, Ser. BB.58, fol. 90, report of the deputies sent to the court, Aug. 5, 1540.

[61] A.N., Z¹B.62, ordonnances of Jan. 14, 1540, and June 1540 (published Sept. 17, 1540); lettres patentes of Sept. 11, Nov. 15, 1540, in Fontanon, *Édicts et ordonnances,* II, p. 96.

[62] The douzains weighed 92 to the marc and had a fineness of 4 deniers 4 grains

The situation called for drastic remedies. After a series of conferences the extensive monetary reform of March 1541, designed both to readjust the currency and reform the mints, was passed. It was intentionally definitive, so much so that when it was found that the rates for douzains, liards, and deniers had been overlooked, it required another supplementary order of July 12, 1541, to give them legal currency. Its publication, however, was not warmly received, especially in the southwest, since it meant something of reversal of policy: the royal edict now favored silver. The rates for gold écu were left at the levels of 1533 while the teston was raised from 10 sols 6 deniers to 10 sols 8 deniers. The adjustment of the ratio between the two metals, in effect, approached more closely 1:12 and showed the desire to "equate silver to the price of the marc of fine gold." The marc of gold was put at 165 livres 7 sols 6 deniers and that of silver at 14 livres.[63] The edict attempted to control, in addition, the operations of money changers: in Paris their cashbooks and registers were subjected to monthly checks by the Chambre des Monnaies. Later, the work of goldsmiths, jewelers, and others working with precious metals was again regulated.[64]

Monetary difficulties over silver were particularly felt, but the results from changing the official bimetallic ratio were on a small scale. Conditions set by the new tariff of March 1541 were part of a wider movement in Europe: in the 1540s the great phase of gold came progressively to a close under the shadow of a war begun by France in 1542 and soon carried to Germany.

At that time, little by little, silver from America made its presence felt. As the imports increased, Spain and then Europe were relieved of the need to draw silver from Germany; this movement had doubtless started in the 1530s with the widespread difficulties in the German mines. In any case, after the ordinance of March 1541, silver currency appeared more frequently in southern France, which formerly had experienced shortages. A letter of November 5, 1541, sent from Paris to Bordeaux and Bayonne drew attention to the silver reals current there at 16 sols. More significant were the notarial acts in Bordeaux mentioning reals in private transactions;[65] although this detail carries some weight, it cannot be assumed beyond doubt that the reals arrived directly from Spain, because "Spanish reals" had been coined in Antwerp since 1516. It is even possible that these reals were of German origin, but circumstances tend not to confirm this.

---

argent-le-roi. A.N., Z¹B.62, ordonnance of Feb. 24, 1540; see also Fontanon, *Édicts et ordonnances,* II, pp. 97–107, ordonnance of Mar. 19, 1541, Article 9; and A.N. Z¹B.365, letter of Jan. 23, 1541, from Montpellier to Paris.

[63] A.N., Z¹B.62; Fontanon, *Édicts et ordonnances,* II, p. 97; A.N., Z¹B.365, letter of June 22, 1541, from Bordeaux to Paris. The mints were Paris, Lyons, Troyes, Rouen, La Rochelle, Bordeaux, Bayonne, Limoges, Toulouse, Montpellier, Angers, Tours, Nantes, Rennes, Dijon, Grenoble, and Marseilles; Poitiers and Turin were opened in 1541; Aix, Chambéry, Romans, Crémieu, and Montélimar in 1542.

[64] A.N., Z¹B.63, ordonnance of Feb. 15, 1542.

[65] *Ibid.,* letter of Nov. 5, 1541, from Généraux des Monnaies to Bordeaux and Bayonne.

The fourth war between Charles V and Francis I broke out in 1542. Francis I allied himself with the Duke of Cleves and with Suleiman the Magnificent. The combined fleets of France and Turkey attacked Nice; Charles V advanced as far as Soissons. The Turkish armies invaded Hungary and menaced Austria. As was logical, from the opening of hostilities the monetary struggle appeared on the northern frontier: between France and Flanders. The decade of the 1530s, when France had been more inclined to attract gold, had seen a decline in the coinage of gold in Flanders and Spain and a "shortage of circulating medium in gold . . . in Spain." As a remedy, Charles V ordered on December 10, 1541, that all bills of exchange should be paid two-thirds in gold. Was this necessary? In the beginning of 1542 the city of Burgos pleaded for the withdrawal of the measure "because the whole trade and traffic of this kingdom and of all the other nations trading in the said province of Flanders and Brabant cease completely on account of the fact that it entails too much cost and effort to raise the gold necessary for payments to conform with the said order." On May 31, Mary of Hungary, the regent of the Low Countries, announced to Charles V that there was an abundance of specie at the Easter fair, notably gold, "to which only those accustomed to trade in silver objected." [66] Between the mints in Paris and Antwerp, moreover, the change in direction was also fairly clearly marked: after 1543, Paris turned to silver while Antwerp became more concerned with gold. There were other signs of change, for example, the differences between the prices of gold and silver. In February 1542 the price of silver in France and the Low Countries was considerably different. In Flanders the legal price converted into French money came to 15 livres 15 sols tournois for the marc of fine silver, while the market rate came to about 16 livres 1 sol 3 deniers. On December 19, 1549, however, reports from Antwerp estimated that gold was worth 168 livres, and silver 15 livres 7 sols 2 deniers.[67] In this last war between Charles V and Francis I France was already beginning to attract silver.

As the lettres missives of July 25, 1543, showed, in France the war levies brought increasing amounts of billon into the tax collectors' hands. In order to avoid the difficulties and costs of transport, the government attempted to put larger quantities of heavier silver coin into circulation. The rate for the teston was raised to 11 sols. In addition, as the levies of war taxes also brought in considerable amounts of silver plate, the coinage of testons was renewed. In September 1542 the order was given to the mint in Paris "and nowhere else" to coin testons from the "large quantity of silver plate." By the order of Sep-

---

[66] *Recueil des ordonnances des Pays-Bas, 1536–1543,* ed. Lameere, pp. 338–339, cited by Federico Chabod, *Note e documenti per la storia economico-finanziera dell'Impero di Carlo V* (Padua, 1937), p. 5.

[67] *Ibid.* For the repercussions in Antwerp, see the report of Stephen Vaughan to the Council in London, Aug. 12, 1546, published in *Tudor Economic Documents,* ed. R. H. Tawney and Eileen Power (3 vols., London, 1924), II, p. 140; and A.N., Z¹B.64, Dec. 19, 1549, reply from Flanders to letter sent by Philippe de l'Aultier on the price of gold and silver.

tember 1543 further controls were put on goldsmiths and silversmiths. Gold ware was to be made at a fineness of 23 and 22 karats; any coin of 21 karats was to be seized and broken; and silverware was to be manufactured at the fineness of argent-le-roi.[68]

The coinage of testons was a further sign of the importance of silver. As the war between Francis I and Charles V worsened, the financial center, Lyons, found itself more and more concerned with filling the royal coffers. The mint there was given special permission to issue large quantities of silver testons. François Guilhen, the mint master of Lyons, when about to sign the contract, argued in favor of raising the mint prices of precious metals. With the authority of a man at the center of finance, he observed that silver in Germany was worth 14 livres 10 sols the marc and that the German "merchants and bankers," formerly accustomed to bring it to fairs in large quantities and at low prices to pay for goods and use in foreign exchanges, were now taking it to Antwerp where they could receive higher prices. No doubt this was the effect of imperial policy. In reply to Guilhen's proposals, the Conseil Privé agreed to raise the price of the marc of silver to 14 livres 10 sols.[69] On these conditions Guilhen accepted a contract (August 4, 1543) to coin 24,000 marcs of testons. Because of the war his monopoly did not last long, and permission to coin testons was extended to other mints.[70] He complained of these infractions, and on April 28, 1544, the minimum in his contract was reduced to 12,000 marcs. On October 31, 1545, the contract was increased by another 12,000 marcs, thus restoring its earlier level. Actually the contracts for testons were still given by preference to Lyons, where the mint was very active. On February 25, 1547, its mint master announced that he had agreements with some German merchants to deliver in the fair of Pentecost 300 marcs of refined silver from Germany; later (October 1, 1548) he received permission to issue a further lot of 1,000 marcs.[71]

The coinage of gold did not stop in Bayonne. In spite of the official prices set in 1541 which favored silver, the mints in this region continued to make gold currency, although at an ever slower rate. In the same way the mint in Villeneuve-lès-Avignon was reopened on August 2, 1543; in the following December it reported that its operations were largely concerned with the placer gold of the rivers of Cèze and Gardon.[72]

Circulation of silver in Europe in the 1540s was a complicated phenomenon, and France did not escape the general slowing down of the customary arbitrage of gold against silver. As a result of the weakening of these main currents,

---

[68] Fontanon, *Édicts et ordonnances,* II, p. 110, lettres missives of July 25, 1543; A.N., Z¹B.63, ordonnances of Sept. 20, 1542, Sept. 21, 1543.

[69] A.N., Z¹B.63, letter of July 25, 1543, to Guilhen.

[70] *Ibid.,* letter of Aug. 4, 1543, to Guilhen. The permission to coin testons was also extended to Limoges, Tours, Rennes, Paris, Bordeaux, Toulouse, La Rochelle, Marseilles, Nantes, and Rouen by lettres patentes of Oct. 24, 1543, Feb. 26, 27, 28, Mar. 18, May 7, 10, 16, 29, June 2, 11, July 9, 1544, July 5, 1546.

[71] *Ibid.,* letters of Apr. 28, Oct. 31, 1544, Feb. 25, 1547, Oct. 1, 1548.

[72] *Ibid.,* commission of inquiry of Dec. 3, 1543; and material in Chap. 4 on Bayonne.

France became more susceptible to the short-term exchange movements of its neighbors. A veritable invasion of foreign currency of all sorts and descriptions followed. In July and August 1541 there were complaints, largely from the north and east, about Flemish écus, gros from Lorraine, and *onzains* from Savoy. At this point, permission as legal tender was given in France to lighter écus weighing 2 deniers 14 grains and 2 deniers 15 grains; this, given at first for a year, became permanent by the order of March 6, 1542. This actually meant that clipped coins were accepted. Along this line, it was officially proposed on February 17, 1542, to accept the écus of Portugal, weighing at least 2 deniers 17 grains, of which numbers were also circulating in France. After June 3, 1542, the fractional coins of Italy similar to the douzains and liards of France began to penetrate "our province of Piedmont and neighboring regions." But these were forbidden currency. At this time proposals were made for a gold devaluation. Some suggested the issue of an écu of 22 karats, to be used to convert Spanish *pistoles* into French coin, but this was not supported by the Chambre des Monnaies which, on February 17, 1542, asserted, among other reasons, that French engravers were not sufficiently skilled to produce the dies for such coins.[73]

Foreign currency continued to invade the country. On March 22, 1544, écus of 22 karats from Castile, Sicily, Lucca, Geneva, and Genoa became forbidden currency. The war no doubt played a part in this, but the position of the French monarchy could not be maintained for long. Finally it succumbed on January 6, 1545, when it confirmed officially the rise in gold prices by authorizing the circulation of écus weighing 2 deniers 15 grains at the same rates as those weighing 2 deniers 16 grains. This amounted to a devaluation of the standard gold coin of France and regularized a situation where different types of gold currency circulated at "excessive" rates.[74]

These solutions did not mean that the outlook for silver in these years was any brighter. The heavier, more valuable, silver coins tended to be replaced by billon, especially in the frontier zones of the northeast. This was true of the silver carolus "recently coined in Besançon," noted by the ordinance of April 15, 1546, and of the silver *gros de Metz en Lorraine,* allowed to circulate in 1541, having a fineness of 10 deniers 18 grains and weighing 96 to the marc. The latter was declared illegal on September 20, 1543, when it came to weigh only between 104 and 105 to the marc at a fineness of 9 deniers 15 grains or 9 deniers 18 grains. Metz, it must be remembered, was at that time outside the frontiers of France, but it came to play an important role through its issues of small coins. Difficult harvest years and the general inflation also helped to undermine the official tariffs. The melting pot offered considerable profits from the more valuable coins. "Black" money became so much in evidence that on

---

[73] A.N., Z¹B.63, ordonnances of July 12, Aug. 2, Nov. 19, 1541; déclaration of Mar. 6, 1542; avis of the Généraux des Monnaies of Feb. 17, 1542.

[74] *Ibid.,* ordonnances of Mar. 22, 1544, Jan. 6, 1545; Fontanon, *Édicts et ordonnances,* II, p. 112, lettres patentes of Apr. 15, 1546.

July 8, 1546, the coinage of doubles and deniers was stopped. A further sign of the troubled times was the appointment of a commission of inquiry to investigate the coinage of deniers in Marseilles and Toulouse.[75]

The debasement of the coinage in England complicated the situation. At first it appeared to be a simple reply to the raising of silver prices in France, but then, by manipulating the currency, Henry VIII coined money of increasingly lower intrinsic content to bring profits to the royal coffers. Between 1542 and 1547 and, above all, from the beginning of 1544, the standard fineness of gold was lowered from 23 to 20 karats and of silver from 8.3 ounces to 4 ounces fine. This coincided with the disappearance of full-bodied silver coins in France. The silver of Central Europe, for example, seemed to be taking the road to Antwerp, a distribution center for the cloth of England. The last debasement in this series in England took place in 1551, which was when silver from America was beginning to make its presence felt. These debasements finally produced the inevitable effects of Gresham's law: quantities of English currency, largely silver but also some gold, found their way abroad to Antwerp, to Normandy, and to other provinces in France bordering on the Channel. In 1546 numbers of English coins were reported in this region of France. And almost in vain, it seemed, the circulation of new types of English coin — the gold rose nobles, for example — was forbidden.[76]

Gold now seemed to attract attention. An English observer, somewhat downcast by the situation, reported from Normandy, beginning in October 1550, that gold had disappeared from circulation. William Lane wrote to Cecil on January 18, 1551, after the devaluation in France, that the écu soleil was "carried away as all other gold is." He also stated that the excessive value put on silver coin north of the Channel was going "to rob England and carry away all the gold in the land into foreign realms, for that it is to a more profit than the exchange." [77]

This, at first, seemed only one more fluctuation in a series of monetary movements, but it soon had long-term repercussions in France. Silver was beginning to predominate in the exports of bullion from Spain; France could not fail to experience the change. The first consequences were masked to some extent perhaps by the presence of English gold coins. The Spanish silver may have had effects opposite to those required in France. On February 8, 1549, the order was given to issue the gold henri, a heavier coin than the écu although having the same fineness; it was made current at 50 sols. The rise in the price of gold and the clipping of gold écus were demonstrated in the ordinance of July 29;

[75] Fontanon, *Édicts et ordonnances*, II, p. 110, lettres patentes of Sept. 20, 1543; A.N., Z¹B.1011, repayment to Alexandre de Faulcon of Mar. 15, 1549.

[76] Sir Albert Feavearyear, *The Pound Sterling* (Oxford, 1931) pp. 47–66; A.N., Z¹B.63, ordonnance of Nov. 18, 1546.

[77] Calendar of State Papers [hereafter cited as C.S.P.], Foreign, letter of Oct. 21, 1550, from Sir John Masone to the Council in London; *Tudor Economic Documents,* ed. Tawney and Power, II, pp. 182–183, letter of Jan. 18, 1551, from William Lane to Cecil.

on this occasion the absence of any mention of silver was significant.[78] The attempt to issue a heavier gold coin at this juncture, when the trend ahead was already in the reverse direction, showed the uncertainty of the basic movements, even though the presence of English gold currency after the debasement in England may have disguised the situation.

In Bayonne the progressive decline in coinage after the great issues of gold currency indicated clearly that the new movement was beginning to take effect. The mint in Paris was making the smaller fractional money at an ever slower rate. The situation was further complicated by the closure of some mints by royal order in 1547.[79] Although their cases were reconsidered in 1548, the general collapse of the provincial mints in 1548 and 1549 coincided with major monetary changes. A complete end to the export of precious metals was ordered in August 1548, and lettres missives were sent on this subject to the governors, lieutenants generals, bailiffs, seneschals, and provosts. Harbor masters were promised a quota of the confiscations.[80]

In summary, then, the decade of the 1540s at first saw efforts to attract silver, but at its close there were growing preoccupations with gold. After 1548 and until the critical summer of 1554 France experienced increased pressure from silver in the south. It would be difficult, in view of the inherent disparity of France, to establish the exact turning point, even for such a sharp change as that in the mid-sixteenth century. The year 1550 has been taken as a convenient date since it was a year of devaluations and reforms of billon currency. If, however, war was the deciding factor in drawing bullion to the campaigns in the north,[81] then the year 1552 could be taken as the crucial moment. Abroad on the political scene that year was also dramatic, with the flight of Charles V from Innsbruck and with the winter siege of Metz. These years can also be considered as a further stage in the rivalry between the Hapsburgs and the Valois. Indeed, the invasion of France by the silver of the New World was promoted by the Emperor's struggle against the Very Christian King, never won, but then again, never entirely lost.

2. The Phase of Silver in France

During the period outlined in the section above, France seemed to play the role of an intermediary; it shared, consequently the activity of others. Some of its regions tended to favor silver; others were noticeably more open to gold. As a result, these years were marked by a mutual adjustment among the different regions in France.

After 1550, however, the trend was reversed, and the arrival of silver

---

[78] A.N., Z¹B.64, ordonnance of Feb. 8, 1549; Fontanon, *Édicts et ordonnances*, II, p. 114, ordonnance of July 29, 1549.

[79] A.N., Z¹B.63, lettres patentes of Sept. 3, 1548.

[80] *Ibid.*, lettres missives of Aug. 21, 1548, and ordonnance of Sept. 3, 1548.

[81] The currency rates were raised in Flanders on July 11, 1548. Witte, *Histoire monétaire*, II, p. 185.

brought something more than a reorientation. Both monetary and economic structures witnessed a profound change. New lines of expansion were determined, and here and there were signs of decline. Some aspects had a certain dramatic quality, for example, the rise to power and fortune of the maritime cities and their dependent regions in the west of France. As these complex changes became clearer, the traditional cities of medieval France tended to lose some of their importance. There was a crumbling away, more or less pronounced, along the network of routes which served them, the counterpart of the emergence of the Atlantic at the expense of continental and Mediterranean France.

The transformation of monetary structures of France had other consequences. During the preceding phase, the frontiers of France had been able to compose both zones of silver and zones of gold, within the general context of the monetary activity of Europe. With the arrival of silver from America, however, there was a shift of axis, a disharmony of one area with another outside this customary arrangement. In place of a fairly balanced France, there emerged a hierarchy of zones with different rates of growth: of prime importance, the maritime zones; of secondary importance, the provinces of the east. Here were the conditions of disequilibrium already noted; their importance is, in my opinion, considerable and extends well beyond the history of money itself.

In France this silver phase can be divided for convenience into three periods: 1550–1575, years of organization; 1575–1588, the time when the silver "inflation" had its more powerful effects; 1589–1609, the culminating point in the surge of silver.

After the disturbances of the 1540s Henry II attempted to reestablish order. The ordinance of January 14, 1550, fixed the number of mints in operation. Coinage of the écu was formally stopped, and that of the gold henri was begun. The rate for the écu itself was increased in face value to 46 sols and the teston to 11 sols 4 deniers. Because of these new rates, the mint prices for gold and silver bullion were raised, gold to 172 livres and silver at a minimum fineness of 10 deniers to 15 livres the marc. The anxiety to retain a bimetallic ratio close to 1:12 was shown in the use of a basic fineness of 10 deniers, rather than the usual 12 deniers. This devaluation of the French livre tournois also necessitated an increase in the rates for foreign coin circulating in France, from Spain, Italy, Flanders, England, Switzerland, Hungary, and Portugal, to name the more important currencies mentioned.[82] Attempts were made to improve the techniques of coinage. Finally, by the edict of January 1552, the Chambre des Monnaies became a sovereign court, the Cour des Monnaies.[83] All these measures coincided with the first signs of the new silver in France.

[82] A.N., Z¹B.64, *passim;* Fontanon, *Édicts et ordonnances,* II, pp. 115, 119.
[83] See Chap. 2, n. 80. After 1549 Marc Béchot and Pierre Milan were engraving dies.

The arrival of silver did not become clear until after the outbreak of war against Charles V in 1552. All Europe was experiencing the same movement in some measure. In France the mints began to coin testons without hindrance, aided by the silverware which war levies and taxes brought to the melting pot. For this reason the operations of the new mint in Paris, the Étuves, were particularly impressive. Requests for permission to coin testons also came, for example, from Villeneuve-lès-Avignon in 1550 and from Angers in 1551. In March 1553 the gardes of the mint in Bayonne, with the same purpose in mind, reported the seizure of a large quantity of silver from seamen in Saint Jean-de-Luz. The first testons in Bayonne were coined in 1553.[84] All these towns, from Villeneuve-lès-Avignon to Bayonne, were able to take advantage of the close proximity to Spain and its silver. But the situation was not the same everywhere. The mint of Moulins complained in 1554 about a general shortage of currency, which was partly due to the fact that merchants were not delivering locally mined silver to the mint. In Lyons in 1550, in contrast to the emerging conditions, the mint master reported that testons were scarce but that there were many silver Joachimstalers (coming probably from Germany) and gold scudi from Italy.[85]

During these years France was extending political pressures to the east and northeast. The bishoprics of Metz, Toul, and Verdun were occupied in 1552. The coinage of silver money at Vic, near Metz, was, in fact, concerned largely with converting French currency. Though the governor of Metz had ordered that only silver bullion from Germany or from the local mines should be used, on June 11, 1555, the mint master protested that it was impossible to conform to these regulations, since the price of silver in Germany had risen to equal 16 livres 13 sols 4 deniers when calculated in livres tournois. The governor, the Sieur de Vieilleville, stated that because the mines were only a day's distance from Vic, they ought to provide silver cheaper than that available in France. He was obviously unaware that Spain was becoming the center for silver.

With the first signs of silver, what happened to billon? As silver became more abundant, the relative price of copper also began to rise. These troubled years were not particularly advantageous to the small states, neighbors of France — Béarn, Navarre, Avignon, Piedmont, Geneva, Savoy, Besançon, Lorraine, Dombes. They unloaded a sizable quantity of billon in France at a time when its monetary system was disturbed. It is possible that during these years the more substantial coins were finding their way eastward or to the melting pot; in compensation, some billon currency found its way into France. In some of the frontier zones the billon was almost entirely of foreign origin.

---

[84] A.N., Z¹B.367, request from Villeneuve-lès-Avignon of Nov. 17, 1550; A.N., Z¹B.368, requests from Angers of Nov. 20, 1551, and letter of Mar. 9, 1552, from the gardes of the mint in Bayonne to the Cour des Monnaies.

[85] A.N., Z¹B.369, request of Apr. 1, 1554, from Moulins; A.N., Z¹B.367, letter of Feb. 11, 1550, from Guilhen to the Généraux des Monnaies in Paris; Fontanon, *Édicts et ordonnances,* **II,** p. 121.

On October 8, 1552, for example, the money from Geneva was prohibited. A report of December 2, 1552, from the mint of Franquemont showed how easy it was to manipulate inferior currency. Although these coins were forbidden circulation, they were observed again in Champagne in the town of Troyes, then again in the valley of the Rhône, in Lyons. The same debasement of fractional money took place at Vic, already mentioned, where the mint melted down French silver coins for conversion into gros of Metz and gold coins into florins.[86] Besançon also produced similar billon.

Eastern and northeastern France — the Paris basin, the duchy of Burgundy, Charolais, Auxerrois, Bresse (then under French occupation), Mâconnais, Bar-sur-Seine — were particularly concerned with this type of currency. In these regions, the coins with a face value of less than 3 sols, which in France generally had been depreciated by the order of July 27, 1555, were given currency for a further period of six months. This recurrence of billon was no doubt inevitable since it implied the absence of sufficient full-bodied currency. The same situation, however, reappeared to some extent in southwestern France, where on the request of the King of Béarn the fractional currency of Béarn was allowed to circulate for a further period of six months in the cities of Toulouse and Bordeaux and in the provinces of Agenais, Perigord, and Quercy. Again later (July 24, 1557) douzains and liards were continued in circulation for it was difficult to find substitutes.

The situation had to wait for the reinforcements of silver from the New World before a full reform could be effected. Henry II had been concerned with the problem of billon and, by the ordinance of January 23, 1550, prohibited the currency of *treizains,* douzains, and dixains. This was the negative side of cleaning up the monetary circulation. An earlier ordinance of January 14, 1550, proposed to issue douzains "of a new type" weighing 94 to the marc. On March 2 the mint master of Lyons protested against this on the grounds that at the going rates it was impossible to mint such coins. And so the new coins were set at 93½ to the marc. The older types, depreciated on January 23, were to be handed in at the mints. Because billon was the coin of the poor, who stood to lose in the process, the whole operation of conversion presented some difficulty. City authorities in Rouen were, in fact, obliged to put money changers under official surveillance during the operations.[87]

In order to cope with this huge conversion, a new mint, the Hôtel de Nesle,

---

[86] A.N., Z'B.369, ordonnance of June 6, 1555; avis du roi of June 22, 1555; procès-verbal of Dec. 2, 1554; procès-verbal in Grenoble of July 2, 1555. For German silver, see also A. Chamberland, "Le commerce d'importation en France au milieu du XVIe siècle," *Revue de géographie,* XXXI (1892), p. 226; A.N., Z'B.64, ordonnance of Oct. 8, 1552.

[87] A.N., Z'B.64, lettres patentes of Jan. 23, 1550, Sept. 5, 1555; A.N., Z'B.65, lettres missives of Feb. 1, Apr. 18, 1556, July 24, 1557. In Rouen on May 8, 1550, the municipal authorities ordered the sale of 20 *muids* of wheat "to be sold bushel by bushel . . . under instruction not to take billon." A.M., Rouen, *Journal des Échevins,* 1, and A.16, délibération of Feb. 27, 1550.

was opened in Paris on March 25, 1550, for the coinage of *doubles sols parisis.* This particular mint operated for only two years in Paris and was then replaced by the Étuves, established by the letters patent of January 27, 1552. The terms "Nesle," "Étuves," and "Moulin" were, however, used without great discrimination. By the end of the year only single sols parisis were coined, a further sign that the heavy pieces of billon were unsuitable for circulation. It has often been thought that the *gros de Nesle* was a prime cause of inflation, but a distinction must be drawn between the doubles sols parisis coined in Paris in the 1550s and the coins of the same name but of different weights and fineness struck at first after 1564 and then again during the troubled years of the League. The important thing to note is that these gros de Nesle were not the coins required at the beginning of the silver phase in France. As a high-grade type of billon in circulation, the sols parisis had a silver content of 4 deniers and were coined at 41 to the marc. The devaluation of the money of account meant that their intrinsic value soon exceeded the face value of 2 sols 6 deniers and 1 sol 3 deniers (for the double and single sol). Indeed, the reports of the royal commissioners who toured France in 1556 rarely mentioned the gros de Nesle, which was in itself significant. In the spiral of inflation they soon passed to the melting pot. Fifteen years later Bodin commented on their disappearance from circulation.[88]

The reform and conversion of inferior coins into douzains (and into sols parisis in Paris) were carried on in fifteen towns. Paris provided the largest contribution; then came Lyons, Rennes, Poitiers, La Rochelle, Limoges, and Tours. The shares of Bourges, Aix, Bayonne, and Villeneuve-lès-Avignon were relatively small. In 1556 the commission of inquiry revealed that the tax collectors received huge quantities of billon, probably douzains, in settlement of taxes; the least desirable type of money was, of course, given in payment. As a result, the monarchy was anxious to settle the matter of billon, if only to recoup the losses it suffered in revenue.

Operations of credit were involved in these reforms. The "merchants" of Paris themselves were not apparently in a position to finance the whole conversion of billon, but "some bankers" were prepared to put up the capital at 8 percent interest, on condition that the Hôtel de Nesle worked for them alone. They proposed to buy the existing specie by weight, which probably involved a loss for the monarchy. The avis of June 20, 1550, even suggested that the low-grade metal should be sold to England where the standard was even lower. Another suggestion was to raise a loan with the "bankers" of Lyons at the rate of 4 percent for the fair (that is, at 16 percent per year). A further scheme proposed to raise the money by issuing rentes on the *Hôtel*

---

[88] Fontanon, *Édicts et ordonnances,* I, pp. 122–123; A.N., Z'B.64, lettres patentes of Dec. 9, 1550; see also Jean Bodin, *Les Six livres de la république de I. Bodin, Angevin* (Paris, 1583) [hereafter cited as *République*], VI, p. 932, and in particular his remarks on Jacques Pinatel.

de Ville in Paris; this solution was finally chosen as the most appropriate.[89]

All these proposals did not produce a complete answer to the difficulties of the monetary system. In June 1550 it was necessary to prolong the circulation of douzains and treizains by a period of four months. On June 2 the tax collectors were authorized to receive these coins, without being obliged to accept more than a sixth of the total payment made. There were further prolongations: on September 5, so long as the coins were not clipped or worn; on October 11, another delay to December 31, 1550. By July 1551 a report from Lyons showed that almost all the coins of these denominations were below the statutory weights.[90]

On December 5, 1552, the coinage of all billon — liards, doubles, and deniers — was stopped, since it was considered (by order of January 22, 1553) that this currency was responsible for the disappearance of full-bodied gold and silver coins. In June 1556 Lyons complained again of the deterioration of douzains. On March 3, 1558, it was ordered that all light or clipped coins be delivered to the nearest mint. There were even reports in Scotland, as on August 29, 1559, that "clipped and rowngeit sous" had been sent from France to pay the newly arrived garrison.[91]

While these incidents were occurring, the position of billon in the currency began to recede. In the guise of billon, copper had managed to play a larger role in the period of undecided flows of bullion. After 1550, however, the arrivals of silver from the New World made it progressively unnecessary to the monetary circulation, while the continued depreciation of the livre tournois meant that a part of the billon inevitably disappeared into the melting pot.

The increasing amounts of silver in the circulation also affected the position of gold. During the early sixteenth century, demand made silver convenient for hoarding. The documents repeatedly refer to the melting down of silver plate in times of particular urgency. And this state of affairs was augmented by the particular efforts made in France during the 1540s to attract silver into the country. When the basic structures changed abruptly in the middle of the sixteenth century, the monetary system of France was ill prepared, indeed, almost off balance. After 1550 there was no doubt some dishoarding of silver, and the gold hunger increased appreciably. Although the official response to the new state of affairs was slow, that in financial quarters was, by contrast, quick. In Lyons the merchants "who were solely engaged in exchange and deposit transactions" since 1551 required two-thirds of all settlements in gold.[92]

[89] A.N., Z¹B.367, June 20, 1550. "Moiene mys en avant en la Chambre des Monnoyes du Roy notre seigneur pour le convertissement du billon provenant des finances dudit sieur."

[90] A.N., Z¹B.64, ordonnances of June 2, 9, Sept. 5, Oct. 11, 1550; A.M., Lyons, Ser. BB.72, fol. 52, délibération of July 2, 1551.

[91] A.N., Z.¹B.64, lettres patentes of Dec. 5, 1552 and lettres missives of the Cour des Monnaies of Jan. 22, 1553; A.N., Z¹B.65, ordonnance of Mar. 3, 1558; A.N., Z¹B.370, arrêt of Mar. 27, 1557; C.S.P., Foreign, Aug. 29, 1559.

[92] *"Memoyres faicts par les marchans de la ville de Lyon contre l'accord et articles*

A rise in the current market price of gold further indicates the growing demand for it. By the edict of January 1550 the rate of the écu soleil was raised from 45 to 46 sols. On June 5, when an order was made that this new rate should be strictly followed, it was also mentioned that higher rates were being quoted for Spanish pistoles and English rose nobles and angels. Gold prices thus continued to move upward in spite of royal commands, but, in reality, the monarchy was not free to act. Policies of stability and deflation vanished before the financial demands of war. In March 1552, when Henry II invaded Germany, there was the equivalent of a debasement. From this year, and only in Paris, a lighter écu was coined in the Hôtel des Étuves, at 23 karats, and 72½ to the marc. This was officially current at 46 sols, the same rate as the customary écu soleil weighing 71⅙ to the marc.[93]

Another sign of wartime problems was that the crown wanted to collect its taxes in full-bodied coins; it thus ordered registers to be kept of the types of coins received in payment. The legal currency rates were republished in April 1553, but clearly regulations were not observed. A year later (March 24, 1554) the Cour des Monnaies complained to the King that he had given permission for the écu to go for 47 sols in payments to the Swiss mercenaries, when the legal rate was still only 46 sols. In May of the same year the order was given in Paris to resist the general tendency of currency prices to rise, but this was in vain. On July 5, 1554, in order to raise 75,000 livres tournois in rentes in Paris, Henry II increased the rates for foreign gold: ducats, double ducats, and pistolets (the latter fixed at 45 sols). The same maneuver was followed on March 29, 1555, in order to raise 180,000 livres tournois of rentes. The Cour des Monnaies protested in vain. In September it required a proclamation to dispel the rumor that the government was even considering putting the écu at 48 sols.[94]

The prelude to the financial crisis of 1557 in France was thus marked by a prolonged flight of gold. According to some commercial observers, the gold currency was leaving for Spain and then going to Genoa, in order, curiously enough, to settle imperial debts in the war against France.[95] This dramatic war in the 1550s covered the reversal of monetary movements and aggravated their effects. The French monarchy wavered between its desire to maintain

---

faictz par les banquiers marchans estrangiers" (1551), published by Marc Brésard, in *Les foires de Lyon aux XVe et XVIe siècles* (Paris, 1914), *pièce justificative* 18; Chabod, *Note e documenti*, p. 5.

[93] A.N., Z¹B.64, ordonnances of June 5, 1551, Jan. 29, 1552, and Apr. 19, 1553; A.N., Z¹B.368, déclaration of Feb. 4, 1551, and letter of Apr. 18, 1553, from the Cour des Monnaies to Tourette; A.N., Z¹B.369, request of Feb. 28, 1554, from Poitiers.

[94] A.N., Z¹B.64, ordonnance of Apr. 11, 1553; lettres patentes of May 12, July 5, 1554, Mar. 29, 1555; letter of Apr. 17, 1555, from the Cour des Monnaies to the Connétable and royal déclaration of Sept. 3, 1555; A.N., Z¹B.369, letter of Mar. 27, 1554, from the Généraux des Monnaies to the Garde des Sceaux.

[95] In the same way, Thomas Gresham found it easier to send money to England in French and imperial gold crowns. C.S.P., Foreign, letters of Jan. 8, 13, 1554, to the Council in London.

currency rates and an inflationary policy of extending credit to finance the war.

With the purpose of maintaining order, commissions of inquiry were established to tour the provinces. Their combined reports, perhaps the only collective document of the time, gave a full review of the regional monetary conditions in France, at the turning point in the middle of the century.

The principal fact which emerged from their investigations was the disappearance of gold currency in France; it astonished all observers. It was particularly clear in the collection of taxes, and this dismayed the crown as it grappled with a costly war. These events formed part of the royal insolvency of 1557.

One of the inquiries began in Lyons in the summer of 1556. There were, inevitably, questions relating to money changers and to the mint, where the huge coinage of 1556 had been entirely composed of silver, mainly testons.[96] The mint master complained of the impossibility of coining gold; for silver he had to rely on Spanish reals which merchants brought in large quantities. On the matter of rising gold prices, it was observed in Lyons that gold was rated at one or two sols more in the Paris area, and it was thought that the inflation came largely from the direction of Rouen and Paris.[97] No doubt Lyons could have drawn on some supplies of bullion from the adjacent areas, the Rhône Valley and the Midi, but unfortunately, most of the mints near Lyons were inactive. In Montélimar there was complete inactivity; in Romans no issues had been made since the mint officially overshadowed its operations. While the mint master in Lyons exerted himself to meet the royal demands for currency, the mint in Avignon deliberately played the situation to its advantage, issuing lighter gold coins of 22 karats under the stamp of Julius III and Alexander Farnese, valued in March 1556 at 46 sols.[98]

Piedmont provided a more revealing investigation. At the entrance to Italy and closely tied to the affairs of Genoa, Piedmont played the role of a buffer state, and intermediary. By May 1556 écus, that were below the required standards — those of the Val d'Aosta, for example — had already been forbidden currency.[99] Payments for the war also offered considerable opportunities for fraud, as the activities of François de Chalvet revealed. By the contract of November 23, 1554, the King had appointed him as treasurer "of the extraordinary expenditures of his wars in Piedmont and Italy, Corsica and other places" for the year 1555. The money for the war was to be paid to Albisse Del Bene by deposit in Lyons for transfer to Italy by bill of exchange either on Venice or Ferrara. The monarchy feared that under cover of these arrangements there would be further loss of gold, and so it was stipulated that Chalvet should not convert any of the levies into gold, unless

---

[96] A.N., Z¹B.276, fol. 82ᵛᵒ, inquiry in Lyons on June 12, 1556.

[97] *Ibid.,* fols. 79ᵛᵒ, 139ᵛᵒ; A.N., Z¹B.369, June 29, 1556.

[98] A.N., Z¹B.64, lettres patentes of Oct. 4, 1550; A.N., Z¹B.65, lettres patentes of July 24, 1557, and ordonnance of Mar. 27, 1556; A.N., Z¹B.369, 1556 request to the Cour des Monnaies.

[99] A.N., Z¹B.65, ordonnance of May 23, 1556.

they were of foreign origin. Chalvet, on the other hand, received authority to lay out sums up to 60,000 livres tournois, quoting the silver real at 4 sols 6 deniers and the écu at 48 sols. The official rate of the latter in France was 46 sols. In spite of these relatively simple instructions, the commission of inquiry found that payments had reached 2,000,000 livres tournois, without including the expense of more complicated exchange operations.[100] Moreover, they found at Chambéry that, under cover of the transactions, merchants trading with Geneva and the Val d'Aosta were unloading depreciated currency in France.[101]

The inquiries in Italy by the commissioners Tourette and Espiard brought to light the huge speculation in foreign exchange. The opportunities for arbitrage, when dealing in Spanish silver reals in Italy, were at the root of the matter. In Milan, for example, then under Spanish dominion, the last monetary ordinance had been issued on October 8, 1549, with a revision on September 3, 1554. Between the dates 1549 (for the ordinance in Milan) and 1556 (for the inquiry into the scandal of French war finances) came the reversal in monetary trends. In Milan, the monetary situation was further complicated by the luxury trades using precious metals, such as gold leaf, to make gold and silver cloth and other products. According to one estimate, about 40,000 persons were employed in these trades; even allowing for exaggeration, the industrial capacity was still relatively high. Under such conditions it was noticed that although silver prices remained more or less in line with the regulations, those of gold spiraled upward. Milan indeed was a great commercial center, and the merchants of Casale, then under French control, often complained of the losses of silver which their dealings in Milan entailed.[102] Similar conditions prevailed in Genoa. Observers reported huge arrivals of silver and a demand for gold even more persistent than that in France.

At this juncture, Piedmont held a key position for France: the war against Milan made it a French stronghold. French gold specie was acceptable particularly since the French écu soleil had a consistently higher degree of fineness, so it was said, than almost any similar coin in Europe — Germany, Flanders, Portugal, Spain, or England. Piedmont, moreover, was open to the inflation of Spanish reals, from the nearest relay point, Milan. The French finance officers had fixed the real at 4 sols 6 deniers, but in Milan and Genoa it was current for the cheaper rate of 4 sols 3 deniers when converted into livres tournois. In Piedmont the écu soleil was valued at 48 sols, but in August 1556 in Genoa, the écu, in terms of livres tournois, was current at

---

[100] A.N., Z¹B.265, fols. 309ᵛᵒ, 313, 345ᵛᵒ. Michel François *Albisse Del Bene* (Paris, 1934), pp. 16, 23, has shown that the payments by Albisse Del Bene in 1552–1555 amounted to 6,831,953 livres tournois.

[101] A.N., Z¹B.265, fol. 226, report of the commissioners A. de la Tourette and M. Espiard of July 30, 1556.

[102] *Ibid.*, fol. 251ᵛᵒ, inquiry in Milan; fol. 234, inquiries in Turin and Casale.

49 sols and the silver real at 4 sols 4 deniers.[103] In Turin during the same month the silver real circulated officially at 4 sols 6 deniers, and the écu soleil at 52 sols, but the market generally was prepared to accept the écu at 51 sols. Reals, because of their abundance, were current at rates lower than in Lyons, Milan, or Genoa. They arrived in considerable quantities from Milan, via Genoa and sometimes from France. A year earlier the mass of reals transferred from France to Piedmont had been estimated at some 4,000,-000 to 5,000,000 livres tournois. And it was said that the merchants, like the treasurers, paid out only in reals; thus the operations were accompanied by a regular loss of gold from France.[104]

François de Chalvet, the treasurer, claimed that he received Spanish reals "by information from bankers," but the commissioners, for their part, inferred that through his exchange operations the Spaniards managed to transfer gold écus from France to Italy, and the Emperor paid a large part of his debts in this coin. The fact was evident enough, they declared: a letter of August 1555, on the subject of the exchange rates allowed the treasurer, asserted that French gold écus were being transferred to Spain while the silver reals went to Italy and were even being paid to the French army. In order to terminate these transactions the lieutenant general revised the rates in September 1556: écus at 51 and 52 sols and reals at 4 sols 6 deniers. After the inquiry, however, the commissioner, De la Tourette, suggested 4 sols 3 deniers for the reals (the rate at which they passed in Genoa and Milan) and 48 sols for the écu.[105]

Another commission of inquiry in 1556 investigated the south of France, centered on Montpellier. There the mint master revealed the absence of gold coinage and complained that the placer gold from the local rivers found its way to Lyons and Avignon. At Alès, in August 1556, the commissioners tried to ensure that this gold dust was converted into coin. At Saint-Ambroix they fined Pierre de Joufresques 15 livres for fraud. At Anduze they ordered the gold washed from the rivers Cèze and Gardon to be sent to Montpellier; there, the register of "purchases" showed that during the first seven months of 1556 the mint had produced some 26 marcs of gold (the greater part "placer gold") against 37 marcs of silver and 5 marcs 6 ounces of fractional money.[106]

In the total payment at Clermont, of 2000 livres tournois of taxes, only 49 gold écus soleil had been received, the remainder being silver and billon

---

[103] *Ibid.,* fol. 457ᵛᵒ; fols. 234, 240, inquiry in Turin of Aug. 7, 8, 1556; fol. 262ᵛᵒ, inquiry in Genoa of Aug. 19, 1556; fol. 347, report of Sept. 11, 1556, from Turin.

[104] *Ibid.,* fols. 347ᵛᵒ, 349ᵛᵒ, 361ᵛᵒ, report of Sept. 11, 1556, from Turin.

[105] *Ibid.,* fols. 350ᵛᵒ, 351ᵛᵒ, report of Sept. 11, 1556, from Turin; fol. 332, report of Sept. 9, 1556; fol. 454, letter of Oct. 5, 1556, from Tourette (in Valence) to the King.

[106] *Ibid.,* fol. 207ᵛᵒ, inquiry in Nîmes of July 24, 1556; fol. 323, inquiry in Saint-Ambroix of Aug. 29, 1556; fol. 331, inquiry in Alès of Aug. 27, 1556; fol. 332ᵛᵒ, inquiry in Anduze of Aug. 28, 1556; fol. 239ᵛᵒ, in Montpellier of July 31, 1556; A.N., Z¹B.369, registre des achapts of the mint in Montpellier.

"with a quantity of double and single reals and several douzains." The same state of affairs was noted at Riom, where only 28 gold coins were received in the tax receipts out of a total of 9000 livres. The mint master reported that it was more and more difficult to obtain silver from the local mines. It was considered appropriate to open the mint at Villefranche to deal with local silver, but, even though it was in good supply, the price on the open market put it out of reach of the mint.[107]

As the commissioners went up the valley of the Rhône, they noticed progressively fewer payments in Spanish reals, and even less in gold. Along the Saône, only small quantities of full-bodied currency found their way into the official coffers; by far the greater part of the currency received was billon. In Beaune the mayor, aldermen, "and the people of the Third Estate of the town" felt that the écu could easily be set at 48 sols, and this in agreement with other local bodies. The problem of gold in Dijon was much the same: no gold and little silver arrived from the local mines during the year 1555, while up to April 1556 few écus had been received. The region used the money of Franche-Comté and Besançon, which according to the merchants of Dijon, was indispensable for trade.[108]

The tax collectors in Troyes had received some 70,000 livres up to May 1556; among them they found a mere dozen gold coins, some testons, and no Spanish reals, but an abundance of billon. It was always possible that some of the testons had been converted from reals, but even these were of negligible importance. Such a situation apparently put the city on the fringe of the new tendencies spreading from the west and south of France.[109]

In Provins in May 1556 the tax collectors similarly reported minute quantities of gold: only 40 écus for the whole tax year, a small quantity of silver, and the rest in douzains.[110] Like conditions were found in Moulins where the taxes had brought only small amounts of full-bodied gold or silver coins into the royal coffers.

On the Atlantic coast of France (from Rouen to Bayonne) the different ports and their hinterlands were directly open to the silver money of Spain. Gold was in growing demand. In Rouen in February 1554 a goldsmith, François Halle, was accused of having clipped gold pistoles in his possession.[111] The écu in Amboise passed everywhere for 48 sols, but the lieutenant general received no complaints. There were similar difficulties in Saintes over gold, as well as over billon arriving from Béarn, while in Melle the small local

---

[107] A.N., Z¹B.270, fols. 148, 152ᵛᵒ, inquiry in Clermont of May 30, 1556; fol. 121ᵛᵒ, inquiry in Riom of May 27, 1556; fol. 612, inquiry in Villefranche of Sept. 29, 1556.

[108] A.N., Z¹B.265, fol. 126ᵛᵒ, inquiry in Beaune; fol. 156, inquiry in Mâcon of June 17, 1556; fol. 75ᵛᵒ, inquiry in Dijon of May 28, 1556.

[109] *Ibid.*, fol. 22ᵛᵒ, inquiry in Troyes of May 9, 1556.

[110] *Ibid.*, fol. 16ᵛᵒ, inquiry in Provins of May 5, 1556; A.N., Z¹B.270, fol. 82ᵛᵒ, inquiry in Moulins of May 20, 1556.

[111] A.N., A¹B.369, letter of Feb. 14, 1554, from the Généraux des Monnaies (destination not indicated).

silver mines had stopped working. In Poitiers the royal taxes were paid mostly in testons and reals, but very little in gold. In Châteaurenault the écu was current at 47, 48, and then 50 sols tournois. The same conditions existed in other cities: Orléans, Blois, Étampes. It may be said in conclusion that gold currency had practically disappeared from tax payments.[112]

The mint in Bayonne was closed in 1555, but in 1556 there were requests that it should be reopened; otherwise, it was claimed, bullion would find its way to Pamplona, which seemed likely, for two ships had been captured at Saint-Jean-de-Luz, almost fully laden with silver. La Rochelle also requested the reopening of its mint. In Toulouse the money in circulation consisted largely of billon from Béarn and Navarre; apart from douzains and liards, there was nothing worth reporting. The situation was such that the local authorities did not dare publish the royal edict forbidding these coins to circulate for fear of a popular riot. The full-bodied coins disappeared more and more from circulation, "through information from several persons who have dealings and financial operations in it." At the same time, the port master of Toulouse arrested several Portuguese merchants who were carrying out gold écus. A report on this matter, written in Lyons, revealed a whole network of exchanges and secret transfers. The flight of gold was apparently related to the abundance of billon.[113]

During the 1550s, therefore, silver was everywhere, notably in the big cities and financial centers. The presence of full-bodied silver coins was evidence of direct contact with Spain, as in the case of Lyons, where the fairs brought this currency in abundance. This situation reached a critical point in the quarterly "payments" of March 1557, after the royal bankruptcy. On April 22, 1557, the exchange brokers representing the Florentine and Luchese bankers declared that during the preceding three or four weeks the conversion of silver reals into money of account could only be made at a charge of 3 percent.[114]

The year 1557, which was financially disastrous for France, culminated in the collapse of royal credit, when the finances of Charles V crashed. These bankruptcies prepared the way for the Peace of Cateau-Cambrésis. The war with the Emperor that began in 1552 quickly disrupted the financial system in France, just as it broke down the imperial system in the Low Countries. And all the specie sent from Spain, both officially and secretly, was in vain.[115]

[112] A.N., Z¹B.270, fols. 40, 51, inquiry in Bourges of May 9–12, 1556; A.N., Z¹B.269, fol. 52, inquiry in Orléans of Aug. 27; fol. 39ᵛᵒ, inquiry in Étampes; fol. 126ᵛᵒ, inquiry in Blois of Aug. 30; fol. 142ᵛᵒ, inquiry in Amboise of Sept. 2; fol. 172ᵛᵒ, inquiry in Châteaurenault of Sept. 5; fols. 177, 188, inquiry in Châteauroux of Sept. 7; fols. 228, 361, inquiry in Melle and Poitiers of Oct. 9; fol. 626, inquiry in Saintes of Nov. 21, 1556.
[113] A.N., Z¹B.266, fol. 6; A.N., Z¹B.267, fol. 80ᵛᵒ, inquiry in Lyons of June 12, 1556; A.N., Z¹B.269, fol. 483, inquiry in Bayonne of Nov. 7, 1556; fols. 637ᵛᵒ, 682, 686ᵛᵒ, inquiries in La Rochelle of Nov. 26, Dec. 1, 1556; A.N., Z¹B.270, fols. 247ᵛᵒ, 249ᵛᵒ, 309ᵛᵒ, 519ᵛᵒ, inquiries in Toulouse of July 3, 12, Sept. 3, 1556.
[114] A.D., Rhône, Ser. 3E, 4497, Apr. 22, 1557.
[115] Ehrenberg, *Das Zeitalter der Fugger*, I, pp. 152–155; C.S.P., Spanish, letters of Sept. 13, Dec. 30, 1552, from the Queen Mother to Charles V; and of Jan. 29, 1554, from Francisco de Aresto to Juan Vásquez de Molina.

The monetary movements were thus marked by the flow of silver through France and were complicated by the war. Speculation in foreign exchanges was part of this network of transactions, the repercussions of which were sharply felt on the financial markets of Lyons and Antwerp. For France the war in Germany meant a series of public and private bankruptcies which became increasingly frequent from the summer of 1554.[116] Issues from the mints began to decline in this year and continued into 1555. Though this growing monetary crisis affected the richest cities in France, at the same time the mints in ports such as Bayonne and La Rochelle appeared better placed to stand the strain.

The flight of gold from France was part of the growing extension and instability of public credit. During the war years this instability expanded under the combined pressure of royal finance and the disruption of the customary circuits of bullion in international payments. The crisis of 1557 arose not merely because the French monarchy refused to honor the interest payments on its debts; it was also the outcome of the difficulties which the merchants and financiers experienced in adjusting to new monetary structures in the international economy. The financial markets were obliged to exercise prudence, to withdraw from unsatisfactory credit positions rather than add, as in earlier years, new loans to those already contracted. Thus the establishment of the phase of silver in France was accomplished in an atmosphere of crisis and tension. The second phase of this movement resulted in a sort of equilibrium between the consolidation and funding of the royal debts, on the one hand, and the settlement in the demand for gold, on the other.[117]

It may not be too much of an exaggeration to suggest, that up to 1557 the monetary system of France was the first in Europe to experience the full effects of the "silver crisis." This was no doubt due to the proximity to Spain and its silver. In order to find monetary equilibrium, France was obliged to recover gold. The foreign exchange position of the écu soleil reflected the demand of the French market. Thus in 1553 and 1554 the English agent in Antwerp had offered to send large sums in French écus soleil from Antwerp to England. Five years later, in London, however, the purchase of French écus soleil for use in the war against Scotland presented considerable difficulties.[118] The comparison of these two incidents serves to stress the changes in the circulation of gold

---

[116] Roger Doucet, "Le Grand Parti de Lyon au XVIᵉ siècle," *Revue historique,* CLXXI–CLXXII (1933); Ramón Carande, *El crédito de Castilla en el precio de la política imperial* (Madrid, 1949), p. 66. Gresham reported the purchase of gold by Germans in Antwerp, C.S.P., Foreign, letter of Nov. 18, 1553, to the Council in London; Public Record Office, State Papers [hereafter cited as P.R.O., S.P.], E.101/324/27, Investigation before the Audencia in Seville, May 4, 1558; *Third Report of the Royal Commission of Historical MSS.,* Appendix (London, 1872), p. 37, cited by F. J. Fisher, "Commercial Trends and Government Policy in Sixteenth-Century England," *Economic History Review,* X (1940).

[117] See, for example, A.D., Rhône, Ser. 3E, 4497, Apr. 1, 1557.

[118] C.S.P., Foreign, letters of Jan. 13, 1554, from Gresham to the Council in London; Oct. 6, 1559, from Cecil to Sir Ralph Sadler.

in France: relatively easy in 1553–1554, but difficult in 1559. Was there a solution to the problem of gold?

One result of the rise in gold prices was to divert attention to Portugal. Breton seamen sailing between Lisbon and France returned with silver reals, as the Spanish observers noted in January 1554. By December 1559 they were also returning with gold coin, the most frequent cargo from Lisbon, according to the French ambassador, Jean Nicot. Because these gold coins offered such opportunities for profit, the merchants of Antwerp were also active in the market after 1560. Juan Lopez de Gallo, for example, bought up all the gold he could for transfer to France.[119] A further solution to France's demand for gold can be seen in the expeditions to the coast of Guinea in spite of Portuguese opposition.[120]

Thus there were two simultaneous movements in France: a long-term inflation of the monetary system with silver; and a shorter cycle to redress the balance of gold. These two movements were not in opposition, but were, rather, complementary. Silver was more in evidence toward the south, but gold was apparently more available in the north. From the documentation of the mints seems to indicate that a greater degree of convergence between north and south prevailed once the Low Countries and Flanders began to be submerged with silver.

The restoration of this monetary equilibrium was no doubt partly due to the flows of moneys from abroad — established in 1556 when the order was given for foreign currency to be reassessed every three months.[121] Foreign merchants anxious to buy silver (although the situation was not the same for the whole of Europe) were perhaps also prepared through the mechanism of trade to offer gold in return. This complex movement was also aided by foreign exchange in which the different currencies were adjusted under cover of quotations in gold. In Languedoc and Gascony on February 27, 1560, German and Italian merchants were reported to be trading from fair to fair buying up silver reals with depreciated gold coins. Such exchanges offered profits of about 3½ to 4 percent.[122] The injunctions against the defective gold coins from Spain and Portugal (as in March 1561 and again in May 1563) were particularly severe in the case of the 10 ducat piece, the *peso,* known in France as the *portugaise.* This suggests that foreign coin was not shut out merely by the official prohibition of the coins in question. An inquiry at Lyons in May 1561 revealed a group of

---

[119] See Chap. 1, n. 99; Jean Nicot, *Sa correspondance diplomatique,* ed. Edmond Falgairolle (Paris, 1897), pp. 41–46, letter of Dec. 12, 1559; C.S.P., Spanish, letter of Jan. 29, 1554, from Francisco de Aresto (Antwerp) to Vásquez de Molina; C.S.P., Foreign, letter of Feb. 25, 1560, from Gresham to Cecil in London. See also Witte, *Histoire monétaire,* II, p. 230.

[120] There was, for example, the expedition led by the famous "Salamandre." C.S.P., Foreign, letter of Dec. 12, 1559, from Francis Edwards to Cecil; Braudel, *Méditerranée,* p. 477.

[121] A.N., Z¹B.65, Feb. 1, 1556.

[122] A.N., Z¹B.371, letter of Feb. 27, 1560, from the gardes of the mint in Toulouse to the Cour des Monnaies; see also A.N., Z¹B.271, fol. 67.

Italian bankers, including Baptiste Didato and Paulo Benedicti, counterfeiting gold portugaises, henris, pistoles, and ducats to be passed in their banking operations. In July 1561 another inquiry into the operations of Didato, by then established in Paris, brought to light the irregularities committed by Benedicti in Lyons. The latter, having obligations to pay in gold currency, was making settlements in counterfeit coin.[123] This particular instance involved movements of gold toward Paris. There were also arrivals of gold from Germany. On November 23, 1559, the Cour des Monnaies wrote to Charles de Guise, cardinal of Lorraine, about the monetary difficulties over the circulation of German gold coin of a fineness of less than 22 karats. There was further information on these gold movements in the letters patent of August 11, 1561, which refused currency to portugaises, English angels, double ducats of Nijmegen, and ducats "à la marionette" from Germany, which were similar to the old ducats of Hungary. A few years later Malestroit spoke of the losses caused by the circulation of counterfeit English angels, coined by the abbess of Thorn.[124] All these incidents reveal something of a new situation of gold in France, a comparison between the mints of Paris and Antwerp confirms this. From 1543 to 1559 Paris mostly issued silver, while Antwerp was more concerned with gold up to 1553. After 1560 these positions were reversed.[125]

The French monarchy progressively addressed itself to the gold problem. Solutions were necessary, but it was difficult for the mints to operate at the prices of legal bullion. The mint master of Nantes, for example, announced that at the going rates it was impossible for him to make issues. The death of Henry II, the short reign of Francis II, the minority of Charles IX, and the progressive disintegration of civil order did not make the problem any easier, but decisions were still necessary. In order to ease the collection of taxes, in February 1560 the teston was raised to 12 sols; this was soon followed by a rapid rise in gold prices. On November 22, 1560, the Cour des Monnaies reported that the écu (officially at 46 sols) had reached 51 sols and the Spanish pistollet 49 sols. These prices also prevailed in Dieppe in January 1561. According to some observers, the écu at 51 sols was still not sufficiently high to attract gold from abroad. As a result the Cour des Monnaies appealed to the cardinal of Lorraine to make an adjustment. In December 1560 the Estates General of Orléans considered the problem of defective currency and coin clipping — further signs of the depreciation of the livre tournois.[126]

[123] A.N., Z¹B.272, fols. 1, 59, 98, inquiry in Lyons, May–July 1561; A.N., Z¹B.371, Mar. 21, 1561.

[124] A.N., Z¹B.370, letter of Oct. 23, 1559, from the Cour des Monnaies to the Cardinal of Lorraine; Fontanon, *Édicts et ordonnances*, II, p. 146, lettres patentes of Aug. 17, 1561; A.N., Z¹B.372, remonstrance du procureur-général of May 17, 1561; Sieur de Malestroit, les *Paradoxes du Seigneur de Malestroit, conseiller du Roi et Maistre ordinaire de ses comptes sur le faict des Monnoyes presentez à Sa Majesté au mois de Mars MDLXVI* (Paris, 1566), in *Ecrits notables sur le monnaie*, ed. Jean-Yves Le Branchu (2 vols., Paris, 1934), p. 106.

[125] See Chap. 5.

[126] A. N., Z¹B.65, letter of Sept. 2, 1559, from the Cour des Monnaies to the cardinal

The *lettres closes* of January 27, 1561, set a new rate for the écu at 50 sols, but the Cour des Monnaies nevertheless reported "the greater disorder . . . in several foreign currencies especially the portugaises, angels, and double ducats, which rise in price every day." In February 1561 in Rouen French écus and Spanish pistollets exceeded the new currency rates; at these increased prices gold reappeared in the city from all areas. Silver also was more in evidence: there was particular attention to this after the depreciation of the Joachimstaler, coined with the arms of the Prince of Orange (January 30, 1561, and August 1563). However, the écu soleil in Paris and Lyons circulated at 51 and 52 sols. The letters patent of July 15, 1561, maintained the price of the écu at 50 sols and the teston at 12 sols. If the protests of the Cour des Monnaies were any indication, this official rate overestimated foreign gold coins by comparison with those of France.[127]

In August 1561 the great edict on monetary reform was published. It grouped together a series of trial measures and dealt at length with questions of some urgency, such as the currency of foreign gold coins, ducats from Spain, Portugal, Italy, Hungary, Scotland, Lorraine, England, and Flanders, together with a number of silver coins. The portugaises and the counterfeit angels of the abbess of Thorn and the double ducats of Nijmegen were refused currency. The mint price of bullion was raised, gold from 172 to 182 livres the marc, and silver from 15 livres to 15 livres 15 sols. This increased the ratio of silver to gold and was probably based on conditions in Paris. In the south the ratio was even slightly higher. The costs of brassage were raised to meet the rising costs of coinage, including the price of copper. Finally a new series of écus was begun, of 23 karats fine and weighing 72½ to the marc. This presented a certain number of technical problems, including new dies, and so there were delays. Coinage was relatively limited for 1561 and 1562.[128] The écu soleil of 1561 was the last standard gold coin to be designed in France before the great reform of 1640; it may be called the French gold coin of the phase of silver in Europe.

What were the immediate effects of the ordinance of 1561? For the mints it meant a revival of activity after the stagnation of 1558 and 1559, especially in the towns of the interior. There were social consequences: the devaluation

---

of Lorraine; mandement of Feb. 1560; arrêt of Sept. 3, 1560; A.N., Z¹B.370, letter of May 2, 1559, from the gardes of the mint in Nantes to the Cour des Monnaies; A.N., Z¹B.371, letters of Mar. 8, 1560, from the Cour des Monnaies to the cardinal of Lorraine, and Nov. 22, 1560, from the Cour des Monnaies to the King: C.S.P., Foreign, letter of Jan. 17, 1561, from Francis Edwards to Cecil; Georges Picot, *Histoire des États Généraux considérés au point de vue de leur influence sur le gouvernement de la France de 1355–1614* (4 vols., Paris, 1872), II, p. 295.

[127] A.N., Z¹B.65, Aug. 27, 1563; A.N., Z¹B.371, letter of Feb. 1, 1561, from the Cour des Monnaies to the King; and "Remonstrance très humbles que la court des monnoyes faict au Royne" of July 19, 1561; A.N., Z¹B.372, mémoire of Feb. 6, 1563; C.S.P., Foreign, letters of Mar. 8, 1560, Feb. 20, 1561, from Francis Edwards in Rouen to Cecil.

[128] A.N., Z¹B.65, ordonnance of Aug. 17, 1561, and avis of the Cour des Monnaies of Dec. 9, 1562; A.N., Z¹B.371, report to the Cour des Monnaies by Alexandre de la Tourette and Thomas Turquaim of Aug. 18, 1561.

Plate 3.

Écu d'or au soleil of Charles IX, coined in Paris in 1564 (actual size 2.40 cm., enlarged photograph by the Bibliothèque Nationale, Paris).

and the issues of an écu at a lower intrinsic value affected the real value of debts established in écus, which would therefore be repaid in écus of lesser value.[129]

The reform above all aimed at converting foreign into French gold coin. In Rouen in January 1563 there appeared gold florins of 19 karats, current at 50 sols; on February 17 they were refused currency. In La Rochelle on January 24, 1564, gold mazonettes of 19 karats and 64 to the marc were current; on September 12, 1564, the angels counterfeited by the abbess of Thorn, the ducat *à la marionette,* and other angels recently issued in Flanders were also decried. During the following month the Cour des Monnaies advised a new valuation of angels from England. There were also complaints that the gold real and the silver philippus from Flanders were both officially over-valued by comparison with French money. Nevertheless, the appreciation of gold currency continued, and this tendency was compensated in some measure by clipping the coins. Letters patent of June 15, 1566, set the écu soleil weighing 2 deniers 14 grains (in place of 2 deniers 15 grains) at the same rate as the écu à la couronne. Though in June 1566 English angels, Portuguese ducats, and Flemish talers and Joachimstaler were refused currency in Bordeaux and Rouen, the great centers of trade with England and the north, these coins were still circulating freely in La Rochelle in September. However, the rise in market prices of coins, notably gold coins, continued. On October 24, 1564, the free rate for the écu had reached 52 sols. To meet its financial obligations, the crown compromised and found itself obliged to countenance currency at rates higher than those officially allowed. In July 1565, nevertheless, it re-published the official rates.[130]

In the southwest and in the region around Paris the problem of full-bodied currency, both gold and silver, soon became apparent. On the other hand, in the northeast and east, the question of billon was more pressing. In Dijon in July 1561 the mint master announced that the carolus from Geneva, Besançon, and Lorraine was driving French currency from circulation. Gold was put at excessive prices in the regions near Dole, Besançon, Geneva, Chambéry, and Bourg. In Troyes in 1563 large quantities of billon from Lorraine, Franche-Comté, Savoy, and Geneva circulated. Because of this large invasion of foreign billon, coins up to a face value of 3 sols were forbidden. However, it is interesting in this context that Burgundy and Champagne were exempted for six months from this order. Though the coins of Savoy were forbidden in

---

[129] See Paul Cauwès, "Les commencements du crédit public en France," *Revue d'économie politique,* IX (1895); X (1896).

[130] A.N., Z¹B.65, lettres patentes of July 3, 1565; edict of June 15, 1566; lettres patentes of June 28, 1566; ordonnance of Aug. 27, 1563; A.N., Z¹B.276, fols. 89–93ᵛᵒ, inquiry in Bordeaux of Sept. 28–Oct. 2, 1566; A.N., Z¹B.372, letter of Jan. 15, 1563, from Pierre de Houppeville to the Cour des Monnaies; letter of Oct. 19, 1564, from the Cour des Monnaies to the King; report of the procureur-général of Jan. 24, 1565; A.N., Z¹B.373, report of the procureur-général of Oct. 5, 1566; Fontanon, *Édicts et ordonnances,* II, pp. 149–150; A.M., Rouen, A.19, fol. 13.

March 1565, they were still in evidence in the following May. In Langres on September 29, 1565, it was said that billon from Besançon, Geneva, Vic, and the Val d'Aosta was largely responsible for the rise in the quotations of French coin. The écu was current for 53 sols 4 deniers and even 54 sols, while the teston moved between 12 sols 6 deniers and 13 sols. Much research still needs to be done on the circulation of foreign money in the eastern provinces of France.[131]

During this period of financial embarrassment for the monarchy, two facts became clear: more and more merchants were offering to take over the operations of the different mints; there were increasing levies on the wealth of the Church. The monarchy tried to improve its financial position in both these directions.

First I will discuss the organization of the mints. On December 31, 1563, Pierre Assezat, a merchant of Toulouse, with his "partners," obtained a contract for the issue of new silver coins of a face value of one livre parisis in the mints of Lyons, Bordeaux, Toulouse, and Bayonne. The Cour des Monnaies fiercely opposed the introduction of this new coin, which, being valued at over 10 sols, would be thick and therefore liable to counterfeiting. The Cour would have preferred to limit the issues of billon and to make a clear distinction between high- and low-grade silver. After these objections, the order was given on October 5, 1564, to limit the new issues to 42,000 sols parisis a year for a period of two years. The crown clearly was looking on coinage as a source of revenue, just as when, not long afterward, the Sieur de Malus proposed to take over the farm of all the mints. The strenuous opposition of the Cour des Monnaies also overruled this move.[132]

In the second place the crown turned to the wealth of the Church to help fight the growing anarchy and the threat of Calvinism. The Church, as is well known, was naturally inclined to absorb precious metals, in silver and gold ornaments, chalices, crucifixes, reliquaries, and so forth; the famous silver grille in Saint-Martin-de-Tours, melted down in 1522, was a striking example. From time to time taxation, especially in wartime, reversed this trend.[133]

The provincial estates of Normandy proposed a levy on the Church's wealth in 1560. In August 1561 the Estates General gave the matter closer attention; this led to the Contract of Poissy (October 21, 1561) by which the

---

[131] A.N., Z¹B.65, ordonnance of Mar. 27, 1565, and letter of May 8, 1565, from the Cour des Monnaies to the King; A.N., Z¹B.274, fol. 150, inquiry in Langres of Sept. 29, 1565; A.N., Z¹B.372, requests of Claude le Double, Dijon, of May 10, 1564, and Jehan de Rieu, Troyes, of May 25, 1563.

[132] A.N., Z¹B.65, remonstrance of the Cour des Monnaies to the King of May 17, 1564; A.N., Z¹B.372, lettres patentes of Oct. 5, 1564.

[133] See Chap. 2, n. 42. For an example of the religious objects of gold and silver in private hands, see the "Inventaire des biens meubles dépendant de la succession de Maître Jehan Miffant et de celle de Nicolas Miffant, son fils," of Sept. 18, 1559, ed. Charles Leroy, in *Société de l'histoire de Normandie, Mélanges,* 13th Ser. (Rouen, 1937), pp. 7–55.

Church took over the responsibility for the crown's debts.[134] In order to pay the levies, the clergy in many cases pawned silverware and sold or mortgaged land. Thus, the cathedral of Nevers on March 31, 1562, sent ornaments worth some 5,980 livres tournois to Bourges. According to an inquiry of September 1562, some 514 marcs in silverplate had been received in Montpellier. In Troyes as on September 18 and in Dijon in October 1565, there were further reports of sales of silverplate. The letters patent of June 2, 1562, authorized the cathedrals of Rheims, Sens, and Rouen to convert their silverware into money, most of which was sent to the old "hammer" mint in Paris.[135]

It is difficult to estimate the volume of this dishoarding, but in 1581 Nicolas Froumenteau calculated the losses of the clergy in "silverplate, jewels, and reliquaries raised on the Churches or clergy" (in addition to the value of landed property) at 9,000,000 livres tournois.[136] The figure is unlikely to be exact but it gives an order of size, and certainly the levies coincided with activity in the mints. The raising of the mint prices in the ordinance of 1561, the inflow of bullion and specie from abroad, and the effects of the levies on Church property combined to revive the operations of the mints. In Paris the old "hammer" mint was reopened by order of the Surintendant des Finances to meet the demand; it also acted as an annex to the Hôtel des Étuves.[137] It should be noted that in this period issues of gold coin were evident in La Rochelle, Lyons, Poitiers, Rennes, and Paris, while this metal played a minor part in the key town of Bayonne. This movement reached a peak about 1566, while the years of 1567, 1568, and 1569, particularly, were marked by decline.

The year 1566 is a convenient date to close the period of reorganization observed since about 1550. During these sixteen years France experienced the spontaneous inflow of silver from Spain, probably in advance of other countries further away from the peninsula. This precocious position was not without points in its favor. With silver, France was able to recover some of its gold circulation from the north. Gold also arrived in Spain from the New World, and in Lisbon from the Portuguese colonies and outposts, but it is probable that France relied particularly on the markets of the north, notably Flanders, to balance out the silver problems facing it.

This suggests that in the first phase of silver inflation France retained some of the advantages of an intermediary. In effect the first waves of silver

---

[134] Victor Carrière, *Les épreuves de l'église de France au XVIᵉ siècle* (Paris, 1936), pp. 396, 403; Henri Prentout, *Les États Provinciaux de Normandie* (3 vols., Rouen, 1925–1927), I, p. 285.

[135] A.N., Z¹B.65, ordonnance of June 2, 1562, and letter of Nov. 16, 1562; see also examples of these sales in B.N., MSS., Nouvelles Acquisitions Françaises, 11968, fols. 2/20 ff.; Catherine de Médicis, *Lettres* (10 vols., Paris, 1880–1895), I, p. 377; A.N., Z¹B.273, fol. 58ᵛᵒ; A.N., Z¹B.274, fols. 86, 126, 169; A.N., Z¹B.372, request of the Dean and Chapter of Nevers of July 29, 1563.

[136] Nicolas Froumenteau, *Le Secret des finances de France* (3 pts., in 1 vol., n.p., 1581), Pt., p. 8.

[137] A.N., Z¹B.65, ordonnance of May 23, 1562.

penetrated its western provinces, while the monetary structures in the preceding phase of gold had stressed towns such as Limoges, Poitiers, Tours, and Orléans. The masters and officers of some mints went over to the Protestant side;[138] in this aspect the monetary drama of these years was most apparent, with money changers and merchants, especially in the Low Countries, playing a critical role. In December 1566 in Limoges the money changers were accused of exporting silver reals and testons to Flanders during the preceding four or five years, leaving in their place the inferior silver philippus. The same remarks and complaints were made in Tours in October 1565, and in Poitiers in 1566. There were the same suspicions at Saintes and at Marseilles in December 1566, favored by maritime trade. In Dijon and in Lyons in 1565, inquiries revealed the same state of affairs.[139] Beyond these characteristic details, the monetary geography stressed contrasts between the south and the north with a sort of zone of compensation in between. In reality the situation was far more complex and anything but easily defined.

The years 1567–1575 were marked by a veritable flood of silver. Under this pressure monetary structures were bound to change: for the opposition between north and south was substituted a more characteristic distinction between west and east, between the Atlantic and continental France. The final break probably took place in the early 1570s and was marked by the crisis of 1575.

The Duke of Alba's arrival in Flanders in 1567 produced changes of considerable importance to France. His military campaigns were sustained by massive transfers of bullion from Spain. Up to the time of the rupture between Spain and England in 1568, these transfers used chiefly the sea route, although even before this the land route across France was sometimes employed. Thus during the summer and autumn of 1567 two huge convoys (the second carrying 120,000 marcs in silver money and bars) made their way via Bayonne and Paris to Flanders.[140] By 1568 the sea route had become dangerous and was finally abandoned after 1572 and the successes of the Sea Beggars. Following these, large sums of money passed through France in transit for the north.[141]

As a result, silver currency — notably the silver philippus — was issued in large quantities by the mint of Antwerp, in the period 1567–1572. After some difficulties in 1567 and 1569 the large expenditures in the Low Countries began to have effects on the monetary circulation of neighboring France. Thus, in addition to the inflation from the south and west, an inflation of silver

---

[138] *Ibid.,* report of Aug. 5, 1569.

[139] See, for example, A.N., Z¹B.275, fol. 433ᵛᵒ; A.N., Z¹B.276, fols. 91, 288ᵛᵒ; A.N., Z¹B.372, remonstrance of Oct. 11, 1565; A.N., Z¹B.373, remonstrance of May 10, 1566.

[140] Catherine de Médicis, *Lettres,* I, p. 464, letter of Jan. 2, 1563, from Chantonnay to the Duchess of Parma; A.N., Z¹B.65, procès-verbal of Apr. 29, 1567; A.N., Z¹B.373, ordonnance of Feb. 11, 1568.

[141] For the detour through France, see Braudel, *Méditerranée,* pp. 376–385.

began to penetrate France from Flanders. The proof of this state of affairs can be found in the reopening of the mint of Amiens, with the purpose of converting the quantities of foreign currency forbidden circulation in 1577, but still abundant in the northern provinces. In this way, France was pressed between two important sources of inflation, directly from the south and west and indirectly from the northwest. After 1567, and above all after 1575, the mints were more and more concerned with silver. It was not until 1630–1640, almost half a century later, that gold was again issued in large quantities. Only Paris, the political and therefore fiscal capital, could claim to be an exception to this reign of silver in France.

A new monetary geography in France, then, was beginning to take shape, infiltrated both in the north and in the southwest by the silver exported from Spain. The line of division, once again approximate, can be placed for convenience along the valley of the Loire, that great line of demarcation which has appeared so often in the history of France. And to this scheme must be added the increasingly close relationship between Aquitaine and the Mediterranean south, marked by the rise in activity in the mints of Aix-en-Provence and Villeneuve-lès-Avignon after 1567. They had been reopened in 1553, but their early operations were at a low level. Later, at the beginning of the seventeenth century, the mints of Bayonne and Aix reached their peak activity at the same time, and it may be inferred that they tended to conform closely to monetary movements in Spain. To be more complete the scheme must take note, on the one hand, of the privileged position assumed by Brittany in the west in the profitable export trade in wheat and linens, which will be considered later, and, on the other hand, the zones relatively ill furnished with silver in the east, marked by the confusion of billon and copper money.

It would be interesting to compare the monetary map in Graph 22 (showing the new and the more traditional regions) with that of the political and religious wars of the period. The divisions, after one makes allowances for basic differences, show curious similarities. Clearly the problem is complex and cannot be explained by simple arguments. However, the role of government and public affairs must nevertheless be taken in association with monetary conditions.

Toward the end of the period 1567–1575 currency rates rose rapidly, and the monarchy gave ground before the irresistible upsurge. There were at first some piecemeal changes, which were ultimately insufficient, and then the periodic general settlements, which in the end also survived for only a short time.

The letters patent of October 20, 1567, mentioned the seizure of a large quantity of Spanish silver reals in Paris and that in the payments connected with the *rentes sur l'Hôtel de Ville* the silver real should be set at 4 sols 4 deniers. This was an increase over the official rate of 4 sols 2 deniers. It was similar to the rise in the rate for the gold écu circulating in the market at 53 sols in July 1568, but authorized by letters patent at only 52 sols. Even this valuation of the real brought loud protests from the Cour des Monnaies, although it was a question only of the circulation of the real, and no mention was made of the French teston. It was as good as suggesting that the silver real was a standard means of payment. The rising currency rates for the écu followed. In July 1569 it circulated in the markets at 54 sols; in August it was given an official rate of 53 sols. In view of the delays in making payments to the holders of rentes, a payment of 20,000 écus was authorized on April 10, 1570, at 54 sols. On August 30 this rate became official, but already, apparently, the market rate had passed it, for on September 16 and November 22, 1570, and again on April 21, 1571, orders were given that the official rate should be respected. Then, in May 1571, there was a fresh upward shift, with the écu fluctuating between 55 and 56 sols "in some parts of the kingdom"; by October it had reached 56 and 57 sols. An Assembly of Notables was held in Paris in October 1571; present at it were the Conseil, the Parlement of Paris, and the members of the Chambre des Comptes and the Cour des Monnaies. The Assembly decided to keep the écu at the rate of 54 sols for six months, then reduce it to 52 sols, and finally to 50 sols, the rate set in the ordinance of 1561. During all this, however, no change was allowed for the teston. A further attempt in June 1572 brought the écu to 54 sols, with the intention of reducing it to 50 sols by January 1, 1573. But the ordinance had scarcely been published when it was followed by another of July 4, 1572, forbidding a rise in the currency rate above 54 sols; it declared that the premium on gold was such that silver and silver billon had been chiefly used for paying taxes "during the past twenty years." These fluctuations in currency rates formed the prelude to St. Bartholomew and the crisis of 1575.[142]

The royal government did not abandon the hope of an eventual revaluation. The letters patent of September 2, 1572, "tolerated" the rate of 54 sols until January 1, 1573, but required another prohibition on September 26 to check a renewed advance in the rate. In December the "tolerated" rate was continued until July 1, 1573, but already after January 1573 this was no longer valid. At the end of January a new effort was made to keep the écu at 54 sols. In April the general rate was 57 sols, but by the letters patent of April 20, 1573, a rate of 56 sols was "tolerated." On May 26, 1573, "in order to adjust gold and silver money," the teston was set at 13 sols, the real at 4 sols 6 deniers, and the mint prices were raised, gold to 200 livres and silver to 17 livres the marc. These conditions were particularly applicable in Picardy, Burgundy, and Champagne, as well as in Brittany with its important trading contacts with Spain.

[142] A.N. Z^{1}B.65, report of commissioners of July 21, 1568; remonstrances of the Cour des Monnaies of July 27, 1568, July 29, 1569, Apr. 22, 1570; lettres patentes of Aug. 11, 1568; A.N., Z^{1}B.66, remonstrance of the Cour des Monnaies of May 17, 1571, and ordonnance of Apr. 2, 1571; A.N., Z^{1}B.69, remonstrances of the Cour des Monnaies of May 17, 1571, Dec. 3, 1571, Aug. 17, 1572; ordonnances of Apr. 21, 1571; lettres patentes of Oct. 16, 1571; déclaration of June 14, 1571; prohibition of July 4, 1572.

On July 15, as the royal government started negotiations to raise a loan of 300,000 livres tournois to pay the Swiss troops, the merchant-financiers concerned were not prepared to accept the terms except with the ecu at 60 sols and the teston at 15 sols. The official rate of 54 sols was announced on June 9, 1574, but this rate was not strictly adhered to. The Cour des Monnaies protested on August 3, 1574, that the rate would soon rise to 60 sols and that the legal rates would not keep both types of currency in circulation. This state of affairs was confirmed by the letters patent of September 22, 1574. In October 1574 the commercial rate was between 60 and 63 sols, sometimes even as high as 65 sols. The écu was reported at 60 sols in Montpellier in the following October.[143]

The price of gold and silver, clearly, continued to figure prominently in governmental policies. There were differences between the official rates and the free market; thus after April 1570 the silver philippus passed between merchants at 44 sols, well above the official rate of 38 sols 6 deniers. On April 5, 1571, the Cour des Monnaies expressed the paradoxical opinion that this situation accounted for the disappearance of silver from circulation. On the other hand, the royal Conseil claimed that there were already many official instructions on the subject and that it was only a matter of enforcement. A pious hope! However, it agreed to send a deputation to the Duke of Alençon, then in Flanders, to find a solution. On December 3, 1571, the conclusion was reached that the conversion of silver reals into testons would stop the disappearance of silver. In January 1573 an inquiry in Rennes revealed the traffic in silver reals, a problem which remained for many years.[144]

The crown eventually accepted devaluation, and on September 2, 1572, the teston was set at 12 sols 6 deniers. The mint price of bullion, however, remained unchanged. The price of silver, it was thought, could not be altered without disturbing the rate for gold. Three weeks after the devaluation the money changers in Paris declared that, at the going market rate, silver still disappeared. When the master of the Paris mint asked on the following day for permission to buy gold at 74 écus the marc and silver at 26¼ testons the marc, the Cour des Monnaies reexamined the causes of the apparent maladjustment between gold and silver and concluded that it was better to lower the price of gold than to run the risk, just as great, of raising both types of money at the same time.[145]

---

[143] A.N., Z¹B.69, lettres patentes of Sept. 2, 1572, Jan. 30, 1573; remonstrances of the Cour des Monnaies of Sept. 10, 1572, Apr. 20, 1573, ordonnance of May 26, 1573; A.N., Z¹B.70, reply of the Chancelier to the Cour des Monnaies of July 15, 1574; ordonnance of July 7, 1574; report to the Conseil of Aug. 3, 1574; lettres patentes of Sept. 22, 1574; remonstrance of the Cour des Monnaies of Oct. 2, 1574; Ehrenberg, *Das Zeitalter der Fugger,* I, pp. 178–183, 348–350.

[144] A.N., Z¹B.65, remonstrance of the Prévôt, Marchands, and Échevins of Paris of Apr. 22, 1570; remonstrance of the mint master of Toulouse of Feb. 11, 1568; A.N., Z¹B.374, report of Apr. 5, 1571; remonstrance of the Cour des Monnaies of Dec. 3, 1571; A.N., Z¹B.280B, fol. 73ᵛᵒ, inquiry in Rennes of Jan. 16, 1573.

[145] A.N., Z¹B.69, lettres patentes of Sept. 2, 1572; inquiry of Sept. 24, 1572; request of

The pressure of necessity can be seen in the ordinance of July 7, 1574, which raised the teston to 13 sols and the real to 4 sols 6 deniers. For the first time since 1561 a general review of mint prices was considered, and permission was given to the mints to buy gold at 200 livres and silver at 17 livres the marc. This, however, did not pass without protest from the Cour des Monnaies. Soon afterward the Conseil raised the écu to 58 sols, but as Thomas Turquaim, a conseiller-général of the Cour des Monnaies and a well-known expert, wrote on September 23, 1574, the maladjustment between gold and silver led to the export of silver.[146]

In the meetings of the Conseil on April 8 and 12, 1575, more proposals were made that the écu should be raised to 60 sols and that the teston should be replaced by the silver franc (having a fineness of 10 deniers and weighing 17¼ to the marc). The letters patent of May 31, 1575, made these measures official; the teston was set at 14 sols 6 deniers and the real at 5 sols. In order to end exchange manipulations, it was decided that the phrase "the remainder paid in testons and douzains" should not figure in contracts. A declaration set the écu at the official rate of 60 sols from June 14, 1575. By these regulations of 1575 the ratio of gold to silver was lowered slightly, indicating a policy to attract silver; this ratio was not changed until the ordinance of 1602.[147]

Another measure was passed in an attempt to restrain exports: in Paris loans were raised on silver plate and jewelry. The conversion of this bullion into testons was continued in May. Similar decisions were taken at Tours on July 26, 1575, and at La Rochelle on July 7 of the following year: the mints were authorized to coin testons. Large quantities were issued in Paris between 1574 and 1576, above all in 1575, for the total sum of 297,151 livres tournois. However, in Bayonne in 1577, the franc at 10 deniers fine was considered unsuitable for local currency, but the silver quart d'écu issued in 1579, at 11 deniers fine and weighing 25⅕ to the marc, admirably met the need to convert silver reals from Spain into French money.[148]

With the crisis of 1575, the period of reorganization at the opening of the silver phase in France ended. The growing tension of the period 1567–1575 had been marked, in addition, by difficulties over gold. During the following years (1575–1588) France experienced is boom of the second half of the sixteenth century.

---

the mint master of Paris of Sept. 10, 1572; remonstrance of the Cour des Monnaies of Apr. 20, 1573; ordonnance of May 26, 1573.

[146] A.N., Z¹B.70, ordonnance of July 7, 1574; A.N., Z¹B.374, letter of Sept. 23, 1574, from Turquaim to the Cour des Monnaies.

[147] A.N., Z¹B.70, remonstrance of the Cour des Monnaies of Oct. 2, 1574; avis of the Cour des Monnaies to the Conseil of Apr. 8–12, 1575; ordonnance of May 31, 1575; déclaration of June 14, 1575.

[148] A.N., Z¹B.376, arrêt of the Cour des Monnaies of May 14, 1576; A.N., Z¹B.70, July 7, 1576; Paul Bordeaux, "La fabrication des deniers testons de Henri III à Paris en 1576," *Revue numismatique,* 4th Ser., X (1905).

Plate 4.

Silver franc of Henry III, coined in Paris in 1577 (actual size 3.90 cm., enlarged photograph by the Bibliothèque Nationale, Paris).

Measures at the beginning of the decade 1570–1580 did not succeed in stabilizing the situation once and for all, and when the Estates General met on December 6, 1576, monetary affairs were again on the agenda. One result was the important ordinance of March 1577. The écu, set at 60 sols by the ordinance of March 22, 1575, was raised to 65 sols. From the month of June the rate was again set officially at 66 sols, while the teston found currency at 16 sols 6 deniers, although the market was already above these rates. During the summer of 1577 the rates rose rapidly. The merchants of Lyons pressed the King to hold back prices. There followed the important ordinance of September 1577 which apparently was effective.[149] After January 1, 1578, the écu was to replace the livre tournois as the accounting unit, and thus became officially both a real coin and a money of account. Fractional money was legal tender up to one-third of payments made, which had already been prescribed in the ordinance of March 22, 1577, after a long series of proposals, but from the beginning it met with hesitation and resistance, and the order was renewed on May 5, 1579. Until January 1, 1578, the écu was to pass at 66 sols and after that date at 60 sols, the minimum level proposed by the Cour des Monnaies. To mitigate the sharpness of this order, letters patent of April 30, 1578, stipulated that all debts contracted during 1577 were to be calculated with the écu at 66 sols. As a last measure to end the short-term manipulation of foreign exchanges and traffic in gold and silver, especially in Lyons, the use of agio and the discounting of bills of exchange from fair to fair were prohibited. This was a heavy blow for Lyons; although it remained a center of banking activities, it found itself less and less well placed to dominate the French economy.[150]

Billon provided the clearest indication of the situation of gold and silver coins. In 1578 (following the edict of September 1577) the first pure copper currency of France in the sixteenth century was issued.[151] Though the presence of copper mailles from Flanders had already been reported in Amiens and Abbeville, now it was proposed that the Paris mint should coin copper deniers and doubles up to a total of 20,000 livres tournois, with legal tender throughout France in payments up to 20 sols. At the outset they were unwelcome. Three years after the beginning of these issues, there were complaints of excessive quantities of copper in circulation, and four years later (March 11, 1585) the coinage was stopped. However, this was started again

---

[149] Picot, *Histoire des États Généraux*, II, p. 309; A.N., Z¹B.70, ordonnances of Mar. 22, July 21, 1577; remonstrance of the Cour des Monnaies, Nov. 20, 1577. Between Nantes and Lyons the difference in commercial rates often reached 35 percent. Henri Lapeyre, *Une famille de marchands: Les Ruiz* (Paris, 1955), pp. 449–450.

[150] A.N. Z¹B.71, prohibition of May 5, 1570; Fontanon, *Édicts et ordonnances*, pp. 177–178; A.N., J.971–972, Mémoire au Roi of July 1577, which indicated that near the royal residence there were premiums of 20 to 30 percent while the currency remained at par in the Rhône Valley.

[151] Although some of the early versions bore the date 1577, the first issue of copper coins was registered in Paris from September 13, 1578, to July 9, 1580. A.N., Z¹B.327.

during the troubles of the League in spite of the difficulties in obtaining copper. The monarchy evidently was ready to exploit the situation to the full, but the watchful Cour des Monnates acted to a limited extent as a restraining force: copper during this period supplemented the circulation of gold and silver currency.[152]

The great reforms of 1577–1579 settled some of the problems of silver inflation. Too much silver was pouring into Spain through Seville for nearby France not to feel its immediate effects. Through the simple mechanism of relative costs, the transfer of goods and services from France to Spain was encouraged. This was clear in the case of wheat, a necessity for Spain, which Breton ships loaded and carried to the peninsula. In return, fleets from Spain (François Garrault mentions Portuguese merchants, but in 1581 they were "ships from Spain") arrived about Easter, as one report declared, in the ports of Brittany loaded with silver reals, and these in turn flowed into the operations of the mint in Rennes.[153] It was clear also, as Bodin observed, in the migration of laborers from Auvergne, across the Pyrenees, to Aragon.

What about gold? It is possible that it began to find its way out of circulation, either through hoarding or the manipulations of changers and bankers. The 1580s opened with further signs of the disappearance of gold. In 1584 there was a fresh alert on the subject of the flight of precious metals, gold in particular, to Flanders.[154] The Cour des Monnaies addressed a long remonstrance on this subject to the Conseil on January 28. The rapid rise in currency rates — an endemic state of affairs — was noted later in the letters patent of June 1584. Attempts were made to return to the conditions of 1577. Note was also taken that the gold pistollet circulated at a rate above its official bullion rate, which excluded it from being converted into French coins. It is difficult to state these conditions precisely, but the evidence tends to show that silver was the standard means of payment.

Few periods were more disturbed, more violent, more dramatic than the years 1589–1606. The purpose here is to confine the discussion to monetary problems, which were not the least important. In order to explain these problems fully the movement must be set in the general context of the Atlantic economy.

Philip's conquest of Portugal in 1580 and the establishment and expansion of the United Provinces were striking features of the development of the Atlantic economy. The Dutch asserted their power more and more after these critical years; in France (and also in Germany) the presence of "Flemings"

---

[152] A.N., Z¹B.65, May 28, 1568; A.N. Z¹B.378, report of the procureur-général of Feb. 23, 1581; A.N., Z¹B.71, ordonnance of Mar. 11, 1581; A.N., Z¹B.377, Mar 17, May 14, 1579.

[153] A.N., Z¹B.378, request of July 29, 1581; A.N. Z¹B.381, request of Mar. 29, 1588.

[154] A.N., Z¹B.72, remonstrance of the Cour des Monnaies of Jan. 28, 1584.

became increasingly noticeable during the last two decades of the century.[155] Amsterdam became a great commercial and financial center whose many activities featured, significantly enough, the redistribution of silver from America. In time, with the East India Company of 1602 trading with Asia and the West India Company of 1621 trading with America, the Dutch Republic became an axis in the international circuit of bullion. In the war against Spain in Europe, bullion passed indiscriminately from allies to enemies.

France also became involved in this complex network based in the north; indeed, the powerful movements of the Atlantic pushed it in this direction. In this, certain characteristics must be kept in mind. Rouen was, for example, included in the 1585 list of exchange centers in direct relationship with Amsterdam. Another new feature involved, by 1585–1590, the direct export of wheat from the north, from the plains of Prussia and Poland, by Dutch merchants. Against such competitive prices, even with the shorter haul to Spain, the small sailing vessels of Brittany were naturally at a disadvantage. As a result there may have been sharp competition for wheat exported from the Breton farms and, perhaps as a result, a decline in the exchange of wheat for silver. The Dutch also made their presence felt along the Atlantic coast of France, where competition was tough and unrelenting. These newcomers were able to take advantage of the flow of silver. There were constant complaints against them, for example, in Bayonne in May 1587. In La Rochelle in April 1590 the mint master reported the disappearance of silver: the "Flemings" were scooping up silver reals — the famous pieces of eight — officially rated at 40 sols but which the market quoted at 42 sols. The quarts d'écu of France, minted in 1587, 1588, and 1589, had already risen above the legal rate by 2 sols in the écu. On March 8, 1594, the Cour des Monnaies reported that the mint of Middleburg, employing about a hundred workers, issued more than 150,000 marcs of coin and used silver specie almost entirely drawn from France. The Cour observed that the Dutch and English together controlled what little trade existed with Spain at that time. The presence of the Dutch was noted even more in monetary transactions in Bayonne and Saint-Jean-de-Luz, on the frontier of Spain, just as further north the ports of Brittany such as Saint-Malo were another vital relay point en route from Spain. It was no mere coincidence that some of the early French expeditions to the Far East were promoted in Brittany with the aid of Dutch seamen.[156]

The monetary situation was again discussed at Blois where the Estates met on September 17, 1588. Complaints were voiced about the large quantities of sols parisis, douzains, and liards below the official standards (later their

---

[155] Braudel, *Méditerranée*, pp. 494 ff.; and see *The Fugger News-Letters*, ed. Victor von Klarwill, 2nd Ser. (London, 1926), p. 94, letter from Lisbon of Aug. 17, 1585.

[156] B.N., MSS., Nouvelles Acquisitions Françaises, 733, fol. 84, session of the parlement of Rennes of Aug. 7, 1589; A.N., Z¹B.382, letter of Apr. 29, 1590; A.N., Z¹B.385, letters of Feb. 20, 1590, Mar. 8, 1594, from the Cour des Monnaies to the parlements of Rouen and Caen.

coinage was stopped, but only in 1596). The problem was particularly severe in Brittany, where the abundance of inferior currency was the counterpart of the drain of specie by the Dutch to the Low Countries.[157]

From 1588 to 1606 France felt the monetary effects of Spanish politics. According to the agreement of Joinville (December 31, 1584) between Philip II and the Guises, the League was assured of a yearly subsidy of 600,000 écus. After 1588 more impressive sums of money were expended to influence the course of affairs of France, and although rumor probably exaggerated their size, it is possible that a large part was sent in silver species. No doubt the region of Paris, the center of political pressures, received the biggest share, and there the mint during this period of public disturbances experienced an exceptional prosperity. The issues of coin certainly exceeded those of 1587, the preceding peak year. In Paris these issues continued until 1592, but not without difficulty and complaints. The report of December 15, 1589, officially condemned the silver *philippus dalles* from Flanders used in paying the Spanish troops, and this only a month after the order of November 3 to assay the reals issued "in the Indies." It is possible that the policy of Spain did not hesitate to unload currency of inferior standards in France. On December 22, 1589, a remonstrance of the Cour des Monnaies drew the attention of the Duke of Mayenne to the silver philippus which, although not having legal currency, was employed by the Conseil of the League at the high rate of 50 sols to pay the troops.[158] In all, these large expenditures created a further inflationary force in the general confusion of civil war. The silver *philippus* had thus risen from 40 to 48 sols and then to 50 sols; this rise was particularly marked in Burgundy. An order from the Duke of Mayenne (February 8, 1592) confirmed the official rate of 50 sols in those areas controlled by the League. The gold écu was officially set at 60 sols in the ordinance of 1577, but passed for 63 sols and the teston for 15 sols.[159] The rates were naturally higher in the free market. In January 1592, in the region of the lower Rhône, the rate for the écu rose to 90 sols, and, in August 1592, to the exceptional level of 100

---

[157] Picot, *Histoire des États Généraux,* III, p. 91; A.N., Z^{1}B.72, remonstrance of the Cour des Monnaies of Sept. 9, 1588; A.N., Z^{1}B.381, letter of Mar. 29, 1588, from François Mezart to the mint master of Saint-Lô, and request of Philippe Varice of Apr. 8, 1588.

[158] A.N., Z^{1}B.72, procès-verbal of Dec. 15, 1589; ordonnance of Nov. 3, 1589; remonstrance of the Cour des Monnaies of Dec. 22, 1589; A.N., Z^{1}B.382, arrêt of the Cour des Monnaies of Dec. 20, 1590.

[159] *The Fugger News-Letters,* ed. Victor von Klarwill, 1st Ser. (London, 1928), Feb. 9, 1590, reported that the Genoese bankers, the Spinolas, offered to put their reserves in Paris amounting to 400,000 crowns at the disposal of Philip II for repayment in Spain; see also A.N., Z^{1}B.72, lettres patentes of July 18, 1591; ordonnance of Feb. 8, 1592; remonstrances of the Cour des Monnaies of Feb. 19, 1592, Mar. 30, 1594. See also the articles of Jean Bailhache, "Un atelier monétaire inconnu, Maringues, 1591–1593," *Revue numismatique,* 4th Ser., XXXII (1929), "Le monnayage de Montmorency pendant la Ligue à Montpellier, Beaucaire, Béziers, et Villeneuve d'Avignon," *ibid.,* XXXV (1932), "L'atelier monétaire d'Orange pendant la Ligue, 1591–1592," *ibid.,* XXXVI (1933).

sols. At the same time the teston and the quart d'écu went for 25 sols. In Montpellier in November 1594 the écu was quoted at 72 sols; when payment was made in terms of silver reals, it was quoted at 66 sols. This must be taken as a further indication of the inflationary effects of billion (notably of douzains and sols parisis) in the south.[160]

The Spanish royal bankruptcy of 1596–1597 also had repercussions on the general rates for gold and silver currency in France. In Montpellier a report of July 5, 1596, noted that the silver ducaton passed for 55 sols, the piece of eight reals for 44 sols, and the écu for 66 sols. In the Easter payments of the Lyons fairs the ducaton was quoted at 57 sols 6 deniers. In Toulouse "and all through this region of Languedoc, le Puy, and Rouergue" the ducaton circulated at 55 sols and at the same time as the disappearance of French currency was noted. Nothing took place under normal conditions.[161]

Even before the official bankruptcy of the Spanish monarchy the monetary situation deteriorated. There the exportation of silver was forbidden in December 1596 and in March 1597. At the same time the official rate for the silver real was raised from 30 to 40 maravedis. It is difficult to ascertain the precise effects of this crisis on economic activity of France, but by coincidence or otherwise, wheat from Brittany, for example, apparently no longer sold so easily in the peninsula. Was this difficult market accompanied by a glut in Brittany? In any case, the Parlement in Rennes considered it appropriate, on March 3, 1600, to forbid the payment of dues in grain unless this means of payment was the accepted custom.[162]

An appreciation of gold followed these events. In January 1598 the master of the mint at Trévoux, which was outside French monetary control, offered 66 sols 4 deniers for the gold écu d'or soleil. In Toulouse on September 22 the écu also passed for 66 sols. In 1601 the commercial price for the gold ducat was 75 sols, and the marc was assessed at 90 écus that is, in terms of the écus, the accounting unit imposed by the edict of 1577. On June 9, 1601, the écu apparently circulated at 64 sols and the ducaton at 50 sols, while in Lyons the écu was at 65 sols and the ducaton at 52 to 53 sols. In Rouen in the same year the écu was rated at 64 sols but the philippus at 50 sols. Once more it must be noted that these currencies tended to appreciate in con-

---

[160] A.N., Z¹B.73, remonstrance de la Cour des Monnaies of Nov. 18, 1595; A.N., Z¹B.384, "Informations faictes en ceste ville d'Aix par nous Thomas Estienne conseiller du Roy au siège général et principal estably audit Aix et commissaires à ce depputés par messieurs tenans la court des monnoyes à Parys," Aug. 1, 1592; A.N., Z¹B.385, letter of Nov. 17, 1594, from the mint master of Montpellier to the Cour des Monnaies.

[161] *The Fugger News-Letters,* 1st Ser., letter of Oct. 15, 1594, indicates bankruptcies; A.N., Z¹B.387, letter of July 5, 1596, from the mint master of Montpellier to the Cours des Monnaies; A.N., Z¹B.388, request of the mint master of Toulouse of Sept. 3, 1597; A.N., Z¹B.389, letters of Sept. 1, 22, Dec. 2, 1598, from the mint master of Toulouse to the Cour des Monnaies.

[162] *The Fugger News-Letters,* 1st Ser., letters of Mar. 29, Aug. 15, 1597, Nov. 20, 1598; A.N., Z¹B.388, remonstrance of the Cour des Monnaies of Jan. 29, 1597; B.N., Nouvelles Acquisitions Françaises, 734, fol. 56, arrêt of the Parlement of Rennes.

tinental France. The restoration of the authority of the monarchy under Henry IV, especially after 1598, no doubt helped to stabilize the situation.[163]

Yet, as the gap widened between the official and the market rates, speculation increased on the frontiers of France. It was assumed in Lyons that the better types of currency were disappearing, for example, in the direction of Trévoux, to be exchanged for small coins of three deniers. In Aix on February 13, 1599, again there were reports of the disappearance of money, to such an extent that the Cour des Monnaies felt obliged to intervene. The mint in Montpellier found it difficult after November 1599 to make issues on account of the activity of the rival mints of Carpentras and Avignon, coining ducatons and douzains. From on all sides came protests and precautionary measures against foreign coins. Again, in spite of the opposition of the Cour des Monnaies, the succession of Henry of Navarre to the throne meant free access after October 1594 for the coins of Béarn and Navarre into the circulation of France.[164]

France under Henry IV at first seemed beset with difficulties, and a practical solution was not to be found immediately. The currency rates were clearly so much out of line that in June 1601 the Parlements of Bordeaux and Toulouse agreed on their own authority to allow the rates current "between merchants." All this meant opportunities for foreign merchants to exploit. In March 1601 the monetary operations of the "Flemings" were again under review. Germans and Swiss were reported on June 20, 1601, in the Rhône Valley and in Lyons buying up silver ducatons for export. There were similar situations in Brittany. In order to check the export of bullion from Saint-Malo, the Conseil d'État proposed in August 1597 to set up a mint in this key port.[165]

Through all this, the monarchy tried to control the inflation. The system imposed in 1577 was repeated by orders in April 1590, in March 1594, in December 1599, in June 1600, in May 1601, and in April 1602. The remonstrance of the Cour des Monnaies of January 29, 1597, asserted that merchants and bankers were responsible. But, the difficulties went much deeper; it had become impossible to retain the old system, and this the Conseil was in the end forced to face. It considered sweeping remedies. Sully disapproved of raising the official currency rates and suggested at the time the expansion of

[163] A.N., Z¹B.74, fol. 279, lettres patentes of Sept. 15, 1601; A.N., Z¹B.389, letters of Jan. 26, 1598; A.N., Z¹B.391, letter of Mar. 31, July 4, 1601; A.N., Z¹B.391, letter of Mar. 31, July 4, 1601; A.N., Z¹B.392, request of the mint master of Saint-Lô, and letters of June 9, 1601, Apr. 13, 1602.

[164] A.N., Z¹B.387, letter of July 5, 1596, from the mint master of Montpellier to the Cour des Monnaies; A.N., Z¹B.389, letter of Nov. 27, 1599, from the mint master of Montpellier to Cour des Monnaies; letter of Jan. 26, 1598, from the mint master in Lyons to the Cour des Monnaies; A.N., Z¹B.390, report of the commission in Aix, Feb. 13, 1599.

[165] A.N., Z¹B.73, arrêt of the Conseil d'État of Aug. 31, 1597; A.N., Z¹B.74, remonstrance of the Cour des Monnaies of July 9, 1601; A. N., Z¹B.391, letters of Mar. 31, June 20, 1601.

certain industries, which would adjust the balance of trade and stabilize the monetary situation. But the inevitable devaluation came in the edict of September 1602. The écu was raised officially to 65 sols, the silver franc to 21 sols 4 deniers; other gold and silver coins changed proportionally. In this scheme the mint ratio of gold to silver was raised, as the new mint prices for bullion confirmed: gold at 240 livres 10 sols and silver at 20 livres 5 sols 4 deniers the marc. At the same time accounting in livres tournois was restored, although in bills of exchange the écu was kept at the former rate of three livres tournois. An attempt also was made to eliminate the disturbances caused by money changers: their offices were abolished in towns where there was a mint, and their functions were transferred to the mint master. This important edict was unwillingly accepted.[166] The Parlement of Toulouse, for example, on June 20, 1602, ignored the order concerning changers, and it required an *arrêt* from the Conseil on August 13, 1602, to insist on their suppression.

At the turn of the sixteenth century the deterioration of civil peace because of the wars of the League and monetary difficulties opened the way to increased circulation of billon. The net result was an appreciation of gold and silver. Monetary circulation also suffered from the pressure of Holland. Billon thus appeared as a sign of imperfection. The civil wars in the south saw the coining of large quantities of sols parisis; the mint at Montpellier also secretly coined this money, but was eventually closed because of it.

In order to understand the gravity of the problem, one should note that the Cour des Monnaies was informed on June 1, 1590, that defective sols parisis, a quarter below the official weight, were being produced in the mints of Toulouse, Narbonne, and Montpellier. This was also accompanied by a rising premium on gold, and the market rate for the écu fluctuated between 70 and 72 sols. In Provence, also, unauthorized mints appeared in Tarascon, Arles, Toulouse, Martigues, and Marseilles, coining sols parisis and setting silver bullion at 30 and 33 livres the marc, while the gold écu rose to 90 sols and the Spanish pistollet to 88 sols. These prices certainly exceeded the legal prices by half, while in Paris the premium was about 20 to 30 percent. In Lyons and Marseilles, paradoxically enough, the rates were reported to conform to the list of 1577. Conditions thus showed considerable differences and probably indicated the particular breakdown in Languedoc and Provence, which was long in evidence. It should also be noted that the Estates of the League, which had been assembled in Paris since January 26, 1593, appointed a commission of inquiry to investigate "the number of counterfeit *six blancs* and douzains carrying our arms and mark" from Languedoc, Provence, Dauphiné, and Auvergne and mentioned in particular Montpellier, Toulouse, Arles,

---

[166] A.N., Z¹B.73, Mar. 30, 1594, and remonstrance of the Cour des Monnaies of Jan. 29, 1597; A.N., Z¹B.74, Dec. 1599, May 24, 1601, Apr. 18, 1602, and edict of Sept. 1602, verified Sept. 16, 1602; A.N., Z¹B.382, Apr. 6, 1590. See also *Voyage de Barthélemy Joly en Espagne, 1603–1604,* ed. L. Barrau-Dihigo (Paris, 1909), indicating that in 1603, after the devaluation, gold was worth more in France than in Spain.

Tarascon, Narbonne, Grenoble, Martigues, Marseilles, Avignon, Carpentras, Orange, Le Puy, and Alban, mints which had mushroomed in the anarchy of the League and issued currency without let or hindrance. The haste shown in Provence and Languedoc to issue sols parisis can be explained to some extent by their trade with North Africa, which was always ready, so it seemed, to take these coins. In addition, there were the copper coins which also played their part in raising the premium on gold and silver, particularly in Paris. Part of the trouble, according to observers, was the poor quality of copper (the mint master reported in January 1589 that it came from Germany). Everywhere the invasion of copper was organized more or less for reasons of necessity. On August 12, 1592, copper money valued at 10,000 écus was ordered in Paris for distribution in cities dependent on the capital. Another sign was the report that in Tours on March 7, 1594, copper doubles minted in Rennes in 1593 were refused currency.[167]

The circulation of copper was increased from both official and counterfeit sources, and it weighed heavily on the France which Henry IV set out to restore. The first measure was to stop further coinage of this currency by the ordinance of March 30, 1596.

The situation concerning gold also required attention. Even after the reform of 1602 the price of gold and silver continued to rise. This problem was reported from Rouen in February 1603, and measures were take non February 4, 1604, to republish the edict of 1602. In Bordeaux in October 1603 the pistole reached 7 livres tournois. The situation concerning silver was no better, particularly in the south and southeast, which used this currency in trade with the Levant. In Villeneuve-lès-Avignon on December 28, 1602, it was difficult to find a silver quart d'écu, traditionally in heavy demand for this trade. The law courts give some evidence of the importance of these clandestine monetary movements; for example, the master of the mint in Villeneuve was arrested in 1607 in the act of carrying bullion out of the town. In Montpellier, with a premium of 7 sols in the écu the mint in May 1604 found it difficult to continue the coinage. This premium rose to 8 sols in Marseilles. In addition, currency received in Limoges from Toulouse, according to a letter of July 25, 1607, often weighed only half the required weight. In Dijon in April 1605 the price of silver bullion had risen to 21 livres 5 sols the marc.[168]

The period 1589–1606 thus contrasts with the preceding two decades. After the serious conflicts of the League most mints found themselves in difficulties.

---

[167] A.N., Z¹B.76, avis of the Cour des Monnaies of June 16, 1609; A.N., Z¹B.382, Jan. 26, 1589, June 1, 1590; A.N., Z¹B.383, Jan. 30, 1592, Feb. 2, 1591; A.N., Z¹B.384, lettres patentes of Mar. 22, 1593; A.N., Z¹B.385, remonstrance of the procureur-général of Mar. 7, 1594.

[168] A.N., Z¹B.74, ordonnance of Feb. 4, 1604; A.N., Z¹B, 392, letter of Dec. 28, 1602, and report of the commission in Villeneuve-lès-Avignon; A.N., Z¹B.394, letter of May 12, 1604, from the gardes of the mint in Montpellier to the Cour des Monnaies; A.N., Z¹B.396, letter of July 25, 1607, from the mint master in Limoges to the Cour des Monnaies.

However, following the political upheaval, some of the mints — in Bayonne, La Rochelle, Villeneuve-lès-Avignon, Aix, and Rennes — reached the peak of their operations in the first decade of the seventeenth century. In general, though, the mints became increasingly inactive in the north and above all in continental France. This state of affairs in eastern France is not surprising. In the north stagnation probably indicated both a decline in the coin coming from Spain via the southern Low Countries and the increase in the trade of Holland. However, the expenditures of Spain in the Low Countries did not end with the opening of the seventeenth century; evidence from Antwerp shows that in 1605 the mint there was extremely successful.

How can we explain this downturn in the activity of the majority of the mints of France? How, indeed, can we do so without citing the rise of the United Provinces, built on the operations of astute merchants all over Europe and not least in the markets of western France, those major points of entry for silver into the country? The development of Dutch trade in the Baltic and then in the Far East at the end of the sixteenth century was essentially part of the market mechanism for the general flow of silver. It influenced their success to the detriment of others by funneling silver either through war expenditures from Spain or by trade with its neighbors, especially France. Spanish currency which appeared in France was almost at once acquired by Dutch traders. In the much larger economic perspective, the last decade of the sixteenth century was, moreover, a period of difficulty and slowing down in the economic activity of France, which the problems of silver or copper naturally aggravated. The France of Henry IV, though in many fields of activity marked by success, was considerably troubled in its economy and was indeed vulnerable. It needed fresh orientation. Along with the rapid rise in gold rates, the references to the dearth of silver in the south and east of the country increased in the seventeenth century.

Perhaps, in all this, sufficient attention has not been given to the traditional date of 1598, so critical in French history. It is important as long as it is not taken as an exclusively decisive point in the economic history of France, whose monetary structures were at this time more dependent on outside considerations. The critical dates outside France are more probably 1607, when the Spanish monarchy under Philip III again declared itself insolvent, and 1609, when the Twelve Years' Truce was signed between Spain and the United Provinces. These two moments were at the threshhold of a period when copper began to play a larger role. France, in general, did not have its own particular chronology.

3. The Phase of Copper and Credit from 1607

This phase, essentially the greater part of the seventeenth century, followed from a weakening of the silver structures in European and world trade, and in consequence, of the links with Spain. For France there were a slowing down of the pressures of bullion from outside and, as has been seen, a readjustment in monetary differences between the various regions of the country.[169] These differences continued to exist, but in a more attenuated form, and France tended to become, at least from a monetary point of view, more homogeneous. In Europe there was a general relaxation of long-distance relationships, in favor of more independent and more regionalized movements. These movements of the seventeenth century tended to prefer national governments, which were more limited in immediate aims. In brief, France experienced greater balance, increasingly national in character, under the control of Paris, which was growing in power and fame.

Why choose the year 1607 as a turning point in the history of silver? Clearly the date is approximate even though there are reasons for thinking it has some validity. At the beginning of this phase, the inflation in the "southern" economies of Europe showed signs of slackening, insofar as the evidence of price movements in Spain and Italy is indicative of the general problem. The full effects were realized slowly. In the northwest, for example in Britain and Holland, the rising trend in silver prices continued to the second quarter of the seventeenth century. It was thus a very complex long-term movement, with little comparable to the abrupt reversal in the middle of the sixteenth century, when gold gave way to silver. In general it has been called the "crisis" of the seventeenth century, and, by implication, of Spain and its prestigious empire.

In this context, therefore, the choice of the year 1607 can only be justified in general terms. For France it marked the introduction of a modified policy toward billon and copper money. Fractional money tended to play the role of a substitute.

The crux of the matter was the decline in additions to the stocks of bullion, shared by Europe and the world. However, other dates are also possible: the crisis of 1619–1620, or perhaps even 1629–1630 at the time of crop failures in Europe and on the eve of the appreciation of gold in France (gold prices began to rise in 1628 and noticeably in 1630). The years 1636,[170] 1640,[171] or 1648 in other respects may be appropriate. Nevertheless, the first date, 1607–1609, had a preparatory role and shaped the years to come. It could be compared, *mutasis mutandis*, to the experience in the Second World War after the crisis of 1929–1933. The years 1607–1609, at the beginning of the Twelve Years' Truce, were a prelude to more serious events, although the comparison requires considerable allowances.

By 1607 some markets already quoted silver above the legal rate, par-

---

[169] See series of maps in Chap. 4. The gold currency rates were raised in Spain on November 23, 1609 (Hamilton, *American Treasure*, p. 65); in England in 1611 (Feavearyear, *Pound Sterling*, p. 81); in Flanders on May 13, 1609 (*Les ordonnances monétaires du XVIIᵉ siècle*, ed. Victor Brants [Brussels, 1914], suppl. vol. to *Recueil des ordonnances des Pays Bas.* 2d Ser., ed. Laurent, Lameere, *et al.*, p. 64).

[170] Jean Meuvret, "Conjoncture et crise au XVIIᵉ siècle: L'exemple des prix milanais," *Annales: Economies, Sociétés, Civilisations,* VIII (1953).

[171] Hamilton, *American Treasure, passim.*

ticularly in the south, in Montpellier and Marseilles. During the following years a similar rise was reported in the west, linked by sea to Spain, the source of silver bullion. With the growing gap between the market and official bullion prices, the mints themselves found their activity in decline. Angers and Tours were authorized to buy silver reals in Saint-Malo and Sables d'Olonne, where trade with Spain was active. This gave some relief to those conveniently placed, but the future was by no means assured. In due course the smaller mints such as Tours and Troyes became idle, and even the bigger mints complained of increasing difficulties. In Toulouse in April 1610, trade to the Levant was blamed for the disappearance of bullion. In La Rochelle the mint master protested that since the truce of 1609 the Dutch had commandeered the grain trade through their connections in Danzig and Poland.[172] In Rouen on January 1, 1611, the officers of the mint reported that the "traffic in money is remarkable amongst the people" and that the price of silver reals rose even though they could be obtained easily enough in Saint-Malo. The inhabitants of Saint-Malo asked on February 9, 1611, for permission to send their bullion and specie to those mints which offered the best terms.[173]

These scraps of evidence tend to focus attention on the Atlantic trade, particularly on the trade between Spain and Holland. In this, Brittany had its place as an export sector more or less on its own, having a role apart from the general movement of the French economy. Brittany was deeply involved in trade with the Spanish peninsula; this was evident in 1611 when the prohibition of clipped and defective reals in Spain and Portugal was followed by protests and complaints about this currency in France, particularly in Brittany.

Nevertheless, it would be too much to believe that the bullion imported into Brittany passed immediately into circulation in France. Dutch activity explains much of the complex, indeed international, role of a port such as Saint-Malo. The disassociation of this region from the rest of the kingdom appears clearly in an inquiry dated October 4, 1607, which concerned the possibility of setting up a mint in Morlaix. The reaction of the mint master at Rennes (February 3, 1608) was typical of the monetary situation in Brittany: he indicated that in general, the bullion and specie went to Morlaix in return for cargoes of wheat and linen sent to Spain; almost immediately the precious metals were sent on to Rennes. The mint there, however, received little or no metal from Saint-Malo. The latter, though experiencing a low level of trade, nevertheless customarily sent any bullion by

---

[172] A.N., Z¹B.397, request of the mint master of La Rochelle of July 5, 1610. The exports of wheat from Danzig reached a record figure in the exceptional year of 1618, Jan Rutkowski, *Historia gospodarcza Polski* (Poznan, 1947), I, p. 167; Stanisaw Hoszowski, *Les Prix à Lwow* (Paris, 1954), Tables, for low grain prices in 1618.

[173] A.N., Z¹B.398, letter of Jan. 1, 1611, from the gardes of the mint in Rouen to the Cour des Monnaies, and request of Saint-Malo of Feb. 9, 1611.

sea to Saint-Lô, Rouen, and other ports.[174] There was little to say against such movements, but it also happened that the bullion went abroad. On December 2, 1606, the city of Saint-Malo itself complained of the ever increasing number of aliens who, it was alleged, traded "from overseas to overseas" to the detriment of the inhabitants. In February 1611, however, the town asked for the right to export bullion to ease its trade.

Actually the Dutch made their presence felt all along the west coast: in Rouen and La Rochelle they dominated the wheat trade; in Bayonne and Saint-Jean-de-Luz they manipulated the exchanges to profit from silver. The master of the Bayonne mint complained of the activities of "a number of merchants and other persons" who prevented silver from finding its way into his mint. Though on March 11, 1605, such practices were prohibited, on April 23, 1607, the same mint master renewed his complaints about the obstacles in converting Spanish reals into French currency. These coins were either carried away to Béarn or bought up in Bayonne by the masters of the Dutch ships who offered 67 sols for the écu. In the same way, silver was loaded on Dutch ships anchored in the harbor of Saint-Jean-de-Luz. An inquiry in Bayonne in January 1614 revealed that silver reals were arriving from Spain by the land route, but were almost immediately scooped up by the Dutch ships.[175] The Dutch concentrated their attention on two points of entry into France: in the southwest on the frontier of Spain; and in the ports of Brittany. Silver, by the process of trade and exchange, thus left France. Paris, not so well placed as Bayonne or La Rochelle, depended on specie from the provinces and even more on the flow of tax payments. Taxation by the government was outstanding in bringing flows of currency to the capital.

The mints in the interior of the country declined. Silver seemed to brush past the Atlantic coast. As a result, the expedient of using copper was not far away. After the edict of 1602, operations of the mint revived, but the crown began to entertain the idea of issuing copper currency. On December 21, 1602, the Conseil d'État gave permission to the mint of Paris and "nowhere else" to issue copper doubles and deniers up to the sum of 15,000 livres, but there were difficulties in putting them into circulation. On the other hand the, issues of gold and silver began to slow down in 1607 and visibly in 1609. In order to ease the conversion of the precious metals, the money changers (whose offices, it will be recalled, were suppressed in 1602) were officially reinstated by edict in April 1607. The royal government was by no means satisfied with the decline in revenue through the fall in coinage. Copper provided an easy solution.

On January 20, 1609, the establishment of four mints was envisaged to

[174] A.N., Z¹B.396, avis of Feb. 3, 1608.
[175] A.M., Saint-Malo, Ser. BB.11, Dec. 2, 1606; A.N., Z¹B.394, request of the mint master in Bayonne of Nov. 28, 1605; A.N., Z¹B.396, inquiry of the town of Saint-Malo of Feb. 9, 1611; A.N., Z¹B.77, avis of the Cour des Monnaies of Dec. 14, 1613.

coin copper doubles and deniers. Confronted with the possibility of large issues, the Cour des Monnaies immediately objected, drawing attention, with good reason, to the experience of copper *cuartillos* in Spain in 1603, which had driven the full-bodied gold and silver coins from circulation. The final measures to increase the volume of currency were not instituted until after the assassination of Henry IV. The letters patent, finally imposed on the Cour des Monnaies by lettres de jussion, which were direct orders to override opposition, gave permission to the Sieur de Vitry to set up mints for two years at Dijon and then at Bordeaux for coining copper to the amount of 30,000 livres tournois. Later, permission was given for 15,000 livres in Aix and for 30,000 livres in Paris. The pace of the copper coinage thus increased. During the first decade of the seventeenth century four towns coined copper: Bordeaux and Nantes in small quantities; Lyons for 63,623 livres; and Paris for 91,560 livres. In the second decade of the century the quantities almost doubled: from Paris (93,594 livres); from Bordeaux (44,102 livres); and large amounts also from Lyons, Nantes, Amiens, and Toulouse.[176] A new monetary period was beginning.

The issues of copper currency coincided with growing civil unrest during the minority of Louis XIII. The position of royal authority was revealed to some extent in the way in which contracts were given to the great nobles. For example, the letters patent of September 30, 1612, authorized André de Vivonne, "captain of the Queen's guards," to issue 30,000 livres tournois of copper currency in each of the towns of Nantes, Saint-Lô, and Amiens for six years; in May 1615 Christophe Poisat, agent of the Sieur de la Grange St. Vivien, found himself with similar permission for La Rochelle, which was later transferred to Poitiers, when the mint in La Rochelle was moved to the latter town.[177]

Difficulties appeared quickly. A report of January 12, 1611, from Nantes and the neighboring district noted quantities of defective copper coins, probably from Lyons. Though the issues there were stopped on June 3, later in 1614 the master of the mint, Daniel de Chambye, was arrested in Auvergne in the act of transporting copper currency by mule to Limoges; he was accused of having issued defective currency.[178]

Under such conditions, it was by no means surprising that the more valuable gold and silver currencies tended to appreciate; their market rates rose, and "monetary disorders" began to reappear. An attempt was made to prohibit the export of bullion in January 1611. The gold pistole, which was officially set at 7 livres 4 sols, went for 7 livres 5 sols on the open market.

---

[176] A.N., Z¹B.74, arrêt of the Conseil d'État of Dec. 21, 1602; A.N., Z¹B.76, edict of Apr. 1607; avis of the Cour des Monnaies of Jan. 20, 1609; lettres patentes of Jan. 31, May 28, 1610; arrêt of the Conseil d'État of Sept. 25, 1610.

[177] A.N., Z¹B.77, lettres patentes of Sept. 30, 1612; A.N., Z¹B.78, May 13, 1615.

[178] A.N., Z¹B.76, inquiry of Jan. 12, 1611; report of Aug. 21, 1613, and remonstrance of the Cour des Monnaies of Mar. 20, 1614.

There were more and more complaints of clipped and worn coins, above all from Normandy, Picardy, Champagne, and Burgundy. In August 1613, further efforts were made to restrain the rise in currency rates, especially of silver. Such a situation became much clearer during the payments of rentes on the Paris Hôtel de Ville on October 9, 1613, when the écus were counted at 76 sols and the pistoles at 7 livres 8 sols "but not without protests from many citizens." [179]

During the critical years 1607–1609 Nicolas de Coquerel published his famous Mémoire. The Cour des Monnaies replied officially on June 16, 1609, that much of Coquerel's argument came from Bodin, in particular his strenuous support of the use of the mill and of returning to a mint ratio of 1:12. Almost two weeks later, on June 28, it made further recommendations, and on September 5 (after the July conference held at Fontainebleau) the Cour des Monnaies supported the formulation of a new monetary edict to stabilize the situation. It proposed a new series of coins and a readjustment of gold and silver prices in terms of the livre tournois.[180]

Nevertheless, there were delays in accepting such proposals. When a move was finally made in 1614, the devaluation was almost double that anticipated in 1610. The edict of December 5, 1614, followed the closure of the famous Estates General of 1614, assembled on October 27, the last to meet before 1789. The reform was delayed by the proposal to forbid all foreign currency to circulate and to settle on friendly terms the rate for the English gold *jacobus,* also called the *unite,* current since 1604. The latter was arranged between the Chancelier and the English ambassador.[181]

The edict, as it finally appeared, raised the price of gold, but left the rates for silver currency unchanged at the levels set in 1602. Thus the écu was put at 75 sols, the pistole at 72 sols, and the marc of gold at 278 livres 8 sols 6 deniers, while the marc of silver remained at 20 livres 5 sols 4 deniers. This monetary system favoring gold had a considerable influence on the position of Paris, which in the early seventeenth century found it easier to acquire this money.[182]

Silver currency, now undervalued by comparison with gold, tended to disappear. In Angers in 1615 the mint master complained of smugglers and asked for permission to purchase bullion in Anjou, Normandy, and Brittany. Also with the same intentions, in 1617, the mint master of Saint-Lô requested that he be able to buy up silver in Normandy and in Saint-Malo as he had done in the preceding year. The mint masters of Nantes and La Rochelle com-

---

[179] A.N., Z¹B.77, report of the Premier Président of the Cour des Monnaies of Dec. 22, 1611, and his letter of Oct. 9, 1613.

[180] A.N., Z¹B.76, avis of the Cour des Monnaies of June 16, 28, 1609, and remonstrance of Sept. 5, 1609. See also Paul Harsin, *Les doctrines monétaires et financières en France du XVIᵉ au XVIIᵉ siècle* (Paris, 1928), p. 51, n. 3.

[181] P.R.O., S.P., 78/62, letter of Dec. 1, 1614; B.N., MSS., Nouvelles Acquistions Françaises, 2011, fol. 150, report of the Chancelier of Dec. 4, 1614.

[182] A.N., Z¹B.77, edict of Dec. 5, 1614; A.N., Z¹B.399, remonstrance of the procureur-général of Dec. 10, 1615.

peted with each other for the monopoly of purchasing precious metals in Sables d'Olonne and the neighboring ports.[183]

The difficulties of the commercial crisis of 1619–1620 were particularly felt by the mint master of Rennes. It was even suggested that the mint be shifted to Morlaix, for when the fleets from Spain arrived in the spring the silver money brought by them went mainly to the fairs held in mid-August at Guibray near Caen.[184]

Further south the situation was much the same. In Bordeaux in November 1617 there were complaints that some merchants from Toulouse, Lyons, Marseilles, and even from Italy were collecting silver reals. During that same month Bayonne reported that the market rates for silver currency were constantly rising while the quality of the coins tended to deteriorate; the mint master suggested that the quart d'écu be coined at 26 to the marc in order to compensate for the rise in silver prices. In December 1619 he reported the rising price of gold as well as the continued disappearance of the silver real in Bayonne and Bordeaux. At this time the mints in Montpellier and Villeneuve were idle. This situation had developed about May 1615, no doubt as a result of being near Avignon, where the mint was turning out coins of 10 sols, which were quickly sent to Marseilles.[185]

In Lyons it was reported on May 17, 1616, that merchants entirely disregarded the regulations, and so the edict of December 1614 was expressly republished in Paris and Lyons. In Troyes in October 1617 the écu had risen one sol above the legal rate, while the pistollet paradoxically had fallen by two sols, no doubt owing to particular conditions existing in Lyons and Franche-Comté. Amiens had to satisfy its needs with currency from Flanders, for want of a better supply.[186]

These conditions were also marked by another surge of copper coinage under Louis XIII. On February 17, 1617, Henri du Plessis, Sieur de Richelieu — the family name was not without significance — received a contract to issue copper currency for a sum of 60,000 livres tournois in six years, in each of the cities of Lyons, Toulouse, Aix, and Nantes. The contract for the mint of Dijon was later transferred to Bordeaux, while that for Nantes went to Poitiers, and later still to La Rochelle. In addition, on February 7, 1625, the brother-in-law of Plessis attempted to transfer the contract to his own name.[187]

---

[183] A.N., Z^{1}B.78, request of the mint master of Angers of Apr. 9, 1615, and of Saint-Lô of Feb. 20, 1617; A.N., Z^{1}B.401, request of the mint master of Nantes of Feb. 4, 1619.

[184] A.N., Z^{1}B.402, letter of June 1, 1623, of the procureur-général; A.N., Z^{1}B.403, requests of the mint master of Saint-Lô of May 24, 1628, Sept. 5, 1629.

[185] A.N., Z^{1}B.400, request of the mint master of Bordeaux of Nov. 24, 1617; letter of May 23, 1618, from the gardes of the mint in Villeneuve-lès-Avignon to the Cour des Monnaies; A.N., Z^{1}B.78, request of the mint master of Bayonne of Nov. 22, 1618.

[186] A.N., Z^{1}B.78, remonstrance of the procureur-général of May 17, 1616; A.N., Z^{1}B.277, inquiry in Troyes of Oct. 7–8, 1617, and in Amiens of Nov. 11–12, 1617.

[187] A.N., Z^{1}B.78, lettres patentes of Feb. 17, 1617; A.N., Z^{1}B.313, Feb. 27, 1617; A.M., Nantes, Ser. HH, 26, délibération of Oct. 20, 1617, and request of the Sieur de Richelieu of Feb. 7, 1625.

Keeping in mind the remarks already made on the rise of copper mining in Sweden, one should note that on August 19, 1621, the master of the mint in Poitiers reported that he was bringing copper from Germany by way of La Rochelle.[188]

Whether or not the copper came from Sweden, a certain number of measures were taken to restrict its more serious monetary effects. On June 26, 1624, the procureau-général of the Cour des Monnaies reduced the maximum of copper money allowed to Paris from 45,000 to 30,000 livres tournois and ordered that the coins "could not be sent to the provinces of Normandy, Picardy, and Champagne except on the express demand of the aldermen of those towns which had requirements."[189] In 1626, a year of exceptional importance for copper in Spain, the Cour des Monnaies sent to the *sénéchal* in Bayonne a prohibition on foreign billon as a result of the "report that in the town of Bayonne and elsewhere in the neighborhood, there are large amounts of foreign currency of copper and billon issued in Spain and other foreign countries in circulation which are called *quartes, quartilles* . . . and others with which the country could become loaded."[190] During that same year an inquiry opened in Morlaix "against several persons accused of having made counterfeit doubles in Flanders and brought them to Brittany to put them in circulation, and that one of the counselors of the Parlement was found to be implicated in the affair," the latter trying to use his influence to cover up the proceedings.[191] The difficulties in acquiring currency continued to favor copper to the point of using bags of this small currency for settling accounts. Copper currency appeared everywhere, sometimes coming from abroad. In the northern provinces there were vain attempts to bring a half to the invasion of patars (of patards) from Flanders: "in contravention of the prohibition previously made, the bad habit is continuing of making payments of douzains by bag and by weight without counting them, and in them are mixed a large number of patars and other billon coins."[192] Further protests came from the Cour des Monnaies on July 6, 1628, against the flow of billon coins arriving from Liège, Orange, Dombes, and Avignon and that "by the great and frequent grants of coinage of doubles, such large abuses and excesses are committed over and beyond the loss of silver given up to foreigners for copper as also for doubles which are being issued without royal permission in Châteregnault and Dombes which are brought in by the sack and are retailed by the roll at the rate of 74 sols for 4 livres."[193]

What was the use of good intentions in such circumstances? Suggestions

---

[188] A.N., Z¹B.401, request of Christofle Poisat of Aug. 19, 1621.
[189] A.N., Z¹B.402, avis of the procureur-général on the request of the Prévôt, Marchands, and Échevins of Paris of June 26, 1624.
[190] A.N., Z¹B.80, remonstrance of the procureur-général of Mar. 3, 1626.
[191] A.N., Z¹B.402, inquiry in Brittany of Aug. 26, 1626.
[192] A.N., Z¹B.80, remonstrance of the procureur-général of Sept. 7, 1628.
[193] *Ibid.,* remonstrance of the Cour des Monnaies of July 6, 1628. The location of "Châteregnault" has not yet been established.

were not lacking, as in the case of Nicolas Briot who on March 1, 1622, proposed to coin gold at 22 karats. On May 31, 1623, he received letters patent for a new press for the mint, but the Cour des Monnaies did not confirm this until June 17, 1624, and then only after lettres de jussion. He had been authorized on May 23, 1623, to mint douzains "of new type" in agreement with the Cour des Monnaies — an innovation since these coins were to have the same fineness as the full-bodied coins. Thus, the idea of reform was already in the air. The Cour des Monnaies was considering the conversion of the large number of gold pistoles in circulation, but still seemed to favor the coinage at 23 karats, even though in its avis of March 17, 1622, it had noted that "what gold does exist in France is largely made up more in pistoles than in écus." [194] Was a solution possible? The Thirty Years' War brought far-reaching changes, particularly the further appreciation of gold; the hostilities greatly aggravated the situation.

In 1628 there were signs of a rapid rise in gold prices. In July the gold pistole found currency at between 7 livres 12 sols and 7 livres 14 sols, and the French écu (officially still at 75 sols) circulated at 4 livres. The silver real, legally set at 5 sols 4 deniers actually passed at 6 sols. Faced with this inflation the government was compelled to revise the official currency rates. A partial solution of raising the rate for the pistole was discussed, but the Cour des Monnaies declared that this would inevitably entail a further change in the rate of the écu. Similar anxieties were expressed in September 1628.[195] The discussions resulted on February 5, 1630, in a readjustment of the legal currency rates. The écu was fixed at 4 livres until the end of March, then at 3 livres 18 sols until the end of June when the rate would fall to 3 livres 15 sols, the level prescribed by the edict of 1614. But in Bayonne by March 1630 a new ordinance was already forecast. On January 28, 1631, "in the discussion in our conseil . . . we have agreed to tolerate" the écu at 4 livres and the pistollet at 3 livres 17 sols. These rates were to remain in force until June 30, when the écu was to circulate for three months at 3 livres 18 sols before returning to the rate of the edict of 1614. The half scudo of Italy was forbidden currency at this time — evidence from France of the great crisis in Italy, harassed by famine first, then plague.[196] By July 23, 1631, the Conseil d'État abandoned hopes for a return to the old rates. The écu was authorized at 4 livres 2 sols until October 31, with an arrangement to revert to the old rates of 1614. On August 13, "while awaiting a more extensive rule for the monetary disorders," the écu circulated at 4 livres 3 sols, still in the hope of

[194] A.N., Z¹B.79, lettres patentes of May 31, 1623; A.N., Z¹B.402, avis of the Cour des Monnaies of Mar. 17, 1622.

[195] A.N., Z¹B.80, remonstrance of the Cour des Monnaies of July 6, 1628, and of the procureur-général of Sept. 7, 1628.

[196] *Ibid.,* déclaration of Feb. 5, 1630; A.N., Z¹B.403, letter of Mar. 12, 1630, from the sénéchal of Lyons and of Mar. 20, 1630, from the gardes et juges of the mint in Bayonne; déclaration of Jan. 28, 1631.

returning to the levels of 1614 by April 30. Again this hope was soon dis-
pelled. On September 9, 1631, the "treasurer of the rentes on the clergy of
France" received permission to set the pistole at 8 livres 2 sols in spite of the
fact that the legal rate of 8 livres had been set on August 13. In December
1632 the rate authorized for the écu was 4 livres 6 sols, and for the pistole 8
livres 6 sols; these rates were confirmed in 1633. At this same time the commercial price of the pistole in Paris was 8 livres 8 sols, and the écu was at 4
livres 10 sols; in Picardy and Champagne the pistole circulated at 8 livres 10
sols.[197] On each occasion the market rates were ahead of the monetary ordinances, while the mint prices for bullion remained at the levels of 1614.

The situation in northern France during the 1630s attracted most attention. From 1633 it was noted in Brittany, but most particularly in Picardy,
Champagne, and Normandy, that the pistole rose to 8 livres 12 sols and even
sometimes to 8 livres 14 sols. The gold écu circulated at a market rate of between 4 livres 10 sols and 4 livres 12 sols. In January 1634 the rates continued to be higher in the northern provinces, where the veteran quart d'écu
rose to between 17 and 18 sols. On June 17, 1634, the rate of 4 livres 6 sols
was authorized for the écu and 8 livres 6 sols for the pistole. At the same time
the English jacobus and the Flemish *riddes* and *albertines* were still officially
recognized and at higher rates than before. These details are significant because, after 1633, through the operation of favorable rates of exchange, English gold currency began to appear more in the monetary circulation of France.
Was there any prospect that this upward spiral would come to a halt? After
November 1663 the *receveur des rentes,* in making payments, already set the
pistole at 8 livres 10 sols. The inflation was further accentuated in the northeastern provinces: in February 1636, at Vitry-le-François, the price of the
pistole reached 8 livres 15 sols and the gold écu 4 livrès 16 sols.[198]

The gold crisis in France was part of a general appreciation of gold in Europe during the first half of the seventeenth century. It was particularly evident
in the movement of exchange rates during the 1630s. To demonstrate the
crisis, it is sufficient to show the deterioration after 1630. The situation was
clear in Lyons, where, on March 12, 1630, the unfavorable exchange rates
affected the transfer of several million livres tournois to pay the army in Italy.
The foreign policy of Richelieu entailed subsidies on a large scale, transferred
mainly by bills of exchange on Amsterdam. These payments abroad must be
related to the general crisis in Europe and France, but the heavy commitment
of the French government to wield the purse rather than the sword aggravated

---

[197] A.N., Z¹B.81, déclarations of July 23, Aug. 13, 1631; arrêts of the Conseil d'État of
Dec. 16, 1632, June 20, 1633; A.N., Z¹B.404, interrogation of Laurens Pepin of Sept. 9,
1631.

[198] A.N., Z¹B.81, "Advis donne au Roy et à nos seigneurs de son conseil par la Cour
des Monnoyes sur les désordres qui sont de présent au fait des monnoyes" of Jan. 7,
1634, and arrêt of the Conseil d'État of June 17, 1634; A.N., Z¹B.404, Nov. 23, 1633;
A.N., Z¹B.405, request of the widow of the "receveur des consignations de Vitry-le-
François" of Feb. 8, 1636.

the instability of the livre tournois. Eventually it became almost impossible to carry the heavy expenditures of paying for other countries to fight the war. Open hostilities finally began against Spain in May 1635, immediately followed by a series of reverses inflicted by the hardened Spanish troops. France was invaded, the Spanish armies overrunning the north and advancing as far as Corbie. The monetary system in 1635 reflected these critical events; devaluation was necessary. On January 7, 1634, the Cour des Monnaies drew up a list of the problems to be solved: the abundance of foreign currency in circulation; the raising of the official monetary rates; the change in rates for foreign coin; the disappearance of French currency; the inactivity of the mints; and, finally, the series of disorders, notably in Normandy, Picardy, and Champagne. The Cour also proposed remedies: an end to the circulation of foreign coins; and the restriction of bullion movements out of France and of the industrial use of precious metals.

The military setbacks suffered soon after this, however, made remedies even more urgent. An indication of the development of the crisis was the rapid rise in monetary rates, especially for gold. Under these circumstances, the edict of 1636 raised gold prices and allowed the circulation of a number of foreign coins from Europe — Bohemia, Hungary, Poland, Turkey — and included pistoles from Spain and scudi from Italy. It seemed as if all the trouble spots of Europe were losing their gold and that France benefited. The presence of scudi from Italy no doubt reflected the famine in 1628–1629 and the plague in 1630. Free circulation in France was granted to these gold coins, but the edict was less generous to the silver coins from the Italian states or from Atlantic countries, such as Spain, England, and Holland. New tariffs were established: the French écu was set at 4 livres 14 sols; the pistole at 9 livres; and the quart d'écu at 20 sols. The Cour des Monnaies protested against this reversal in monetary policy, but in vain, for the Conseil d'État had decided. The Chancelier declared, that it "was not a devaluation . . . and the King demands obedience." [199]

This edict, of course, did not settle everything. On the open market, according to a report of April 28, 1636, monetary rates continued to rise. Jewelers, goldsmiths, and refiners were said to be buying silver at 27 livres the marc and gold at more than 350 livres. This set the ratio between the two metals at about 1 : 13. The Conseil soon ordered that the official prices at the mints should be 320 livres for gold and 23 livres 10 sols for silver, which, although below the market rate, implicitly favored gold. A further modification came on June 25, 1636: the écu was set at 5 livres 4 sols; the pistole at 10 livres; and other currency in proportion. Accounts, it was stipulated, were to be kept in livres tournois. However, silver money remained at the rates set in the previous ordinance, except in the case of the piece of eight reals, which was advanced from 57 sols 6 deniers to 58 sols. The official purchase prices

[199] A.N., Z¹B.81, edict of Mar. (verified Mar. 5) 1636, and remonstrances of the Cour des Monnaies, Mar. 5, 1636.

for bullion after September 10, 1636, were 384 livres for the marc of gold and 25 livres for the marc of silver. Thus gold had again appreciated by comparison with the preceding edict.[200] These devaluations offered an opportunity for speculation on French money, especially in Venice, where the exchange rates on Amsterdam, up to that moment unfavorable, after 1636 began to improve.[201] The Cour des Monnaies attempted in vain to check the situation in France, insisting that the order of June for accounting in livres tournois should be extended to bills of exchange "while waiting for a general regulation for monetary reform." However, the upward spiral in monetary rates continued, especially for gold. In December 1636 the pistole went to 10 livres 4 sols and even in some instances to 10 livres 5 sols, while the old quart d'écu reached 21 sols. Despite rumors the crown declared itself opposed to any renewed devaluation: "our intention is not and has not been to raise currency rates." [202] But what good were such promises?

The official increase in gold monetary rates (the official ratio was now 1 : 15) and the wide diversity of gold coins authorized to circulate ended in giving France a strange assortment of money, largely from Spain, Flanders, and Italy, all zones of Spanish influence. This gold was noticeable in continental France, especially in the case of scudi from the Italian states. The maritime towns of western France were less able to obtain the bullion which had marked their earlier fortune. The mints of Bayonne, Bordeaux, La Rochelle, Nantes, and Rennes hardly operated at all. In Toulouse on July 19, 1634, the mint master asked for permission to go to Spain to buy gold and silver, returning by way of Bayonne, on condition that he would not be obliged to have the bullion converted into coin there. In continental France, by contrast, the mints in Aix and Lyons had some profitable years, though they also complained, for example on September 14, 1636, about the damage done to their operations by their rivals in Avignon and Orange.[203]

This period of difficulties ended with an attempt to restore the gold system of France and to "nationalize" this diversity of coins. The need for the famous reform of 1640 was felt well in advance. On December 4, 1639, the order was given to convert underweight écus, and on December 9 the coinage of 10,000 écus was authorized. These were at a fineness of 23 karats, in contrast to the larger part of the foreign currency which was at 22 karats. It was finally decided on March 31, 1640 to create a new series of French gold coins of 22 karats, the famous Louis d'or weighing 36¼ to the marc, with a face value of

[200] *Ibid.,* edict of June 25, 1636, and arrêts of the Conseil d'État of Apr. 26, Sept. 10, 1636.

[201] See Chap. 5; Giulio Mandich, "Di una tentata speculazione cambiaria in Venezia nel 1636," *Rivista di storia economica* (1942); Nicolaus W. Posthumus, *Inquiry into the History of Prices in Holland* (2 vols., Leiden, 1946–1964), I, Appendix.

[202] A.N., Z¹B.81, arrêt du Conseil d'État of Sept. 10, 1636, and lettres patentes of Dec. 20, 29, 1636.

[203] A.N., Z¹B.405, request of the mint master of Toulouse of July 19, 1634; letter of Sept. 14, 1636, from the gardes of the mint in Aix, and of Sept. 16, 1636, from the procureur-général.

Plate 5.

Louis d'or of Louis XIV, coined in Lyons in 1644 (actual size 3.10 cm., enlarged photograph by the Bibliothèque Nationale, Paris).

10 livres tournois. By this means a large part of the foreign currency (above all, Spanish pistoles and Italian scudi) was converted into French coin.[204]

It was further decided to refuse circulation, after three months, to coins which did not meet French requirements; this order was delayed until September 1640 and then again to December. However, by an order of June 24, 1640, exchange bureaus were opened in Lyons, Toulouse, Bordeaux, and Rennes in October 1640 and in Angers in 1641.[205]

What became of silver during this time? Overlooked in the arrangements of 1636, most silver coins soon found themselves undervalued. As a result, there were loud complaints about coin clipping, counterfeiting, and the clandestine export of silver bullion. In the Rhône Valley, where the mint of Lyons was active in coining the new gold, there were reports in December 1640 of movements of silver abroad. An adjustment had to wait until 1641, when the edict of September raised the mint price of silver to 26 livres 10 sols the marc, "in order to set the value of the marc of silver in proportion to that of gold." The coinage of the silver franc stopped, but the currency rates were raised: the quart d'écu to 21 sols; the franc to 28 sols; and the teston to 20 sols 6 deniers. It was finally decided to coin a new silver écu of 11 deniers fineness, $8^{11}/_{12}$ to the marc, with a face value of 3 livres. Gold prices remained unaltered, and, in effect, the edict lowered the official gold-silver ratio. At the same time arbitrage in gold became more profitable. The Cour des Monnaies reported that in the fairs of Lyons, during the "payments" of Epiphany and Easter 1641, there were profits of 3¼ to 4 percent on gold but only 1½ to 2 percent on silver. Thus the new rates offered more favorable conditions to pay abroad in gold, and that metal was used by the Spaniards for their military operations in Piedmont and Catalonia. As a result, further difficulties concerning gold emerged.[206]

During these years the conversion of foreign currency offered various mints a new lease of life. When the price of gold was raised in the 1630s the mints in Paris, Amiens, Lyons, Troyes, and Aix increased their operations. Bayonne, by contrast, decreased its operations. The raising of silver prices in 1641, however, allowed the mints on the west coast to expand their activity, and Bayonne revived. The work of conversion, however, was far more important than the usual run of monetary issues, above all in the capital, where the issues reached a total of some 15,000,000 livres in 1640, 25,000,000 livres in

---

[204] A.N., Z¹B.82, déclarations of Nov. 17, 1639, Mar. 31, 1640; lettres patentes of Dec. 4, 1636; A.N., Z¹B.83, arrêt of Jan. 12, 1641; Witte, *Histoire monétaire,* II, p. 107; Hamilton, *American Treasure,* p. 68, n. 2.

[205] A.N., Z¹B.82, lettres patentes of May 29, June 24, 1640, and déclaration of Oct. 11, 1640; A.N., Z¹B.83, déclaration of June 13, 1641. It should be noted that in 1644 the mint master of Paris, Varin, also took over the operations in Lyons. A.N., Z¹B.321.

[206] A.N., Z¹B.82, ordonnance of Dec. 4, 1640, and déclaration of Oct. 18, 1640; A.N., Z¹B.83, edict of Sept. (verified Nov. 18) 1641; A.N., Z¹B.408, remonstrance of the Cour des Monnaies of Oct. 30, 1641.

1641, and 20,000,000 livres in 1642. These sums vastly exceeded the combined activity of all the other mints.

What part did copper play during this period? After 1636 there were repeated attempts to counteract this expedient.[207] Richelieu's policy concerning Germany was designed to take advantage of the ambitions of Sweden. Sweden required subsidies, and the Treaty of Berwald (January 13, 1631) was the prototype for a long series of these payments. Military aid from Sweden was not achieved, it appears, without a package deal including the purchase of copper either for coinage or for the manufacture of bronze cannon. After 1626 Gustavus Adolphus considered the French market an excellent prospect for his royal copper; hardly a year passed without attempts to pass Swedish copper into France.[208] In 1631 Gustavus Adolphus presented firm proposals. A French dispatch of March 14, 1631, reported:

> He sent for M. de Charnacé [the ambassador of Louis XIII] in order to propose a matter which he said was of great importance. It was that having need of funds in recent years and seeing that it seemed to him that copper was too low in price, he did not want to sell what he had but he had an agreement with a merchant of Amsterdam named Trip for six thousand skeppund for 290 thousand rixdollars . . . ; in order to avoid this loss which he greatly suffered, and to bring these Dutch gentlemen to their senses, he would like to beg the King [his words] to take these 6 thousand skeppund from the merchant for himself and to pay him the 290 thousand rixdollars of the contract and so that the copper would be worth more . . . which he would consider a very outstanding favor from His Majesty and more profitable to him than the aid given by our treaty . . . this large quantity of copper coming into His Majesty's hands, which it would never leave, he could for five or six years set the price he wanted on his own copper."

In June there was another appeal from the Swedish King citing "the embarrassment which he has to raise the matter of the copper with the King, about which he has already written and about which he has had no reply." [209] Similar remarks were made in January and February 1633; the sale of copper was to be linked to French subsidies in Amsterdam.

In the course of these negotiations (on December 17, 1635) César de Cambont, Sieur du Tremblay, was given the right to coin copper money up to a value of 10,000 livres tournois in Toulouse and Montpellier during six years. The name Tremblay gives a further sidelight on the politics of Richelieu, just as in the same way the other beneficiaries of contracts for copper currency, the

---

[207] A.N., Z^{1}B.81, lettres patentes of Aug. 20, 1636; A.N., Z^{1}B.82, edicts of Feb., June 1640.

[208] For the contracts for Swedish copper in France, see Georg Wittrock, *Svenska Handelskompaniet och Kopparhandeln under Gustaf II Adolf* (Uppsala, 1919), pp. 121–122, 134–135, 139.

[209] A.N., Affaires Étrangères, Correspondance Politique, Suède, 2, fol. 46, reports of M. de Charnacé of Mar. 14, 1631, and fol. 84, of June 6, 1631; see also Chap. 1, n. 181.

Sieur de la Grange and the Sieur de la Brèze, were former envoys in Germany in the negotiations with the Swedes. The connections were clear enough and should not be discarded out of hand. A report from Stockholm dated April 16 and 26, 1636, again showed the efforts of the Swedes to unload copper in France "but inasmuch as copper is the most precious commodity of all Sweden, these Gentlemen want to let me know, as last year, that this crown had agreed to send the whole lot during three years to a company of Dutch merchants, associated for that purpose. And if the King were agreeable (now that the three years are up) that another company should be set up in France to receive and distribute this commodity, Sweden would be very appreciative." [210]

The purchase of copper was one step toward its coinage. The issue of copper currency had been stopped in August 1636, but by January 17, 1637, the crown made an attempt to start it again. Isaac Texier "and his associates" were given a contract to issue 1,800,000 livres tournois of copper coins during three years, using forty presses in the towns of their choice, but especially Tours, Bordeaux, Lyons, Vienne, Riom, Villeneuve, Mâcon, Toulouse, Saint-Esprit, Corbeil, Melun, Troyes, and Rouen. The letters patent for this were sent to the Cour des Monnaies on June 26, 1637, at the last moment, when the presses in Lyons were already working. The Cour reacted sharply, and the contract was withdrawn on July 4, 1637. The subsequent inquiry showed that the presses had already worked for six weeks, producing 14,227 marcs of copper money. Among its complaints, the Cour noted that the copper came from Sweden.[211]

The circulation of these coins did not depend solely on Sweden and its copper, nor indeed on the wishes of the royal authorities, divided as they were between the desire to extract the maximum revenue from coinage and the aim to stem the inflation of billon. But, as in the case of gold and silver, France was not wholly independent. Foreign copper currency constantly found its way into the country either through trade or under cover of counterfeit coins. In January 1637 a report from Nantes drew attention to the "very light" doubles which had come from Flanders and were circulating in Brittany. Elsewhere payments for large amounts were being made in Flemish patars and, in the frontier region next to Spain, in cuartillos. Everywhere, apparently, the role of copper in transactions was increasing. It was noted actively in the region of Saint-Jean-de-Luz in 1636–1637 and in Paris after July 1637, where all sorts of counterfeit copper coins — of French or foreign origin — passed unnoticed in the growing habit of making payments by weight ("by rolls"), which led, it was said, to losses of between 14 and 15 sols in the livre (by weight).

[210] Johannes G. van Dillen, "Amsterdamsche notarieele acten betreffende den koperhandel en de uitoefening van mijnbouw en metaalindustrie in Zweden," *Bijdragen en Mededeelingen van het Historisch Genootschap,* LVIII (1937), pp. 255, 260; A.N., Affaires Étrangères, Correspondance Politique, Suède, 4, fol. 186ᵛᵒ, reports of Apr. 16–26, 1636; A.N., Z¹B.81, lettres patentes of Dec. 17, 1635.

[211] A.N., Z¹B.406, inquiry and remonstrance of the procureur-général of July 4, 1637; letter of June 26, 1637, from the gardes of the mint in Lyons; procès-verbal of July 17, 1637.

The situation was even more impressive in the east of France, loaded with coin from transactions across the frontiers. There were copper doubles from Avignon, which were refused circulation in 1633; from Dombes, which flooded into Lyonnais in 1636; from Charleville, which circulated in Saint-Rémy in October 1636. During the following year, on April 24, the pieces of 5 sols together with the doubles and liards from Avignon, Dombes, Orange, Sedan, Charleville, Henrichemont, and Stenay were refused currency. The problem was huge and apparently without solution.[212] The mints in Avignon (with six presses operating) and Orange (with twelve presses operating) had literally flooded the whole Rhône Valley; the doubles they turned out were taken by carriers to Lyons and from there distributed throughout France. Popular riots occurred in Marseilles.[213] Can this phenomenon be at least partially explained by the monetary tension in France at a time of war? Must an explanation be sought, as Earl J. Hamilton has shown, in the declining imports of bullion through Seville? Under such conditions, copper played a role in balancing the monetary system more than in the preceding century.

If the copper money encumbered the lower ranges of the monetary circulation in France, the responsibility did not rest entirely on the French mints. Officially at least they were moderate in their issues. As we have seen, the attempt of 1637 was restricted. The project was successfully resumed only five years later. An arrêt of the Conseil d'État (March 12, 1642) authorized copper currency for 1,800,000 livres tournois in three years, with forty presses, three of which were to be in the region of Paris, but several leagues from the capital, and thirty-seven in the provinces. In addition it was stipulated that "all the arrêts of the said Conseil in favor of Isaac Texier, formerly undertaker of similar production, will be effective for the said [Simon] Mathieu." A week afterward, the latter complained that "it would be impossible for him to set up the presses for the first of July next . . . on account of the scarcity of copper and of the fact that to acquire it from abroad would take same considerable time." [214]

Thus the authorities in France should not be held responsible too soon. From the time that Mathieu was authorized to make these issues, there were doubts as to whether it was the soundest means to aid the poor. The interests of the government were therefore mixed. Was the abundance of copper largely due to fraud and counterfeiting? There was an abundance of doubles, "defective and of much less weight than that stipulated in the regulations," so much so that an order was made on August 5, 1643, to halve their face value: a double

---

[212] *Ibid.*, letter of Jan. 27, 1637 from the général provincial des monnaies in Brittany; A.N., Z¹B.405, letter of Nov. 15, 1636.

[213] A.N., Z¹B.81, remonstrance of the procureur-général of Oct. 1, 1636, and arrêt of the Cour des Monnaies of Apr. 24, 1637; A.N., Z¹B.406, letter of Jan. 6, 1637, from the town of Aramon, and arrêt of the Cour des Monnaies of Apr. 24, 1637.

[214] A.N., Z¹B.83, arrêt of the Conseil d'État of Mar. 12, 1642; P. Bordeaux, "Les ateliers temporaires établis en 1642 et années suivantes à Feurs, Lay, Valence, Vienne, Roquemaure, Corbeil, etc.," *Revue numismatique*, 4th Ser., XIV (1910).

became a denier. A month later another order reiterated the decision that doubles were to circulate as deniers. The royal government was no doubt making an effort to complete the silver reform of 1641 by regulating copper money, but this only opened the way to a further expansion of copper. In any case the crown did not look for a more adventurous copper policy until the situation abroad had been settled favorably. This came with the Battle of Rocroi (May 18, 1643) and finally with the Peace of Westphalia (1648). A fresh authorization to issue 60,000 livres tournois in copper money was granted to the mint in Paris on May 12, 1643, for two years, the coins to weigh 150 to the marc.[215] Thereafter the government was more cautious. It is likely that these particular problems of copper money played their part in the troubles of the Fronde.

Yet, before we enter this new period, a few words must be said about the 1640s and about the measures taken on the subject of silver, the importance of which is reasonably clear. The raising of the price of silver in 1641 favored coinage in France, but the orders for conversion to the light silver coins brought reports of quantities exported abroad. Both the southern and northern Low Countries reported the presence of French francs, quarts d'écu, and testons. There were accounts from Amsterdam on April 15, 1644, about defective quarts d'écu and from Flanders on March 27, 1645, about the "great quantity of the billon of France such as quarts d'écus, testons, and francs all light in weight." [216] The raising of the rates in 1641 nevertheless made silver currency more available in France, especially after the devaluations in Spain and its territories. In February 1643 in the payments at the fairs in Lyons transactions were often settled in silver ducatons. Disorders followed; "the greatest disorders in our currency," declared the edict of March 1645, "come from the provinces more distant from our city Paris and from the frontiers of our realm." [217] In the middle of these "disorders" silver reals arrived from Peru and Mexico and attracted considerable attention. They were reported in Nantes, Rennes, and Bayonne after January 1645; their arrival may have been aided by the fact that they had been refused currency in Flanders (August 8, 1641). Slowly the situation became clearer. On December 12, 1646, the Cour des Monnaies declared that "for some time are seen used in payment a quantity of Spanish reals said to be coined in Peru and which are very defective." These coins again appeared in Marseilles in 1648 through the operations of Genoese merchants, and their quantity increased with the years. Although on December 11, 1650, they were finally refused currency, they were still circulating in the provinces in February 1651, encouraged evidently by civil disorder. A further report from Bordeaux of March 1651 noted the appearance of particularly defective coins: "there is

---

[215] A.N., Z¹B.83, arrêts of the Conseil d'État of Aug. 5, Sept. 26, 1643.

[216] Johannes G. van Dillen, *Bronnen tot de geschiedenis der Wisselbanken* (2 vols., The Hague, 1925), I, p. 87; *Les ordonnances monétaires, du XVIIᵉ siècle*, ed. Brants, pp. 181–204.

[217] A.N., Z¹B.409, letter of Feb. 17, 1643, from N. Fremile; A.N., Z¹B.84, edict of Mar. 1645.

a great trade in the present town with the Spaniards during the two famous fairs held here in March and August and the Spanish merchants and others trading with Spain cull out the worst Peruvian coins and take them to change at the mint and leave the better Peruvian coins in the mints of Madrid, Saragossa, Aragon, Pamplona in Upper Navarre and others in the said Kingdom of Spain." [218] Whether they were good or bad, these silver reals flowed into the mints of France, especially in Paris, and offered material for coinage.

From the end of the Fronde to the Peace of Nijmegen (August 1678), the phase of copper culminated during the great years of Louis XIV. The list of successes, real and apparent, from the beginning of the personal reign of Louis XIV (1661) would be long indeed. Military and diplomatic honors followed in an almost unbroken stream: the precedence of the ambassadors of France over those of Spain (1661); the humiliation of the Pope (1662); the War of Devolution (1667); the acquisition of Lille, Tournai, and Charleroi by the Treaty of Aix-la-Chapelle (1668); the isolation of Holland as a result of treaties with England (1670), the Empire (1671), and Sweden (1672). At this time the great work of Colbert began to give France the elegant economic structures of the *ancien régime*. And mercantilism aimed to attract bullion to the country. Although the early years of Colbert's ministry were apparently crowned with success in restoring the French economy after the civil disturbances of the Fronde, his system finally coincided with a period of favorable foreign payments. The quotations of the livre tournois (the unit of the écu was fixed at 3 livres tournois) in Amsterdam followed an upward trend. It is clear from the available data that this had begun about ten years before Colbert assumed power, and, before his death in 1683, there were unmistakable signs of a trend in the opposite direction.

What was seen at the time — although it should not obstruct the observation of other factors — was the multiplication of inferior money. The monetary reforms themselves were signs of change. The letters patent of June 12, 1649, authorized the issue of copper liards (of 3 deniers face value) at a weight of 66 to the marc. They met with opposition. On two occasions lettres de jussion were sent, on September 27, 1649, and again after the Fronde, on April 1, 1654. The declaration of July 1, 1654, ordered the new series of copper currency, but only after the complaints from Paris were heard, when the weight of 60 to the marc was proposed.[219]

The plan envisaged the use of eighty presses for a period of nine months; the coins already in circulation were to be converted into French liards with 120 presses working over a period of two years and three months. On August

---

[218] A.N., Z¹B.83, report of the procureur-général of Jan. 14, 1645; A.N., Z¹B.84, arrêt of the Conseil d'État of Dec. 12, 1646; A.N., Z¹B.410, report of Oct. 16, 1648; remonstrance of the procureur-général of Dec. 31, 1648; A.N., Z¹B.85, edict of Dec. 11, 1650; mémoire of the Cour des Monnaies, Dec. 22, 1651, and prohibition of Feb. 1, 1651.

[219] A.N., Z¹B.85, arrêt of June 12, 1649; A.N., Z¹B.411, lettres patentes of July 11, 1654.

7, 1649, however, it was decided to limit the number of presses to forty for a period of six months (Corbeil, eight; Pont-de-l'Arche, five; La Rochelle, five; Meung, five; Bordeaux, five; Caen, four; Vienne, four; Nîmes, four) and to "transform" with sixty presses for a period of eighteen months. In 1654, after more lettres de jussion, the Cour des Monnaies finally agreed to begin the operations with forty presses. Among the mints, Paris alone was authorized to issue copper, and then only 100 marcs (an extra issue to be included in those recorded at Corbeil). This was done on October 27, 1654, and the operations were finally completed in 1658.[220] In October 1658 a further order limited the circulation of copper coins to those with legal currency.[221]

These issues of copper coins coincided also with an attempt to coin silver billon — the six blancs, ordered in August 1656. These, however, were stopped by the letters patent of November 19, 1657, and replaced by sols and doubles sols, but these again were revoked by an arrêt of Conseil d'État, at the request of the *prévôt* and *échevins* of Paris, as being injurious to trade.

This copper currency acted like yeast in everyday transactions. The order of May 28, 1658, was not, therefore, surprising; it forbade, among other things, the transporting of liards to Paris.[222] No doubt this was an act of political prudence, for copper money had to be controlled lest it disturb the newly restored monetary edifice. The liards, originally current at 3 deniers, were reduced to 2 deniers by the letters patent of July 4, 1658, and then, on November 14, 1664, to 1½ deniers.[223] At the same time these coins were flooding the provinces. A remonstrance of the Cour des Monnaies of March 28, 1665, declared that "the copper money is almost the only one which remains in the provinces in the hands of the people." [224]

Foreign billon also increased the volume of fractional money. Reports confirmed the arrival of defective coins from Charleville in January 1647, from Artois in September 1650, and from Orange in June 1658 and November 1660, in addition to the issues from Sedan and Dombes.[225] A fairly long series of ordinances (July 4, 1653, July 1, 1654, September 16, 1654, May 26, 1655) aimed to restrict the circulation to French currency, but the repetition of these orders implied that they were ineffective and that the small coins continued to arrive from abroad.[226]

The circulation of the coins worth 5 sols (that is, a twelfth part of a silver écu) also presented difficulties. By the arrêt of the Conseil of April 22, 1660, the issue of these coins was forbidden for a year, but this prohibition raised a protest from the Cour des Monnaies on November 15, 1660: "these coins are the most convenient coins of trade and have become absolutely necessary by

---

[220] A.N., Z¹B.917, lettres patentes of May 12, 1648; A.N., Z¹B.412, Jan. 11, 1655.

[221] A.N., Z¹B.88, arrêt of Oct. 23, 1658.

[222] A.N., Z¹B.413, arrêt of the Cour des Monnaies of May 28, 1658.

[223] A.N., Z¹B.88, lettres patentes of July 4, 1658, Dec. 14, 1664.

[224] A.N., Z¹B.416, remonstrance of the Cour des Monnaies of Mar. 28, 1665.

[225] A.N., Z¹B.84, arrêt of Jan. 17, 1648; A.N., Z¹B.85, arrêt of Sept. 17, 1650; A.N., Z¹B.88, arrêts of June 30, 1658, Nov. 20, 1660.

[226] A.N., Z¹B.90, arrêt of the Cour des Monnaies of May 18, 1665.

reason of the scarcity [the use of the term scarcity should be carefully noted in this context] of billon and the fifteen-sols pieces." On May 23, 1663, the lieutenant of the admiralty of Marseilles confiscated — the incident was by no means surprising — "a certain quantity of five-sol pieces issued by the mints of Orange and Avignon." [227]

Was the Cour des Monnaies well informed concerning the scarcity of billon? The Conseil d'État was obliged, for its own part, on August 5, 1665, to forbid making more than a twentieth part of payments with bags of douzains; this was no sign of shortage. In the following year, on October 7, 1666, the King noted "the disorder which has crept into the settlement of bills of exchange, merchandise, and other obligations in which the majority of debtors who were of difficult commercial procedure compelled those who were receiving payment to accept bags of sols called douzains." According to the report of Colbert, payments by bags was forbidden: the coins were to be counted one by one, under pain of a fine of 3,000 livres and confiscation of the coin. However, between what the government wanted and what the country was prepared to accept lay a gulf.[228]

The flow of billon seemed to be an unsatisfactory expedient, and not at all surprising in view of the increasing number of counterfeit coins. It is possible to understand this from some brief examples. A report of the Procureur-Général of January 9, 1663, stated that there were counterfeit coins at Lyons; another, dated February 15, 1663, noted that "in the neighborhood of the towns of Bayonne and Toulouse there has been produced a large amount of counterfeit coins which has filled the channels of trade." On May 15, 1665, the Cour des Monnaies, faced with disorders, forbade the currency of doubles (which had become deniers) as well as deniers issued by French mints. The Procureur-Général (on March 11, 1671) again reported the presence of copper doubles from Rouen, dated 1656, "like those," he declared, "which were coined at that time but which are much smaller and lighter, and which have most likely been brought from abroad and are now being circulated in the province of Normandy." [229] Whether accepted or rejected, copper currency found a range of activity beyond the reach of governmental measures.

The war between France and Holland was another occasion for the issue of billon, this time the famous coins of 4 and 2 sols, although by definition these were not strictly billon. The silver écus issued in 1641 at 3 livres had also been coined in fractions of 30, 15, and 5 sols. On this occasion the 4 sols pieces were at a fineness of 10 deniers, instead of the 11 deniers for the silver écus; their weight was 150 to the marc, and those of 2 and 3 sols were in proportion. The coinage, authorized by the order of April 8, 1674, was given to Paris and Lyons, to be carried out with seven balance presses, four in Lyons and three

---

[227] A.N., $Z^1B.88$, remonstrance of the Cour des Monnaies of Nov. 15, 1660, *passim;* A.N., $Z^1B.89$, report of May 23, 1663.

[228] A.N., $Z^1B.90$, arrêt of Oct. 7, 1666.

[229] A.N., $Z^1B.89$, remonstrances of the procureur-général of Jan. 19, Feb. 15, 1663; A.N., $Z^1B.90$, arrêt of the Cour des Monnaies of Mar. 11, 1671.

in Paris; coinage was to begin in September 1674 and end in September 1677. Already before the former date, counterfeit versions began to circulate as the trial and execution of one culprit, Jean Gallot, revealed; later François Crosnier was convicted of the same crime.[230]

This coinage was stopped by an arrêt of the Conseil d'État of September 21, 1677. The greater part of the coins had been issued by Lyons, for a total of 12,753,461 livres; these were coined, in all probability, at Vimy-Neuville, in the neighborhood of Lyons. Paris produced 7,459,036 livres. These issues again coincided with the pressing needs of wartime finance. In the meantime an arrêt of the Conseil d'État of November 14, 1676, increased the coinage "in order to find a timely aid to the affairs of state and to contribute to the pressing expenses of the war." Colbert explained on March 7, 1679, in the Conseil that "the same abuse had been made in the use of sols which were being circulated in bags in large payments for considerable sums." A scale was fixed limiting the legal tender of these coins: up to 10 livres, it was considered full legal tender; from 10 to 500 livres, a quarter could be paid in 4 sols and a tenth in douzains.[231] No doubt this control of the use of 4 sols was part of the difficulties of the war, but the reappearance of a silver billon coin rather than a renewal of the issues of copper was perhaps evidence of changes for the better in the circulation of gold and silver.

The period of the Fronde (1648–1653) was marked by sharp increases in the rates for gold and silver. This was probably due in part to a breakdown in civil order. On August 1, 1650, the écu circulated between 105 and 106 sols, the louis at 10 livres 8 sols, the pistole at 10 livres 10 sols, while the silver écu arrived at 61 sols. Gold rates tended to advance even more than those of silver. In Paris, the center of the revolt, this inflation was apparently severe, but in the majority of the provinces, such as Lyonnais, Auvergne, and Bourbonnais, gold coins also circulated at levels above those officially established. On January 10, 1652, the Parlement of Paris proposed that the gold pistole should be fixed at 11 livres 10 sols; in April the gold louis was raised to 11 livres and the écu to 5 livres 14 sols. The Procureur-Général further confirmed the inflation on January 16, 1652, when he noted that it was part of a general trend in the preceding two years. On March 7, 1653, the louis was raised to 12 livres, the pistole to 11 livres 16 sols, and the silver écu was set at 3 livres 10 sols. These rates, which greatly favored gold, lasted until June. After May 1653 reports circulated of gold pistoles weighing an eighth below the official weight.[232] Also in 1653 there was an abrupt fall in the exchanges of French

---

[230] A.N., Z¹B.92, lettres patentes of Apr. 8, 1674; A.N., Z¹B.93, arrêts of the Cour des Monnaies of May 16, Sept. 23, 1676.

[231] A.N., Z¹B.93, arrêts of the Conseil d'État of Nov. 14, 1676, Sept. 21, 1677; A.N., Z¹B.94, arrêt of the Conseil d'État of Mar. 7, 1679.

[232] A.N., Z¹B.85, remonstrances of the procureur-général of Aug. 1, 1650, Jan. 16, 1652; lettres patentes of Apr. 4, 1652; arrêt of the Conseil d'État of Mar. 7, 1653; A.N., Z¹B.86, remonstrance of the Cour des Monnaies of May 19, 1653.

money on the Amsterdam bourse: the quotations for the écu soleil (since 1602 fixed at 3 livres tournois) reached their lowest point of the seventeenth century.

Some time was required to emerge from these difficulties. By the edict of December 1655 a new series of coins was started: the gold and silver *lys,* of a high fineness, but weighing less and current at lower rates than the earlier series of coins. The gold lys was coined at 23¼ karats and 60½ to the marc; it was current at 7 livres. The silver lys of a fineness of 11 deniers 12 grains weighed 30½ to the marc; it was current at 1 livre tournois. The issues of these coins did not, however, last very long. The silver coins were issued only in 1656, and the gold coins only in 1656 and 1657. After these dates the previous series of gold and silver coins continued to be used. On April 8, 1656, the louis was rated at 11 livres, the gold écu at 5 livres 14 sols, and the silver écu at 3 livres.[233] These changes thus revealed a rise in the bimetallic ratio of gold to silver as compared with that set in 1641.

After the Fronde, as has already been noted, the exchange rate for the livre tournois in Amsterdam for a time became unfavorable. In December 1660 it was said that currency rates would be raised again, but nothing came of it; and the various coins remained at their former rates. But in 1662, although these rates continued, the price of the marc of fine gold in bullion was raised to 423 livres 10 sols 11 deniers. Colbert's policy was, in effect, to try to lower the official currency rates. On December 7, 1665, he succeeded in making a reduction of the gold louis to 10 livres 15 sols. But on September 16, 1666, as a result of "requests and importunities made to the King by merchant-bankers and other traders in the chief towns of his kingdom, together with the different information which had been collected on his orders about the amount of gold and silver in specie and bullion which has left the country since the deflation," [234] the rate was raised to 11 livres.

The silver problem concerned, without specifying, the silver reals of Spain. Good or bad, they appeared in France. Light and defective reals were refused currency at the beginning of the 1650s, yet this effort was in vain. They were again prohibited by the Cour des Monnaies on October 23, 1658, and still they continued to circulate. Their presence was noted in the report of June 10, 1666, on the activities of goldsmiths and other craftsmen. They made a further appearance and were on July 16, 1672, refused circulation in the province of Artois on order of the Conseil d'État.[235]

The war in Holland also directed attention to the strategic question of stocks of bullion. On April 11, 1673, the Conseil d'État noted that "as from the beginning of the war, much gold and silver specie has left the kingdom, and those

---

[233] A.N., Z¹B.88, edict of Dec. (verified Dec. 23) 1655 and déclaration of Apr. 8, 1956.

[234] *Ibid.,* report of the procureur-général of Dec. 16, 1660; A.N., Z¹B.89, arrêt of the Conseil d'État of July 7, 1662; A.N., Z¹B.90, arrêt of the Conseil d'État of Sept. 16, 1666.

[235] A.N., Z¹B.90, arrêt of the Conseil d'État of June 10, 1666; A.N. Z¹B.92, arrêt of the Conseil d'État of July 16, 1672.

provinces which trade with Spain would have difficulty in continuing." At the same time the rate for pieces of eight reals was raised to 58 sols in Paris, and in the following month to 60 sols. Elsewhere reals were current at the same rates. How was it possible in southwestern France, so dependent on Spain, to get by without them? On November 24, 1676, "various private individuals of the region of Béarn, Bayonne, and other frontier zones" passed reals in circulation at 56 sols.[236] They were ordered to follow the official rates, but the incident points out the disparity of zones in France and the effect of the pressures of war.

Under such circumstances, any general reform faced considerable difficulties. Colbert nevertheless tried by a series of regulations to achieve two results: to keep a certain balance in the monetary circulation, a typically mercantilist endeavor; and to simplify the system. A step in this direction was taken in the order of April 26, 1672, which established restrictions on the use of gold and silver in manufacture. Gold plate for the table was forbidden, and silverware was limited to 12 marcs for basins and 8 marcs for plates. There were more important measures in 1668 to reform the monetary circulation by converting pistolles into gold louis; as a result the mints increased the issues of the latter coin, but gold currency from abroad also continued to find its way into the country.[237]

Actually new policies were impossible as long as the war against Holland continued, but once this was ended, a further series of measures was attempted. By the declaration of March 28, 1679, a number of coins were refused currency. Only gold louis, écus, and pistoles and silver écus remained officially in circulation. The operations of conversion were in advance made easy: the marc of gold was set at 437 livres 9 sols 8½ deniers, and the King, for a period at least, waived his claims to seigniorage. The Conseil d'État also gave instructions for more mints to be opened; by the arrêt of April 4, 1679, the mints of Amiens, Rouen, La Rochelle, Aix, Montpellier, and Metz were opened to effect conversions. Later the arrêt of April 15, 1679, gave similar permission to Tours and Limoges, and by the edict of April (registered May 5) 1679 the old mint in Troyes was transferred to Rheims. The declaration of March 28, 1679, reduced the face value of the pieces of 4 sols to 3 sols and 9 deniers; a month afterward there was a further revaluation to 3 sols and 6 deniers.[238]

The measures concerning gold did not mention the relative bullion prices of gold and silver. In 1662, with gold at 423 livres 10 sols 11 deniers and silver at 27 livres 13 sols the marc, the ratio of fine gold to fine silver had been 1 : 15.32. In July 1692, with gold at 450 livres and silver at 30 livres the marc, the mint ratio was 1 : 15. Because there was an absence of precautionary

---

[236] A.N., Z¹B.92, arrêts of the Conseil d'État of Apr. 11, May 12, 1673; A.N., Z¹B.93, arrêt of the Conseil d'État of Nov. 24, 1676.

[237] A.N., Z¹B.92, déclaration of Apr. 26, 1672, and ordonnance of Aug. 3, 1672.

[238] A.N., Z¹B.94, déclaration of Mar. 28, 1679; edict of Apr. 1679; arrêts of the Conseil d'État of Apr. 4, 15, 29, Sept. 28, 1679.

measures in 1679 for silver, considerable exports may have followed. In Villeneuve-lès-Avignon on September 5, 1679, a report drew attention to the fact that "reals which were all from Mexico and Seville" were finding their way to Avignon and Italy. During the same month the Cour des Monnaies heard that sols and other coins no longer having currency were leaving the country for Flanders. In compensation foreign coins were appearing in Provence, Languedoc, and Dauphiné, "a very large number of deniers from Orange, Dombes, Monaco, and other foreign money." Into Champagne, Picardy, and neighboring provinces went *escalins* from Flanders.[239]

From the Fronde to the Peace of Nijmegen, increasingly stable monetary conditions apparently prevailed, no doubt encouraged by the centralization of the administration. Already present in the reforms of 1640s, this tendency toward rationalization was further accentuated by the letters patent of August 19, 1656, which granted Samuel Pannier the lease of the mints of Paris and of five other towns. Colbert aided this policy even though he did not initiate it. In May 1662 Denis Génisseau was granted a general farm of the mints for six towns: Paris, Rouen, Lyons, Bayonne, Aix, and Rennes. Two of these towns, Bayonne and Rennes, were important transit points in the west for bullion movements among France, Spain, and Portugal; the other four were on the great route from the Channel to the Mediterranean. On January 28, 1666, the Conseil d'État revoked this lease and gave the contract to Claude Thomas; on September 28, 1672, they gave it in turn, to Vincent Fortier.[240]

As this last period came to a close there was increasing concern with the problems of gold and silver, accentuated by greater pressure from governmental controls. Repeated efforts were made to prevent the export of bullion and to control the domestic circulation: orders in March 1644, in March 1654, in January 1657, in August 1660, in November 1662, and so forth. Soon after Colbert assumed his position, he attempted to simplify the internal monetary relationships of France. Yet these were not simple matters to arrange.[241]

The seventeenth-century expansion of the operations of the mint in Lyons symbolized, to some extent at least, the resurgence of continental France. It issued large quantities of gold currency and made the largest production of pieces of 4 sols. In July 1660 the master of the mint, however, admitted that his operations depended on the bullion available in the ports of the west and that he had agents in Paris and Saint-Malo for this purpose. As the years passed, conditions long experienced in Lyons continued to be evident. On November 21, 1670, Jean Tourvielle, a merchant of Dauphiné, made a request to the Cour des Monnaies and mentioned that fourteen sacks of silver tokens made in Germany had been bought in Lyons for export to the Levant.

[239] *Ibid.*, remonstrance of the procureur-général of Sept. 5, 1679, and arrêts of the Cour des Monnaies of Sept. 20, 1679, Apr. 28, 1681, Jan. 28, 1682.
[240] A.N., Z¹B.89, lettres patentes of May 1662; A.N., Z¹B.90, arrêt of the Conseil d'État of Jan. 28, 1666; A.N., Z¹B.92, arrêt of the Conseil d'État of Sept. 28, 1672.
[241] A.N., Z¹B.89, arrêt of Sept. 10, 1663.

On June 23, 1670, the West India Company (*Compagnie des Indes Occidentales*) was authorized to coin and export 30,000 livres of silver pieces of 5 sols, 10,000 livres of sols, and 10,000 livres of copper doubles. In the west the mint of Rennes continued to be predominantly concerned with issues of silver: on February 16, 1682, they still spoke of "the operations of the mint in Rennes since the arrival of the fleet." In contrast, Bayonne, which had been so closely tied to the silver of Spain during the silver phase, proved itself able, after 1668, to make issues of gold currency.[242] This coinage of gold louis was no doubt the conversion of light pistoles, but their presence in the southwest, customarily so attached to silver, was an important sign for the future. This new trend to the changing situation, both in the Spanish colonies, where gold was the first time coined in Mexico, and in the Portuguese colonies in the Brazilian interior, where the discoveries and exports of gold soon made their mark on the monetary circulations of Europe.

4. The Beginnings of the Eighteenth Century: The Age of Gold (1681–1725)

In this section I shall review briefly the half century to the eve of 1726. The great reform of that year set a bench mark in the monetary history of France, virtually establishing the structures that would last for the duration of the *ancien régime*. Certain aspects are clear enough. There were rising imports of gold into Europe after discoveries in Brazil, a trade in which Britain managed to acquire a dominant share. There were the wars fought bitterly on sea and land which were to draw the last, relentless veil over the territorial dreams of Louis XIV. And there were the speculative projects of John Law, framed in the context of coinage and credit. All these set the tone of the period. The reform of 1726 confirmed the basic tendencies which were emerging in the preceding decades, but this great settlement did not signify the close of a phase. To be more precise, the years under discussion belong to a much larger monetary phase, which rightly extends to the middle of the eighteenth century. In this period, what was the particular experience of France?

It must be emphasized at the outset that the reactions in France were colored by the fact that these years belong to a pivotal period in the widest historical sense. In one respect the eighteenth century, the Enlightenment, benefited from scientific discoveries and far-reaching transformations in the cultural climate of Europe, themselves deriving from the endeavors of many scholars and empiricists in the previous century. The "Age of Newton" — an apt label chosen from among many possible ones — implied a transition to the acquired rationalism of the eighteenth century. In the area of coinage, new skills and techniques brought improvements in the accuracy of coins issued. The presses,

---

[242] A.N., Z¹B.414, request of the mint master of Lyons of July 20, 1660; A.N., Z¹B.92, request of Tourvielle of Nov. 21, 1670; arrêt of the Conseil d'État of June 23, 1670; A.N., Z¹B.94, arrêt of the Cour des Monnaies of Feb. 16, 1682.

the dies, and the refining of metals all benefited in their own way. The techniques used by the mints at the time of John Law's administration represented great improvements over methods employed when Charles VIII fabricated gold écus in preparation for his descent on Italy.

In the wider context of the European economy, the years from 1680 to the mid-eighteenth century also formed a turning point. The convergence of grain prices in terms of silver was particularly marked in the early decades of the eighteenth century. At the same time a price rise slowly asserted itself: some areas showed precocious tendencies toward inflation by the 1680s; others hesitated until the second quarter of the following century before joining the long-term trend.[243]

In another respect the end of the seventeenth century marked a further departure, which has already been mentioned: the improved availability of gold. Although the established sources of gold, especially Africa, showed evidence of increasing trade, the western Atlantic largely disgorged the new supplies. Along with sugar and other products, gold began to flow into Europe, certainly after 1700 and impressively in the 1720s. Another turning point in monetary history had been reached.

Some gold was produced in Mexico, but the main new source was Brazil. There the Portuguese plied the alluvial deposits of Minas Gerais with the slaves from Africa. Portuguese influence and control spread into the interior with the establishment of the captaincies of Minas Gerais (1720), Matto Grosso (1744), and Goyaz (1748). Lisbon returned for a time to preeminence as a market for gold, a reflection of its experience on the eve of the great days of Seville. The prestige of Portugal was such that in 1750, in the Treaty of Madrid, Spain finally agreed to a bold correction in Portugal's favor of the Treaty of Tordesillas (1494), which had set the line of demarcation between the two spheres of empire building.

France was caught in the backwash of these important changes. During the last two decades of the seventeenth century the proportion of gold issued by the mints followed a rising trend: by the late 1690s about three-quarters of the total value of the currency issued in France was gold, an average level exceeded only in the early sixteenth century and again during the great reforms of the 1630s and the early 1640s.

The monetary system of France, indeed, was adjusted to attract gold, and the bimetallic ratio tended to be set higher during these years. The complement to this, a recurring theme of reports to the Cour des Monnaies, was a tendency for silver to disappear. It emerged in the discussion of the reform of 1686, and the edict of 1687 attempted a remedy, by lowering the rates for gold coins. Yet, as the statistics show, the rising proportion of gold in the coinage remained unchecked.

[243] Fernand Braudel and Frank Spooner, "Prices in Europe from 1450 to 1750," in *The Cambridge Economic History of Europe*, IV, ed. E. E. Rich and C. H. Wilson (Cambridge, Eng., 1967).

The experience of France, however, was not confined to the flows of bullion adjusted by international markets. The policies of states had their part to play, and not least the conduct of monetary affairs across the Channel. The situation in Britain contrasted with that in France. In London the mint coined large quantities of silver in the 1690s, taking into account the great silver recoinage of 1696–1698 when coins were also issued in Bristol, Chester, Exeter, Norwich, and York. In the decade as a whole (1691–1700), out of a total coinage of £7,216,632 sterling, 29.98 percent was in gold compared with 78.53 percent in 1681–1690.[244] The opposite was true in France, where an average of 51.94 percent of the total coinage in 1681–1690 and of 66.50 percent in 1691–1700 was in gold.

A trend in the opposite direction, toward the coinage of silver, emerged during the truce between the two countries (1699–1701); and this trend was further confirmed with the renewed conflict over the Spanish succession. On November 1, 1700, Charles II of Spain died, leaving the throne to the French claimant, the Duke of Anjou, who in turn became Philip V. France swept away the Pyrenees at the price of war with Holland, Britain, and the Empire (1701–1713). The monetary implications of these hostilities soon became evident. While the Bourbon monarchy, through the dynastic link with Spain, had access to the Empire in the New World with its great mines, particularly of silver, Britain turned toward Portugal, the mistress of Brazil and its flourishing gold fields. The latter association culminated in the famous Methuen Treaty, signed on December 27, 1703, by Don Emmanuel Telles Silvias and John Methuen, the British ambassador extraordinary in Portugal. By the first article British woolen cloth entered Portugal on preferential terms, and by the second article Portuguese wines went to Britain at rates lower than those from France. The treaty became one of the great commercial events of the eighteenth century and later provided David Ricardo with a case study of comparative advantage.[245]

The effects of this alignment became apparent in France both in the coinage and in the monetary administration. The latter has already been mentioned. The change in trends gave Lyons the opportunity to acquire a separate Cour des Monnaies, with control over the mints in Aix, Bayonne, Grenoble, Lyons, Montpellier, Riom, and Toulouse.[246] The change in the coinage was even more rapid: the trend toward issues in silver was accelerated. By 1708 the coinage of gold had fallen to only 7.3 percent of the total output for France, and then from the reform of 1709 until the time of John Law[247] fluctuated between one-

---

[244] Sir John Craig, *The Mint* (Cambridge, Eng., 1953), pp. 184–197.

[245] David Ricardo, *On the Principles of Political Economy and Taxation* in *The Works and Correspondence of David Ricardo,* ed. Piero Sraffa (10 vols., Cambridge, Eng., 1951–1955), I, Chap. 7.

[246] See Chap. 2, Section 3.

[247] See Chap. 5, Section 2. John Law expressed the view in "Restablissement du commerce, September 1715," in *Œuvres complètes,* ed. Paul Harsin (3 vols., Paris, 1934), II, p. 111, that "the union of France and Spain gave us the fond hope of promoting our trade . . . in this respect we exhausted ourselves of gold and silver."

fifth and one-third. Thus, it seems that the hostilities between the two countries brought a special crop of monetary troubles. Through its connection with Portugal, Britain gained an advantage in the flows of gold. Observers remarked that no Portuguese gold was imported into England before 1703 but that this soon changed. In the years 1710–1713 the mint in London coined 3,550,008 ¾ gold cruzados, and in some cities of England Portuguese gold coins were standard currency.[248] France continued the war in conditions largely dominated by silver. With the hostilities ended in the Treaty of Utrecht (1713) and with the experience of the extraordinary John Law endured and then assimilated, France returned to the trend typified by the role of gold in the early eighteenth century. This was confirmed in the reform of 1726.

During the years 1681–1725 both the types of coin and the currency rates underwent frequent changes, only the main alterations will be indicated here. First came two decades leading to the reversal of 1700–1701, which was confirmed in the Methuen Treaty and rationalized in the reform of 1709. The second period included the peace and early years of the administration of John Law. Finally there were the debacle of the East India Company (*Compagnie des Indes*) and the restoration of the monetary system, achieved in 1726.

Until 1709 coins were issued at the same standards as those of 1640–1641, that is, the gold louis at 22 karats fine and 36¼ to the marc and the silver écu at 12 deniers argent-le-roi and $8\frac{11}{12}$ to the marc. Although redesigned coins were ordered in 1686, 1687, 1689, 1693, 1701, and 1704, they all met these basic requirements for weight and fineness.

However, the key to the situation lay in the price of gold. In 1679 the marc of gold had been put at 437 livres 9 sols 8 deniers and silver at 29 livres 6 sols 11 deniers the marc, implying a bimetallic ratio of 14.91. Then came the revocation of the Edict of Nantes (1685), associated, as Herbert Lüthy has clearly demonstrated, with the financial operations of the Protestant merchants and bankers.[249] In any case, on July 27, 1686, the price of gold was raised to 457 livres 7 sols 5 deniers; silver remained unchanged, thus raising the ratio to 1 : 15.57.

The War of the League of Augsburg also brought some small adjustments. The declaration of January 3, 1690, set the marc of gold at 457 livres 16 sols and the marc of silver at 30 livres, thus lowering the ratio to 1 : 15.26. Then, on May 20, 1692, the price of gold was reduced to 450 livres, which reduced the ratio to 1 : 15. It is interesting to note how often in the succeeding years the monetary authorities, particularly under the administration of John Law, attempted to maintain this relationship; it was retained in the order of December 12, 1693, which put the marc of gold at 465 livres and silver at 31 livres, and the same ratio was again attempted in 1699.

---

[248] Alan D. Francis, *The Methuens and Portugal, 1691–1708* (Cambridge, Eng., 1966), p. 217.
[249] Herbert Lüthy, *La Banque Protestante en France* (2 vols., Paris, 1959–1961).

At this point the monetary situation began to change rapidly. The peace signed at Ryswick in 1697 almost at once opened a new monetary conflict over the control of gold. The arrêt of September 22, 1699, raised the price to 502 livres 10 sols and that of silver to 33 livres 10 sols, keeping the ratio at 1 : 15. Three months later, however, this was radically modified. With the price of gold raised to 518 livres 10 sols and silver lowered to 32 livres 15 sols by the arrêt of March 23, 1700, the ratio rose to 1 : 15.83. The monetary system of France was thus officially adjusted to attract gold, and the alteration conformed to the progressive decline in the proportion of gold in the total coinage issued by French mints. Although every effort was made to return to the currency rates of 1693 — by June 1701 the price of gold was set at 462 livres 6 sols and silver at 30 livres 16 sols, making a ratio of 1 : 15.01 — the situation could not be maintained. As France embarked on the adventure of the Spanish succession and the Duke of Anjou became Philip V (November 1, 1701), bullion prices rose, and the battle was joined for the control of gold. By the declaration of September 27 gold was raised to 514 livres 1 sol 2 deniers the marc, at a bimetallic ratio of 15.02. Then the underlying intentions of French monetary policy became clear: to draw bullion, particularly gold, from Spain. By the arrêt of the Conseil of February 4, 1702, the marcs of gold and silver "coming from Spain" and entering France through the ports of Rouen, Saint-Malo, Bayonne, and Marseilles were put at 553 livres 12 sols 8 8/11 deniers and 36 livres 19 sols 3 deniers, respectively, instead of the rates fixed on September 27, 1701.[250] These special rates were lowered slightly by the arrêt of the Conseil of August 22 to 543 livres 15 sols and 35 livres 19 sols 10 deniers, referring this time to the gold and silver entering by the ports of Rouen, Saint-Malo, Nantes, La Rochelle, Bayonne, and Marseilles.[251] As the military campaigns began, the monetary purpose of France was clearly underlined in the arrêt of November 18 which set higher rates for gold and silver "marked from Spain" than for the gold and silver "without mark." The arrêt of July 14, 1703,[252] again mentioned the same ports, but set the preferential rates at 523 livres 19 sols 6 deniers and 34 livres 10 sols 7 deniers, and, finally, by the arrêt of August 21 the rate became 514 livres 1 sol 9 deniers and 34 livres 10 deniers.

In addition to these, as the following table shows, the bullion "marked from Spain" was given a higher bimetallic ratio than the bullion "without mark." In other words France was attempting to attract gold from the peninsula. By autumn the struggle had been decided. The arrêt of October 30, 1703,[253] mentioned only bullion "without mark" and raised both gold and silver prices to the same levels as "Spanish" on August 21. The Methuen Treaty dealt the final

---

[250] A.N., Z¹B.101, fol. 21.
[251] *Ibid.*, fol. 139.
[252] *Ibid.*, fols. 337–339.
[253] *Ibid.*, fol. 393.

blow: Portugal passed into the English sphere of influence. For France, the Spanish connection meant a currency system based largely on silver.

Table 4. Different Prices of Gold and Silver, 1702–1703

Date of arrêt du Conseil	Percentage premium of "Spanish" over bullion "without mark"		Bimetallic ratio for bullion	
	Gold	Silver	"Spanish"	"Without mark"
November 18, 1702	8.00	6.66	15.25	15.06
July 14, 1703	8.16	6.82	15.17	14.99
August 21, 1703	8.33	7.69	15.10	15.01

This development expressed itself in two ways: in the increasing proportions of silver coined by the mints of France; and in the higher bimetallic ratios. In the seven important adjustments of bullion prices in 1704–1708 a ratio of 1 : 15.25 was reached in January 1705 and again in November 1708.

One aspect of the monetary affairs of the period 1691–1721 has not yet received attention — billon coined after 1691. The need for small change was pressing. The declaration of August 28, 1691, ordered the first "reform" of the coins of 4 sols; they were reissued to the old standards of 10 deniers fine and 150 to the marc. As this was a "reform," the details did not appear in the customary records of the mints. The old coins current at 3 sols 6 deniers were received at the mints at 3 sols 7 deniers tournois. The edict of May 1709 continued them in circulation, this time at 3 sols 9 deniers, but they were forbidden currency by the arrêt of the Conseil d'État of November 29, 1712, and ordered to be carried to the mints. In addition, the coinage of douzains was resumed by the edict of October 1692 at a fineness of 2 deniers 12 grains, weighing 132 to the marc and current at 1 sols 3 deniers tournois.[254] Finally the coinage of copper liards was renewed by the declaration of June 9, 1693; they were to the same standards as the liards of 1654, of pure copper and weighing 64 to the marc.[255] Evidence is lacking on the volume of these issues, for again, as in the mid-seventeenth century, the coinage took place outside the official mints, but the machinery was often set up close to them, and, in some cases, the coins carried the same distinguishing marks as those of the nearby mint.

The edict of May 1709, one of the great monetary reforms of the early eighteenth century, confirmed these tendencies. In the first place, new series of gold and silver coins were issued; they were based on the gold louis *aux 8 L* at 22 karats fine, 30 to the marc and current at 10 livres. The counterpart in

[254] A.N., Z¹B.419. François Abot de Bazinghen defined billon as silver below a fineness of 10 deniers.

[255] Little information is given about the origins of the copper used. In the special case of Strasbourg, however, copper coins were struck in 1699 from "red copper of Saxony" and "red copper of Münster."

silver was the écu 3 *couronnes* at 12 deniers argent-le-roi, 8 to the marc and current at 5 livres. Different versions of the same coins appeared in December 1715: the gold louis *insignes* and the silver écu *vertugadin*.

However, one significant feature of the reform of May 1709 was the fixing of the prices of gold and silver. The marc of gold was put at 531 livres 16 sols $4\frac{4}{11}$ deniers, that of silver at 35 livres 9 sols $1\frac{1}{11}$ deniers; this produced a bimetallic ratio of 1 : 15. It is worth noting that this ratio was maintained during the next decade and was abandoned only after the collapse of the "system" of John Law in 1720.

Another feature of the reform was the concern with copper billon. The edict of November 19 authorized the coinage of up to 2,000,000 marcs weight of double liards (current at 6 deniers) in the mints of Aix, Bordeaux, Montpellier, Nantes, and La Rochelle. These coins were to weigh 40 to the marc, thus representing a devaluation of copper of the order of 25 percent by comparison with those issued in 1693 (64 single liards to the marc). In the south of France these coins often went by the name of *Dardennes,* for they were minted in the Château de Dardenne near Toulon.[256] The bronze from old naval guns was prepared as raw material, and the coinage was completed in the mints of Aix, Montpellier, and La Rochelle. When peace returned in 1713 the authorities opposed a renewal of this type of coinage.[257]

Later, the difficulties of John Law pressed him to reverse this policy. The edict of July 1719 ordered coinage of liards at 80 to the marc. In February 1720, when speculation was at its height, sols, demis-sols, and quarts de sols (that is, liards) of copper were allowed. The sols were popularly named after John Law himself. However, the depreciation of copper in terms of silver was on a relatively small scale in the long run. With the new silver écu set at 6 livres in 1726, the nominal ratio between silver and copper was about 1 : 49.8. Later, François Abot de Bazinghen recorded in his dictionary in 1764 a ratio of 1 : 54. The discount was thus of the order of 8½ percent.[258]

A satisfactory explanation of the years 1716–1720 inevitably revolves around the projects of John Law.[259] These projects were conditioned partly by his theories of credit, explained at length in *Money and Trade Considered* (1705), which took shape with the founding of the Banque Générale (May 1716), and partly also by the development of the system of credit and public debts in the preceding quarter of a century.

This system emerged under the impact of war. Pressing financial needs were met by raising loans. The huge volume of coinage and of restamping old coins necessitated credit. The length of the interval between the handing in of the old

[256] Maurice Raimbault, "La Dardenne," *Revue numismatique,* V (1901), p. 370.

[257] *Ibid.,* p. 374.

[258] François Abot de Bazinghen, *Traité des Monnoies* (2 vols., Paris, 1764), sv. "Liards."

[259] For the full discussion of these projects, we must wait for the forthcoming publications of Earl J. Hamilton.

coin and the issue of the new clearly depended on the techniques and equipment of the mints, as well as on the financial standing of the entrepreneurs concerned. In order to cover this interval, credit notes were issued — in reality, receipts — to be reimbursed in new coin. This method was used in 1693 when *billets de monnaie* were issued, valid for periods of a month. Again in September 1701 the directors of the mints issued similar notes to meet the same need. Up to this point the notes were simple receipts without interest, but as the clouds of war gathered over the Spanish succession and the delays in delivering new coin became more troublesome, a new departure was taken. On October 25, 1701, the billets de monnaie were issued as bonds bearing 4 percent interest. In February 1702 these became *rentes immobilières,* and in December 1703 the interest was raised to 8 percent. At the time an estimate put the volume of these notes in circulation at 6,700,000 livres, and in late 1705 they still stood at par. By October 1706 the volume had expanded to 180,000,000 livres, and depreciation soon followed. By the last quarter of 1706, the notes had already fallen to a discount of over 50 percent and the depreciation continued.[260] The situation was such that the government made a serious attempt to set the matter right in the edict of May 1709, this ordered 72,000,000 livres of billets de monnaie to be withdrawn from circulation and to be repaid in new coin.[261]

In the interim John Law published his *Money and Trade Considered.* One of his basic concepts was that the inflexibility of metallic currency could be overcome by the use of bank notes and credit. Since they would be convertible into a fixed quantity of bullion they would be superior to coins subject to debasement. It seems that the history of the billets de monnaie sets his theories in relief and thus form a prelude to his exploits under the regency (1715).

The regency opened the way for Law to return to Paris. At that time, a review of the accumulated royal debts determined that extensive recoinage would be necessary — the "reformation," as it was called, of the currency by restamping the coins in circulation. The realization of Law's schemes, however, began in earnest with the founding of the Banque Générale by letters patent of May 2, 1716. At the outset, this was a private company, capitalized at 6,000,000 livres. A few months afterward followed the issue of a heavier gold coin, the *louis Noailles,* at 22 karats, weighing 20 to the marc and current at 30 livres. The marc of gold was put at 515 livres 9 sols $1\frac{1}{11}$ deniers and of silver at 34 livres 7 sols $3\frac{3}{11}$ deniers, thus maintaining the ratio of 1 : 15 prevailing since 1709.

At first the conduct of the affairs of the Banque was sound enough. During the first year and a half, 61,000,000 livres were issued in notes against a satisfactory reserve of 31,000,000 livres in gold and silver specie.[262] In August

[260] Lüthy, *La banque protestante,* I, p. 103.
[261] A.N., Z¹B.104, fol. 186.
[262] Émile Levasseur, *Recherches Historiques sur le Système de Law* (Paris, 1854), p. 196.

1717 Law's operations widened with the creation of the "Louisiana" or "Western" Company (*Compagnie de la Louisiane ou d'Occident*), capitalized at 100,000,000 livres, the shares payable a quarter in coin and three-quarters in *billets d'état*.

Along with this came alterations in the standard coins. A gold coin (the *louis Malte*) was issued in May 1718 in lighter form at 25 to the marc, but current at the higher rate of 36 livres. The mints were ordered to coin a new and lighter silver *écu de Navarre* at 12 deniers argent-le-roi, weighing 10 to the marc and current at 6 livres. The price of gold and silver made a spectacular leap, the former to 654 livres 10 sols $11\frac{1}{11}$ deniers, the latter to 43 livres 12 sols $8\frac{8}{11}$ deniers, this maintaining the ratio of 1 : 15. By August 20 there was further inflation: gold was put at 785 livres 9 sols $1\frac{1}{11}$ deniers the marc and silver at 52 livres 7 sols $3\frac{3}{11}$ deniers, thus keeping the ratio at 1 : 15.

Law's achievements led to an opposition which at first had some success. The Frères Paris set up an "antisystem" company to farm the taxes, but Law continued to pursue his objectives. On December 4, 1718, the Banque Générale became the Banque Royale, this time as a state corporation with a note issue guaranteed by the government. The Louisiana Company was merged with the *Compagnie des Indes* (founded in 1644) and with the China Company (*Compagnie de Chine,* founded in 1713); in May 1719 it was given exclusive right to trade from the Cape of Good Hope to the South Seas. Printing notes was the method used to meet the demands for capital. This meant a departure from the policy of the Banque Royale, which at first had restricted the issue of notes. The volumes of notes issued in 1719 were as follows:[263]

Table 5. Issue of Notes of the Banque Royale in 1719

Date	Issues in millions of livres tournois
January 5	18
February 11	20
April 1	21
June 10	50
July 25	240
September 12	120
October 24	120
December 29	360
Total	949

Law's projects continued to expand: on August 27 he took over the rival company farming taxes; he controlled the coinage as Directeur Général des Monnaies du Royaume; in February 1720 the Banque Royale merged with the Compagnie des Indes. The edifice of finance seemed to be complete.

[263] *Ibid.,* pp. 196–197.

During all this activity, irresistible inflation began to take its toll. On the one hand, there was the situation in the mints and in the currency circulation generally. By an arrêt of August 3, 1719, the marc of gold was set at 774 livres 10 sols $10^{10}/_{11}$ deniers from September 15, with provision to decrease this to 720 livres by November 16, but the inflation of bullion prices continued. On February 25, 1720, the marc of gold was put at 981 livres 16 sols 4 deniers. Two days later an order forbade hoarding more than 500 livres in specie from March 1 in Paris and from March 15 in the provinces. A selection of the official prices for the marcs of gold and silver in 1720 gives an outline of the final surge of inflation. By the summer of that year the price of gold had almost quadrupled since 1709.

As speculation gathered momentum, a further experiment was tried with coins of pure gold and silver, the gold quinzain at 65 5/11 to the marc, current at 15 livres, and the silver petit louis at 30 to the marc, current at 3 livres. These apparently provided only an interlude. Examples exist of the silver louis, but the *Cabinet de Médailles* does not have a gold quinzain in its collections, and the records do not reveal its coinage. The plan was lost in the final collapse.

The inflation of the total stock of money, both specie and credit instruments, also implied shifts in the level of commodity prices. Earl J. Hamilton has long since examined the problem in a classic article; according to his careful estimates, the volume of currency (specie, bills of credit, and notes) had slightly more than doubled by May 1720, while prices had risen 88.4 percent.[264] It was "modern" inflation in the true Wicksellian sense: the official rate of interest, set below the market rate, acted as a further stimulus to the inflationary movement.[265] Although Law fought to save the situation by restrictions on hoarding — in March he ordered that gold should cease to circulate on May 1 and silver by the end of the year — the end was inevitable. By November the system had collapsed.

Nevertheless, the liquidation, as Hamilton has also shown, was not immediate. The arrêt of the Conseil d'État of October 10, 1720, recognized a total

Table 6. Prices of Gold and Silver in 1720 (in livres tournois)

Date	Price of silver per marc	Price of gold per marc	Bimetallic ratio
May, 5, 1720	87-5-5	1309-1-9	1:15
May 29, 1720	90-0-0	1350-0-0	1:15
June 10, 1720	91-16-4 $^4/_{11}$	1227-5-5 $^5/_{11}$	1:13.37
July 30, 1720	130-18-2	1963-12-8	1:15
October 24, 1720	85-1-9	1276-7-3	1:15
November 8, 1720	68-14-6	1030-18-2	1:15

[264] Earl J. Hamilton, "Prices and Wages at Paris under John Law's System," *Quarterly Journal of Economics,* LI (1936–1937), p. 59; see also "Prices and Wages in Southern France under John Law's System," *Economic Journal Supplement,* III (1934–1937).

[265] Hamilton, "Prices and Wages at Paris," p. 63.

issues of notes of 2,696,400,000 livres and allowed them to circulate until November 1. The notes were not discarded as worthless, but were held for redemption. By December, Hamilton concludes, "the country had apparently returned to a specie basis." [266]

Monetary stability gradually emerged in the period 1720–1725. By September 1720 a new series of coins had been introduced, the gold louis *aux 2 L* at 22 karats and 25 to the marc, current at 54 livres, together with the silver écu at 12 deniers argent-le-roi, weighing 10 to the marc and current at 9 livres. At this point the bimetallic ratio of 1 : 15 still held good. The edict of August 1723, however, brought a change. There were new gold coins: the *louis mirliton* (22 karats, 37 to the marc and current at 27 livres). And the new official prices for gold and silver bullion set a bimetallic ratio of 1 : 14.66, approaching a situation which formed the basis of the reforms of 1726. In September of the following year came the silver écu *aux 8 L* (12 deniers argent-le-roi, 10⅜ to the marc and current at 4 livres). The price of silver, set at 44 livres 8 sols, implied a ratio of 1 : 14.45. Subsequent adjustments in the prices of bullion retained this state of affairs, as the following table demonstrates:

Table 7. Prices of Gold and Silver, 1723–1726 (in livres tournois)

Date	Price of silver per marc	Price of gold per marc	Bimetallic ratio
August 1723 (edict)	74-3-7 $\frac{7}{11}$	1087-12-8 $\frac{8}{11}$	14.66
February 4, 1724	66-0-0	965-9-1 $\frac{1}{11}$	14.63
March 27, 1724	53-9-1 $\frac{1}{11}$	801-16-4 $\frac{4}{11}$	15.00
September 22, 1724	42-15-3 $\frac{3}{11}$	641-9-1 $\frac{1}{11}$	15.00
" " "	44-8-0	" " " "	14.45
December 4, 1725	38-17-0	561-5-5 $\frac{5}{11}$	14.45
January 1726 (edict)	37-1-9 $\frac{9}{11}$	536-14-6 $\frac{6}{11}$	14.47
May 26, 1726	48-0-0	695-9-1 $\frac{1}{11}$	14.49
June 15, 1726	53-3-3 $\frac{3}{11}$	740-9-1 $\frac{1}{11}$	14.47

And, finally, there was the great monetary settlement of 1726 which emerged in three distinct steps. First, the edict of January proposed new coins, the gold *louis lunettes* (22 karats, 30 to the marc and current at 20 livres) and the silver *écu aux lauriers* (11 deniers argent-le-roi, 8³⁄₁₀ to the marc and current at 5 livres). This edict set gold bullion at 536 livres 14 sols 6⁶⁄₁₁ deniers the marc and silver at 37 livres 1 sol 9⁹⁄₁₁ deniers, at a ratio, therefore, of 1 : 14.49. Then the arrêt of May 26 raised these gold and silver prices, respectively, to 695 livres 9 sols and 1¹⁄₁₁ deniers and 48 livres, also at a ratio of 1 : 14.49. At the same time the louis was priced at 24 livres and the écu at 6 livres. Finally the arrêt of June 15 raised these prices again to 740 livres 9 sols 1¹⁄₁₁ deniers and 51 livres 3 sols 3³⁄₁₁ deniers, at a ratio of 1 : 14.47.

[266] *Ibid.,* p. 61.

Thus emerged the monetary structures which were to prevail in the eighteenth century. They meant a currency system which was standard for France and recognized across Europe. They also implied that a solution had been found to the problem of gold which was experienced in the first decades of the century. The ratio of 14.47 effectively confirmed this. In itself, the French experience was significant, for it represented the achievement of a major country, holding a strategic position on the Continent. Yet that achievement could not have been so easily attained, nor so successfully entrenched, had it not been for the conditions of relative economic stability generally prevailing in Europe. The convergence of price levels on the Continent[267] and the pause in secular price movements of the second quarter of the eighteenth century assured France of an underlying tendency in favor of stabilization. And beyond 1726 were foreshadowed the great expansions and the pervasive economic growth characteristic of the *ancien régime*.

[267] Braudel and Spooner, "Prices in Europe from 1450 to 1750," pp. 470–471.

Chapter 4

Coinage in France: An Essay in Differential Geography

The point has now been reached in this study of the monetary development of France when it is necessary to deal in more detail with the activity of the different mints. It is also necessary to set this activity in a framework of the economic geography of the country. The task is not easy because, as in many quantitative studies for the modern period, the data are incomplete and much of the basic complementary material is unavailable. This naturally entails the difficulties usually associated with processing such statistics, over and above the inherent nature of the problem, both expressed and implicit in this book. Although the main purpose is to provide some quantitative estimates of changes in the monetary stock of France, the question has been approached from the standpoint of the different regions, associated one with another. It is clear that in a country such as France in the sixteenth and seventeenth centuries — endowed with an extensive territory and, relative to other states in Europe, a large population — the agreements or disagreements of the various regional movements raise fundamental questions of the differential geography of the country. This regionalism conditioned, in varying measure, the monetary movements in France and their harmony or disharmony with the general movements in Europe. France proved to be a mosaic, combining many different forms of activity. The implications of this are crucial. They prepare the way to study later the economic relevance of the movements of money and lead to the conclusions of the book. The fundamental question is whether this disparity was overcome or whether it remained a significant barrier to further development.

This present edition, as has been explained earlier, is a version in English of the book published in Paris in 1956, but at the same time, it is also a second edition in the strict sense, because it incorporates a new section of data for the period 1681–1725 as well as further sections of interpretation. These additions and alterations here particularly concern Chapter 4, which deals with the performance of the mints, both in time and magnitude. In this second edition, as in the first, I have decided to restrict this section to the five groups of mints, with a brief comment on their combined activity. This is followed by a section on the coinage of copper. The data then assembled in ten-year series are presented in map form; these maps are perhaps the focal point of this study of the monetary history of France. The chapter concludes with a review of the economic "viscosity" of the different zones of France and the variations in life which they reflect.

1. Coinage in France

Before embarking on this analysis, I shall make a few remarks on the sources. The data relating to the monetary affairs of France are drawn largely from the archives of the Cour des Monnaies (Series Z^1B in the Archives Nationales, Paris) which controlled and supervised monetary operations in France. The statistical series come from the états des délivrances, or registers in which the mint masters' operations were recorded precisely; and the contrôle des boîtes, which recorded the samples of coin sent to Paris, the samples representing customary proportions of the total coinage issued.

The issues of coins were recorded in the états des délivrances either by number or weight. The value of these coins was calculated at the official rates given in the royal edicts and ordinances. When the reporting period was different from the calendar year, as happened during the early sixteenth century, the totals have been adjusted on a monthly basis. Issues which ended in the first half of the month (first to fifteenth day) were included in the preceding month; those which ended in the second half of the month (sixteenth to the last day) were added to those of the following month.

The issues of coin have been divided into four main groups: gold; silver; silver billon (the fractional coins up to and including the sols parisis, and including also the pieces of 4 sols of the 1670s); and copper.

The series of the contrôle des boîtes is statistically inferior to the états des délivrances. It originated in the requirement by the Cour des Monnaies to verify the quantity and quality of the coinage. It nevertheless acts as a check on the états des délivrances and fills the gaps in this series. Out of the total issues made in the different mints, a certain proportion was sent to Paris, at the beginning, for example, 1 piece in 200 for gold money; 1 piece in 18 marcs for silver money; 1 coin in 720 for the silver billon. By the ordinance of 1682 these proportions were changed to 1 gold coin in 400 and 1 silver coin in 72 marcs weight. These data in turn have been valued in livres tournois and assigned to annual periods.

This study, when first published in 1956, took the account to 1680 for two reasons. First, it conformed to a hypothesis that a new phase in the monetary history of Europe began with the closing decades of the seventeenth century. Under such conditions, the choice of a precise date was arbitrary, but I felt that the year 1680 was as convenient as any of those possible. Second, the nature of the data and the way they were reported changed. This is always a matter of some importance in dealing with long series of statistical information. The registers of the états des délivrances are not as continuous as in the earlier period. In the case of Paris, the best series preserved, they end early in 1714. The gaps have been completed, first, from the *cahiers des délivrances,* the separate notebooks sent to the Cour des Monnaies each year by the individual mints, from which the états were compiled, which by their nature are often discontinuous; and, second, from the contrôle des boîtes for which the registers continue until 1723. The last two years, 1724–1725, have been completed from separate reports of the contrôle, filed in the general administrative papers of the Cour des Monnaies.[1]

A further complication affecting the survival of data came in 1705. At this point, as already seen, the monetary jurisdiction of France was split by the establishment of a second Cour des Monnaies in Lyons. The explanation of this change is complex, but must no doubt take into account the events associated with the Methuen Treaty (1703), as well as the financial implications of the sales of offices. As a result of this change, the mints in the Midi — Aix, Bayonne, Grenoble, Lyons, Montpellier, Toulouse, and Riom, in addition to Pau — sent their annual reports to Lyons and not to Paris. The archives of Lyons do not preserve the main series of États; at least I have not yet found them. However, the method of reporting is clear from the records of some of the mints, kept in the Archives Départmentales of the different towns. Montpellier is a case in point: the title page of the register recorded that it was a copy of the "original sent with the sample coins to the registry of the Cour des Monnaies in Lyons."[2] In some instances the records have found their way to the Archives Nationales in Paris, as for example in the case of Toulouse and Riom. The box for the latter contains an original label: "Cour des Monnaies de Lyons: registres des délivrances, Riom."[3]

Even in these various sources two gaps remain for the period 1706–1725: Aix and Bayonne, both important mints. To these may be added Toulouse for the period 1718–1725, Lyons for 1721–1722, and Riom for 1718. In these instances it has been necessary to make estimates in order to complete the aggregate series for France.[4]

---

[1] Archives Nationales [hereafter cited as A.N.], Z¹B.421. The relevant volumes of the contrôle des boîtes to 1723 are A.N., Z¹B.297, 298. For the sources used for the supplementary period 1681–1725, see Appendix D.

[2] Archives Départmentales [hereafter cited as A.D.], Hérault, B.470.

[3] A.N., Z¹B.949.

[4] The manuscript series used are: Grenoble, A.D., Isère, 19B.61–64, communicated on microfilm through the kindness of Monsieur Marcel Gouron, Director of the Archives Départmentales; and A.N., Z¹B.879A, cahiers des délivrances; Lyons, Jean Tricou, *Recherches sur les monnaies frappées à Lyon de 1664 à 1800* (3 vols., Lyons, 1959), to which Monsieur Jacques Yvon has most kindly drawn my attention; Montpellier, A.D., Hérault, B.470–471, B.475–476, cahiers des délivrances, communicated on microfilm through the kindness of Monsieur Robert Azevou, Director of the Archives Départmentales; Riom, A.N., Z¹B.949, cahiers des délivrances; Toulouse, A.N., Z¹B.966, cahiers des délivrances. The remaining gaps have been filled by estimates. The hypotheses on which these estimates have been based are (a) for the total coinage, that the issues of a particular mint in question keep the same share of the aggregate issues for the rest of France as in the period before 1705; (b) for the proportion of gold to silver in the coinage, that the same ratio prevails as in the period before 1706. In the case of Aix, Bayonne, and Toulouse these ratios have been averaged with the performance of three other mints in the "southern" group, Lyons, Montpellier, and Toulouse. The resulting coefficients are:

(a) for total coinage (given as estimated percentages of the aggregate coinage for France, less Aix, Bayonne, Grenoble, Lyons, Montpellier, Riom, and Toulouse):

Finally, the coinages of the mints in Metz, Pau, and Perpignan have not been included in the series because the statistics series are largely lacking, and from the time of their inclusion under French sovereignty these mints tended to play separate roles.[5] In the case of Metz, an arrêt of the Conseil d'État of January 11, 1663, forbade the city to coin its own money, and another arrêt of May 5, 1663, finally revoked this municipal privilege. The mint came under the administration of the Cour des Monnaies in Paris. Those in Pau and Perpignan were in turn allocated to Lyons after 1705. The mint in Pau opened in 1589, and its history belonged to the union of the House of Navarre with the French crown. This mint of "Béarn and Navarre" was active until the Revolution. The mint in Perpignan officially replaced Narbonne in 1710.

In summary, it will be readily seen that the source material for the years 1681–1725, and especially for 1706–1725, no longer has the simplicity enjoyed by the previous period.

For the period 1493–1680 the collected data have been divided into two representative categories; this method has been continued for 1681–1725. The first relates to fifteen towns: Paris, Amiens, and Troyes; Bayonne, La Rochelle, and Rennes; Limoges and Poitiers; Tours, Bourges, and Saint-Pourçain (moved to Moulins and then to Riom); Lyons and Grenoble; Aix-en-Provence and Villeneuve-lès-Avignon. From about 1555 the data for these have been drawn from the états des délivrances, which record the precise quantities of coin issued.

The mints in the other towns (as in the case of the majority of the fifteen

---

Aix	5.01	(base = 1691–1705)
Bayonne	8.86	(base = 1691–1705)
Lyons	7.20	(base = 1711–1718 and 1723–1725)
Riom	1.68	(base = 1718 and 1720)
Toulouse	2.51	(base = 1703–1717)

(b) proportion of gold and silver (given as estimated percentages of gold in the total coinage of each mint):

Aix	(1706–1710) = 43.63
	(1711–1720) = 44.27
	(1721–1725) = 70.72
Bayonne	(1706–1710) = 45.73
	(1711–1720) = 46.40
	(1721–1725) = 74.12
Toulouse	(1719–1725) = 68.36.

There is the possibility of single-year assessments of total coinage in France at the time of the ministry of John Law; for this we must wait for the definitive work on the period by Earl J. Hamilton. The difficult problem remains of establishing a precise series for total coinage in France during the first quarter of the eighteenth century.

[5] For Metz, see Eustache Le Noble, *Traité de la monnaie de Metz avec un tarif de la réduction en monnaie de France* (Paris, 1675); and Félicien de Saulcy, *Recherches sur les monnaies des Évêques de la Cité de Metz* (Metz, 1833–1836). Some information has also been preserved in the A. D., Moselle, Ser. B, 2415–2416, for the period 1695–1754. This has been kindly shown by Monsieur Jean Colnat, Director of the Archives Départementales.

towns above for the period before 1555) have the approximate data of the series of the contrôle des boîtes. This series contains most of the information for the first half of the sixteenth century and records particularly the different type of coin put into circulation. As in most similar series, the validity of the data rests on the efficiency of the organization and the honesty of the royal officials of the mints, notably the gardes, whose main task was to supervise the operations of the mint master. The administrative history of France, as of other countries, shows that such a system was far from infallible, and a margin of error is to be expected. Moreover, it must be repeated that the issues have been valued at the legal rates listed in the royal edicts and ordinances, the annual totals beginning with January 1 of each year.[6] For the first half of the sixteenth century the documentary sources refer to irregular periods and have been adjusted on a monthly basis.[7]

The coinage has been valued in terms of the livre tournois in order to estimate the total value of issues made.[8] Clearly, in this matter, a certain caution must be exercised. In the short run the calculation involves lags since the royal edicts and ordinances represent devaluations which have already often run their course for several years in the commercial market. In the long run the progressive devaluation of the livre tournois in terms of precious metals must be kept in mind. The use of the semilogarithmic scale takes account of the factor of inflation so that fluctuations are comparable over the whole period. Movements in different towns naturally remain directly comparable among themselves.

The operations of the three mints in the Paris Basin (Paris, Amiens, and Troyes) show similarities and differences, inevitably, since Paris was the focus of the monetary system of France (see Graph 14). By reason of its place as the capital for government and taxation and of the volume and continuity of its operations — it was the only mint which did not miss a year of coinage in the whole period of 233 years — Paris held the dominant position. In converting foreign currency or in executing monetary reforms, however, the three mints were in unison. (This contrasted with more normal periods when there were

---

[6] See Chap. 4, Section 4. The calendar year was used officially in France from January 1, 1565.

[7] Partial data that fall in the period from the first to the fifteenth day of the month are given for that month, and from the sixteenth to the last day are given in the following month.

[8] The extensive section devoted to a detailed account of the operations of the individual mints which was included in the French edition has been almost entirely eliminated from this present edition. Nevertheless it is necessary to give some indication of the statistical sources for the coinage during the years 1681–1725. In addition to the major series utilized from the états des délivrances and the contrôle des boîtes in the Archives Nationales, the following sources have been used: Paris, cahiers des délivrances (A.N., Z¹B.940); Bordeaux, cahiers des délivrances (A.N., Z¹B.839); Montpellier, cahiers des délivrances (A.D., Hérault B.470–471, B.475–476); Nantes, cahiers des délivrances (A.N., Z¹B.905); Toulouse, cahiers des délivrances (A.N., Z¹B.966). In the case of Lyons, reference has also been made to Tricou, *Recherches sur les monnaies frappées à Lyon*.

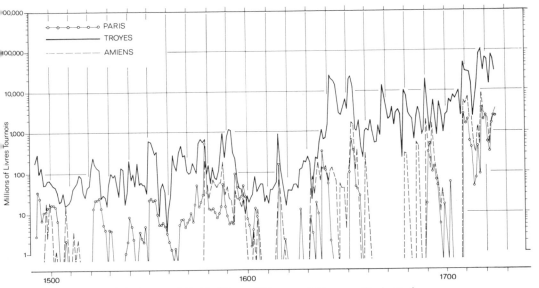

14. Total Annual Coinage of Gold, Silver, Billon, and Copper: Paris Basin

considerable differences.) Such unison can be detected in 1578, 1587, 1615, 1637, 1652–1653, and during the time of John Law. Paris and Amiens were closely linked in 1578–1587 and 1650–1660.

During the period 1681–1725 no great similarity marked the coinage in Paris, Amiens, and Troyes. The activity of the early 1690s (the mint in Troyes reopened in 1691) gave way to idleness in 1699 in both Troyes and Amiens. And in contrast to the huge issues in Paris, neither of the other mints produced sizable quantities of coin until after the reform of 1709. In the subsequent period to 1725, these two mints remained in unison. Paris made outstanding issues, especially in 1718.

The three towns of Bayonne, La Rochelle, and Rennes represented the exceptional group of maritime towns of western France (see Graph 15). Basically their movements showed a degree of similarity. During the first half of the sixteenth century, the mints in Bayonne and La Rochelle, without having a close relationship, tended to be similar in years of crisis and especially after 1553 and until the first decade of the seventeenth century (excepting the years of the League). Along with the majority of the mints in France at the beginning of the seventeenth century, the coinage in both Bayonne and La Rochelle tended to increase. After 1640 a similar movement continued until the closure of the mint in La Rochelle between 1662 and 1678.

The movement of the mint in Rennes apparently showed a greater degree of independence, especially in the first and second phases. The break in the years 1567–1574, however, found a response at Rennes. In contrast, the great ex-

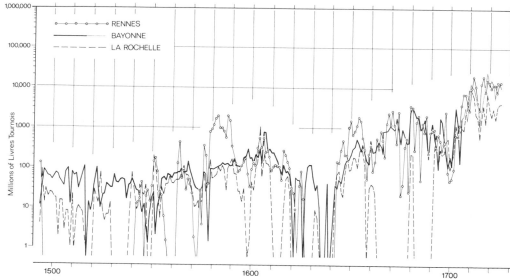

15. Total Annual Coinage of Gold, Silver, Billon, and Copper: Maritime Towns of the West

pansion of monetary issues in 1575–1587 is peculiar to Rennes. It was only after 1590, with the catastrophe of the League, that a greater degree of correlation appeared among the three movements, notably between Bayonne and Rennes, although the latter remained subject to wider fluctuations during the third quarter of the century.

After 1680 the general movement of the western seaboard seemed to divide into two fairly clear periods: a falling trend to 1699, and then a long phase of rise and recovery. The divide came during the period of peace, between the Treaty of Ryswick (1697) and the renewal of war in 1701. At first the mint in Bayonne made the best sustained performance, but Rennes supplanted it in 1704. The monetary policy in favor of gold seemed to stimulate the activity of Bayonne; while that of silver supported the expansion of Rennes.

Until the decade 1520–1530 the issues of Poitiers and Limoges followed similar movements, with Poitiers the slightly more active of the two (see Graph 16). After 1550 Limoges showed a tendency to lead, but the two movements again became similar during the period 1570–1590. During the last decade of the sixteenth century and again in the decade 1640–1650, Limoges was clearly the more important, and this superiority did not end until 1718–1725.

The case of Tours, here given alone, represents the Loire Valley: its success during the sixteenth century which lasted until 1604 (see Graph 17). After this, an uncertain period followed, lasting until 1708; then began a period of sustained activity which continued until the reforms of 1726.

In the areas of Berry, Bourbonnais, and Auvergne (Bourges; and Saint-

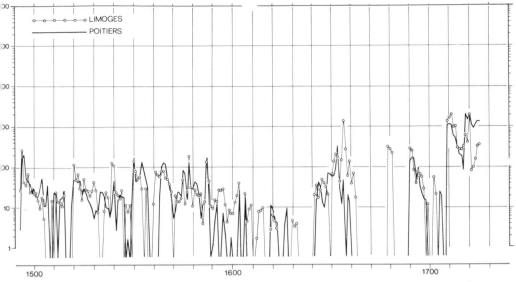

16. Total Annual Coinage of Gold, Silver, Billon, and Copper: Limousin and Poitou

Pourçain, Moulins, and Riom) the movements of Bourges and Riom reveal contrasts (see Graph 18). The coinage in Bourges was on the whole larger than that in Saint-Pourçain and Moulins, with the exception of the 1520s. In the second half of the sixteenth century, however, Riom, the regional tax center, took first place. After 1640 the issues in Bourges were, nevertheless,

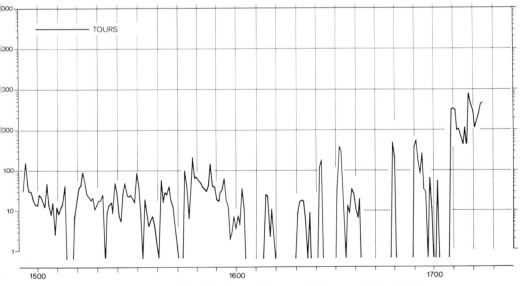

17. Total Annual Coinage of Gold, Silver, Billon, and Copper: Loire Valley

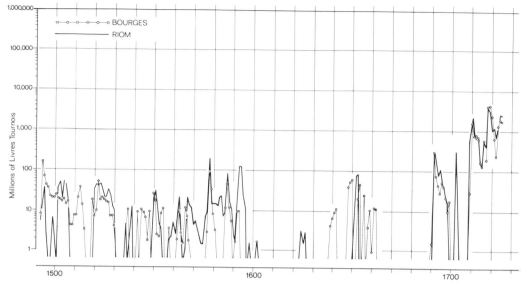

18. Total Annual Coinage of Gold, Silver, Billon, and Copper: Berry, Bourbonnais, and Auvergne

relatively more continuous than those in Riom; the performances in these two mints were similar in the period after 1690.

In Lyonnais and Dauphiné, represented by Lyons and Grenoble, scarcely any agreement existed, either in quantity or in movement (see Graph 19). An

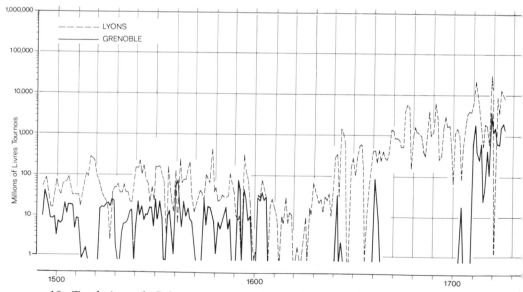

19. Total Annual Coinage of Gold, Silver, Billon, and Copper: Lyonnais and Dauphiné

exception to this may be found perhaps in the difficult years 1594–1605. At the beginning of the sixteenth century the divergence appeared more clearly in the first fifteen years of the reign of Francis I. Lyons was very active after 1520 and then tended to stagnate whereas in Grenoble the reverse was the case. In the second, third, and fourth phases, both Grenoble and Lyons appeared to respond poorly to the monetary movements affecting France generally and Grenoble in particular. The issues from Lyons were substantial after 1706; Grenoble improved its performance particularly after 1718.

In Provence and Languedoc (Aix-en-Provence and Villeneuve-Saint-André-lès-Avignon) there was similarity of movements during the first three-quarters of the sixteenth century between Aix and Villeneuve, and again in the first decade of the seventeenth century, with Villeneuve in a short lead (see Graph 20). After 1643 Aix was clearly dominant.

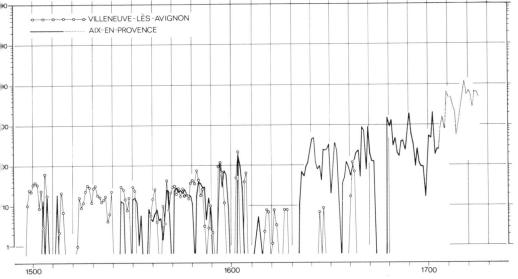

20. Total Annual Coinage of Gold, Silver, Billon, and Copper: Provence and Languedoc

2. Copper Money and Gold and Silver Money

If the coinage of copper is compared with that of gold, and silver, two phases appear, divided about the year 1606. In the first period, the issues of copper tended to follow those of gold and silver, particularly in the case of Paris. In other words, the movements of expansion and contraction were largely in sympathy between the coinage of copper and that of precious metals. Copper coins, it may be said, were an addition to ease the circulation of gold and silver.

After 1606, however, the expansion in copper coinage tends to be negatively correlated to gold and silver, to be more significant when gold and silver coin-

ATLAS I

Key to the scale used in livres tournois

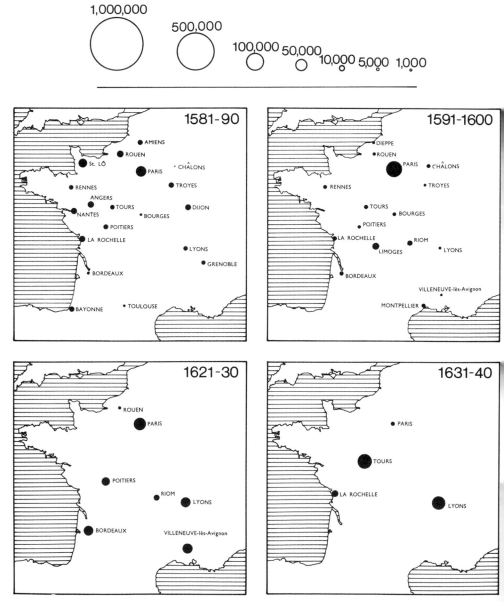

Atlas 1: *Copper Coinage in France, Ten-year Totals (1578–1660)*

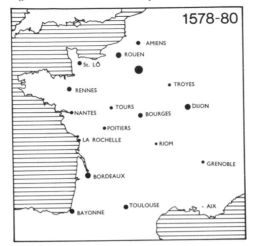

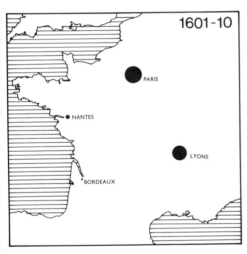

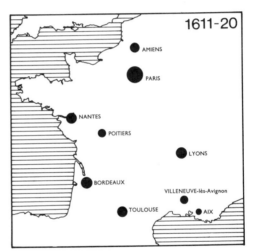

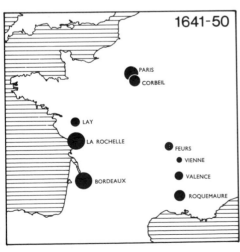

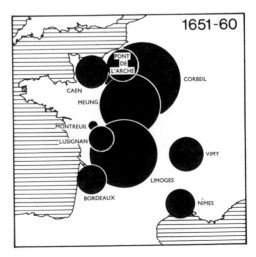

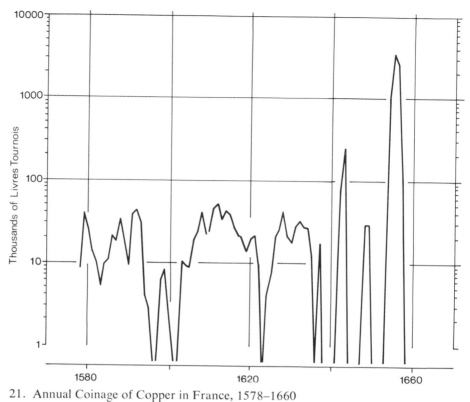

21. Annual Coinage of Copper in France, 1578–1660

ages were falling, such as in 1608, 1612, 1621, 1632, and 1648–1649. In this, copper tends to appear more as a substitute for gold and silver.

This section aims to consider the problems of France, using an atlas of twenty-four maps which should be consulted as a sequence. I have simplified the presentation to show gold, silver and billon, and in consequence, particular attention should be given to the documentary sources from which the data have been assembled.

This second edition includes a supplementary period 1681–1725 which has imposed a problem of scale. The proportions of the circles adopted in the first series of maps (1493–1680) were chosen with the particular purpose of showing changes in monetary phase, firstly in the mid-sixteenth century and secondly at the beginning of the seventeenth century. The progressive inflation and the resulting increase in the total value of coinage — for example, in the decade 1641–1650 — demonstrated the implicit difficulty of retaining this scale for the second half of the seventeenth century. In the period 1681–1725, and particularly during the time of John Law, the totals of coinage were often considerable, with the result that the continuation of the earlier scale is clearly in question. In an attempt to achieve unity for the whole two and a half centuries under study, and at the same time, to feature the changes in monetary phase, I experimented with various other schemes, including the conversion of the whole series of data into logarithms. After finding the results of these attempts unsatisfactory, I decided to retain the original series as published in the first edition, and to give the supplementary series 1681–1725, drawn to a tenth of the area used for 1493–1680. The break between 1680 and 1681, therefore, must be kept clearly in mind when making any visual comparisons over the whole period from 1493 to 1725. In order to mitigate some of the difficulties in bridging the gap between the two series, I have included in each map for the period 1681–1725 an inset which shows the total coinage in Paris in the same relationship to the area of France as in the series 1493–1680. The frontiers of France in 1493 and 1789 have been added to provide a framework of reference.

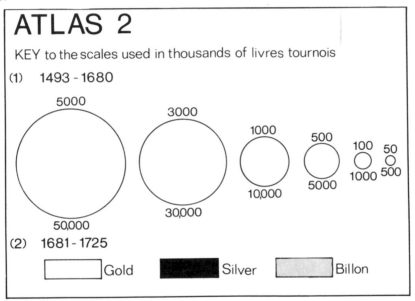

Scale used in Atlas 2.

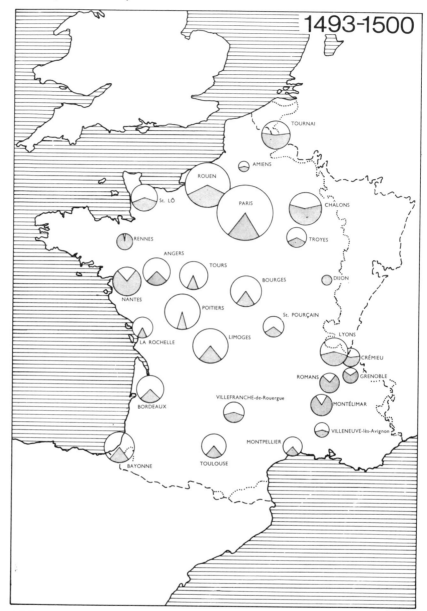

1493–1500 The coinage reflects the beginning of the campaign by Charles VIII in Italy. The mints responded to the financial needs of the monarchy in converting foreign currency and collecting taxes. The importance of Paris is clearly shown, although at this time Lyons provided the great bourse of France. In turn the contribution of the towns of the west and center should be noted, especially Poitiers, Limoges, and Rouen, but also Tours, Bourges, Lyons, Bayonne, and probably Tournai, Châlons, Angers, Nantes, and Toulouse. The small towns of the Rhône Valley — Romans, Montélimar, and Crémieu — were also active. In general, gold predominated in the coinage of Paris, Bayonne, La Rochelle, Poitiers, Limoges, Tours, and probably Angers, Bordeaux, Montpellier, Toulouse, Villefranche, and Saint-Lô. With the exception of Rennes and Nantes, silver currency was more prominent in the towns of the east and north east of continental France. Dijon was concerned solely with silver billon, which predominated in Tournai, Châlons, Montélimar, Romans, Crémieu, Nantes, and Rennes; the last two, under the provincial administration of Brittany, were probably concerned with the conversion of silverware. The activity of Bayonne, largely involved in gold, indicates the influence of Spain.

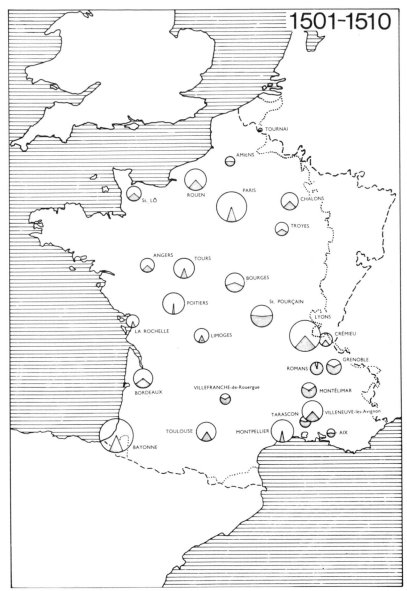

1501–1510 The rising prices of bullion in the commercial markets led to a general decline in the total coinage, although some towns — Bayonne, Ville-neuve, Saint-Pourçain, and Lyons — managed to escape this restriction. Bayonne largely overshadowed Bordeaux and La Rochelle; Toulouse showed a slight reduction, but this was not as severe as that in Bordeaux and Villefranche-de-Rouergue. The coinage in Lyons was slightly greater than that in Paris, which suffered a setback by comparison with the preceding period. In contrast, in the direction of the Mediterranean, the movements seemed more active: Villeneuve and Aix had just opened; and Montélimar increased the volume of its coinage. The primacy of gold remained a feature of this map, but the proportion of silver currency issued tended to increase in Montélimar and Romans.

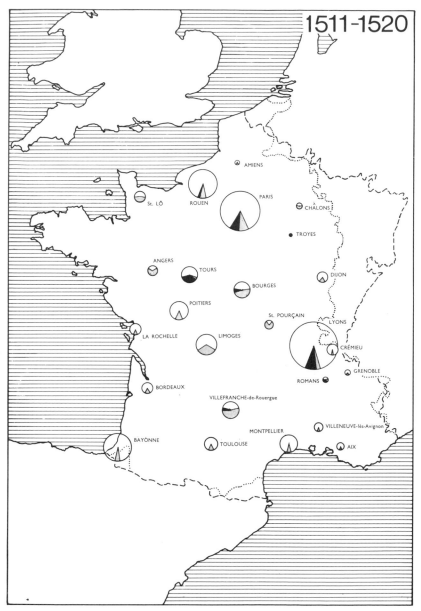

1511–1520 This decade shows the response to the ordinances of 1516 and 1519 which raised the price of gold while containing that of silver. It also reflects the first coinage of testons in 1514. The situation was tense in view of the financial levies entailed by the costly candidature of Francis I in the imperial election of 1519. Some of the mints had been closed after the accession of Francis I in 1515, and, in many others, coinage declined, for example, in Poitiers, Tours, Saint-Pourçain, Bordeaux, and Montpellier. However, some exceptions (Lyons, Paris, and Rouen) were linked to the financial needs of the monarchy. In Bayonne the situation scarcely changed by comparison with the preceding decade. The coinage of gold was important especially in Paris, Bayonne, La Rochelle, Rouen, and perhaps also in Montpellier. The coinage of fullbodied silver was more marked in certain towns — Rouen, Bourges, Villefranche, Romans, Lyons, Paris, Tours — most of which were located near silver mines or had trading centers. In this decade Lyons was dominant.

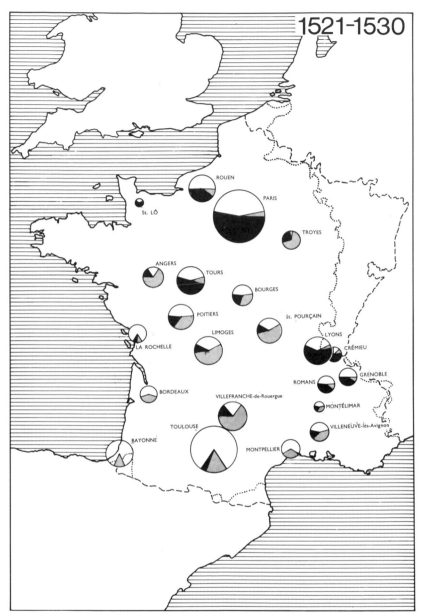

1521–1530 By the ordinance of 1521 the monetary system of France was adjusted in favor of silver. The lowering of the intrinsic content of the teston was another important change. As a result a larger number of mints issued these coins, including Villeneuve, Angers, La Rochelle, Toulouse (the last two for only small amounts), and Villefranche. With the exception of Rouen the coinage of testons, strikingly enough, was largely a feature of the interior of France — Poitiers, Tours (where the trellis of St. Martin was melted down), Limoges, Bourges, Saint-Pourçain, Lyons, Troyes, Crémieu, and Montélimar. Romans and Paris issued the largest quantities of silver testons. The situation of the "gold" towns (Bayonne, Bordeaux, La Rochelle, Toulouse, which was probably more important for gold even than Paris, and Montpellier) remained roughly the same. This was also a period of war finance and tax levies, but on this occasion Paris expanded at the expense of Lyons.

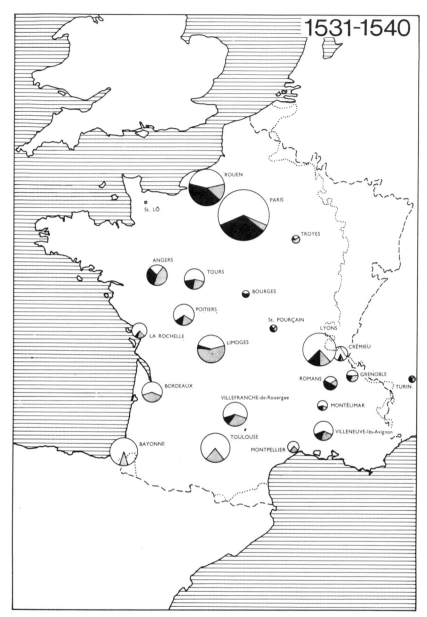

1531–1540 During the years 1531–1540 the demand for gold increased after the payment of the ransom for Francis I and the ordinance of 1533. Consequently, in contrast with the preceding decade, higher proportions of gold currency were issued, especially in Paris and Lyons. As might have been expected, there was a significant increase in coinage in the towns which were in contact with Spain, but Bayonne and Bordeaux only slightly increased their total coinage. Toulouse and Montpellier were less active though they were attached to gold. In contrast, the towns of the north and northeast again showed their command over silver: Bourges, Troyes, Saint-Pourçain, Paris, Rouen (in the wake of Paris, where the larger part of the issues were in silver billon and testons), and, especially, Lyons. Paris retained the dominant position.

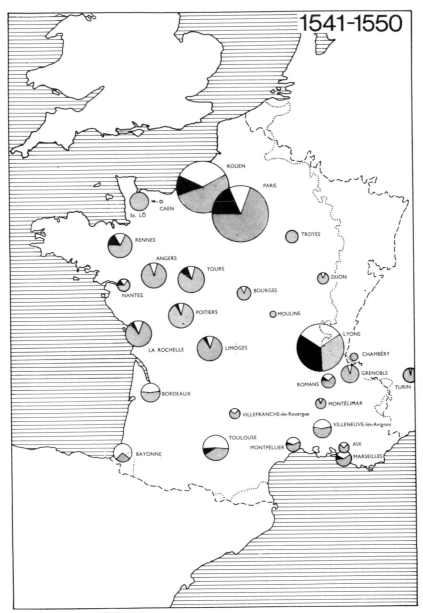

1541–1550 This map records the decline of the gold phase in France. The demand for silver money was accentuated in the war of Francis I against Charles V, and the coinage of silver billon increased. Bayonne provides the best example of the end of the phase; in contrast to the majority of other mints, which were occupied with silver billon and silver currency, Bayonne had the largest proportion of gold in the coinage, although the total coined was lower than in the preceding decade. For the rest of France the increase in silver coinage is clear and scarcely requires comment. The issue of billon, and in some cases of testons, was widespread: in Bordeaux (all billon); in Montpellier (some testons); in Toulouse (preponderantly billon, with the total silver issued probably exceeding that of gold). The same situation prevailed in Aix and Villeneuve. Paris remained a center for taxation, the conversion of silverplate, and the reform of silver billon. In Rouen, also, silver predominated, especially billon.

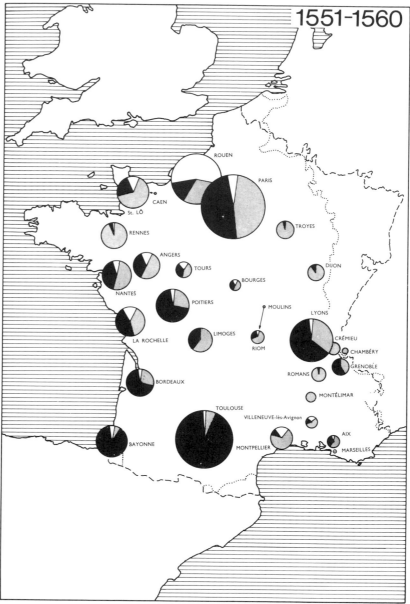

1551–1560 This marks the beginning of the phase of silver from the New World. The new situation in coining silver, however, gives a balanced appearance, and the differences between north and south, east and west, tended to diminish. Toward the north and east billon was largely in evidence; Dijon was occupied entirely with silver, mainly billon. The same situation appears in both Romans and Crémieu, where the mints were finally closed in 1557 and 1552, respectively. The issues of testons took place in proximity to Spain, in Bayonne (360,889 livres), in La Rochelle (158,582 livres), and especially in Toulouse. Rouen, in contrast to Paris, was the largest contributor to the coinage of gold. On the whole western France tended to gain slightly at the expense of continental France. Paris was dominant, followed by Toulouse, Rouen, and Lyons.

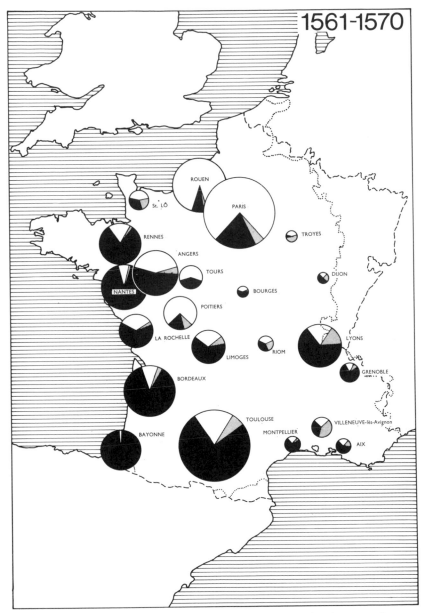

1561–1570 The edict of 1561 favored gold; consequently, the general structure of silver coinage was modified to take into account the inflow of gold into France. The mints of the south and west (Bayonne, Toulouse, Bordeaux, Rennes, La Rochelle, Nantes, Angers, and Limoges) revealed a solid attachment to silver. The towns of the western seaboard tended to increase in importance. By contrast, the mints in the north and northeast were concerned with gold currency: Tours, Poitiers, Bourges, Troyes, Riom, Lyons, Grenoble, and, above all, Rouen and Paris. The mints of Crémieu, Montélimar, and Romans disappeared; Villeneuve, Aix, and Montpellier operated on a small scale.

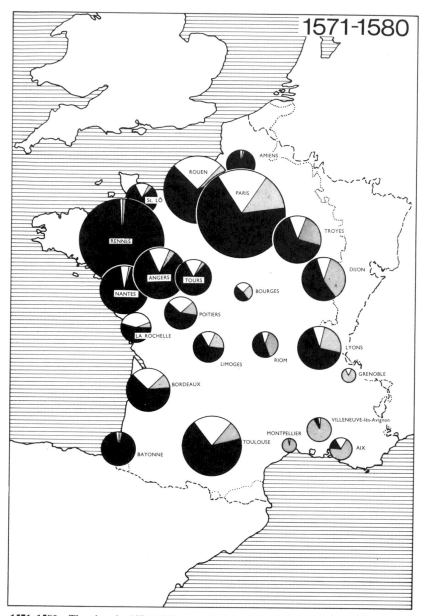

1571–1580   The decade 1571–1580 responded to several factors: the raising of the ratio of gold to silver by the ordinance of 1573; the ordinance and reform of 1575, again more favorable to silver; and the conversions of foreign specie in 1577–1578. Paris remained the most important mint, but the growth of Rennes, apparent after 1575, was remarkable. A huge movement favoring silver appeared in Angers, Nantes, Saint-Lô, Rouen, and Paris. The invasion of foreign money on the northern and northeastern frontiers was shown in the expansion of Troyes and Dijon and also in the reappearance of Amiens. The expansion of Villeneuve and Aix probably indicated a mutual attachment to the economy of the southwest. The less favored position of silver in France at the beginning of the decade explains the relative eclipse of Bayonne, Bordeaux, and Toulouse compared with the preceding period. However, in contrast, those ports which served a hinterland, such as Bordeaux and Rouen, increased their offerings of gold. La Rochelle also followed that trend. In all the towns, especially Paris, silver predominated. The issues of silver billon also showed certain differences: in the maritime towns of the west, the issues were largely concerned with silver money and only to a small extent with silver billon, while in the towns of the east and in the Rhône Valley, more silver billon was in evidence. The issue of copper currency, begun in 1578, formed the counterpart of these billon coins. Paris was the most important center (18,291 livres). Copper was coined in seventeen other towns; four (Dijon, Rouen, Bordeaux, and Bourges) contributed 10,000 livres.

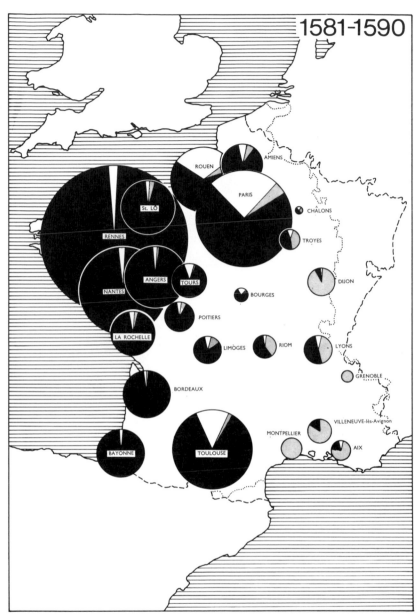

1581–1590 The decade 1581–1590 was a boom period for the mints, largely to the advantage of the western seaboard. Paris remained important, but the total coinage of the capital was largely overshadowed by that of Rennes. Nantes, Angers, and Saint-Lô were also associated with this astonishing movement, while, in the southwest, Bayonne and Bordeaux followed the same trend. Rouen was also active. In contrast, the continental towns tended to languish: Dijon (especially after the conversions of 1578), Lyons, Riom, Grenoble. The coinage of *billon* also provided contrasts. Nantes, Rennes, and Bayonne did not issue this currency, but the reverse was the case in Villeneuve, Aix, Montpellier, Grenoble, and Dijon. Billon had an important place in Lyons, Troyes, and Riom. Copper was issued widely, notably in Paris (31,902 livres); of the eighteen other towns the most important in the west were Saint-Lô (20,262 livres), Rouen, and Nantes. There were small signs of gold everywhere, but Bayonne, Montpellier, Villeneuve, and Grenoble were exceptions. Paris was most important in coining gold, among a group including Rennes, Amiens, Troyes, Lyons, Limoges, Poitiers, La Rochelle, and Aix.

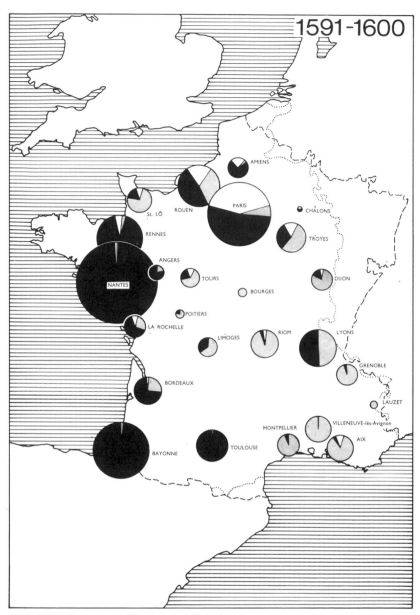

1591–1600 The years 1591–1600 included the bitter struggles with the League. The revolutionary movements upset all accounting procedures, and the data must be accepted with caution. As recorded, the issues in Paris remained important although in decline. Nantes assumed an outstanding position and, along with Rennes, Rouen, and Bayonne, constituted the main effort in the west during the decade. By comparison with the preceding decade, the activity of Bayonne, Lyons, and Aix increased, in spite of the rise in commercial currency rates tending to lead to a decline in the total coinage. A large quantity of gold was coined in Paris, but elsewhere silver predominated. In the south, Bayonne, Toulouse, Montpellier, and Villeneuve, together with Lyons, Grenoble, and Lauzet, were concerned with silver alone. In contrast Aix issued a small amount of gold coin.

This decline in the availability of silver for coinage was compensated to some extent by increased issues of silver billon, which generally continued until 1596. Villeneuve, Aix, Troyes, Tours, Riom, Poitiers, Limoges, Grenoble, Bourges, and Lyons as well were important in this respect. Full-bodied silver currency predominated almost entirely in Bayonne, Bordeaux, Toulouse, La Rochelle, Nantes, and Rennes. Rouen, Paris, and Lyons devoted about half their volume to this currency.

Seventeen towns continued to coin copper. Paris was first (87,553 livres annually), followed by Limoges (12,521 livres). The other towns remained below the level of 50,000 livres annually. In general copper coinage was more important in the west.

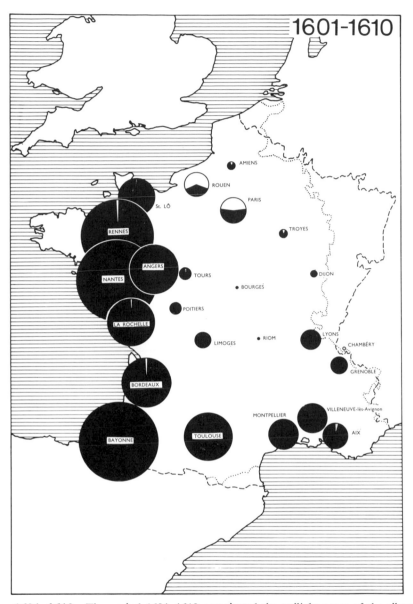

1601–1610 The period 1601–1610 constituted the twilight years of the silver phase. The end of the coinage of billon, generally in effect from 1596, meant that the towns of the west became the important centers for coining silver. Issues continued to grow in Bayonne, Bordeaux, La Rochelle, and Toulouse; they were also important in Brittany and its associated regions, in Nantes, Angers, and Rennes, the last improving its performance of the preceding decade. Recession, however, was evident in Paris and Rouen. Although a number of towns were devoted entirely to silver issues — Bayonne, Nantes, Angers, Tours, Toulouse, Montpellier, Villeneuve, Aix, Lyons, Grenoble, Limoges, Poitiers, Dijon — some issued gold. There were traces in Bordeaux, La Rochelle, Rennes, Saint-Lô, Troyes, Amiens, but issues were relatively important only in Paris and Rouen. The coinage of copper in this decade was concentrated in four towns: Paris (63,623 livres); Lyons (91,560 livres); and Bordeaux and Nantes (very small quantities).

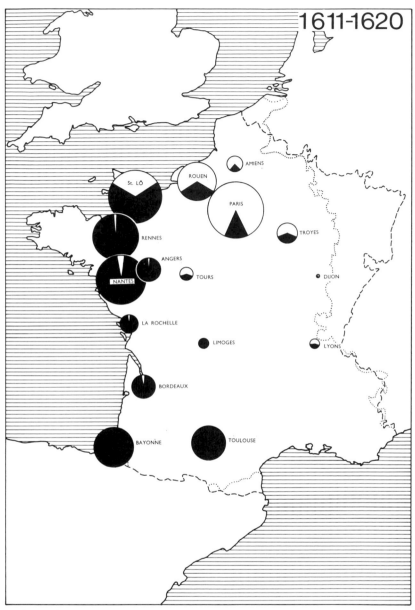

1611-1620 The overall movement of the decade 1611–1620 was under the influence of the edict of 1614 which raised the currency rates for gold, leaving those of silver at the levels of 1602. Where convenient, the mints produced gold coin: in Paris in the first instance, but also in Tours, Lyons, Dijon, and particularly in Amiens, Rouen, Saint-Lô, and Troyes, all in the north. Bayonne, Toulouse, and Limoges (showing a decline in comparison with the preceding decade) were entirely devoted to silver. Though there were traces of gold in Bordeaux, La Rochelle, Nantes, Angers, and Rennes, silver predominated. The issues of copper doubled by comparison with the preceding decade. Nine towns contributed: Paris (93,594 livres); Bordeaux (44,102 livres); Lyons (36,397 livres); Nantes (36,285 livres); and also Toulouse, Amiens, Poitiers, Ville-neuve, and Aix.

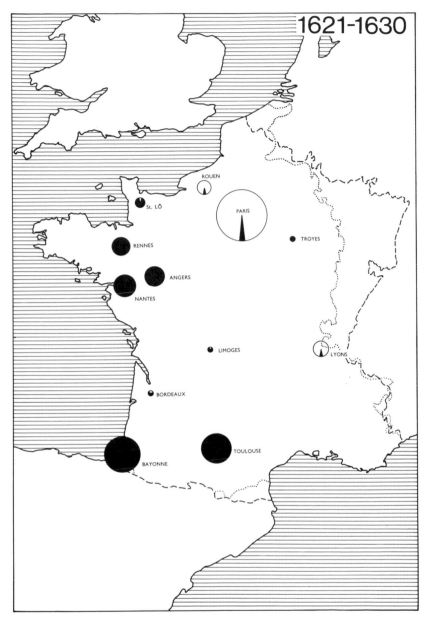

1621–1630 The crisis of 1619–1620 was followed by a general decline in coinage, particularly in the maritime towns of the west. Bayonne and Toulouse were exceptions to this rule. La Rochelle, Montpellier, and Aix do not figure at all on the map, while Rennes, Nantes, and Angers experienced reduced activity. The difficulties owing to the movements of silver were aggravated by the Thirty Years' War, and Spain again directed its financial and monetary power toward the Low Countries. There were some traces of gold in Bordeaux, Limoges, and Saint-Lô, but the principal signs of that metal were on the route from the Mediterranean to the Channel, notably in Lyons, Rouen, and Paris. The last was almost entirely devoted to gold. The coinage of copper consti-tuted about half that of the preceding decade. Of the seven towns involved, the most important were Paris (51,687 livres), Lyons (32,915 livres), Bor-deaux (30,385 livres), Villeneuve (26,433 livres) and Poitiers (22,911 livres).

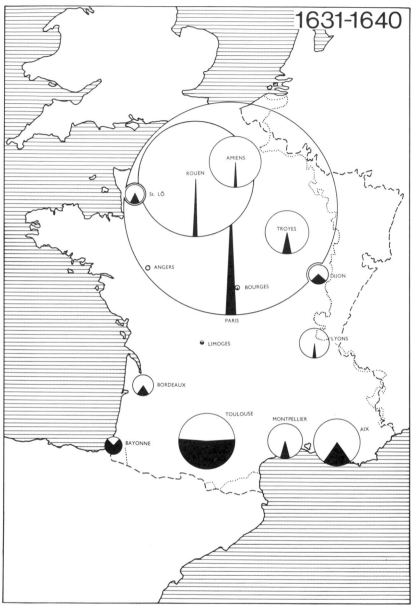

1631–1640 The sharp rise in the commercial rate for gold at the beginning of the decade 1631–1640 was finally confirmed in the ordinance of 1636. The mints open to gold were thus favored. Operations in Bayonne and Limoges were again reduced; Rennes and Nantes disappeared from the map while Angers was greatly reduced. Gold predominated in Bordeaux, Montpellier, Aix and accounted for about half in Toulouse. The route from the Channel to the Mediterranean was also featured, Paris being by far the most important, followed by Rouen, Amiens, Troyes, Lyons, Aix, and Montpellier. There were small issues of gold in Angers, Saint-Lô, Bourges, and Dijon. These issues above all accentuated eastern France. Four towns were active in copper coinage: Tours (73,487 livres); Lyons (59,328 livres); La Rochelle (12,712 livres); and Paris (4,167 livres).

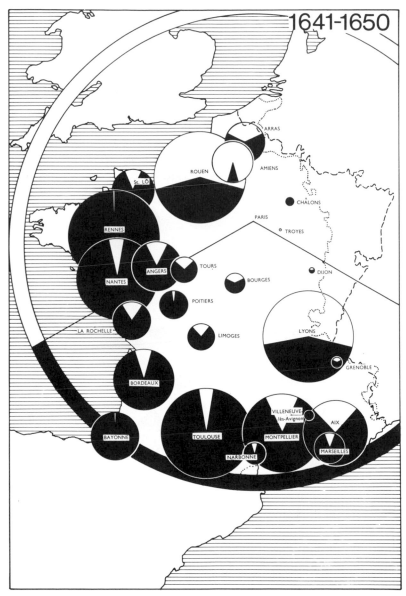

1641–1650 The period 1641–1650 was dominated by the conversions ordered by the ordinance of 1640 and by the raising of silver prices in 1641.
These factors explain to some extent the general expansion of coinage and
above all the extensive activity of Paris. The towns of the west and south —
Rennes, La Rochelle, Bordeaux, Bayonne, Nantes, Angers, Saint-Lô, Toulouse,
Montpellier, Narbonne, Marseilles, Villeneuve — remained tied to silver. There
seems to have been a renewed division between the east and west of France,
with the large issues of gold being confined to Paris, Rouen, Lyons, Amiens,
Arras, and, to some extent, Aix. The total of copper coinage rose considerably,
with La Rochelle producing 98, 858 livres, Bordeaux, 85,108 livres, and Paris,
60,065 livres, followed by Corbeil, Roquemaure, Valence, Tours, Lay, and
Vienne.

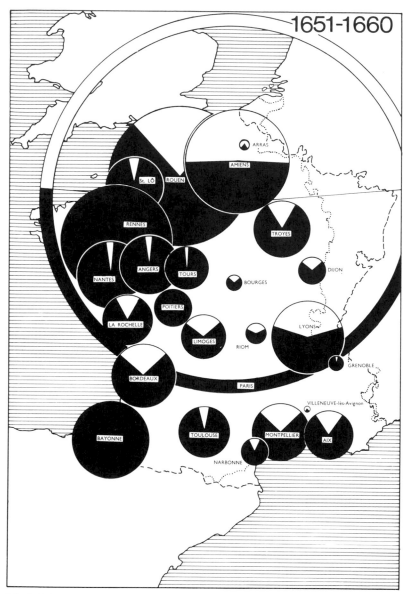

1651–1660 The beginning of the decade 1651–1660 was marked by the conversion of silver reals from Spain and by a decline in the proportion of gold issued. The end of the Thirty Years' War (hostilities were finally settled in 1659) restored to some extent the relations between France and Spain. Rennes and Bayonne were solely concerned with silver. In towns such as Paris, Amiens, and Lyons, however, gold constituted about half the issues; in others, such as Bordeaux, Aix, Montpellier, and Rouen, it was important. The maritime towns of the west expanded at the expense of the east. Paris dominated the scene.

Eleven towns coined copper liards. The first group, in order of importance, was Corbeil (2,077,819 livres), Limoges (1,632,807 livres), and Meung-sur-Loire (1,264,688 livres). After the troubles of the Fronde, the coinage of copper was executed outside Paris, and on condition that this currency not be carried into the capital.

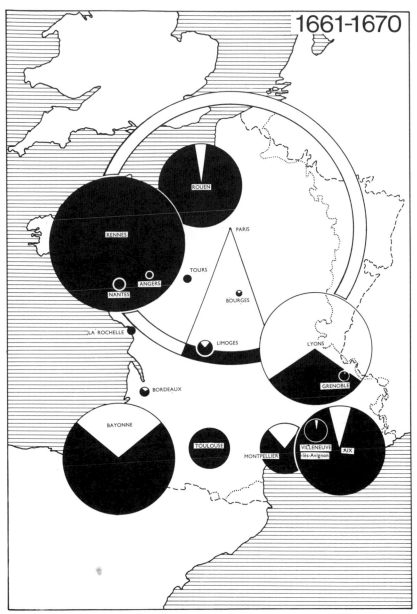

1661–1670 Again the ordinances raised the price of gold. Paris remained dominant, but its volume was lower than in the preceding decade. The difference emerged from the fall in the value of silver coined. It is difficult to compare the zones, for six mints made large issues: Paris, Lyons, Rennes, Bayonne, Rouen, and Aix. Of these, the first four operated continuously. The majority of the other mints were closed in 1662–1663, which contributed to the reduction of coinage in La Rochelle, Nantes, Angers, Rouen, Limoges, Bourges, Grenoble, and Villeneuve. On the other hand, operations in Bayonne increased and were marked by the reappearance of gold in quantity (the result of coinage from 1688). The presence of this money contrasts with the long attachment to silver since the 1550s. Rennes was more active than in the preceding decade and was wholly concerned with silver. Toulouse also produced only silver. Rouen declined by comparison with the 1650s. Further east, Aix, Montpellier, and Villeneuve concentrated largely on silver. The great gold centers were Paris and Lyons.

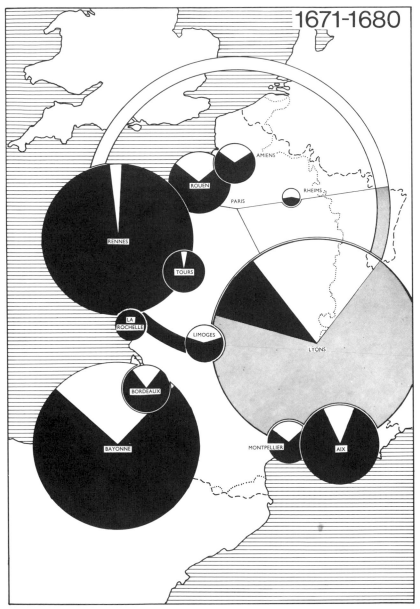

1671–1680 The years 1671–1680 proved to be a decade of confused movements, as was evidenced by the reopening of the mints closed in 1662–1663 and by the issues of the pieces of 4 and 2 sols in Paris (7,459,036 livres) and Lyons (12,753,461 livres) which are shown here as billon in order to mark the difference. Paris, Lyons, and Bayonne were, though others issued some quantities of this currency, most important towns in the production of gold. The maritime towns of the west — Rouen, Rennes, La Rochelle, Bordeaux, and Bayonne — and Montpellier and Aix remained the great producers of full-bodied silver currency during this decade.

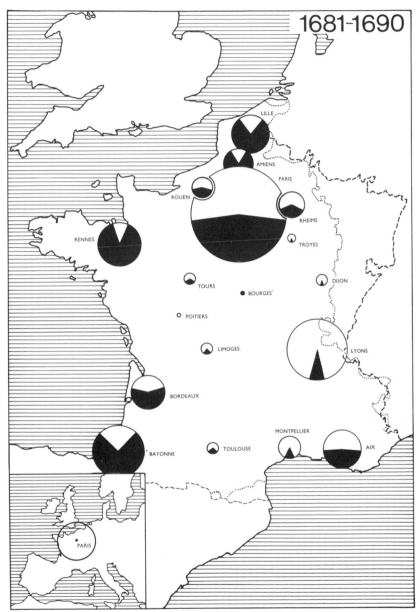

1681–1690 By comparison with the preceding decade, 1681–1690 shows a slight decline in coinage. The notable exception was Paris which increased its issue from 37,437,488 to 39,023,641 livres. Paris, Lyons, and Bayonne were the most important mints; taking into account the end to the official coinage of pieces of 2 and 4 sols, the first two were dominant. La Rochelle and Nantes were completely inactive.

This decade marked the beginning of war (1688–1697), and this particularly affected the performance of the mint in Lille newly opened in 1686. The coinage of gold should be noted, for it occupied more than half the sizable issues of Paris, Lyons, Aix, and Rheims.

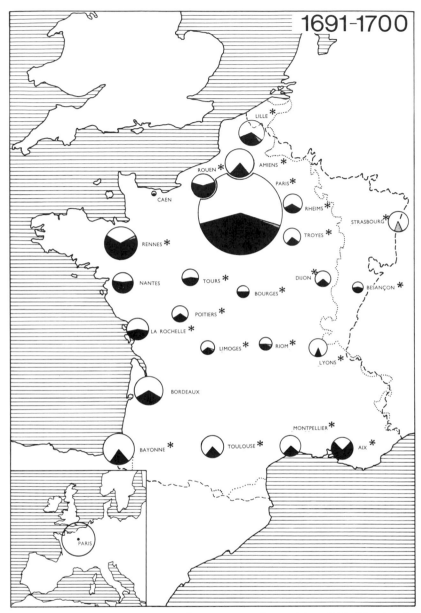

1691–1700 Hostilities lasted until the Treaty of Ryswick (1697). The decade 1691–1700 was marked by three important features: the outstanding position of Paris and Lyons, although below the level of 1681–1690; the relatively more even spread of coinage among the mints of France, attenuating the differences between east and west, north and south; the high proportion of gold in the coinage, with only Rouen, Rennes, and Nantes having it constitute less than half their issues. The coinage of billon was widely dispersed and reported from Aix, Amiens, Bayonne, Besançon, Bourges, Dijon, Lille, Limoges, Lyons, Montpellier, Paris, Poitiers, Rennes, Rheims, Riom, La Rochelle, Rouen, Strasbourg, Toulouse, Tours, and Troyes. Since in the majority of cases the amounts were relatively insignificant, they have been marked with asterisks.

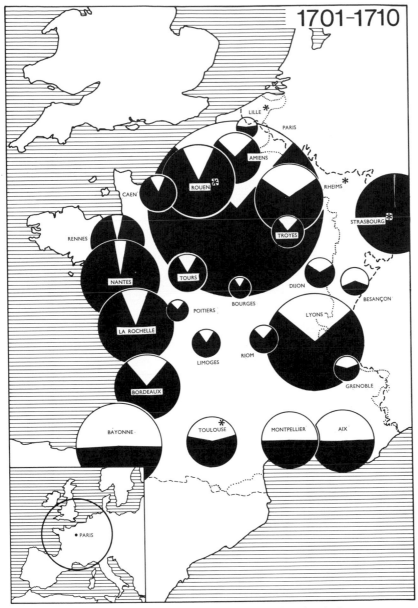

1701–1710 This map shows a reversal over the preceding decade in two respects. It reveals, first, a different structure in the size of issues. In place of an even spread over the entire country, there was an expansion of coinage in the western regions from Bordeaux to Rouen; in the north where, in addition to Paris (the largest), Amiens, Rheims, and Strasbourg were important; and in the south — Bayonne, Toulouse, Montpellier, Aix, and Lyons. The poor performance of the central towns was matched by Lille, lost to France in 1708.

The second feature was the difference between the coinage of gold and silver. Foreign affairs partly explain this change, for example, the possible contrasts between, on the one hand, the Methuen Treaty of 1703, which confirmed trading privileges between Britain and Portugal, mistress of the Brazilian goldfields, and, on the other hand, the dynastic connection which linked France to Spain and its empire. Silver was predominant for more than half the issues north of a line linking Bordeaux, Riom, Besançon, and Strasbourg; the last produced silver almost completely. Lyons also followed this tendency. In the south, however, the mints in Bayonne, Toulouse, Montpellier, and Aix coined more gold. After 1706 these towns came under the administration of Lyons, and although the figures for Bayonne and Aix have been completed only by estimates, those for Toulouse and Montpellier are reasonably accurate. Their different performances should be noted. Billon was coined in Lille, Rheims, Rouen, and Strasbourg (each marked with an asterisk).

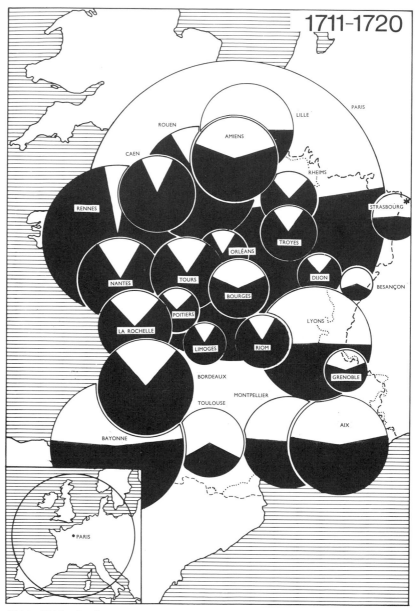

1711–1720 In the decade 1711–1720 monetary affairs were profoundly influenced by the Treaty of Utrecht (1713), and even more by the reforms of John Law. The volume of coinage increased, with the accent on Paris and Rennes, but these increases were also shared by the Atlantic and Channel regions of France from Bordeaux to the north. In this category may be placed Lille (restored to France in 1713) and Amiens. Rennes came second to Paris. In contrast there were declines in Rheims and Strasbourg. The mints generally showed widespread and substantial activity. In this period silver predominated, with the exception of 1717, during the time of John Law. There were, however, regional differences between the northeast and the maritime west. In Paris (with the largest total), Lille, Besançon, Strasbourg, Lyons, and the towns of the south, gold predominated for about half the issues. Billon was coined in Strasbourg (marked with an asterisk).

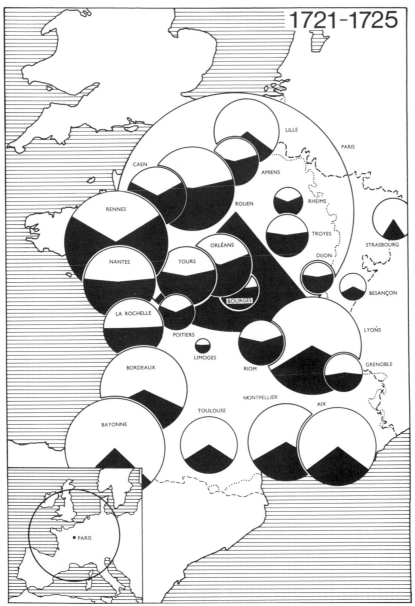

1721–1725 Although covering only half a decade, the period 1721–1725 coincided with the important years following the crash of the Mississippi Company (1720) and formed the prelude to the reform of 1726. In relative terms, the volume of coinage was large; as in the preceding decade, Paris and the western seaboard from Bayonne to Lille predominated. The estimates for the mints in the south — Bayonne, Toulouse, Montpellier, Aix, Riom, Lyons, and Grenoble — give evidence of important activity. These five years showed extensive issues of gold and created the preconditions for the great monetary reform of 1726. In Paris the issues of gold were very large (an estimated 77.07 percent). Even in the great mints of the western seaboard, Rouen, Rennes, and Bordeaux, which were normally attached to silver in the preceding decades, the quantities of gold coined were sizable.

4. France: An Essay in Differential Geography

In the data so far examined, each series of calculations has emphasized the basic diversity of France. That diversity has more or less dictated the methods used and has, indeed, suggested the ultimate conclusions. It is, therefore, worth stressing this aspect of the problem and giving these geographical disparities prominence in the discussion. This entails a review of economic affairs and life in general in France, not an easy task. Using monetary analysis is only one possible line of inquiry, and it has undeniable limitations.

In addition to the quantification of monetary movements, the types (or rather the technical quality) of currency issued are also important indicators. For example, in the silver phase, the issues of sols parisis and of full-bodied silver coins were not the same for the whole of France. There were significant regional differences between the issues of the franc (at a fineness of 10 deniers argent-le-roi) and the quart d'écus (at a fineness of 11 deniers argent-le-roi). The latter were used more directly to convert the silver reals from Spain, on which they were modeled. Their presence in the coinage would tend, therefore, to indicate a closer relationship with Spain and its great silver resources. The silver francs, however, in all probability revealed the use of secondary sources of silver, at a greater distance from Spain, beyond the first line of bullion inflation. The mints particularly concerned with the quart d'écu were Bayonne, La Rochelle, Nantes, Rennes and Saint-Lô; those occupied with the silver franc were Toulouse (with its overland connections with Spain), Limoges, Poitiers, Lyons, Amiens, Riom, Troyes, and Dijon. Some mints were concerned with both types. The Paris mint was notable in this regard; though it issued large quantities of silver francs, the quart d'écu dominated in the years 1589–1593 during the disorders of the League. In Rouen during roughly the same period (1587–1593) the quart d'écu was also issued in larger quantities. Angers and Tours were concerned with silver francs, although the latter mint showed a preference for the quart d'écu in the years 1580–1590. Bordeaux issued only quarts d'écu after 1590. While the mint in Bourges remained firmly attached to the franc, those in Montpellier, Villeneuve, and Aix occupied themselves more with the quart d'écu.

Observations of similar interest can be made about the distribution of coinage of sols parisis. These most important of billon coins tended, in general, to characterize inland areas, at a secondary level. They were issued in large quantities in continental France during the period 1550–1575 in such towns as Dijon, Troyes, Lyons, Grenoble, Aix, Limoges, and Poitiers. By contrast, in the cities taking the brunt of the arrivals of Spanish silver, the issue of these coins was less regular and of relatively less importance. They were issued in Bordeaux only in 1565, 1567–1568, and 1570–1572; in Angers in 1565–1572, 1578, and 1585; in Rennes in 1565–1570 and 1579–1580; in Nantes in 1567 and 1578; and in Bayonne in 1572 and 1586.

Many similar observations could be made. On each occasion, important differences among the issues of gold, silver, and billon can be noted. Besides this repetition of data, there is the fundamental problem of the geography of France, which goes beyond the limits already set.

We must now turn our attention to the geography of France, in its immense variety, in order to set the framework for the political and economic aspects of monetary developments in the sixteenth and seventeenth centuries. Clearly, it is not so much a question here of a *Tableau économique* of François Quesnay or of a *France rurale* of Marc Bloch, or indeed of an itinerary across the different provinces,[9] but rather of a number of remarks in the nature of a summary of conclusions.

The frontiers of France in the sixteenth and seventeenth centuries were not yet fixed, but still in a long process of settlement. These territorial adjustments were sometimes curtailed in summary fashion. The wars of Italy ended finally in a check to French expansion. The dreams of Charles VIII, Louis XII, Francis I, and Henry II to establish an "empire" among the brilliant city-states of Italy, to reach from Milan to Naples, were destined to be unfulfilled. They proposed an empire built by feats of arms and in no way comparable to the rich resources on which the relentless expansion of Spain was founded. They collapsed under a series of rebuffs: Pavia in 1525, the Treaty of Cambrai (1529), and the final liquidation in the Treaty of Cateau-Cambrésis (1559). France abandoned the strongholds it had won so easily since 1536 in Savoy and Piedmont. The Treaty of Lyons in 1601 settled the outstanding differences with the Duke of Savoy and brought important acquisitions in Bresse, Bugey, and Gex.[10] However, this did not restore the great "window" into Italy which France had claimed.

On the frontier of the Pyrenees the same sort of situation occurred. Béarn and French Navarre were finally brought into the kingdom of France in 1607, and Cerdagne and Roussillon were acquired in 1659 by the Treaty of the Pyrenees. Only then was France able to assert that these mountains separated it from Spain. The northern frontiers of France experienced still longer disputes to mark the boundaries of regions from the Saône to the Channel and the North Sea. At first France lost ground, under the conditions imposed at Senlis (1493), the bargain struck by Charles VIII to leave him a free hand in Italy. He renounced his rights in the Franche-Comté and abandoned Artois north of the Somme Valley, which thus became the French frontier. Afterward came sporadic advances: the occupation of the bishoprics of Metz, Toul, and Verdun (1552); the capture of Calais (1558); and the great acquisitions of Louis XIV which carried the frontier of France north of the Somme (Artois and French Flanders in 1668) into Franche-Comté (occu-

[9] See, for example, the popular sixteenth-century handbook, *Le guide des chemins de France* (1553, and numerous subsequent editions) of Charles Estienne, ed. Jean Bonnerot (2 vols., Paris, 1936).

[10] Auguste Longnon, *La formation de l'unité française* (Paris, 1922), pp. 313–314.

pied in 1672 and ceded in 1678). France had already taken Alsace in the Treaty of 1648.

Nevertheless, I do not intend here to give a résumé of French territorial maneuvers during two centuries, but rather to emphasize the mobility of the unit of estimate when the term "France" is employed. Even when this area was fixed officially by treaty and law, a basic uncertainty still remained. The frontiers in the reign of Henry IV, for example, certainly did not have the characteristics of the frontiers of the present day. They were by no means effective. Men, goods, and money moved constantly to and fro without serious let or hindrance. For example, the Pyrenees were not a barrier to the flow of gold and silver from Spain. The route of Canfranc was a channel for smuggling and illicit trade, under the very noses of the authorities; virtually the same may be said of Lyons with its direct connections with Italy and Germany and its communities of alien merchants. There were the coasts of the Atlantic from Calais to Bayonne and of the Mediterranean from Roussillon to Var. The high seas were open to trade from the four corners of the world. Marseilles prospered as a function not only of its city and traditional hinterland but also of the whole Mediterranean. The avenues of maritime trade, in the same way as the land routes, brought a constant flow of all sorts of money from abroad. France was a meeting place for Europe, an isthmus as geographers would say, between the Mediterranean, the Atlantic, and the North Sea, between Italy and the Low Countries, Germany and Spain.[11] This junction in the currents of international trade brought both advantages and disadvantages; an example of the latter is the way some of the small neighbors of France used it as a place to dump the depreciated currency which they turned out, so it seemed, indiscriminately.

For these small states, neighbors and sometimes even enclaves in France, the opportunities for such arbitrage encouraged coinage operations to almost industrial proportions. It can be seen in the case of Savoy, of Béarn before 1607,[12] of Avignon, where the Papacy still held authority, of the small enclave of Orange, for long a hideout for Protestant forces, of the free imperial city of Besançon, and of Metz before 1552. Though the coinage of these small mints made history on only a small scale, they have a place in the general context. The Great Powers — England, the Low Countries, Spain, Portugal, the German principalities, and Italy — of course controlled the essential relationships of the French monetary system.

It must not be assumed too soon that France enjoyed territorial and economic unity; in the sixteenth and seventeenth centuries, as has already been noted, the country was marked by diversity. It was a conglomeration of zones, a collection of economic compartments often imperfectly linked together, at

---

[11] Fernand Braudel, *La Méditerranée et le monde méditerranéen* (Paris, 1949), pp. 157–161.

[12] Béarn was finally incorporated into the territories of the French crown by the edict of 1607. See Longnon, *Formation de l'unité française,* p. 327.

different levels of activity. Large areas of its economy, in all probability, were given to quasi-subsistence farming, and a "money economy" was by no means necessarily the rule. The penetration of foreign specie into France, or the circulation of French currency, therefore, met with varying degrees of resistance in different parts of the country.

It would be fairly easy to demonstrate this disparity through the gradual evolution of the *ancien régime*. Clearly though, the differences were much greater in the sixteenth, and indeed in the seventeenth, century than at the time of the French Revolution. However we consider the country, whether from the political, administrative, or legal point of view, or in matters concerning the crown and the law, or in questions of language and historical development, France was a mosaic, a composition of provinces. Geography played its part, contributing variations and basic contrasts. The backward, more isolated lands in Brittany were not the same as the rich and brilliant valley of the Loire. The Massif Central was composed of different regions, half shut off from the outside world. There is, indeed, no end to the natural differences, in some places still surviving, elsewhere virtually disappeared.

In this context, it is perhaps worth citing a series of small differences, of little importance in themselves but nevertheless representing larger problems, which, to my knowledge, have rarely been mentioned. Even in the sixteenth century the year did not begin at the same time for the whole of France. In Limoges it took place "on the day of the nativity of Our Lord"; in Poitiers the year opened at Easter "which is the day when the year is changed in Poitou"; in Aix it dated "from Christmas, following the custom of the country": in Bayonne it was "the day of Our Lady in March"; in Grenoble it was calculated "according to the custom of the country which is Christmas"; in Villeneuve-lès-Avignon it was "to date from the Annunciation of Our Lord" and "taken at the Nativity." Only with the royal edict of 1564 did the year begin officially on January 1. In monetary matters, however, this procedure had been followed since 1550, and the accounts of the mints were closed every December 31.[13]

What can be said about the calendar can easily be repeated with greater justice about weights and measures. Fortunately the crown had at an early stage ordered that the Paris marc (equivalent to 244.75 metric grams) be the standard for weighing precious metals. However, it was still necessary to send local measures to Paris for checking against the official standard weights.

In brief, these differences serve the particular purpose of this study to measure the performance of France. Its monetary history rests on documents and data which provide, taking the large and small mints together, some fifty-nine samples. This history is thus essentially marked by variety and dispersions. In order to summarize these movements, it was necessary to combine the coinage of mints very different in operation and character. If it is supposed that

[13] A.N., Z¹B.881 (for 1548); A.N., Z¹B.936 (for 1529); A.N., Z¹B.310; A.N., Z¹B.1011 (for 1546); A.N., Z¹B.877–878 (for 1511); A.N., Z¹B.320 (for 1561).

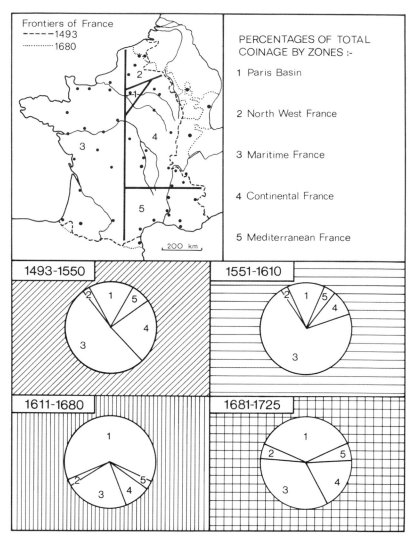

22. Comparison by Zones and Phases of the Coinage in France, 1493–1725 (Reference: Appendix B)

their activities were in some degree a function of local needs — and this was generally valid — then the volume and type of their coinage would reflect the monetary and economic disparity of France in the sixteenth and seventeenth centuries. Furthermore, in order to emphasize these disparities, I shall group these mints, thus dividing France into significant regions. Such a method is clearly arbitrary. For the purpose of simplifying this study, I have divided France into five zones (see Graph 22 and Map 3). Some of the divisions are open to question, for example, the line between Lyons and the Mediterranean

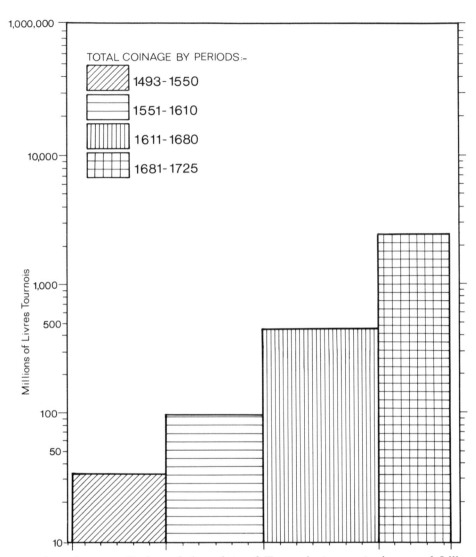

TOTAL COINAGE BY PERIODS:-

1493-1550

1551-1610

1611-1680

1681-1725

Millions of Livres Tournois

south or between Paris and the mints of Tournai, Arras, Amiens, and Lille. In general, however, such fine distinctions call for too much precision and ultimately serve little useful purpose. The crux of the matter, whatever the scale of measures adopted, is to contrast three key zones: the west, the east, and Paris.

The components of the graph have been put in the legend; it should be emphasized that the data are given in livres tournois, which underwent a series of devaluations during the two centuries. This is a disadvantage, but it has been reduced to some extent by dividing the period into four phases: 1493–1550; 1551–1610; 1611–1680; and 1681–1725. Within these phases comparisons are more valid. However, taking the period 1493–1725 as a whole, and bearing in mind the devaluation of the livre tournois, four general observations emerge: a general increase in the value of money issued during the gold coinage in the phase 1493–1550; through the predominance of silver, 1551–1610; and in the seventeenth century, dominated by Paris. The earlier chapters have emphasized the general nature of these factors, but for the present only the implications for the differential geography of France are relevant here. The analysis shows the overwhelming preponderance of Paris in the seventeenth century; during the reigns of Henry IV and Louis XIII it became the monetary, financial, and economic capital of France. The graph also reveals the prosperity of the west of France, from the time of Charles VIII, growing within the development of the Atlantic. These two huge questions — the importance of Paris and the prosperity of the west — demand closer attention.

The wealth of Paris leaves no doubt in the mind of the observer, but this has its own particular problems. It cannot, for example, be separated from the relative decline of Lyons, which is another question. This shift of economic focus from Lyons to Paris appears to be of the same nature as the shift in the Low Countries between the old market in Antwerp and the new, thriving metropolis in Amsterdam, which was the outcome of a series of wars and civil conflicts. It is clear in the case of the Low Countries that both contestants lived directly or indirectly on handouts from Spain, while in the case of the civil wars in France, much less is known about the financial and economic conditions after 1562. If these latter wars did not end in political division as in the Low Countries, they nevertheless assisted the replacement of Lyons by Paris. Does this profound alteration of structures — a part of the complex but continuous development of the French economy — have monetary connotations? From the monetary point of view, the adjustment was not resolved until after the mid-sixteenth century; it was in the second half of the century that Lyons succumbed to Paris. The mint at Lyons had shown exceptional activity in 1504–1510, 1517–1520, and 1541–1543, when the crown summoned its financial market to underwrite its wars and political endeavors.

Yet Lyons had more than a mint; its fame rested on the great fairs, created on March 8, 1463, to compete with Geneva.[14] Because of the fairs, by the end of the fifteenth century, and certainly by the opening of the sixteenth century, Lyons became one of the foremost markets of Christendom. About 1530 a *mémoire* described the exchange dealers in Lyons as "wealthy from large sums of money, all gained in the last twenty years by exchange operations";[15] this date, it must be noted, placed the important days of Lyons after the first opening up of the New World. I do not intend to study here the double fortune of Lyons as a commodity market and as a center

[14] Marc Brésard, *Les foires de Lyon aux XVe et XVIe siècles* (Paris, 1914), p. 261.
[15] A.N., J.971–972, Mémoire au . . . Légat Chancelier (c. 1530), at the time of the payment of the ransom of Francis I.

for finance and capital, for there are already enough excellent studies on the subject. It is more interesting to note the moment when the emphasis shifted toward the north, when Lyons faced political and financial difficulties — the inevitable outcome of the repeated war loans and tax levies necessary to the Valois. Was the economic future of Lyons impaired by the import duties in 1552 on commodities, the lifeblood of the fairs? [16] The financial operations of the market — always difficult but still profitable in 1562,[17] in the opinion of some observers — were not seriously affected (fatally affected would be more appropriate, according to Henri Lapeyre's study) until the crisis of 1575. This sharp break became sooner or later advantageous to other markets and merchants. The first victims were the Luchese and the Florentines through whose hands passed the operations of "exchange and finance" of Lyons.[18] Such upsets help to explain the brilliant fortune of the fairs first held in Besançon, and then after 1579 in Piacenza.[19] They also explain to some extent the fortune of Paris, far more than the mere issues of currency from its mint. It is significant to find in the notarial acts that the merchant bankers of Lyons early established representatives in Paris. Thus, the Florentine Alberto Jacquinoti on October 15, 1570, appointed Bernard Belalbigie as his agent in Paris, and the Luchese banker Paulin Benedicti named Damio Jardini as his representative in Paris. In the summer of 1574 the merchants of Paris even began to establish a bourse in the capital. The ordinance of July 7, 1574, which attempted to fix the rate for the gold écu at 54 sols, drew attention to the illegal meetings of merchants in the Palais de Justice which they called "the change." [20] In 1590, at the time of the Spanish intervention in the wars of the League, the Spinolas — those "wealthy Genoese merchants who did a great deal of business in Paris" [21] — offered to make large sums of money available to Philip II. A whole new study could be made of these early signs of the financial supremacy of Paris and its subsequent urban expansion. Without that financial eminence, it would not have become the Paris of modern times. Paris was not an artifact, created out of nothing; it was, after all, the capital and grew with the power of the monarchy and central administration. The edict of August 1555, which made the changers royal officials, fixed their numbers

[16] Archives Municipales [hereafter cited as A.M.], Lyons, Ser. BB.58, fol. 169; BB.63, fol. 38, 260, 268; BB.68, fol. 181.

[17] An inquiry in Lyons in 1565 (A.N., Z¹B.274, fol. 391, Dec. 2, 1565) asserted that in the fairs the alien financiers had sometimes cleared a million crowns in Spanish silver reals, on the condition of leaving a third in the city.

[18] The Florentine merchants presided over the fixing of the exchange rates for the "payments" in each fair. See Claude de Rubys, *Histoire véritable de la ville de Lyon* (Lyons, 1604), pp. 497–498.

[19] Braudel, *Méditerranée*, pp. 396 ff.

[20] A.D., Rhône, Ser. 3E, 4495, fol. 125; 4499, fol. 56; A.N., Z¹B.70, ordonnance of July 7, 1574. Richard Ehrenberg, *Das Zeitalter der Fugger* (2 vols., Jena, 1896), II, p. 300, cites the report of Ambassador Hieromino Lippomano of 1577 mentioning the existence of this bourse.

[21] See Chap. 3.

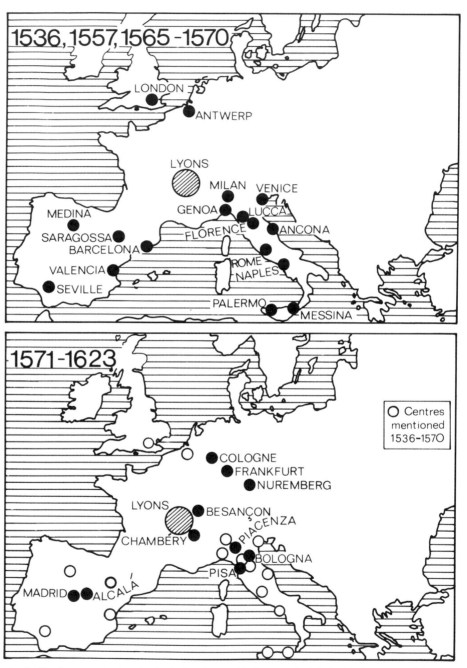

4.–5. Exchange Centers in Relationship with Lyons, 1536–1623 (as quoted in the lists of exchange-rates in the Lyons fairs)

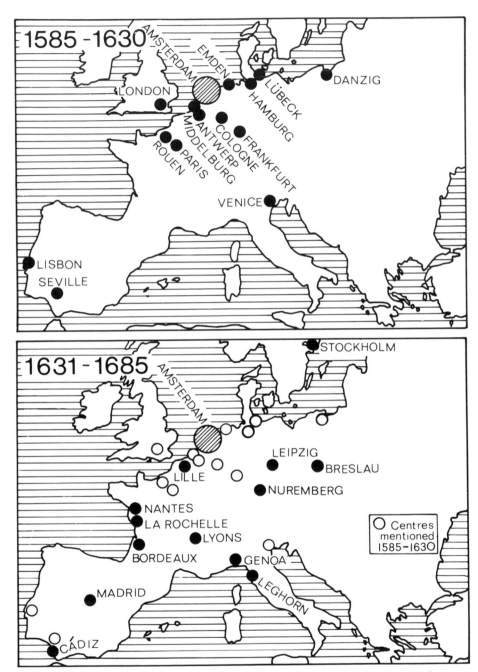

6.–7. Exchange Centers in Relationship with Amsterdam, 1585–1685 (Reference: N. Posthumus)

in all cities except Lyons.[22] By contrast, the letters patent of May 1580 authorized twenty-four in Paris and only twelve in Rouen, Lyons, and Toulouse, cities which were also allowed to have a "bourse couverte." [23] Can this be taken as another sign of the rising financial power of Paris?

There was, no doubt, an underlying movement of point and counterpoint, which is clearly shown (see the accompanying maps 4–7) in the changing structure of the exchange centers in relationship to Lyons and Paris.[24] In the three decades before 1570 Lyons had dealings primarily with the exchange centers of the south (Spain, Italy, and Sicily) and with London and Antwerp in the north. After 1571, with the victory of silver in France, new names appeared in the official lists: Besançon, Chambéry, and Piacenza; Cologne, Frankfort, and Nuremberg. Here may be seen the emergence of the "Spanish corridor" between Italy and the Low Countries. In contrast, Paris found its place more in the network dominated by Amsterdam. During the years 1585–1630 the dependent centers of this young economic giant were, above all, the maritime ports; the exceptions were Paris, Frankfort, and Cologne. Except for Venice, they were all situated on the seaboard of the Atlantic Ocean, the Channel, the North Sea, or the Baltic. Later, in the years 1631–1685, Amsterdam vigorously pushed its contacts south to Nantes, La Rochelle, and Bordeaux and east to Nuremberg, Leipzig, and Breslau. Between these two great spheres, in which both Paris and Lyons found their places, there are some points of transition worth noticing. The quotations of exchange rates for London came to an end in the Lyons fairs in 1601 and began on the Amsterdam market in 1609; Cologne, quoted in Amsterdam in 1585, disappeared from the lists of Lyons in 1601. Nuremberg ended its appearance in Lyons in 1618 at the outbreak of the Thirty Years' War, but emerged in Amsterdam in 1614. The rivalry between Lyons and Paris, carried out discreetly, was thus part of a much larger transformation of the international scene.

The rise of Paris also set in relief the growing power of the west. This second geographical reality is self-evident, but it needs a brief explanation. Graph 22 shows that the percentages of the total issues provided by the western region were 51.45 percent in the years 1493–1550; 72.42 percent in 1551–1610; 24.87 percent in 1611–1680, in spite of the preponderance of the activity of the mint in Paris; and 36.62 percent in 1681–1725. The corresponding percentages for the continental region are, respectively, 23.00 percent, 9.02 percent, 8.02 percent, and 15.33 percent; even if they are combined with the percentages for the Mediterranean south — 6.48 percent, 3.59 percent, 3.90 percent, and 7.07 percent — the portion of the west still

[22] A. Fontanon, *Les edicts et ordonnances des Roys de France* (2 vols., Paris, 1585), II, p. 136.

[23] A.N., Z^{1}B.71, lettres patentes of May 1580, verified Aug. 22, 1581, and remonstrance of the Cour des Monnaies of Aug. 7, 1581.

[24] See Chap. 5.

remains superior. The revival in both cases in the period 1681–1725 recalls the earlier gold phase, here confined to the years 1493–1550. Paris came into its own in the period 1611–1680, after having long been dominated by other regions. During the time of the early Bourbons Paris provided more than three-fifths of the coinage. If the estimates are correct for the years 1681–1725, this share was reduced to 35.34 percent, which was less than that of the western region (37.08 percent). In passing, it should also be noted that the court rivalry of Versailles against Paris coincided in the monetary sphere with renewed tension between Paris and the west of France.

Nevertheless, the problem is not solved by mere figures, telling though they may appear to be. The coinage in the west was by no means the wealth of the west. It went into circulation and passed to other zones. However, the province of Poitou in the sixteenth century, analyzed by Paul Raveau, and the port of La Rochelle, studied by Étienne Trocmé,[25] were regions rich in gold and silver, as the notarial acts record. Yet, on the other hand, we find Franche-Comté, then outside the frontiers of France, with those ill-furnished coffers, so brilliantly described by Lucien Febvre; [26] and Burgundy, which, Henri Hauser has shown, was obliged to rely on low-grade billon.[27]

If conclusions can be drawn from these graphs, then the economic geography of France can be revised. Lucien Romier was perhaps looking to past fortunes in placing the wealth of France in the provinces of Burgundy, Champagne, and Picardy, the bulwarks of the Catholic Counter-Reformation. The fast rate of growth in wealth was more likely in the west, in those regions deeply shaken by the risings of the peasantry who were prone to react against taxes and to support revolution, where with the possible exception of Brittany (still a fringe region, on the margin of French history), the Protestant armies found many supporters.[28]

There is an even more telling example to add to these explanations. The great route across France in the sixteenth and seventeenth centuries and even later perhaps, the great route of wealth, was not the classic "isthmus" of the geographers joining Marseilles and Lyons by way of Burgundy to Paris. There is reason to suggest that, in the sixteenth century, the great road was rather from Paris to Bayonne, the old route taken by pilgrims to the shrine of Santiago de Compostela.[29] It left Notre Dame in Paris, climbed the Rue

[25] Paul Raveau, *L'agriculture et les classes paysannes* (Paris, 1926), *passim,* especially Chap. 1; Étienne Trocmé and Marcel Delafosse, *Le Commerce Rochelais de la fin du XVe siècle au début du XVIIe* (Paris, 1952), pp. 46–56.

[26] Lucien Febvre, *Philippe II et la Franche-Comté* (Paris, 1911), p. 241 *et passim.*

[27] Henri Hauser, "La question des prix et des monnaies en Bourgogne," *Annales de Bourgogne,* IV (1932), p. 5, n. 1.

[28] Lucien Romier, *Le royaume de Catherine de Médicis* (2 vols., Paris, 1922), II, pp. 159, 166; Marc Bloch, *Les caractères originaux de l'histoire rurale française* (Paris, 1952), especially pp. 57–65.

[29] André Varagnac, "Genèse et avenir de Paris," *L'âge nouveau,* LXII (June 1951); see also Yves Renouard, "Le pèlerinage à Saint-Jacques-de-Compostelle et son importance dans le monde médiéval," *Revue historique,* CCVI (1951).

Saint-Jacques, an indication of its destination. Some accounts made it reach the Loire at Orléans, follow the river downstream, cross over by way of the island at Amboise, skirt the shrine of St. Martin in Tours, and then, by way of Poitiers, Angoulême, Bordeaux, and Bayonne, reach "Pontarbie, on the seacoast, the great fortress of this passage of Navarre, the key to Spain," [30] then still a point of contention between France and Spain. Over this frontier, the route took the traveler to Santiago, passing by the towns of Castile which had important fairs. A study of this route, with its traffic and convoys, its relays of merchants, would probably set in relief the stream of activity which Spain directed into France after the discovery of the New World. And such a study would also give more information on the upsurge of wealth in the west.

[30] Estienne, *Guide des chemins,* II, p. 217; J. Vielliard, *Le guide du pèlerin de Saint-Jacques-de-Compostelle* (Mâcon, 1938), Plates II, III.

Chapter 5

Monetary Movements in the French Economy during the Sixteenth and Seventeenth Centuries

The monetary problems of France become much clearer when set in the context of its economic development. At the outset some difficulties must be noted. Apart from questions of the validity of the data, two important reservations qualify any simple assessment of the problem.

In the first place, the physical area of France came increasingly under a centralizing political administration, but its economy was by no means homogeneous. I have already emphasized the point that under existing economic conditions it was difficult to overcome or attenuate regional differences, and they still remained largely valid at the end of the seventeenth century. France was far too complex to be described as a well-defined economic unit. It was a country of many facets rather than an ideal, organic whole.

In the second place, although there is some justification for considering money as having a more or less dynamic role in economic activity, it was nevertheless only one among other possible economic variables. Monetary factors were certainly not sufficient in themselves to explain completely the mechanism of these early agrarian economies, which suffered from the restrictions implicit in metallic currency even though the use of that money became increasingly more extensive. In the final analysis, it is just as important to assign weights to these variables as to variables in more recent periods. Even in the present day, economic theories largely rationalize current human experience.

The first task, perhaps, in such an inquiry is to set the different schools of thought in their historical context: the bullionist theories of the seventeenth century can be better understood, perhaps only understood, against the failure of the astonishing "inflation" of gold and silver of the sixteenth century. This has much the same validity as considering Adam Smith in the light of the expansion of Britain during the late eighteenth century. Again, Knut Wicksell and the Viennese theorists on capital find their place in the growth and progressive industrialization of the late nineteenth century when the rise in the ratio of capital per worker was an indicator of growth. Lord Keynes, in turn, was closely associated with the troubled years between the two world wars, with the great economic crisis of 1929–1933 when unemployment reached high levels and the problems of investment and consumption assumed an exceptional significance. Clearly these are facile conclusions, but they are, for the economic historian, timely reminders that theories float on a wide range of experience.

Yet even though facile, such remarks are by no means unrelated to the sixteenth and seventeenth centuries. Obviously, the short-run explanations are not always directly applicable to the particular period being discussed, even with necessary modifications. It is not so much a question of making a model to fit the situation, but, rather, of using the customary methods of history to review the empirical data. Moreover, it is apparent that the monetary sector was profoundly transformed in the sixteenth and seventeenth centuries and in this sense has particular importance. Neither before nor after were economic questions raised in the same political, social, institutional, or even psychological context.

This chapter attempts a more detailed study of the monetary variable in the activity of the French economy in the sixteenth and seventeenth centuries. The approach here has once more been at the microlevel, dealing in turn with money and its relation to different sectors. In the concluding chapter, the problem will be considered in aggregate. Much of the necessary empirical data for this inquiry is still unavailable, but even a provisional explanation based on partial evidence has some interest. Taking into account these patent difficulties, I have divided the present chapter into three parts: money and price movements; foreign exchanges; and economic movements. In this way, simple considerations lead to the more complex.

1. Money and Price Movements

It has become increasingly fashionable, since the polemics in the wake of the "great" crisis of 1873 and even more since 1929, to reduce the casual role of precious metals. Their direct responsibility for changes in price levels and economic activity[1] has diminished in the context of the expansion of bank deposits and the continuing effects of technological change. In the analysis of shorter movements, money generally defined and the balance of payments retain their place in the explanations. At the present juncture, it is apparent that economic systems largely dominated by planning and governmental considerations are very different in substance from the articulated system of markets and self-sufficient regions existing during the period under study. All this must be kept in mind.

Although in modern economic analysis monetary factors have been given less importance and other considerations brought into prominence, special caution is required in dealing with price movements in the sixteenth centuries; money then remained powerful, but, it must be repeated, was one factor among many. In preindustrial economics, naturally, agriculture was dominant. In addition, the pressure of a growing population — of which the annual rate of increase was low but cumulative — on scarce land resources could exercise a powerful "demand-pull" on prices. Again, money was not a simple entity in itself; it was composed of different types of money in circulation — gold, silver, billon, and instruments of credit. Their general development often followed different lines. As noted in the earlier chapters, the additions of these different forms of money to the aggregate stock did not keep constant proportions. And there is good reason to believe that their

---

[1] Knut Wicksell, *Interest and Prices* (London, 1936), pp. 110, 167.

proportions in active circulation also did not remain constant. In view of these alterations, since money changed in "structure," it is possible to consider the history of prices in the light of the standard money in use; instead of analyzing money through price movements, we can examine prices through the different types of money, each producing its own particular version of the general movement. The task is not entirely without purpose.

Few will doubt the considerable obstacles in the way of reconstituting even the present-day economy of France. Its diversities are, of course, an essential part of its behavior. As a result, there has been a tendency to deal with the subject in studies of particular regions or towns. Everywhere the the economic historian turns he is confronted by an immense richness of subject and sources. The history of prices proves no exception to this basic lack of coherence, although an insufficiency of price series over a complete range of sectors for the period from the late fifteenth to the seventeenth century makes this type of regional study difficult. Consequently, a comparison between a differentiated price system and the operations of the regional mints is scarcely possible. But it is important to establish the framework of the existing data. What was the position of France in the price structures of the international economy?

It is possible to make a rough estimate of the position of France in the general hierarchy of markets in Europe during this period. For a bulky commodity such as wheat estimated in terms of an international standard, silver, there were considerable price differentials (see Graph 10). At the end of the fifteenth century the difference between the "advanced" economies of the Mediterranean and the "backward" economies of the eastern Baltic was of the order of one to six or one to seven.[2] In the ranking of economies by grain prices, France tends to fall in the upper bracket, although it was not an area of "maximum" prices such as Spain, the great center of bullion inflation, nor as Italy, with its wealthy and brilliant cities. However, France, a prominent producer of wheat with an agrarian economy, must be classed among the more prosperous regions of Europe. After about 1600 there is a gradual but noticeable closing of the differential between zones of relatively high and of relatively low grain prices, brought about partly by the price fall in the "advanced" economies, particularly Spain, and partly by the persistent tendency to inflation experienced in the backward regions, such as Poland, with its famous grain-producing lands. At the close of the seventeenth century, Britain, the future dominant economy, appears to have become an area of high wheat prices. By the second quarter of the eighteenth century, a period of low grain prices and "agricultural depression,"[3] the spread between

[2] Fernand Braudel and Frank Spooner, *"Prices in Europe from 1450 to 1750,"* in *The Cambridge Economic History of Europe*, **IV**, ed. E. E. Rich and C. H. Wilson (Cambridge, Eng., 1967).

[3] G. E. Mingay, "The Large Estate in Eighteenth-century England," in *First International Economic History Conference* (Stockholm, 1960).

maximum and minimum wheat prices had closed to about one to two. Although this gap tended to widen during the inflation of the eighteenth century, Europe had in effect reached a stage in the evolution of its international price structures.

What were the general price trends of Europe, the secular phases in which the movements in France found their place? The period under study — the sixteenth and seventeenth centuries — was, in reality, part of a much longer period, which began earlier and ended later. There were three dominant secular trends: the price rise of the sixteenth century — the "price revolution" (a label long subject to debate which can be accepted in general terms); the recession or pause of the seventeenth century; and the renewal of inflation associated with the eighteenth century.

Although I do not intend here to give a detailed description of the experience of these long swings in European prices, it is nevertheless pertinent to consider when the turning points occurred, when the "sixteenth century" began, when there was a definitive break in the price revolution, when the upswing in prices at the end of the seventeenth century was finally confirmed. The evidence so far appears to indicate that these turning points were not abrupt, but, rather, extended over wide periods of about half a century.[4]

The price rise, which later marked the sixteenth century, apparently began early for the less developed economies — in Northern and, above all, Central Europe — which experienced rising prices probably from the mid-1460s. France, if we are to trust the evidence from Limoges and Grenoble, belonged to this group. Micheline Baulant's reconstruction of wheat prices in Paris also tends to confirm a clear trend of rising nominal prices from the 1460s.[5] However, in the case of Spain, as Earl J. Hamilton has clearly established, there is no question of secular rising prices until the beginning of the sixteenth century.

In contrast, the end of the price revolution came early for Spain: silver prices went down after 1601. The data from Udine, Siena, Rome, and Naples show that Italy shared roughly the same experience, perhaps from the 1590s. And some regions of France probably also belonged to this movement, although the conditions of the League confused the situation. In Aix, according to René Baehrel, the prices "peaked" in the 1590s and so may be associated with the movement in Spain and the western Mediterranean. In the north, in the regions of Beauvais, Pierre Goubert places the downturn at 1630. However, a definite dating of the economic downturn in the Mediterranean has not yet been established. More recent studies, such as those of Pierre Vilar on Catalonia and Emmanuel Le Roy Ladurie on Languedoc, would tend to prolong the moment of recession. Growth may have continued in some cases even to the mid-seventeenth century.[6] In the Low Countries and

---

[4] Braudel and Spooner, "Prices in Europe from 1450 to 1750."

[5] Micheline Baulant, "Le prix des grains à Paris de 1431 à 1788," *Annales: Économies, Sociétés, Civilisations,* XXIII (1968), pp. 537–540, Annexes.

[6] René Baehrel, *Une croissance: La Basse-Provence rurale (fin du XVI° siècle —*

Britain the downturn in silver prices was not clear until the 1640s. Germany, Central Europe, and Poland seem even more to confirm this trend.

Finally, there is the third turning point, the upswing at the end of the seventeenth century. Some German cities experienced rising prices in the second half of the seventeenth century: Leipzig, Frankfort, and Speyer in 1656–1660; Würzburg, Augsburg, and Munich after 1671.[7] In nominal prices there was a tendency in Italy, France, and Spain to experience inflation from the 1680s, but in silver prices the countries followed the lead of the advanced economies of Holland and Britain, which did not see the upward trend in both nominal and silver prices until after the agricultural depression of the 1730s and 1740s. The upturn in silver prices (as distinct from nominal prices) was not finally clear in France until after the collapse of the projects of John Law. The tendency of silver relatively to appreciate in the early eighteenth century may have contributed to these movements.

When the economic historian omits the exact nature of regional differences, he may propose the hypothesis that France tended to have an intermediary position, neither holding to the extreme stability of Spain at the end of the fifteenth century nor wholly joining Britain and Holland in the prolonged movement of inflation in the early seventeenth century. The downturn, at the end of the sixteenth and in the early seventeenth centuries, if the evidence from Aix and Beauvais are taken together, tends to show that the different regions of France were not concerted even in the phasing of secular price movements. It may be inferred that by position, territorial size, and fundamental economic diversity France assumed the role not of a leader in prices but rather, within its frontiers, of a microcosm of the wider structural shifts in Europe.

A third large problem remains: that of cycles and short-term fluctuations. It is tenable that the seventeenth century, with its severe dearths, for example, in 1628–1630, 1648–1652, and 1693–1694, experienced short-term fluctuations of greater amplitude than those in the sixteenth century. This may be a question of the availability of information, for there were severe cyclic movements at an earlier date, as in Flanders in the 1490s[8] and in France in the 1540s and 1590s. However, after analyzing the data for Spain, H. T. Davis noted the existence of an increasing amplitude of cycles in the seventeenth century.[9] This also appears to have been the case in the price movements in Udine, which reveals a series of waves of greater amplitude from 1627 to 1659 (1627–1636, 1636–1640, 1640–1646, 1646–1650, 1650–1653, and

---

1789) (Paris, 1961); Pierre Goubert, *Beauvais et le Beauvaisis de 1600 à 1730* (Paris, 1960), p. 388; Pierre Vilar, *La Catalogne dans l'Espagne moderne* (3 vols., Paris, 1962); Emmanuel Le Roy Ladurie, *Les Paysans de Languedoc* (2 vols., Paris, 1966).

[7] Moritz J. Elsas, *Umriss einer Geschichte der Preise und Löhne in Deutschland* (2 vols., Leiden, 1936–1949).

[8] Charles Verlinden *et al.*, *Dokumenten voor geschiedenis van prijzen en lonen in Vlaanderen en Brabant* (*XV*e*–XVIII*e *eeuw*) (Bruges, 1959).

[9] H. T. Davis, *The Analysis of Economic Time Series* (Bloomington, Ind., 1941).

1653–1659). Pierre Goubert's evidence for Beauvais shows that periods of cyclic disturbances occurred there in 1639–1658 (1639–1645, 1645–1650, 1650–1657, 1657–1658). Again, later, the crises in the years 1687–1728 were associated with the difficulties of 1693–1694, 1709–1710, 1720, and 1723–1725. The first group of cycles (1639–1658) coincided with a general crisis in Europe in the mid-seventeenth century, of which the graph published in the *Cambridge Economic History of Europe* is given here as illustration (see Graph 23). More detailed information is required to explain these important movements. The effect of climatic conditions on the cycle of harvests or series of harvests — conditions apparently were unfavorable, for example, in 1649 — must be considered in the explanations.

These affirmations, it must be noted, have been drawn largely from the more complete series of data, those for the prices of wheat. In the case of France, the series for Paris has the great advantage of reflecting a market in the capital city; it merits confidence by reason of the continuity and large number of mentions each year. The prices taken from the official *mercuriale* begin with 1520.[10] In a great agricultural country such as France, furthermore, it can be assumed that the grain market played an exceptional role. The price of grain, together with that of wine, remained central to the French economy.[11] Since they were the dominant prices in the market they require special attention.

Though grain prices have the persuasive advantages of continuity, type, and location, they will not be the sole indicator used for my analysis. Their special character is, nevertheless, critical enough to require a long discussion on their formation. In the equation of exchange there are implicit considerations both of demand and of supply to be kept in mind. In the first place, the demand for cereals — the basic food — was highly inelastic. Over the long run, the relationships of the different cereals within the grain market would almost satisfy the *loi des débouchés* of Jean-Baptiste Say, in that in equilibrium the basic structure of supply fitted the demand. But that equilibrium was largely unpredictable. The more expensive wheat, compared with cheaper cereals such as rye, maize, or the "mixtures" of grains, was a superior food and tended to have a higher income elasticity. When incomes rose, or prices fell, relatively more wheat would be consumed. There was a double advantage: the

---

[10] Henri Hauser, *Recherches et documents sur l'histoire des prix en France, 1500–1800* (Paris, 1936), pp. 107–112. A more recent edition of this mercuriale is published in Micheline Baulant and Jean Meuvret, *Prix des céréales extraits de la mercuriale de Paris, 1520–1698* (2 vols., Paris, 1960–1962). A further elaboration of these data, extended with additional material from 1431 to 1788, has been published by Micheline Baulant, this time for the calendar years; see n. 5; see also R. Latouche, "Le prix du blé à Grenoble du XVᵉ au XVIIIᵉ siècle," *Revue d'histoire économique et sociale*, XX (1932).

[11] C.-Ernest Labrousse. *La crise de l'économie française à la fin de l'Ancien Régime et au début de la Révolution* (Paris, 1944), I, introd., especially pp. XXIII–XXXV.

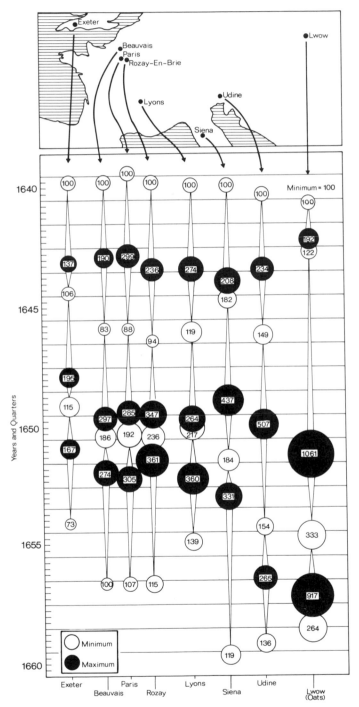

23. A Wheat Crisis in the Mid-Seventeenth Century. Maximum and minimum prices are given as an index to the base period (4th quarter 1639–1st quarter 1641 = 100). (Reference: *Cambridge Economic History of Europe*, Vol. **IV**)

consumption of wheaten bread was something of a status symbol;[12] and in nutritive value wheat was superior to rye or maize, containing 334 calories per 100 grams, as against 319 and 356 (maize, it must be remembered, being low in niacin, has provoked notable cases of nutritional deficiency when used as a standard diet).[13]

Because these details were not known precisely at the time, all that one can say is that in the group of food cereals wheat tended to be slightly less susceptible to wide fluctuations. In the short run, in years of dearth, wheat prices tended to rise less than the cheaper grains, for example, rye and maize, which suggests that as prices rose marginal groups of consumers substituted cheaper foods. Similarly over the long run, in the secular trend, wheat prices tended to rise slightly less than those of rye and maize. And the same tendency prevailed during a long trend of stagnant or falling prices, as in the seventeenth century: wheat prices fell slightly less over the long run. The evidence of prices in Udine bears this out.[14] In all probability, the factors of demand did not necessarily refer to the same market structures for the different cereals. Wheat was much more a cash crop than the others and, being more valuable in relation to bulk, was more susceptible to shipment over longer distances. Regional and even export trade, therefore, could have been significant factors in affecting the demand for wheat.

If certain inelasticities can be observed in the aggregate effective demand for grains, the same cannot be said for their supply. In the short run, the market was fed by the harvest, dependent on the growing cycle, climatic factors, and seasonal fluctuations which conditioned to a large degree the level of agricultural production. This does not necessarily imply, however, that the supply to the market was directly and exclusively dependent on each harvest; there were some reserves. Everywhere in France, as in Europe, the documents speak eloquently of the granaries which town authorities prepared and administered for the grim days of dearth. A mild failure of the harvest could be palliated or even overcome by such stores. A series of successive failures, however, exhausted the reserves on hand and precipitated those famines which repeatedly cloud the history of the preindustrial economies. The crises were not only cumulative but also, often enough, general: the great famines, as is shown in the dearth of 1648–1652, were a phenomenon which spread over Europe (see Graph 23). Even in the normal course of events, agrarian communities lived in a seasonal cycle of prices — rising through the winter to the spring, falling slowly with the prospect of the harvest, and then falling sharply as the new grain arrived or was announced on the market. The movement followed a largely agricultural rhythm, but was influenced by the

[12] Sir William Ashley, *The Bread of Our Forefathers* (Oxford, 1928).
[13] Charlotte Chatfield, *Food Composition Tables* (Rome, 1954).
[14] This is the case for prices in Udine, for which a study by Ruggiero Romano, Frank Spooner, and Ugo Tucci is in progress.

difficulties of transport in winter. The rigidities of the system, however, were different from the fluctuations and structure of industrial prices prevailing in modern economies.

The importance of the harvest in price fluctuations has been the subject of lengthy debates. Should price series be presented in annual data according to harvest years? Or should they be given according to the more conventional calendar years? Clearly in an agrarian society, where the accounting followed the harvest year, the argument that the price averages should be related to such a periodicity carries considerable weight. It should be remembered, nevertheless, that according to this proposition, each harvest decided the total volume of supply of grain for a given year. But this is not entirely correct since in normal years, with the system in relative equilibrium, there were reserves already in hand, and the harvest, instead of determining afresh the entire supply of grain, in reality provided additions to existing stocks. In a series of poor harvests, when these reserves were exhausted, the harvest had a more direct effect, and the market responded immediately with a sharp rise in prices. In the element of continuity in the market, the factor of the level of reserves is, therefore, variable. The presentation of grain prices by harvest years would, in consequence, tend to be significant during famine years.

A more rigorous method can test this problem. The lagged correlation coefficients have been calculated between the prices of wheat in Paris by harvest and by calendar years.[15] The results are as follows:

Table 8. Coefficients of Correlation of Wheat Prices by Calendar Years with Prices by Harvest Years, Lagged by Years

Period	t_{-5}	t_{-4}	t_{-3}	t_{-2}	t_{-1}	t
1520–1680	0.8077	0.8259	0.8340	0.8798	0.9796	0.9522
1520–1550	−0.0901	−0.0141	−0.0616	0.0690	0.8260	0.5088
1551–1610	0.6247	0.6647	0.6489	0.7447	0.9603	0.9027
1611–1680	0.1222	0.2233	0.3761	0.6436	0.9417	0.9092

Period	t_{+1}	t_{+2}	t_{+3}	t_{+4}	t_{+5}
1520–1680	0.8685	0.8406	0.8239	0.7994	0.7953
1520–1550	0.0289	0.0335	−0.1635	−0.2146	−0.0004
1551–1610	0.7205	0.6626	0.6739	0.6127	0.5547
1611–1680	0.6036	0.3927	0.2502	0.1301	0.0019

The column t_{-1} represents the correlation between all prices in calendar years with all prices in the harvest year beginning in the preceding August.

[15] The computations in this chapter have been programmed and calculated through the kindness of the Computer Center, Yale University, and the Computer Unit, University of Durham. Logarithms have been used in order to take into account secular inflation. The formulas used are:

This particular comparison shows a very high correlation between harvest years (that is, August–July) and calendar years, lagged by one year. Only for the test period 1520–1550 does the coefficient fall below .94 and in this case concerns a much shorter period, thirty years.

In the same context it is worth mentioning that, for producers, abundant harvests did not necessarily offer the largest profits, since, accepting the inelasticity of total demand for cereals, they found that the abundant harvests with low prices often would not cover the high costs of transporting it to distant markets. Exceptional profits no doubt came from harvests that were below average. Gregory King's observation of the multiplier effect on grain prices of small shifts in the supplies offered by the yearly harvest has long been quoted. In 1915 G. Udny Yule gave this proposition formal mathematical definition.[16]

Further rigidities were also apparent in the secular trend. During price inflation, it was noticeable that food prices, cereal prices in particular, rose relatively more than other commodity prices. In countries where sufficient data exist — such as England, Germany, Spain, Poland, and Holland, to mention only the most important — the evidence tends to reveal this basic feature in the great price rise of the sixteenth century. It discredits the explanation that the inflation was entirely due to monetary causes and widens the possible explanations to the pressures generated by increasing population on available resources for food. This encouraged the cultivation of marginal lands which were both less productive and at greater distances from the place of consumption. Had monetary factors remained stable, increases in population could have tended to exert a deflationary pressure on prices. All these factors must be kept in mind in any analysis involving grain prices.

The factor of transport in the case of a bulky commodity such as wheat, or, indeed, cereals in general, was central to the problem. The cost of financing

$$r = \frac{1}{n} \sum_{i=1}^{n} \left(\frac{X_i - \overline{X}}{S_x} \right) \left(\frac{Y_i - \overline{Y}}{S_y} \right)$$

where

$$S_x = \sqrt{\frac{1}{n} \sum_{i=1}^{n} (X_i - \overline{X})^2} = \sqrt{\frac{1}{n} \sum_{i=1}^{n} X_i^2 - \overline{X}^2}$$

$$\therefore r = \frac{n \sum_{i=1}^{n} X_i Y_i - \left(\sum_{i=1}^{n} X_i \right) \left(\sum_{i=1}^{n} Y_i \right)}{\sqrt{n \sum_{i=1}^{n} X_i^2 - \left(\sum_{i=1}^{n} X_i \right)^2} \cdot \sqrt{n \sum_{i=1}^{n} Y_i^2 - \left(\sum_{i=1}^{n} Y_i \right)^2}}$$

$$S_k = \frac{\sum_{i=1}^{n-k} (X_i - \overline{X})(X_{i+k} - \overline{X})}{\frac{n-k}{n} \sum_{i=1}^{n} (X_i - \overline{X})^2}$$

[16] G. Udny Yule, "Crop Production and Prices: A Note on Gregory King's Law," *Journal of the Royal Statistical Society,* LXXVIII (1915).

and moving it from where it was produced to the market and where it was to be consumed assumed a relatively important place in the final cost. Adam Smith's observations in this respect were basic to preindustrial economies, namely, that entry into foreign markets for industrial goods required a small advantage while that for grain, a considerable advantage. It is significant that the Dutch developed an economical cargo ship, the *fluit* or flyboat, and used it extensively for the bulky shipments in their Baltic trade. By the end of the seventeenth century there were some eight-hundred of these in this traffic.

In average years, however, there are reasons to suppose that France, a great agrarian economy, lived largely in conditions of self-sufficiency and, in the case of some favored regions, with a surplus for export. The extent to which this economy was served by a market mechanism and was accustomed to the consequent monetary conditions must be considered in the next chapter.

As for transport services, Paris was admirably endowed by geographic position. The capital, moreover, had long been accustomed to the advantages of a central administration which progressively became more effective. In the time of dearth — the difficult years of the Fronde were a case in point — even the diplomatic service was mobilized to bring cargoes of cereals from the Baltic. At the hub of a network of routes, its markets drew in grain supplies from the wheatlands of Beauce, of Champagne, from Brittany by the sea route, and on occasion even from further afield, from the distant grain exchange of Amsterdam and the Baltic.[17] In the economies typical of the *ancien régime,* famines were a recurring disaster, frequent and serious in the seventeenth century.[18]

The Paris market then could be affected directly or indirectly by foreign or long-distance trade. The increasing demand from Spain in the second half of the sixteenth century, as has already been noted, brought the Breton grain lands into the international picture and later stimulated competition between them and the grains from the Baltic, carried to Spain above all by the Dutch.[19] If the markets had been highly efficient, the surpluses and deficits could have been more easily absorbed. An expanding market — as may be supposed in the years 1575–1588, which gave France the apparent opportunity to enjoy a widespread boom — could have had the effect of increasing the area under wheat production in Brittany.[20] This logically, again, would have tended to support the market price. Serious competition from the Dutch and alterations in foreign exchanges or economic structure (as, for example, in the case of

[17] Abbott P. Usher, *The History of the Grain Trade in France, 1400–1710* (Cambridge, Mass., 1913).

[18] Karl Helleiner, "The Vital Revolution Reconsidered," *Canadian Journal of Economic and Political Science,* XXIII (1957).

[19] The municipal authorities in Rouen during dearths bought wheat in Champagne in February 1556 (Archives Municipales [hereafter cited as A.M.], Rouen, A.17; in the Low Countries in May 1563 (*ibid.,* A.18); in Brittany in September 1565 (*ibid.*); and even in Seville on January 24, 1574 (*Ibid.,* A.19, fol. 328).

[20] See Chap. 3. The possibility of a correlation between the prices in Andalusia and the coinage in Rennes requires further study. See Earl J. Hamilton, *American Treasure and the Price Revolution in Spain, 1501–1650* (Cambridge, Mass., 1934), Appendix IV.

Spain) could impose multiplier effects on grain prices in France. Could the lethargy of the wheat market and prices in the years 1590–1620 be attributed, in part at least, to the falling demand in foreign markets for French grain? [21]

Apart from these difficulties peculiar to the grain market, the comparison of wheat prices with the mint issues in Paris brings out mutual agreements and disagreements. It must be emphasized that these two movements were basically very different: the price series formed a cumulative movement; while the mint issues were simply additions or renewals in the total monetary stock. Both movements, however, were in livres tournois and therefore reflected the same basic factor of inflation: the values for the mint issues were a compromise between quantity of bullion and its valuation in changing nominal terms in livres tournois. We shall return later to the question of both the livres tournois and the total monetary circulation in France.

The issues [22] of currency, moreover, were made from bullion and specie of different types and origins. In the early sixteenth century the mints often converted bar metal which merchants brought to France. This suggests that the average costs of converting foreign coin of different degrees of fineness into French coin were then higher than later in the century when the coinage was often of similar fineness. The heavy standard silver coins of Spain were more successfully converted into French currency and thus reduced the need, after the middle of the sixteenth century, to make settlements in bullion rather than specie. In addition, small amounts of precious metals were produced in France itself. The silver mines were still active in the third quarter of the sixteenth century. Here and there bands of gold washers plied their skills to make a meager living along the great rivers; [23] some still survived near Paris in the eighteenth century. In principle at least, all this gold and silver should have been turned into French coinage, but from the frequent complaints it is clear that this ideal often had little reality. An attractive price at the mints was the most effective mechanism to ensure the conversion into French money.

In effect, this conversion became a standard activity of the mints. A certain number of foreign coins were allowed legal currency in France; they were particularly important in the sixteenth century, but in the seventeenth century, as the monarchy increased its competence and centralizing efficiency, there was greater emphasis on French currency in circulation. The gold louis and the silver écu became tokens of the authority of Louis XIV. As a result, it was constantly necessary to melt defective or illegal coins for reissue. The recoinage of billon in 1550–1552, the conversions of 1577–1578, the issue of demis francs in 1586–1587, the great recoinages after 1639, and the "reformations" of 1709 and 1718 were good examples of this. More important still were the

---

[21] See Chap. 3.
[22] See Chap. 2.
[23] Archives Nationales [hereafter cited as A.N.], Z¹B.61; in Bayonne on May 9, 1523, there was an allusion to "fishing for placer gold"; see also Chap. 1, nn. 17, 18.

conversions of foreign money: from Germany during the first half of the sixteenth century and from Flanders during the second half of that century, but most of all from Spain. The exchanges of money in the frontier regions between currency of France and that of adjacent provinces, often more backward from a monetary point of view, also had a part to play. The conversion of foreign money varied according to the type of money. The conversion of gold specie was noticeable after periods of difficulties in foreign exchange (which will be dealt with later); while the conversions of silver currency were perhaps more frequent in periods of exchange stability. In the normal course of events, these were some of the main factors affecting the flows of bullion and specie into the melting pots of the mints.

There were, in addition, exceptional circumstances, such as war and famine. Such crises, involving whole societies, required immediate cash payments. The sudden demands of tax levies for war exerted pressures to end the hoarding of silver plate and coin. In France in the first half of the sixteenth century, when gold currency appeared to be relatively more plentiful, the melting down of silver plate frequently was used to satisfy the royal levies. In the same way, during a crisis of subsistance following a series of bad harvests the melting of gold or silver plate and jewelery often eased the payment of excessively high food prices.[24] These food crises could precipitate exceptional mint issues of coin to satisfy the increased demand for means of payment.

Such crises implied an increase in liquidity preferences and rising premiums on gold and silver currency. Since the mint prices for the purchase of bullion or species were fixed and the market price of bullion tended to rise, the issues of money tended to fall. This was the reverse side of the picture and was an indication of profound changes in the state of monetary circulation. Such a situation could be remedied to some extent by the melting down of silver plate which would keep the mints active, but it would be necessary to study the circulation carefully in order to establish the ultimate destination of these additional issues. In the case of taxation for war, the payments could all too often be made beyond the city and occasionally abroad. In the case of famines, the money issued would pass largely into the hands of the producers, the middlemen, carriers or merchants who organized and financed the distribution. A process of hoarding was possible, but only after some delay would the currency tend to return more actively to the towns.

In this respect, the circulation of money between city and countryside was not the least of the monetary problems of France.[25] (The extent to which the monetary system penetrated the agrarian economy of France will be discussed further later in this book.) At the international level, payments abroad in times

[24] For the remarks of Voltaire on the winter of 1709, see Shelby McCloy, *Government Assistance in Eighteenth-Century France* (Durham, N.C., 1946), p. 20, n. 84.

[25] See also Jean Meuvret, "Circulation monétaire et utilisation économique de la monnaie dans la France du XVIe et du XVIIe siècle," *Études d'histoire moderne et contemporaine,* I (1947).

of stress to the grain markets of Holland and the Baltic must be kept in mind.[26]

After I have given this lengthy but necessary introduction to the problem, I can now compare the two movements, on the one hand of wheat prices in Paris, and on the other of monetary data from the total annual issues of currency. The proportional issues of both gold and silver will be considered later.

During the first half of the sixteenth century — the predominantly gold phase — there was considerable activity in issuing coin, and yet prices tended to rise slowly. At first sight, it appears that the short-term fluctuations from year to year were not more pronounced than in the latter part of the century. Some years (1520–1525, 1531, 1533, 1540, 1544, 1546, 1550–1551) showed rises; others, falls (1498, 1505, 1528, 1535, 1547–1549). The price movements, taken as a whole, show no clear correlation in the short run with issues from the mint. This would be the conclusion for the phase of gold. At the most, here and there, it is possible only to speak of an association, but not of any correlation of statistical significance.

In this period, we can take two particular instances. The first is placed at the beginning of the war between Francis I and Emperor Charles V. At the outbreak of this conflict there were tax levies, sometimes raised in Paris in silver plate; there were additional levies during the dearth of 1521–1522.[27] In view of the observations above, it is possible to state that the issues of silver coins rose considerably; it is even possible that the *setier,* because of its large size as a measure of volume, required payment in silver rather than in billon. Again, it is possible that there was a certain correlation between the two movements, but this is in appearance only for it takes little reflection to imagine the other factors and pressures which went into the formation of this short-run movement.

This accidental character, however, is underlined by a second example during the last war between Francis I and Charles V. In the years 1543 and 1546 the conversion of plate[28] appeared to coincide with high grain prices. The issues of billon in 1546 accompanied a poor harvest in that year. A large part of these issues of billon probably resulted from the conversion of full-bodied silver coins of higher denominations, such as testons. The operation, in itself, could have had an inflationary effect since it amounted to debasement: the billon contained a higher proportion of copper. On the other hand, the issues of billon in 1547 and 1548 coincided with falling wheat prices. Needless to say, the chances of finding a significant correlation between the two movements at this particular juncture are slender.

The silver phase imposed a fundamental reconstruction of the monetary system (see Graph 24). It seems at first sight that during this time a greater sympathy existed between the two movements of mint issues and prices. Two

[26] Axsel Christensen, *Dutch Trade to the Baltic about 1600* (Copenhagen, 1941).
[27] *Le Journal d'un bourgeois de Paris sous le règne de François Iᵉʳ, 1515–1536,* ed. V.-L. Bourrilly (Paris, 1910), p. 82.
[28] See Chap. 3, n. 58.

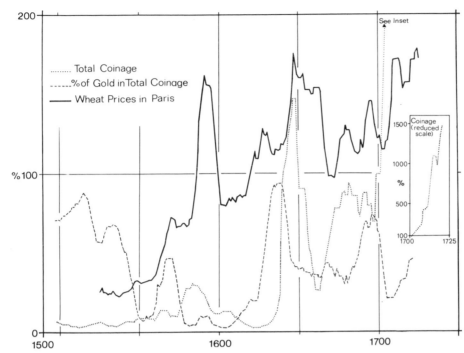

24. Index Numbers of Wheat Prices in Paris, and of Total Coinage, 1525–1710 = 100; and the Percentage of Gold Coined

other periods, 1566–1578 and 1587–1593, show prima facie a more significant short-run concordance between prices and issues. In the longer movement, both tended to reach their high points at the end of the century, in 1591–1592, and then experienced a downturn. This, however, assumes nothing more than the general effect of increases in the total supply of money on prices in the second half of the sixteenth century. Obviously this was not the only factor to be taken into consideration.

In the phase from 1611 to 1680 the divergences were more marked. Paris, the administrative center, assumed an increasing proportion of the mint issues and expanded as a financial center. However, it should be noted that the price movements did not greatly respond to the issues of copper currency. In the decade 1611–1620, when these coins were issued in larger quantities, the level of prices rose slowly. During these years, also, gold currency tended to appreciate. In contrast, in the decade 1631–1640, a price recession coincided with an increased demand for gold currency. After the end of the Thirty Years' War the famine conditions of the winter of 1649–1650 developed; demands for wheat went to Poland, and even as far as Russia.[29] Grain prices rose in a

[29] A.N., Affaires Étrangères, Correspondance Politique, Hamburg, 2, p. 267, letter of Nov. 20, 1649; *ibid.*, p. 209, letter of Nov. 19, 1649; *ibid.*, p. 270vo, letter of Nov. 26, 1649.

clearly defined cycle all over Europe. Something of this composite and concerted crisis can be seen in Graph 23. The famine hit the grain economy in a well-defined cyclic movement, thus making the coordinated effects all the more severe. In France the famine coincided with the troubles of the Fronde and, on the monetary side, with the conversion of silver reals of Mexican and Peruvian origin to French money. Setting aside the large issues at the time of the monetary reform of 1640, the coinage and prices show, nevertheless, some association in the middle of the seventeenth century, but the level of significance appears to have been too low for any categoric affirmations.

Finally, in the forty-five years before the reform of 1726, four instances invite attention — 1693–1694, 1709–1710, 1718, and 1723–1726 — each of which represents a crisis of subsistence of varying severity.[30] Each also coincided with monetary changes: issues of billon in the case of 1693–1694; reforms in the cases of 1701–1710, 1718, and 1723–1726. However, again, it would be stretching this coincidental evidence too far to assume a causal relationship.

A further comparison can be made between the two series of coinage and prices by calculating the correlation coefficients for different periods. This is statistically more elegant, but clearly does not take full account of qualitative variations implicit in historical change. The prices of wheat in Paris (by both harvest and calendar years) have been compared with the total coinage, first annually, then as a thirty-year moving average and finally as a forty-year moving average. The correlations have been lagged each year in turn of the preceding and succeeding by five years. The results are given in the following Table 9 (i) to (vi):

First, for the annual series (Table 9 [i] and [ii]), the coefficients rarely exceed 0.5 and are therefore of low significance. There is a higher correlation between the prices of the harvest year and the coinage in the following calendar year. In the case of the calendar years the highest coefficients are generally synchronized. Apart from this, little difference is shown between using prices by harvest years and those by calendar years. There is, however, a feature of exceptional interest in the coefficients for the second half of the sixteenth century: the highest coefficients are not synchronized, but extremely lagged, and an explanation could be offered that prices were influenced most by coinage in the five previous years. This persistent effect could also be explained by the fact that the economy of France was sufficiently extensive in territory to retard the immediate, direct effects of the imports of bullion in the second half of the sixteenth century. By contrast, in the seventeenth century, with its diminished monetary pressures, the correlation coefficients are extremely low.

In the second place, the correlation coefficients have been calculated be-

---

[30] Jean Meuvret, "Les mouvements des prix de 1661 à 1715 et leurs répercussions," *Journal de la Société Statistique de Paris,* LXXXV (1944), graphs and p. 2, and "Les crises de subsistances et la démographie de la France d'Ancien Régime," *Population,* I (1946).

Table 9. Coefficients of Correlation between Wheat Prices in Paris and Total Coinage in France

Period	t_{-5}	t_{-4}	t_{-3}	t_{-2}	t_{-1}	t	t_{+1}	t_{+2}	t_{+3}	t_{+4}	t_{+5}
(i) *Wheat prices (harvest years) correlated with total annual coinage, lagged by years*											
1520–1680	0.4493	0.4198	0.4299	0.4669	0.4838	0.4653	0.4635	0.4606	0.4514	0.4518	0.4889
1520–1550	0.1561	−0.2348	−0.2545	−0.0546	0.2208	−0.1192	−0.0084	0.0689	−0.0175	0.0722	0.3630
1551–1610	0.1179	0.1139	0.1560	0.2478	0.2941	0.2833	0.2886	0.3426	0.4020	0.4801	0.5157
1611–1680	0.2923	0.2375	0.2644	0.3397	0.3452	0.2973	0.2659	0.2530	0.1639	0.1331	0.2054
(ii) *Wheat prices (calendar years) correlated with total annual coinage, lagged by years*											
1520–1680	0.4515	0.4458	0.4143	0.4423	0.4718	0.4870	0.4541	0.4627	0.4578	0.4469	0.4653
1520–1550	0.0056	0.1375	−0.3923	−0.1920	0.0680	0.3462	−0.0781	0.1897	0.0403	0.6667	0.1729
1551–1610	0.1150	0.1476	0.0989	0.1622	0.2145	0.2366	0.2370	0.2807	0.3592	0.4327	0.5340
1611–1680	0.2867	0.2601	0.2433	0.3018	0.3492	0.3359	0.2594	0.2567	0.2039	0.1261	0.1298
(iii) *Wheat prices (harvest years) correlated with a thirty-year moving average of the total annual coinage, lagged by years*											
1522–1680	0.7029	0.6981	0.6988	0.6984	0.6949	0.6885	0.6817	0.6715	0.6609	0.6539	0.6495
1522–1550	0.2780	0.2440	0.2191	0.2054	0.1968	0.1337	0.2503	0.1339	−0.0902	−0.0172	0.2021
1551–1610	0.7537	0.7477	0.7497	0.7540	0.7485	0.7429	0.7373	0.7227	0.7040	0.6784	0.6455
1611–1680	0.3594	0.3362	0.3313	0.3244	0.3121	0.2867	0.2552	0.2231	0.1895	0.1652	0.1532
(iv) *Wheat prices (harvest years) correlated with a forty-year moving average of total annual coinage, lagged by years*											
1532–1680	0.6915	0.6867	0.6892	0.6899	0.6880	0.6821	0.6742	0.6668	0.6602	0.6533	0.6479
1532–1550	0.8037	0.5507	0.4473	0.3921	0.2964	−0.0440	−0.2073	−0.1918	−0.1086	−0.3330	−0.3846
1551–1610	0.7414	0.7307	0.7308	0.7331	0.7237	0.7182	0.7157	0.7032	0.6859	0.6609	0.6338
1611–1680	0.2717	0.2501	0.2522	0.2509	0.2471	0.2296	0.2045	0.1789	0.1550	0.1403	0.1130
(v) *Wheat prices (calendar years) correlated with a thirty-year moving average of total annual coinage, lagged by years*											
1522–1680	0.7047	0.7000	0.6981	0.6985	0.6983	0.6933	0.6844	0.6752	0.6641	0.6539	0.6482
1522–1550	0.1757	0.3919	0.3097	0.3711	0.4574	0.4693	0.3238	0.2752	0.0502	−0.0788	0.0464
1551–1610	0.7508	0.7442	0.7390	0.7450	0.7459	0.7407	0.7278	0.7195	0.7038	0.6836	0.6543
1611–1680	0.3579	0.3360	0.3249	0.3167	0.3105	0.2892	0.2580	0.2264	0.1931	0.1627	0.1445
(vi) *Wheat prices (calendar years) correlated with a forty-year moving average of total annual coinage, lagged by years*											
1532–1680	0.6905	0.6856	0.6848	0.6858	0.6859	0.6812	0.6727	0.6655	0.6584	0.6513	0.6451
1532–1550	0.7462	0.8204	0.4488	0.4125	0.2857	0.1302	−0.1949	−0.2140	−0.1740	0.2067	−0.3812
1551–1610	0.7413	0.7315	0.7221	0.7266	0.7233	0.7152	0.7026	0.6968	0.6816	0.6597	0.6317
1611–1680	0.2694	0.2485	0.2428	0.2400	0.2422	0.2290	0.2048	0.1795	0.1538	0.1336	0.1242

tween annual prices (harvest and calendar years) and the total coinage in thirty-year and forty-year moving averages. These coefficients are higher than for the annual series, but this is to be expected since the moving average would tend to approximate more closely the changes in the total money stock. Since the moving averages are end positioned, the negatively lagged prices have higher coefficients, particularly in the silver phase of 1551–1610 when a coefficient of 0.75 is reached. It should also be noted that the coefficients are slightly higher for the thirty-year moving average than for the forty-year average.

These series of prices and coinage can be further analyzed for serial correlations, to see whether periodicities exist in the annual data. The prices of wheat and rye in Paris (by harvest years) and the total annual coinage for France have been tested for periods up to thirty-five years in the phases already used (1520–1680; 1520–1550; 1551–1610; 1611–1680). The results (see Graph 25) are by no means clear enough to warrant firm conclusions. The signifi-

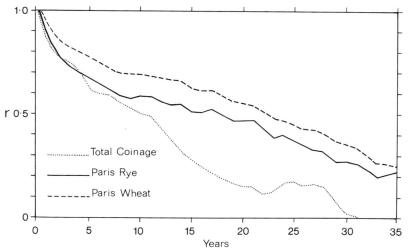

25. Correlograms: Coefficients of Serial Correlations of Wheat and Rye Prices in Paris and Total Annual Coinage in France

cance declines rapidly in all three series, but more in the case of coinage than in that of wheat and rye prices; this can also be explained by the fact that the coinage represented additions or renewals of the total supply of money.

It is possible that there is a greater element of continuity in the wheat series, which was more valuable by about half than rye. The superiority of wheat can also be seen in the market of Udine, where the serial correlations between wheat and maize show comparable results.[31] Thus for Paris there is a slight rise in the coefficients between twenty-four and twenty-nine years,

[31] For the correlograms for wheat and maize in Udine, see Braudel and Spooner, "Prices in Europe from 1450 to 1750."

which suggests that such a cycle possibly existed. However, the order of magnitude is hardly significant enough to assign any real statistical importance to it.

In studying wheat prices, however, the values in terms of the money of account (the livre tournois) are not the only ones to consider. The comparison between money and prices becomes clearer when the latter are expressed in terms of gold and silver (Graph 26). These series are given from the data

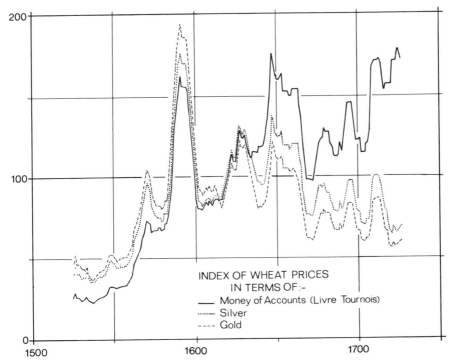

26. Wheat Prices in Paris in Terms of Gold, Silver, and Money of Accounts, 1525–1720 = 100

published by Micheline Baulant and Jean Meuvret, using an index of modified eleven-year moving averages,[32] with a base period of 1525–1720. The conversion of wheat prices in livres tournois into prices in terms of gold and silver at official currency rates entails lags in incorporating the official devaluations of the currency. Nevertheless, the differences between the three series are worth comment.

During the sixteenth century, the fastest rise can be detected in nominal prices, next in terms of silver, and then in terms of gold. This is natural enough, for it is another way of expressing the devaluation of the money of

[32] These modified moving averages are established by discarding the three maximums and three minimums in each set of eleven prices and then averaging the remaining five prices. The moving averages are center positioned and given as percentages of the base period 1525–1720.

accounts in terms of bullion, which already has been mentioned. After the reform of 1561 these differences are not so marked. From 1578 the decision to keep accounts in écus resulted in the combining of the three movements.

After the years of high wheat prices in Paris during the time of the League, a new period opened. The long-term movement of nominal prices showed first a decline and then a progressive rise to the late 1640s, a trend which continued and indeed culminated the inflation of the sixteenth century. In contrast, prices in terms of bullion were falling: the peak in the 1590s was the highest point reached in the two centuries under discussion.

Prices in terms of gold and silver show a clear fall until 1601 and then a recovery to about 1630. A downward movement until about 1640 was followed by a sharp rise during the next decade and then a further fall, slow until 1661 and then fast. And these prices in terms of bullion continued to follow a falling trend during the first quarter of the eighteenth century.

From 1601 to 1636, as the official price of the marc of silver remained unchanged, the movement of prices in nominal and in silver terms converged. It was the passing hey day of silver, with the Dutch extending their trade in the Baltic and the Far East, but with the lengthening shadows of difficulties ahead, featuring the issue of copper currency in Spain.

In contrast, the price of the marc of gold was raised once in 1614 and twice in 1636. On each occasion, the bimetallic ratio became wider. These adjustments appeared in the movement of prices in terms of gold; there was a significant drop after 1614 and again after 1636, which created something of a "Pigou effect": falling prices in terms of gold progressively improved the profitability of producing this metal. The development of gold deposits, notably in Brazil, must be considered in this context. A new phase of gold deliveries to Europe marked the closing decades of the seventeenth century.

As a result of these adjustments, a slight change can be detected in these relative price series. While the trend in terms of money of accounts began to soar, those in terms of bullion continued to fall during the first quarter of the eighteenth century. This was clear in the case of silver; the trough in 1717 was lower than that in 1707, and both were below the level of the 1670s. However, this downward movement was not so marked in the case of the series in terms of gold, which is further evidence of the new phase.

The important feature of this exercise is the changing relationship between nominal prices and prices in terms of gold and silver. The divergence between them (in other words, the depreciation of the livre tournois) relates to a particular aspect of total indebtedness, especially of the French monarchy. The military and political expenditures, above all in time of war, not covered by increased output, were inevitably followed by devaluation. As far as the international economy was concerned, the real value of debts was reduced by the readjustment of the French monetary system. For the domestic economy of France, the debts remained, unless repudiated; an example of this was the war debt accumulated in the 1550s, the Grand Parti of Lyons, on which the monarchy defaulted in 1557. The debt was funded and spread among the various cities of France. A further adjustment was formally made in the devaluation of 1561. After the 1550s the level of nominal prices rose, but was closely followed by those in terms of bullion. From the 1590s, however, the divergence between the curves of nominal prices and bullion prices again indicated a progressive devaluation of the livre tournois in terms of gold and silver. This was particularly clear after 1630, when, in the wake of the great financial operations of Richelieu in foreign subsidies and war expenditures, the devaluation continued apace. The weakening of the monetary standing of France was revealed in the fall in the exchange rates on the market of Amsterdam, discussed later in this chapter. The previously mentioned rise in the domestic price levels in France, however, compensated for it. A subsequent phase of devaluation began in the 1680s, reflecting the costs of the grandiose schemes of Louis XIV and the expansion of public credit.[33] Again this was marked by rising price levels and falling foreign exchange rates.

What conclusions can be reached about the general periodicities in the two series of wheat prices and total coinage? And, while accepting their fundamental differences in character, can they be compared?

First I shall discuss coinage. In general, the movement in the period 1493–1725 appears to indicate three great cycles of combined rise and fall. The first probably began before 1493 and reached a stage, or pause, in 1508; it is also probable that the years until 1559 also belonged to this period. Then a second big cycle began, reaching a peak in 1587, with a downward movement to 1625. A third period of expansion ensued, itself divided into three periods: 1625–1657 (with a peak in 1642); an indeterminate period 1657–1699; and renewed expansion from 1699 to the early 1720s (with a peak, as far as the present data indicate, in 1718).

My second point, the movement of wheat prices in Paris, presents a different picture. The progressive inflation of the sixteenth century tended to submerge the shorter cyclic movements. This is particularly evident after the mid-century; the period 1557–1564, 1564–1570, 1570–1579, 1579–1588, 1588–1594, and 1594–1602 are not very clearly defined against the underlying inflation, which seemed to carry all before it. This phase of rapid "price revolution" gave way to more moderate inflation, in which the cycles of shorter duration appeared with greater clarity. In this respect, the price experience of Paris in the seventeenth century appears to fall into four different periods.

Moderate inflation continued during the 1620s and 1630s, marked by an important cycle 1629–1634 (which peaked in 1631, at the time of the famine crisis). Next there was a period of increasing violence. Pierre Goubert has drawn attention to the "cycle of the Fronde" from the data of Beauvais. In the case of Paris, however, the cycle of 1639–1646 does not appear to have had

[33] Germain Martin and Marcel Bezançon, *L'histoire du crédit en France sous le règne de Louis XIV* (Paris, 1913), I; Herbert Lüthy, *La Banque Protestante en France de la Révocation de l'Édit de Nantes à la Révolution* (2 vols., Paris, 1959–1961).

the same amplitude as that of 1629–1634. By contrast, the two periods 1646–1657 and 1657–1669 were cyclical movements of exceptional severity. This trend, as has been shown in Graph 23, was not confined to France, but was part of the general European experience. Thirdly came a period from 1669 to 1688, when cyclic movements were not clearly marked. Finally there was a period of renewed disturbance in which three important cycles can be detected: 1688–1707 (with a peak in 1694); 1707–1717 (with a peak in 1714); and 1717–1733 (with a peak in 1725).

In general, the comparison of the two series of coinage and prices cannot be said to show a highly significant correlation. It would be an overstatement of the evidence to infer that heavy coinage either followed or preceded directly the sudden shifts in the level of prices. On the other hand, in the longer term, an association exists between periods of violent price changes and periods of heavy coinage. This remains roughly valid for the inflation of the second half of the sixteenth century, when coinage reached a peak in 1587. It also remains pertinent for the period 1625–1657, covering the great recoinages of the 1630s and early 1640s. When one examines this in closer detail, however, it becomes evident that the monetary reforms and coinage following the edicts of 1636, 1640, and 1641 find their place in the context of royal monetary and fiscal policies, while the cyclical movements in prices in 1629–1634 and 1646–1669 cover important harvest failures and social movements. An association between the two series again strikes the observer in the period after 1699 and especially during the recoinages and "reforms" of the currency of 1709 and 1718, at the time of the monetary edict of May 1709 and the currency issues organized by John Law. Yet, once more, care must be exercised, especially in the instance of 1709, when Paris suffered a winter of famine conditions.

Clearly, then, the dating of heavy currency issues and of coinage reform does not coincide exactly with that of the more violent cyclic movements in prices, but, from the present evidence, the association cannot be entirely ruled out. An explanation of the lack of strict correlation must be sought, at lease in part, in the differing quality of the two series. Since the movements of wheat prices were expressions of the "market," they were responsive to economic pressures and were, inevitably, different from those of coinage. The output of coinage is more directly related to the history of administration and institutions. As I have indicated earlier in this book, the official acts, the reforms and the inauguration of new monetary structures, came into effect only after a certain passage of time. Such lags were in themselves sufficient to create differences in timing. In addition, monetary flows cannot have been wholly responsible for the movement of prices; they were important, but their causal nature must not be overstressed. In this, prudence is necessary.

A few remarks are required before Paris can be considered as a sample for France. The capital city had a well-merited importance as the center of administrative and monetary affairs, where the government ordered tax levies and expenditures. In spite of the dominant role of that city, it would be contrary to the basic argument of this book to assume that its market stands alone, outside comparison not to be compared with the provinces — both maritime and continental — of France.[34] A documentation similar to that of Ernest Labrousse in his classic study of eighteenth-century France[35] does not presently exist for the sixteenth and seventeenth centuries. The same opportunity for a precise comparison of maritime and continental prices is largely lacking. However, a certain number of comments on the disparities of the price movements are possible. The scholarly study by Robert Latouche on prices in Grenoble provides such information and deserves careful study. The fluctuations of prices may have been of lesser amplitude there than in Paris. In comparing the data one finds that, in terms of silver, prices were slightly higher in Grenoble than in Paris during the first half of the sixteenth century. The margins of difference, however, are too small to support such statements beyond all doubt, particularly since the conversion of the prices in Grenoble into gold and silver equivalents has been made at rates which were largely valid for Paris. For all that, there could be a differential geography of prices in gold, silver (even in silver billon), and livres tournois, and, according to the region and economic activity, a whole range of results would be possible. This raises problems, which in the present stage of the empirical data, hold out little hope of solution. As will be readily understood, though, they have their importance.

It seems likely from the available data that Paris, after the time of the League and through the seventeenth century, was, by comparison with Grenoble, Briançon, Limoges, Poitiers, Orléans, and Beauvais, a city of high grain prices. It is also possible to assume, though it has not been proved, that during the second half of the sixteenth century, the continental regions showed greater lags in following the trend of rising prices. The progressive inflation may have had some difficulty in penetrating France. The Saône and Rhône Valley, together with Dauphiné, were more well known for the prevalence of inferior billon money. By comparison with the maritime regions of the west, these areas may have remained backward from a monetary point of view, but this requires further investigation.

Another inquiry, not without importance, would compare the prices in Mediterranean France and northern France. As has been mentioned above, this has exceptional interest for the downturn in price trends in the first half of the seventeenth century. The evidence for Aix-en-Provence recently published by René Baehrel shows that after the 1590s wheat prices there were moving downward during the first half of the seventeenth century. Evidence from Beauvais, however, concludes that the decline in this region of northern

---

[34] See the observation of Nassau William Senior cited by Wicksell, *Interest and Prices,* p. 31.

[35] C.-Ernest Labrousse, *Esquisse du mouvement des prix et des revenus en France au XVIIIe siècle* (2 vols., Paris, 1933).

France was realized after 1630. However, the case does not allow simple explanations since the disturbing effects of the Thirty Years' War must be taken into account. Although more ample data are required to confirm such differences, it would seem, in view of the above remarks on the extended nature of the downturn in the early seventeenth century, that the experience of France showed disparities. The "crisis" of the seventeenth century was a general experience for Europe. For the economies of the Mediterranean, it was a decisive turning point, when Spain relinquished its place as the dominant economy. For Holland and Britain, it was more of an interim crisis, a prelude to economic ascendancy. France, within the diversity of its provinces, appeared to share in both of these profound movements.

There were zones in which gold, silver, and credit predominated, each imparting its own characteristics. During the phase of silver, the ports of the west experienced an invasion of this currency, while, on the other hand, the continental regions were obliged to employ larger quantities of billon to satisfy currency requirements. By reason of its fiscal and financial position, Paris may further be supposed to have held the balance of the country, setting a mean between extreme conditions. In any case, after the crisis of 1619–1620, in the phase of copper and credit, the great axis from the Channel to the Mediterranean managed to command greater stocks of gold than the Atlantic west. It may be possible to infer that, in the regions of the east, the level of indebtedness and the bullion reserves in the seventeenth century tended to be higher than in the maritime regions of the west. A century later, in 1764, the reports on the state of municipal finances and debts showed that, after Paris, Lyons carried by far the heaviest load,[36] but that is long after our period.

In addition to these price movements, there is another indicator of economic activity: the price of money or the rate of interest. The movement of the deposit rate for the payments in the fairs of Lyons is available for 1557, and then more or less continuously from 1564 to 1622 (see Graph 27).[37] The money deposits were, in effect, the money borrowed in one fair to be repaid in the following fair. It was, for instance, a means of holding over for another quarter the payment of a bill of exchange. The rate charged for this is therefore to some extent an indication of the state of the credit market. In the absence of the circulation of bank notes and of central banks, the deposit rate played no small role in the overall monetary structure.

The movement of these deposit rates in the Lyons fairs shows fairly clear trends. The first sample for 1557 set the rate for the quarter at between $2\frac{1}{2}$ percent and $2\frac{3}{5}$ percent, according to the group of exchange dealers involved. From 1564 to 1573 ($3\frac{1}{3}$ percent for the August fair) there was a tendency to

[36] A.N., Affaires Étrangères, Mémoires et Documents; I hope later to prepare an edition of this interesting survey.

[37] These data have been drawn from the A.D., Rhône; the relevant data differ only slightly from those since published by Henri Lapeyre, *Une famille de marchands: Les Ruiz* (Paris, 1955), pp. 461–471.

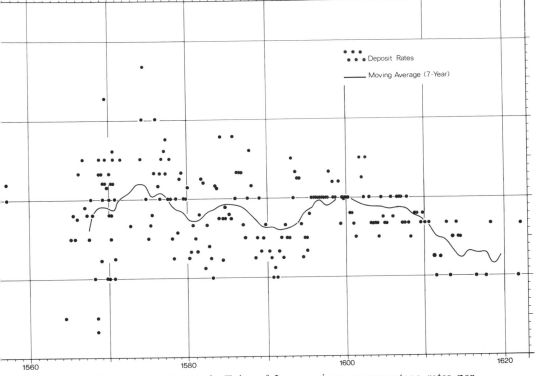

27. Deposit Rates in the Quarterly Fairs of Lyons, given as percentage rates per annum

rise. The trend after 1573 moved downward to 2⅛ percent in the Easter fair of 1578; this rate appeared again in the Easter fair of 1580. Then a renewed rise set in to the Easter fair of 1583 (2⅝ percent), followed by a fall to 1590–1591 (2 percent for the All Saints' Day fair of 1590 and the Easter fair of 1591). There was an upward trend to the All Saints' Day fair of 1601 (2¾ percent, at which time it moved downward, the fall being more pronounced after 1607 (when it stood at about 2½ percent) to reach 2 percent in 1616, 1617, and 1621. By the Epiphany fair of 1622 the rate was 2⅓ percent. It should be noted that these data have been shown in the graph as annual rates.

When we make allowance for geographical differences and the particular conditions of the grain market, we can compare the wheat prices of Paris with the deposit rates. A certain number of interesting features can be observed. In the period to 1587, the heyday of the metallic inflation and transformations in the economy of France and Europe, the movement of deposit rates and of prices generally tend to rise and fall together. These were, nevertheless, the twilight years of the fairs of Lyons, but the great market was still intimately concerned with finance. The rise in prices and the depreciation of silver may explain to some extent a high deposit rate, as a hedge against depreciation.

However, rising prices may also have meant increasing demand for credit in conditions of expanding economic activity, which tended to coincide with higher rates of interest.[38]

A second period occurred after 1589. For more than three decades the general movement was very different: the deposit rate and the price movements tended to diverge. Could such a change represent alterations in the structure of credit? This is possible at the end of the sixteenth century and in the first two decades of the seventeenth century, with greater attempts to use credit instruments. The policies of the Banco dello Spirito Santo of Naples, the use of the patto di ricorsa, the payments by bills of exchange in transactions across the Balkans, the interest rate in the operations of the Bank of Saint George in Genoa — all indicate improved credit conditions in that network of Mediterranean affairs where Lyons found its place. For a time, the offer of credit may have been in excess. Indeed, the situation is so full of possibilities that they cannot all be mentioned, let alone explained, at this particular moment. On the one hand, after the League, there was apparently a decline in the economic pressure of Spain on France. After 1609, and even more after 1620, there was an apparent revival in the east of France, part of an expansion in the financial sectors and land routes between the Mediterranean and the Low Countries.[39] But such statements are mere suppositions and even if verified could not explain the difficulties of credit which so surprised Henri Lapeyre in the market of Lyons.[40] Among the possible explanations, I should prefer to give weight to the slowing down of commercial activity in France after about 1588–1590, particularly in exports. Such activity no longer seemed to provide the profitable outlets which were formerly enjoyed. If insufficient demand for credit proves to be the case, the transfer of commercial and financial capital into land could offer at once a simple but also far-reaching explanation, but that has yet to be proved.

Any review of credit in France cannot avoid considering the important contribution made by foreign merchants and their financial operations. It is evident that after 1573 the deposit rates in Lyons tended to fall, and in this period, as has been observed, the monetary system of France would have been considered a "soft currency" area in the network of transactions of the Genoese merchants. After the 1590s pressures from the Dutch merchants also became more noticeable. These problems will be considered again later.

2. Gold, Silver, and Foreign Exchanges

The study of foreign relations also has much to add to the explanation of bullion and exchanges. Movements of gold and silver in and out of France,

---

[38] See Knut Wicksell, *Lectures on Political Economy* (2 vols., London, 1935), II, p. 168.

[39] Fernand Braudel, *La Méditerranée et le monde méditerranéen* (Paris, 1949), pp. 244–249.

[40] Lapeyre, *Une famille de marchands: Les Ruiz.*

as has been suggested, were largely due to fluctuations connected with trade and services, often originating beyond the frontiers of the country itself. In this respect France found itself all too often in a state of dependence, as part of an economic hierarchy. I have expressed this point of view earlier in the book.

The fluctuations of gold and silver in France did not, by definition, take place in a closed economy. The interdependence in monetary structures meant that an exceptional demand for currency in France was often accompanied by reversed conditions in its neighbors and by alterations in the foreign exchange position of the country. The bimetallic fluctuations and even the simple proportions of currency, either in gold or silver, issued by the mints found a place within these movements. Among the mints, Paris, dominant by virtue of its geographic position and function as a fiscal center, was particularly able to counteract the leading trend of the moment. In the phase of gold during the first half of the sixteenth century the Paris mint made significant issues in silver, while in the phase of silver after the mid-sixteenth century it was able to coin large quantities of gold, at a time when the majority of the mints, willingly or unwillingly, were confined largely to the coinage of silver. The role of government in this context must be emphasized.

Paris can, therefore, be taken as an indicator of movements of wider significance; through its operations one can study the mint in Antwerp in the sixteenth century and in London for the first half of the seventeenth century. From these two points of comparison, the essential characteristics of the fluctuations in France can be placed in another frame of reference.

I shall first discuss the movement of the mint in the Antwerp. The operations of this mint reveal something of the rivalry between the Valois and Hapsburgs,[41] but the comparison between Paris and Antwerp can be continued until the end of the reign of Philip II. Toward the end of the fifteenth century, Antwerp issued more silver than gold, while Paris, at the time of Charles VIII's invasion of Italy, confined its operations largely to gold. Antwerp's in-

---

[41] For Antwerp, the data drawn from Alphonse de Witte, *Histoire monétaire des Comtes de Louvain, Ducs de Brabant* (3 vols., Brussels, 1896–1899), have been calculated in florins. The data for London were drawn from the Public Record Office, E.351, bundles 2030–2059, and A.O.1., 1595–1601. This study was made in 1950, at the time without knowledge of the work of J. D. Gould published in "The Royal Mint in the Early Seventeenth Century," *Economic History Review*, V (1952). See also Sir John Craig, *The Mint* (Cambridge, Eng., 1953). The total of gold and silver coin issued in Antwerp from 1480 settled at 34,482 florins in 1495 and rose to 195,373 florins in 1497, to 366,552 florins in 1501, and to 591,636 florins in 1506. Then there was a decline to 79,240 florins in 1520. After the important year 1521 (1,002,354 florins), the coinage fell to an average of 120,951 florins in 1534–1535. A series of uncertain years followed to 1548 (143,630 florins). Next in the rising trend to 1578, the years 1552 (1,015,065 florins) and 1568 (1,328,680 florins) were outstanding. After this was a short fall to the early 1580s, the occupation of the Duc d'Alençon, and the "French Fury." The documentation is lacking for 1582–1583, but after this the issue rose to 1,768,570 florins in 1593. The value of the coinage culminated in 1605.

terest in silver, however, changed in 1499, and the two cities approached equilibrium conditions by coining quantities of gold. Even so, the proportion of silver still tended to be slightly higher in Antwerp than in Paris. The equilibrium was of short duration; it ended with the famous election of Emperor Charles V. Paris turned to silver, and Antwerp to gold. The break, apparent by 1518, was clear by 1521 with the declaration of open war between the two rulers. However, this disparity was also relatively short lived, and the positions were reversed after 1526, when Antwerp returned to silver and Paris to gold. After 1533, the two cities again approached similar proportions of coinage. Then Paris began to increase the fraction of silver coined, while Antwerp turned abruptly to gold in 1542. This contrast again appeared in 1557, when Antwerp attempted to coin silver, and Paris (after 1560–1561) to coin gold. Antwerp adhered to this trend of issuing silver (which Paris joined after 1567) until 1578–1579, when it returned mainly to gold.

In these contrasts between Paris and Antwerp, the struggle between the Valois and Hapsburgs had a special importance. The conflicts and consequent expenditures in Germany obliged France repeatedly to attract silver, the currency in demand during the gold phase. On the other hand, Antwerp coined gold, which had a natural outlet in the rich cities of southern Germany. It is noticeable, above all in time of peace, that France faced encirclement by the Empire — Spain, the Low Countries, Germany — and preferred to coin gold which was arriving in Europe and which its monetary system appeared more prone to absorb. It is difficult to find the basic explanation for this among the partial data, but the problem will be considered again in the section on foreign exchanges. At first sight it appears that war repeatedly changed the monetary situation in France and pushed the activity of the most important mint, Paris, to coin silver money. This concern of the Paris mint with silver underlined both the fiscal role of the capital since the extraordinary tax levies were often paid in silver plate and also the striking monetary difficulties of France in time of war.

The data for London cover the period 1600–1660.[42] London tended to follow the same course as Paris during the first three decades of this period, with a slight preference for silver in 1615–1620. During the third decade, especially after 1626, gold coinage predominated slightly. The great break between the movements in Paris and London occurred in 1630, when London issued silver, and Paris turned to gold. During the decade 1630–1640 the two movements remained in opposition. After 1646, however, London tended to move in the direction of Paris, toward its interest in issuing gold currency.

---

[42] The output of the Mint in London during the first half of the seventeenth century showed a rising trend. From the total of £50,387 in 1606, the coinage fell to £81,083 in 1610. Then the movement rose to £265,130 in 1616 and fell again in 1619 (£139,-980). It increased to £781,509 in 1624 and fell to £168,632 in 1628; additional increases followed in 1637 (£574,167) and 1640 (£533,003). The documentation from 1641 to 1645 is missing. After £747,250 in 1646, the issues remained at a low level until 1655.

When one recalls that the English East India Company exported gold currency during the 1620s and that the monetary system of France went through a gold crisis as the rise in gold currency rates after 1630 revealed, then the contrasts between London and Paris after 1630 take on some importance. It is possible that the price movements in the two countries were in some measure related. The data for France indicate that the rise in the 1620s was followed by a fall. The tables of Thorold Rogers and Lord Beveridge,[43] show that prices in England tended to level out off the 1620s, but rose sharply in the following decade. This discordance was broken during the difficult years 1629–1630. Later studies may reveal more about this apparent opposition between the two economies.

The movement of foreign exchanges indicated the international standing of the livre tournois; and also reflected to some extent the fluctuations in the prices of gold and silver. Classical economists have long propounded theories of the parity of purchasing power on foreign exchanges. For countries with currencies freely convertible into the international standards of gold and silver, bullion flows would be regulated through the levels of prices and wages and the rates of exchange.[44] A certain amount of information exists on exchange rates in France in the sixteenth and early seventeenth centuries, both in the Lyons fairs and in the market of Amsterdam, the latter from data for the early seventeenth century published by Nicolaus Posthumus.[45] This information points out characteristics of the problem under discussion.

Among the towns that were related to the fairs of Lyons and regularly quoted in the quarterly "acceptances and payments," four of the more important give information on the monetary conditions in France: Antwerp and Venice, which, by stretching a point, can be considered as representing the "old" economies and were particularly active in the phase when gold was relatively more abundant; and Seville and Genoa, the two focal points of the "American" aspects of the silver phase (see Graph 28).[46] What do these four examples reveal?

In Antwerp and Venice the movement of foreign exchanges was probably unfavorable to France from about 1554 to 1557; this lasted until the revolutionary, indeed catastrophic, crisis of the summer of 1575. The rate for the gold *écu de marc* of France in being changed to the *écu d'or au soleil* in 1575 (then

[43] James E. Thorold Rogers, *A History of Agriculture and Prices in England* (7 vols., Oxford, 1892–1902), VI, pp. 5–84; Lord Beveridge, *Prices and Wages in England from the Twelfth to the Nineteenth Century* (London, 1939), I, and "A Statistical Crime in the Seventeenth Century," *Journal of Economics and Business History,* I (1929).

[44] Lord Keynes, *A Treatise on Money* (2 vols., London, 1930), I, p. 72.

[45] Nicolaus W. Posthumus, *Inquiry into the History of Prices in Holland* (2 vols., Leiden, 1946–1964), I, 194, pp. 573 ff. There is a gap in the documentation for 1656–1663.

[46] These have been chosen from the score of exchange centers that were related to Lyons.

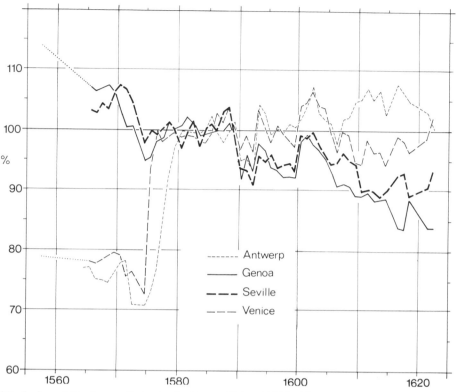

28. Index of Exchange Rates in the Lyons Fairs (1580–1589 = 100)

valued at three livres tournois) rose by about a third on the markets in Venice and Antwerp, Antwerp showing itself to be the weaker of the two. The quotations in the new unit for Antwerp followed a rising trend until 1585 and fell until 1592; they rose again until 1616 and then showed a substantial decline. However, the movement of the exchange in Venice rose until 1588, fell until 1592, rose until 1602, fell until 1610, and finally began to rise again. It is important to note that after 1608 these two towns followed different trends with the exchange rate relatively weak in Antwerp but strong in Venice.

The quotations for Seville and Genoa tended to have a long-term similarity. Their connection underlined the powerful influence which the Genoese bankers had exerted on the finances and economy of Spain; the interrelationship of these two cities constituted an important line in distributing bullion from the New World. They had more substantial claims to bullion reserves than France, and the financial and banking acumen of Genoa was of the first order. Together they were undoubtedly the strongest reference point for the French monetary system and revealed the nature of the crisis of 1575 in relation to the foreign exchange markets of France. This crisis shook Spain and Genoa to their foundations; in 1575 the second bankruptcy of the Spanish monarchy occurred under Philip II. During this crisis the same level of exchange rates was maintained in Lyons, whereas those in Antwerp and Venice rose steeply. It is possible that the difference in exchange rates merely reflected the method of making quotations, but it is also possible for one crisis to compensate for another.

In Seville the general movement of the Lyons exchange was downward until 1574 and upward to 1588. There was a new decline in 1597, followed by a renewed rise to 1600 and then by another fall. The Lyons exchange rates for Genoa show a clear fall until 1574, a slight rise to 1583, a renewed fall to 1597, a rise to 1600–1601, and then an unmistakable decline. The long-term movement of the Lyons exchange in relation to these two centers was, therefore, unfavorable, most clearly in the case of Genoa after 1597, when for the third time, Philip II declared the Spanish crown bankrupt. Did Genoa shift the weight of the crisis to its associates? In any case, there was a change in trend after 1613, when the foreign exchanges of France showed signs of improvement in Seville and Venice.

After 1583, the four series moved roughly in the same direction, but Antwerp after 1602 and Genoa after 1604 showed divergent trends. This may have denoted a change in the bullion and capital markets of Europe.

In order to set the problem in a more general context, I shall also consider trade balances. It may be assumed that in these trade balances France was a creditor to Spain and perhaps also to the Low Countries, but the balances were evidently unfavorable in relation to Venice and Genoa. The present inquiry will consider this particular aspect of the general problem and the character of the monetary fluctuations of France.

These remarks on the exchange movements concern, in effect, the phase of silver. The relationships and connections thus revealed go to the heart of the monetary problems of France. These exchanges, valued in terms of the gold écu de marc and then in écus d'or au soleil at the fixed rate of three livres tournois, give some indication of the extent to which France was dominated by silver during the silver phase.

From this standpoint, the movement of foreign exchanges shows one change of particular importance. While Antwerp was inclined to become a "soft currency" area, the axis of Seville and Genoa tended to increase in strength relative to France and, in effect, constituted a "hard currency" area. Venice also moved toward this position after 1600. Compared with the French monetary system, those of Genoa and Antwerp moved in opposite directions, notably after 1589: Genoa became increasingly stable, while the situation in Antwerp, doubtless influenced by deliveries of silver, tended to deteriorate. It must be noted, however, that there were fundamental differences between the two economies: Genoa, to all appearances, was the dominant financial market. In studying the basic characteristics of these complex economies, one might find it relevant to consider the rise of Holland and the possibility that the Atlantic was more oriented toward silver and the Mediterranean, an area of high prices, toward gold.

For the purpose of the present argument, however, it is important to note the monetary shifts of secondary importance and the position of silver currency during the gold phase and of gold currency during the silver phase. The latter was accompanied by a renewed trade in gold from such sources as Guinea, East Africa, or the New World, as the increases in the arrivals of gold in Seville during the last quarter of the sixteenth century indicates (see Graph 32 on the acceleration of these imports). There is a strong temptation to infer that, through the manipulations of the Genoese bankers in Seville and Genoa, there was some division in the two great streams of bullion, silver going mainly in the direction of the west and gold entering the reserves of the entrepreneurs and great financial markets of the Mediterranean. Since the Western Mediterranean had relatively the highest price levels in Europe, the utility of gold in circulation and in reserves would have tended to be greater. In this respect, the catastrophic crisis of 1575 confirmed the silver phase; it was serious for some of the older economies such as Florence, Lucca, Milan, Naples, and Antwerp, but Genoa emerged in triumph.

In light of this great transformation of 1575 the crisis of 1583 appears as a passing incident, which showed that Genoa was not free from the difficulties of gold facing the international economy. In 1586, it should be remembered, the Banco di San Giorgio in Genoa opened the famous *Cartulario d'oro*.[47] Later, after famine and plague in Italy in 1628–1630 shocked the economy of the peninsula, Italian gold currency appeared in greater quantities in France. These events in themselves could confirm or reject the explanations suggested above, but they show most of all that the situation was complex and not to be explained in simple terms.

In contrast to the fairs of Lyons, the exchanges quoted in Amsterdam for Paris followed the modern system.[48] From 1619 to 1725 the movement of the écu d'or au soleil (continued after the devaluation of 1602 at a token value of three livres tournois) again represented the international position of the French monetary system in Amsterdam (see Graph 29); the livre tournois was, in effect, measured against the guilder of the rising economy of Holland. The slow decline in the years 1620–1630 accelerated with the crisis of 1630, and by 1638 the livre tournois had lost a fifth of its value on the Amsterdam market. There was a slight recovery to about 1650, but during the troubles of the Fronde another sharp fall took place to 1653. The livre tournois followed a clearly favorable trend to the early 1670s, but after 1676 this rising trend faltered once more and gave way, in 1687, to a clear fall. The downward movement gathered momentum during the 1690's, but was checked during the first decade of the eighteenth century. At the time of the Peace of Utrecht and during the operations of John Law there was a further decline; by the early 1720s the value of the livre tournois in Amsterdam was almost half that of

---

[47] See Braudel, *Méditerranée*, pp. 419, 1043–1044.
[48] Posthumus, *Inquiry into the History of Prices in Holland*, I, Sect. III.

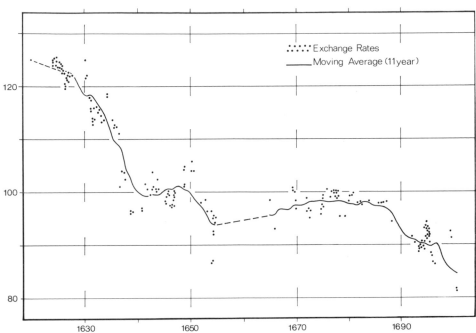

29. Exchange Rates of the écu soleil (= 3 livres tournois) on Amsterdam (Reference: N. Posthumus)

fifty years earlier. The stability of the exchanges between Paris and Amsterdam was not restored until after the great monetary reform of 1726.

These periods of deterioration (1630–1653 and 1687–1724) coincided with difficulties over bullion and, as mentioned above, with phases of more violent fluctuations in prices. In addition they reflected the expansion of credit and increases in governmental spending. The first period was connected with the financial operations of Richelieu and his policy of annual subsidies to the allies of France, above all Holland and Sweden. For these subsidies a flood of bills of exchange passed to the market of Amsterdam. Because these huge expenditures were evidently unmatched by output of the French economy and were uncompensated by exports, the consequences were unavoidable. Two great devaluations in 1636 were necessary to stabilize the sagging value of the livre tournois. These devaluations probably improved the terms of trade, encouraged exports, and thus strengthened the livre tournois (aided no doubt by military successes) during the last stages of the Thirty Years' War.

Again, after 1687, the downward shifts in the exchange rate in Amsterdam were brought to a halt only at the time of the reform of 1726. These shifts once more reflected the extension of governmental finance and indebtedness under Louis XIV, culminating in the schemes of John Law. And, again, as shown in Graph 26, the gap widened between prices in terms of the livre and of bullion. These instabilities in themselves could have contributed substantially to the violence of the fluctuations in prices that we have already observed.

Actually it is not possible to separate the two fundamental aspects of monetary activities: the movement of foreign exchanges; and the coinage of gold and silver in France. These movements show some connection with each other. In examining the different proportions of gold and silver currency issued (Graph 24), one observes that a falling trend in the exchange rate for the livre tournois (that is to say, when the progressive depreciation of the French unit of accounts is assessed in terms of an international standard such as gold) could always be adjusted by an increase of the official nominal rates of gold currency in France. Within the structure of relative costs and the movement of goods and services, this served, first, to draw gold specie from abroad to France and, second, to require the conversion of foreign specie by the French mints. On the other hand, in a period of rising exchange rates, the coinage of silver currency appears to have assumed a larger place. Although the empirical evidence is not complete, the fluctuations in gold and silver coinage must be related to the movements of the exchange; they would tend, therefore, to respond to the general movement of the economy and the "balance of payments."

Between 1536 and 1557 the foreign exchange rates established during the fairs of Lyons probably followed a rising trend:[49] If this trend is compared with the coinage in the Paris mint, it is clear that there was an increase in the proportion of silver issued, even after the raising of the price of gold in 1533 (an adjustment of the bimetallic ratio which tended to favor gold). In the decade 1550–1560 issues were largely made in silver, but from 1554, with the decline in the quantities issued and the appreciation of gold currency, the trend was on the point of being reversed. This was also the time of governmental war borrowing leading to the Grand Parti and eventually to the bankruptcy of 1557. The seriousness of this crisis was thus composed of two developments, firstly the change in basic monetary structures, and secondly a considerable increase in deficit spending by governments. After these difficulties (from 1564 to the crisis of 1575) the foreign exchange rates in Lyons tended to fall. During this period the proportion of gold currency issued by the Paris mint increased, a movement which was further encouraged by the progressive rise in the official prices of gold and gold currency.

During the critical year 1575 the bimetallic ratio was altered slightly to favor

[49] In Lyons the exchange rates were quoted in terms of one gold écu de marc and after 1575 of one hundred écus d'or au soleil (after the devaluation of 1602 the écu was fixed at three livres tournois). In Amsterdam, by contrast, the different units of foreign currency (with the exception of Danzig) were valued in a variable number of guilders or gros. See Posthumus, *Inquiry into the History of Prices in Holland,* I. There is a gap in the documentation for 1656–1663. *Ibid.,* p. 592. The list of exchange rates for 1536 does not give a deposit rate; it is possible that this was lower than that in the crisis and bankruptcy year of 1557.

silver (by comparison with the rates set in 1561). The exchange bankers in Lyons decided to set the rates of foreign currencies in terms of the écu d'or au soleil instead of, as formerly, in the gold écu de marc; then came the regulation that after January 1, 1578, all accounting should be done in écus d'or au soleil. By 1575 the coinage began to show a marked increase in the amounts of silver issued.

The foreign exchanges of France remained fairly stable until 1588, when there was a decline, which was particularly noticeable in the rates for Genoa (after the Epiphany fair of 1589). A slump in the issues of gold currency was evident after 1587. The situation of falling exchange rates in the "strong" economies was finally recognized and to some extent stopped when, in 1614, the official prices of gold were increased sharply, without altering those for silver. During this period the rate for Amsterdam dropped from 125 in 1619 to 122 in 1628, but the trend was not clear until 1625. In the last year the exchange rate in Amsterdam weakened; the catastrophic drop began in 1630. In connection with these changes, the market rates of gold currencies in France began to rise rapidly, and the devaluation was finally confirmed in the great monetary edicts of 1636. There was an increasing proportion of gold coinage during this period.

After the devaluation the exchange rates rose in Amsterdam until about 1650. The rates for silver currency in France were raised in 1641 without altering those for gold; with this change the proportion of silver in the issue increased. A further change came in 1647 and during the troubles and famine years of the Fronde, when the rates of foreign exchange fell once more. The proportion of gold currency began to increase until 1658. Then the exchanges found a period of stability, rose slightly until 1676, and did not fall catastrophically again until after 1686. During these years the proportion of silver currency increased until 1677, when the famous pieces of two and four sols were coined.

The rise in the percentage of gold coined in the last two decades of the seventeenth century was also accompanied by falling exchange rates. The reversal of this trend in 1702–1703 was followed by a decade of relative stability before a renewed phase of coining gold and deteriorating exchange rates occurred in Amsterdam.

On the basis of these observations, one can take another look at the earlier period. It is highly probable that from 1488 to 1516–1519 the exchange rates tended to rise in France's favor, followed later by decline. The monetary edict of 1488 had tended to favor gold currency, and the order of 1516 raised the écu from 36 sols 3 deniers to 40 sols. There was a tendency to coin larger quantities of silver until about 1521 and then gold until 1533–1536.

The comparison of the series of nominal prices, coinage, and rates of exchange tends to show three important turning points: in the mid-sixteenth century, at the beginning of the seventeenth century, and at the end of the seventeenth century. For France these were significant moments, both in secular price trends and in the prevailing monetary structures. On each occasion the monetary system underwent not only changes in the total stock of money but also internal adjustments in its composition. The proportions of gold, silver, copper, and credit, which made up the total stock of money at the disposal of France, changed with the passage of time. Beyond the progressive evolution of the monetary system — the increased availability of gold and silver and the improvement of credit — these changes in composition followed trends and established the phases already indicated. The turning points inevitably imposed instabilities, which emerge from the documents and data studied above.

One must note, in conclusion, that the movement of French foreign exchangers represented structural changes of prime importance. The long-term fluctuations emphasized a persistent depreciation of the livre tournois and focused attention once more on this capital problem. If the international value of the livre tournois reflected the state of the incomes and expenditures in France by comparison with those of its neighbors, the movement of foreign exchange was one rough but effective measure of that condition. The intrinsic value of the livre tournois in terms of bullion was a barometer of the sufficiency — or insufficiency — of the national product of France to meet its expenditures, valued in current prices. A rising trend in the rate for the livre tournois in foreign markets actually resulted in an improvement in the monetary stock of France; a falling trend tended to reflect an increase in the total volume of indebtedness, unmatched by output.

The course of monetary history reveals, in brief, the repeated instability of the livre tournois. During certain periods it was severe and, as a result, demonstrates the repeated weakness in the monetary affairs of France in the sixteenth and seventeenth centuries. This contrasts with the strength of the relationship between Seville and Genoa at the end of the sixteenth and at the beginning of the seventeenth centuries; with the long stability among London, Amsterdam, and Hamburg in the seventeenth and eighteenth centuries; and with the stability between France and Holland in the half century before the French Revolution. The lack of integration in the international economy — a huge problem — was a further factor of uncertainty in the monetary development of France. From the evidence of the exchange markets one finds that the instability was perhaps more apparent in the seventeenth than in the sixteenth century. However, in the sixteenth century, when France had two great international centers of exchange in Paris and Lyons, that instability was just as important.

3. Money and Economic Movements

The diversity of the economy of France, expressed in so many different responses from a relatively wide area, also hampers every attempt to reconstruct its history. The assessment of economic activity in the sixteenth and seventeenth centuries must in the end rest on solid regional studies and must summarize conclusions based on profound contradictions, on differences among regions and towns. And economic activity, according to the particular phase, meant tension or relaxation, diffusion or convergence. Such a method implies a general uncertainty, but tends to give perhaps a truer picture which is more aware of the diversities of fragments and details. In any case, by taking account of such diversities, one can understand the function and presence of France in the historical context of Europe and in the international economy. Behind the instabilities and differences in France loomed the shape of Europe's economic development; in effect, France was a microcosm of this huge history.

The diversity of France almost inevitably produced an exceptional capacity to compensate. An example of this can be found in the second half of the sixteenth century when the difficulties of the towns of continental France were balanced by the expansion and development not only of the ports on the west coast opening directly on the Atlantic but also of the south, particularly Marseilles. This expansion, implying maritime trade, probably had compound effects, especially on agricultural production. In the same way, the difficulties of the maritime regions in the early seventeenth century, particularly after 1620, were to some extent offset by activity in the east of France, the Rhône and Saône valleys. Such compensations entailed important shifts in men and capital. Jean Bodin noted how emigrants from Auvergne found work and high wages in Spain.[50] This was one example among many others of some degree of mobility. In the sixteenth and seventeenth centuries all sorts of pressures — social, political, religious, economic — were mingled together and set up barriers or imposed sudden changes. The civil wars in the second half of the sixteenth century represented a mixture of causes and effects, sometimes contradictory, associated with hardening conditions and restrictions in the older, maturing towns; they aroused social discriminations and even religious persecutions and xenophobia. There were more or less noisy social protests, such as the revolt of the *Croquants* of 1594–1596, or the *Nu-pieds* of 1639 in Normandy, or the attacks on Huguenot privileges under Richelieu and their emigrations to other countries in the wake of the revocation of the Edict of Nantes. All these factors must be taken into account.

Economic theory today, it must be admitted, tends to minimize the role played by changes in stocks of bullion in altering the level of prices and economic activity. Yet classical economics, in conditions more akin to sixteenth- and seventeenth-century France, would not be so hasty in arriving at

[50] Jean Bodin, *La Response de Maistre Iean Bodin, advocat en la Cour, au Paradoxe de Monsieur Malestroit touchant l'encherissement de toutes choses et le moyen d'y remedier* (Paris, 1568), in *Écrits notables sur la monnaie*, ed. Jean-Yves Le Branchu (2 vols., Paris, 1934) [hereafter cited as *Réponse*], p. 92; Émile Giralt and Jorge Nadal, "Inmigración francesa y problemas monetarios en la Cataluña de los siglos XVI y XVII," in *X Congresso Internazionale di Scienze Storiche, Rome,* ed. Aldo Ferrabino (8 vols., Florence, 1955–1957), VII, pp. 298–301.

such conclusions. From the end of the fifteenth to the beginning of the seventeenth century, Europe experienced an economic expansion. At the beginning, the relatively low prices assured high marginal returns for additions to the bullion available for international trade. The phases of gold, of silver, of copper, and of credit represented a concentration of monetary factors which eventually marked the evolution of Europe. France had a substantial part in this long experience. One after another, these forces burnt themselves out, as part of a composite movement of growth. Only in the early eighteenth century did gold again enter the scene to stimulate the economies. Although a similar series of monetary phases seemed to begin again, the economic structures were different. The role was a new one, which was not being replayed.

The progressive price rise in the sixteenth century created, in principle at least, opportunities for entrepreneurial fortunes. In general, the maritime ports and the export sectors were successful in this way. France was prepared, by its position in Europe and by its relatively large territorial size, to respond to such monetary and economic transformations.

In the final analysis it could not have been otherwise. If "bullionist" explanations are required, the basic weakness and strength of France were not the poverty of its land and natural conditions, nor indeed the inevitable difficulties of its size — its "economic viscosity" — and its position for the routes and sea-lanes of Europe. It resulted, rather, from the subsoil. France had resources of precious metals: a few silver mines and some gold dust in the river valleys. But more and more as the years advanced, they were lost in the rising costs and discoveries of more productive fields. And the weakness on the side of monetary supply stressed the output from its most productive sector, agriculture. The facts concerning its mines are nevertheless worth recalling.

The letters patent of Charles VI (May 30, 1413) drew attention to mines, especially in the regions of Lyons and Mâcon.[51] Later, in this same region, Jacques Cœur organized his copper and silver mines from his center of operations in Bourges.[52] Compared with the great revival of activity in the mines of Germany, the output in France remained at a modest level and only assumed a degree of importance at the end of the fifteenth century. A long ordinance of March 18, 1483, renewed the letters patent of Charles VI and placed the jurisdiction in matters relating to the mines in the hands of the Chambre des Monnaies, making particular mention of the mines in Lyonnais, Rouergue, and the Pyrenees.[53] The privileges of the miners were confirmed by the ordinance of Louis XII (November 8, 1498).[54] Toward the end of the fifteenth century the mines of Nivernais were developed — the more

[51] A.N., AD. XI.35, lettres patentes of May 30, 1413.
[52] Gustave Fagniez, *Documents relatifs à l'histoire de l'industrie et du commerce en France* (2 vols., Paris, 1898–1900), II, 141.
[53] A.N., Z¹B.61, ordonnance of Mar. 18, 1483.
[54] *Ibid.,* ordonnance of Nov. 8, 1498.

important were at Citry, Chaumont, and Maxières — with large numbers of miners and laborers. Estienne Burdelot was appointed on April 13, 1516, to the office of "Keeper of the silver mines of the country and county of Nivernais and their adjacent lands." [55] German experts were summoned to help with the project.[56]

All this was soon called to a halt; the increasing flows of silver bullion into Europe from the New World altered the situation, and in the last quarter of the sixteenth century the mines fell into decline. On October 22, 1578, François Garrault, a conseiller of the Cour des Monnaies and author of monetary tracts, reported that the mines of Citry had been abandoned and that their furnaces and stamps had been left to rack and ruin.[57] According to his calculations, these mines had the capacity to produce four ounces of silver for every hundred marcs of lead. During the troubles of the League their owner complained that the metal refined did not cover the cost of production.[58] As a result, France was more dependent than ever on foreign supplies to increase its stocks of precious metals.

France came to rely first on Germany and then on Spain. From the beginning of the sixteenth century Spain became the dominant power by reason of its command of precious metals and an unfavorable balance of trade dependent on bullion. France, too, had export sectors. The export of wheat was one of its chief keys to open the riches of the south, riches largely composed of gold and silver. As Bodin has observed, the embargo on the export of precious metals from Spain was freely raised to allow the import of wheat.[59] Brittany and the adventurous port of Saint-Malo were part of this trade. Money was recoined in the great mints of the region: Rennes, Angers, Saint-Lô, and Rouen. In Rennes after 1575 the issues rose rapidly, reaching totals in 1582 and 1587 which were superior to those of Paris.[60] This sector partially collapsed later. Wheat and bullion — not to mention linen textiles — formed a solid base for the fortunes of Breton merchants. It is not surprising, perhaps, that one of the first attempts to establish a French East India Company developed in this province.

Though France lacked mines, it did have financiers and capital resources. During the great phases of economic expansion, France submitted to the operations of important trading associations from abroad, merchants and financiers from Florence, Lucca, Germany, and Genoa and later from Holland; the ports of Rouen, Saint-Malo, Nantes, La Rochelle, Bordeaux, and Bayonne were familiar to the Dutch shippers. These merchants took advantage of the position of France at the crossroads of Europe; the long history of in-

---

[55] *Ibid.*, mandement of Apr. 13, 1516.
[56] *Ibid.*, ordonnance of Apr. 15, 1484; A.N., Z¹B.64, lettres patentes of Sept. 30, 1548.
[57] A.N., Z¹B.73, lettres patentes of Oct. 29, 1592; A.N., Z¹B.74, edict of Jan. 1597; A.N., Z¹B.377, letter of Oct. 22, 1578, François Garrault to the Cour des Monnaies.
[58] A.N., Z¹B.73, lettres patentes of Oct. 29, 1592; A.N., Z¹B.74, edict of Jan. 1597.
[59] Bodin, *Réponse,* pp. 95–96.
[60] See Chap. 3, n. 153.

ternational fairs shows it to have been a veritable clearinghouse. But France was not weak; in the sixteenth century, in fact, the country was stronger in some respects than its neighbors. Thus, the crisis of 1575 was a severe blow to the prosperity of the Italian cities: Venice, Milan, Florence, Lucca, and Naples. France took advantage of the situation. After 1571–1575 Marseilles rapidly developed its trade with the Levant; at this same time the English Levant Company was being formed, planned (1575), and finally chartered (September 11, 1581).[61] Marseilles, once under the control of the financiers of Lyons, quickly assumed a position of greater liberty and independence. Industries, such as soapmaking, were established there in 1579.[62] Three of its consulates were founded in Barbary on the North African coast.[63] The difficulties of Venice were a further occasion for Marseilles to expand wherever opportunities appeared.

All these observations are worthy of study and reflection. But they do not constitute, in my opinion, the crux of the matter. The livre tournois remains the central question. The instability of the money of account was a constant obstacle to venturing investments when they were established in a monetary terms. Its progressive depreciation, rapid at the beginning of the seventeenth century, was rooted in excessive governmental spending, for the level of taxation mounted at that time. (This will be considered again in the next chapter.) As Adam Smith later observed, excessive taxation was often accompanied by hoarding. Inevitably, there were efforts to find a stable means to store value in order to conserve fortunes. Gold was one outstanding means and had many possibilities. The lethargy of gold prices in the sixteenth century and the rapidity of their fall in the seventeenth century were perhaps both the opportunity and sign of hoarding in France.

It is possible also that the instability of the livre tournois and the risks involved in long-term investment established in terms of this currency may have discouraged capital from abroad. One must not labor the point, however, since institutions to permit the migration of capital on a large scale did not exist. Developed capital markets had not yet been formed, while at the same time dealings in governmental debts were prominent. Nevertheless the infiltration of foreign merchants in France leads the observer to note the paradox of foreign intrusion coupled with domestic hoarding. In addition, this foreign participation, at least initially, was probably concerned with trade, while in France wealth sought the considerable social and material advantages which accrued from investment in land. The large differences in the social distribution of income tended further to encourage spending on luxury goods, and this combined with the later mercantilist theories of overpopulation and

[61] Alfred Wood, *A History of the Levant Company* (Oxford, 1935), pp. 7–9.

[62] Raymond Collier and Joseph Billioud, *Histoire du commerce de Marseille, 1480–1599* (Paris, 1951), p. 505, citing lettres patentes of Oct. 17, 1579 to Georges Prunemoyr.

[63] Braudel, *Méditerrannée,* pp. 712–713.

a whole range of derogatory attitudes toward commercial and industrial activities to limit the development of markets for long-term investment. And such finance represented the life blood of the economy. The policies which Colbert so ably pursued succeeded in giving France the most sophisticated economic structure of the *ancien régime*.

In conclusion, the expansion of the economy continually required an increasing volume of money in order to satisfy the level of transactions as well as the exceptional requirements of years of crisis. It required, moreover, a certain proportion of gold, silver, and billon money. Actually these different types of money were sorts of fuel to be consumed in turn.

France seemed only to advance by spurts, in successive zones, without a concerted movement. Continental France and its relations with Germany, Spain, and Portugal in a cycle of affairs which featured the Mediterranean represented the gold phase. In the mid-sixteenth century, the ports of the west coast came to the forefront. During this period also, as the crises of 1575 and 1583 revealed, the country's economy may have turned gradually once more to revive the life of the Mediterranean. With the difficulties after 1589, competition from the north increased, particularly in the west of France. There were renewed problems after 1607 and later with the opening of the Thirty Years' War and the difficult years of the 1630s. These problems led into a long period of fluctuations and projects until the new turning point in 1676–1686.

All these transformations were extremely important for France. Behind a façade of unified laws and administrative regulations, the range of regional differences imposed their tensions and constant restrictions, which the royal government strove to dominate and reduce to conformity. France was sufficiently complex to allow adjustments and compensations in the changing currents of economic activity. The difficulties of the continental cities opened opportunities in the maritime towns; here and there, the vicissitudes in commercial activity were compensated for by agricultural fertility and fortunes in landholding. A series of balances and counter balances, of contrasts, paradoxes, and adjustments, resulted. Between Germany and Spain and among the traditional Mediterranean, Channel, and Atlantic regions, strengthened by its fertile agriculture, France remained at the confluence of the political and economic development of Europe. In this position, however, the country inevitably suffered shocks. France gave way before stronger economies, but asserted its natural interests and power wherever possible. The compensatory nature of France resulted in exceptional mobility, which was reflected in the history of the livre tournois and its diverse functions.

Chapter 6

Conclusions: Total Coinage and Monetary Structures

So far in the book I have tried to be prudent. However, the closing section must review some problems which, by definition, through the lack of the requisite empirical data, inevitably remain largely unsolved.

There are two such problems, and both are important. In the first place, I was impressed by the diversity, the immense economic disparity, of France; as a result, I set out to study it from the viewpoint of separate regions and cities. This implied a sectional rather than an aggregative method. It was modified, or, rather, coordinated by the function of the livre tournois to which, so far, I have given particular attention. This prepares the way for an essay in aggregation, more in keeping with macrotheory, which estimates economic movements by large, quasi-independent political units. Such a method seems more relevant to the seventeenth and early eighteenth centuries when the imaginative political arithmetic of Sir William Petty, Gregory King, the sieur de Boisguillebert, John Locke, Sébastien Le Prestre, maréchal de Vauban, Charles Dutot, Ferdinando Galiani, and many others was developed. The studies of these men were more than mere flights of intellect; their authors represented an age colored by mercantilist thought and the economic activity of the time. I hesitated to speak of France as an integrated economic unit since, during the long two centuries of this study, its more characteristic features seemed imperfectly knit together. Was France basically an agrarian economy, largely self-subsisting, but slowly organized into a market system and governed by a centralizing monarchy? Or did the market mechanism, dear to the hearts of classical economists, faithfully regulate economic activity at all levels? If such questions are valid for sixteenth- and seventeenth-century France, they can be applied with equal effect to Britain, to Spain, to the sprawling Hapsburg possessions, or even to the Turkish Empire, which under one dominion combined so many diversities.

In the second place, by dealing with the world economy and then the French economy in turn, I also hesitated to deal with the intricate problems of types, systems, and structure. The precious metals arriving in Europe through Spain were shared partly through the vagaries of power politics, but even more substantially through the functioning of trade and services in the international economy. The contribution of international and interregional trade to "total income" was probably small but in effect remained important. Briefly, is it possible to speak of "monetary" structures? How did they function? Did they persist in these centuries of metallic currency, when the emerging, circumscribed credit systems were already signs of future development?

The answers to these two huge questions — the macroeconomic problems of France, and the structural aspects of the monetary experience in the sixteenth and seventeenth centuries — by no means terminate the discussion in this book. They attempt, rather, to open further lines of investigation.

France was, by its very nature, subject to external influences, which belonged implicitly to the general movement of the international economy. It seemed disrupted in every phase of sustained expansion, as if the international economy imposed demands beyond its capacity and strength. In more general terms, this situation could be taken as an indication that the foreign trading sectors of France had a small though significant part in the overall product of France and at the same time endowed the country with high marginal elasticities. As a counterpart, large sectors relegated to quasi-subsistence farming were gradually brought into more open activity. Its huge territory and population (by comparison with other states of the time) presented France with a difficult problem of organization. In order to take this into account, the economic historian can turn to the image of a crossroads, which has often been used by geographers and historians of civilization when dealing with France. Such a meeting place did not create conditions for a coherent or homogeneous economic unit; it was, rather, a complex of regions which acted and reacted with one another. I do not subscribe strongly to the opinion that the monetary activity of France was exactly defined by its frontiers (even when avoiding such famous concepts as "natural" frontiers), that, briefly, France represented a single concept, so necessary to some of the more zealous theorists such as Claude Seyssel in *La Grand' Monarchie de France* (1519), Jean Bodin in *Six livres de la république* (1576), and Antoine de Monchrétien in *Traicté de l'Œconomie Politique* (1615) — in short, the France of Colbert's mercantilism or the power politics of Richelieu and Louis XIV.

All this does not imply a pervasive unity, in contrast to what has already been described as diverse and complex. Much can be said of the unity of France at the level of political economy; there was a centralizing administration, a tax system, and a line of frontiers outlined by tariffs and customs and more directly by national defenses and fortress towns, with which Louis XIV gave practical definition to his kingdom. In the present section, *ceteris paribus,* I propose simply to sum the regions of France using the total coinage of the country. What can these total mint issues tell us?

Before proceeding further, it is necessary to consider the validity of the two main sources from which the total output of the different mints has been computed: the états des délivrances and the contrôle des boîtes. The sum of the mint issues, therefore, reflects the accuracy of these documents; the combination of the two sources tends to reduce the margins of error to manageable proportions. The resulting totals of annual coinage show: the total value of the issues of gold, silver, and billon coin; and the percentages of gold, silver, and billon money in the total coinages, including copper coins.

The first graph (see Graph 30A) in terms of livres tournois includes progressive devaluation, which resulted in an apparent expansion of the coinage, a rising trend. The use of a semilogarithmic scale, however, reduces the short-term fluctuations to proportions comparable throughout the series. A certain number of useful results can be observed. These observations follow the

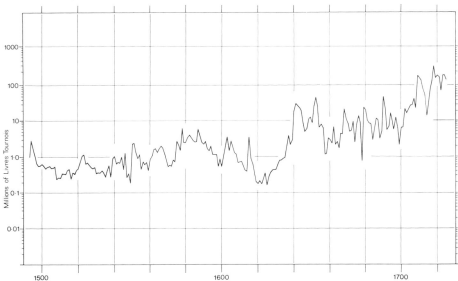

30A. Total Annual Value in Livres Tournois of the Coinage in France (Reference: Appendix C)

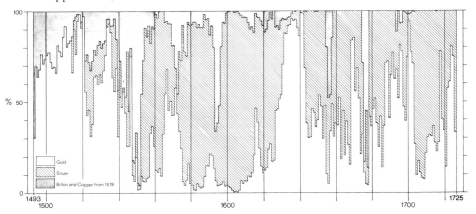

30B. Percentages of Gold, Silver, Billon, and Copper in the Total Annual Coinage (Reference: Appendix C)

general lines of my earlier remarks: a decline to 1508, a rise to 1520, and a recession to 1535. Then came the upsurge of billon in the reform of 1550–1551 and in the activity of the years 1562–1567; it was followed by a sharp fall in 1570–1572. The currency conversion of 1578 succeeded followed by a boom period until 1587 and recession to 1598. After this there was a rise which continued to 1603–1605, followed by a depression which lasted until the 1620s. The recovery after 1626 culminated in the great conversions of 1651–1653. There was a rising trend from about 1657 to 1678, followed by an uncertain period until the slump year of 1699. From 1699 to 1725 the trend increased sharply to a peak in 1709, decreased to a low point in 1714 (the first full year of peace after the Treaty of Utrecht), peaked again in 1718, and continued to rise until the end of the series in 1725.

Graph 30B also gives the percentage issues of gold, silver, silver billon, and copper coinage in the total issues. The graph demonstrates reasonably clearly the phases of gold and of silver, and then, after 1611, the difficult monetary conditions associated with copper coinage and perhaps, in more general terms, with an expansion of total indebtedness in France.

In the first period gold predominated. Silver coins made their appearance on a small scale with the famous testons of 1514, then more importantly after 1521. Silver billon, the only silver issued until 1514, had a larger part to play in the 1540s.

The second period represents the phase dominated by silver coinage: silver billon almost disappeared, except in the 1570s, during a recession in the total value coined, and later in the 1590s, during the disturbances of the League. For the latter period illegal coinage has not been included in these calculations. Copper represented a small proportion of total coinage. Gold, it should be noted, assumed a more important place in the 1560s.

In the third period the structures associated with the silver phase gradually disappeared. After 1626 the increasing proportions of gold coin coincided with a fall in the exchange rates of the French livre abroad. The readjustment of gold prices was confirmed by the edict of 1636. Silver made a recovery after 1642. During the 1650s, 1660s, and 1670s just under two-thirds of the coinage, on the average, was in silver. The fluctuations in the coinage of gold and silver were perhaps not unlike the decade of the 1540s. Finally, the increased importance of copper should be noted for the years 1611 to 1628; billon, in the coinage of pieces of four and two sols, became more significant in the years 1674–1677.

In the fourth period (1681–1725) the share of gold in the total coinage of France followed three main trends. The first began about 1680. The share of gold showed a tendency to rise; by the last two decades of the century it occupied almost three-quarters of the total coinage. At the turn of the century, however, there were signs of impending change, and the reversal was sharp in 1703. Then the share of gold fell abruptly: by 1708 it had dropped to 7.3 percent of the total coinage in France. A third phase opened in 1709. The rising share of gold in the coinage continued through the years of John Law until the end of the series in 1725. This revival probably played a part in underwriting the great, successful stabilization of 1726.

This commentary on the total annual coinage in France, however, leads the discussion back to the point of departure. The data represent increases or renewals of the total stock of money. The basic question remains: what relationship do these increases and renewals have in the total monetary supply in France?

Certainly, the problem of the monetary circulation of France is not simple; at the present moment it is unlikely that a precise estimate can be made. From the discussion in this book it is apparent that the money stock was susceptible to increases and losses imposed by the international economy. First of all, the changes in the supply of money in France were part of the total increments in Europe fed by the stream of bullion passing through Spain from the New World and shared by the different economies. The capacity of governments to expand the total supply of money was very limited. The stocks of precious metals in the early sixteenth century were perhaps larger than often thought,[1] but they were low compared to those in the nineteenth century. Consequently, small bullion flows could assume some importance, for their marginal efficiency was higher. Since foreign subsidies and booty must be considered to have been of minor importance for France, the increases in its bullion stocks were accomplished largely through the mechanism of trade and services.

On the other hand, some of the main losses from circulation in France — apart from direct export, for example, by the *Compagnie des Indes Orientales*[2] or even the random sinking of treasure ships, which never failed to capture the popular imagination — were in industrial uses and in wear and tear. The heavier items of manufactures in gold and silver generally fall into the category of hoarding, and so may be considered as near money.

The problem of wear and wastage in the coinage, on the other hand, remains critical. In the nineteenth century a 3 percent annual loss in some instances was considered a useful working measure for the factor of wear; others have proposed a 1 percent annual loss for gold and 8 percent for silver.[3] For India, before the First World War, Findlay Shirras estimated a figure in the region of 6 percent.[4] This is an anachronistic comparison but nevertheless cites, as an example, a predominantly agrarian economy with a high propensity to hoard gold and silver. In addition, the surreptitious clipping of coins was another important consideration in France, which, as we have seen, was subject to a depreciating money of account; the authorities complained about it, and the documents repeatedly record it. If these clipped coins remained in circulation, they were equivalent to a rough sort of debasement operated by the market. Often enough, as already shown, they were refused circulation and fed back to the mints for recoinage. Such differences were no doubt part of the income velocities of the different moneys, to which we shall return later, and the way they were valued in the market. Again in

---

[1] Fernand Braudel and Frank Spooner, "Prices in Europe from 1450 to 1750," in *The Cambridge Economic History of Europe,* IV, ed. E. E. Rich and C. H. Wilson (Cambridge, Eng., 1967).

[2] Frank Spooner, "La Normandie à l'époque des guerres civiles: Un Problème de l'économie internationale," *Report to the Congress of Anglo-French Historians* (Caen, 1957).

[3] Michael G. Mulhall, *The Dictionary of Statistics* (4th ed., London, 1889), s.v. "Precious metals."

[4] G. Findlay Shirras, *Indian Banking and Finance* (London, 1920), p. 479.

the case of India before the First World War, Shirras noted that new coins retained their maximum face value for about two or three years after issue and then began to fall to a discount.[5] In China in the mid-nineteenth century, certain types of silver dollars, traditionally acceptable as standard means of payment, were given a premium above their relative value to other similar, but less acceptable, coins.[6] Yet, even with these qualifications, the problem of quantifying the rate of wear presents considerable difficulties.

Although these long-term factors in the supply of money depended on the overall supply in Europe and on the performance of France within the context of this international economy, there were also fluctuations of a shorter duration, which were of no small importance. Studies for more recent periods tend to show that in the short run the volume of specie responded to the movement of the balance of foreign trade: coinage tended to increase as the balance became favorable and fall with an adverse balance. In preindustrial economies, however, the harvest was a central feature in such fluctuations. Some aspects of this phenomenon, in conjunction with the movement of exchange rates, have been discussed above. It had direct effects on the level of money supply, and this situation was only to be expected under free, or relatively free, convertibility of gold and silver. Internally, moreover, hoarding and dishoarding were important, and, no less than usury, rarely failed to play a significant part in the life of the agrarian community. Famines and epidemics, notably plague, were disasters which tended to break the habitual tendencies to hoard. Governmental impositions and extraordinary tax levies also exercised powerful pressures to dishoard. Finally there were the velocity of circulation and the different uses of money. During the two centuries of this study it is clear that the monetary system of France underwent these various changes.

In order to establish a general frame of reference, even though grossly approximate, I have attempted to compare estimates of the monetary change with estimates for the total "national income" of France and with total public revenue. The results are shown in Graph 31. Before I discuss these comparisons, some indication must be given of the way in which the series have been established.

First there is the "stock" of money, which is difficult to quantify from the coinage, especially when one remembers that in nineteenth-century Britain, contemporaries, including R. H. Inglis Palgrave, were uncertain about the exact size of the circulation of gold and produced estimates which varied considerably. For an open country such as France in the sixteenth and seventeenth centuries, the calculation is even more hazardous. The operations of the mints responded partly to additions to the circulation and partly to the recoinage of old, worn, or clipped coins.

[5] *Ibid.,* p. 163.
[6] For the premium on the carolus dollar, see Frank King, *Money and Monetary Policy in China, 1845–1895* (Cambridge, Mass., 1965), p. 86.

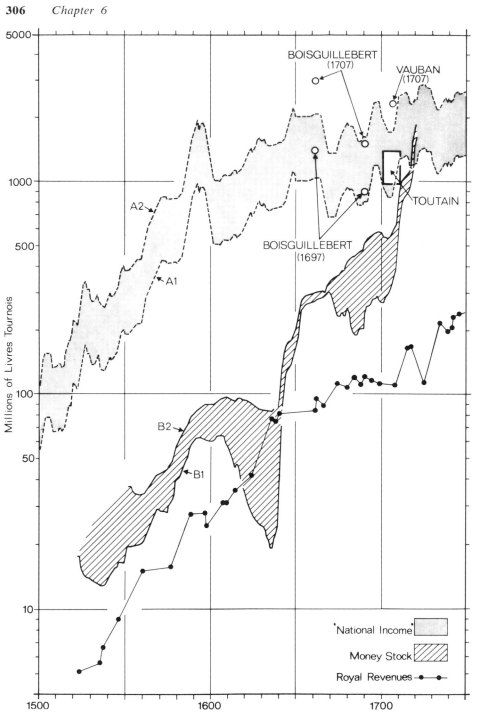

31. Estimates of "National Income" (A.1–A.2), Money Stock (B.1–B.2), and Royal Revenues in France, 1500–1750

The factor of wear has significance; a "law of diminishing stock" at a constant rate could be formulated to account for this, using an equation such as:

$$m = \frac{1}{1 + i^n}$$

where m is the money stock and i the annual rate of loss. Some of the implications of such changes can be seen from the fact that the stock would be reduced below half after the following intervals:

Annual rate of loss (percent)	Approximate interval in years
3	24
6	12
8	9

However, it is fairly clear from the evidence that a coin went to the melting pot long before it had been reduced by half; in consequence, it is probable that the volume of coinage had a higher ratio to the total metallic money stock than is often supposed.

With the purpose of examining these problems further and of establishing orders of magnitude, I began a series of tests for correlations of prices and coinage using thirty-, forty-, fifty-, and sixty-year moving averages of total coinage (see Table 10). The resulting series, using the thirty- and sixty-year intervals, are, in effect, end-positioned moving averages and have been included in Graph 31 to provide a "surface." The assumption here is that the metallic money stock would be renewed by the coinage over, in the first case, thirty years (B1) and, in the second case, sixty years (B2). The cumulative averages would represent a combination of factors, including the total metallic money stock, the rate of new additions, the rate of turnover (that is, the replacement of French coin or the conversion of foreign coin into French coin), and the rate of wear and loss. In the case of the last, the frequency of use of coins would have been one contributing factor, and it will be readily appreciated that this frequency of use could also have been closely associated with, in more technical terms, the velocity of circulation.

The two series give estimates rising, respectively, from 25,000,000 to 30,-000,000 livres in 1555, to 60,000,000 to 89,000,000 in 1600, to 167,000,000 to 201,000,000 in 1650, and to 271,000,000 to 573,000,000 in 1700. At the end of the seventeenth and in the early eighteenth centuries, they can be compared with the estimates which contemporaries made of the metallic stock of money in France. Writing in the mid-eighteenth century, François Véron de Forbonnais suggested a figure of 500,000,000 livres for the money stock in 1683, on the death of Colbert. The thirty-year and sixty-year cumulative series give 211,000,000 and 447,000,000 livres, respectively. Further contemporary estimates were made about the time of the death of Louis XIV (1715) and

Table 10. Coefficients of Correlation between Prices and Coinage by Phases

Price series	Moving average of total coinage	1522–1680	1522–1550	1551–1610	1611–1680
Paris wheat (harvest years)	30-year	0.6885	0.1337	0.7429	0.2867
Paris wheat (calendar years)	30-year	0.6933	0.4693	0.7407	0.2892
Paris rye (harvest years)	30-year	0.6330	0.0778	0.6438	0.2051
Grenoble wheat (calendar years)	30-year	0.7403	0.9168	0.8884	0.4203
Paris wheat (11-year moving average)	30-year	0.6576	0.0213	0.777	0.2107

Price series	Moving average of total coinage	1532–1680	1532–1550	1551–1610	1611–1680
Paris wheat (harvest years)	40-year	0.6821	−0.0440	0.7182	0.2296
Paris wheat (calendar years)	40-year	0.6812	0.1302	0.7152	0.2290
Paris rye (harvest years)	40-year	0.6145	−0.1294	0.6150	0.1526
Grenoble wheat (calendar years)	40-year	0.6409	0.3998	0.7646	0.1250
Paris wheat (11-year moving average)	40-year	0.7436	0.3978	0.8630	0.3370

Price series	Moving average of total coinage	1542–1680	1542–1550	1551–1610	1611–1680
Paris wheat (harvest years)	50-year	0.6699	−0.2626	0.7219	0.2510
Paris wheat (calendar years)	50-year	0.6684	−0.2587	0.7210	0.2554
Paris rye (harvest years)	50-year	0.5826	−0.1824	0.6202	0.1738
Grenoble wheat (calendar years)	50-year	0.6198	−0.2343	0.7626	0.1397
Paris wheat (11-year moving average)	50-year	0.7499	−0.8527	0.8642	0.3641

Table 10 (*continued*)

Price series	Moving average of total coinage	1552–1680	1552–1610	1611–1680
Paris wheat (harvest years)	60-year	0.6139	0.6884	0.2643
Paris wheat (calendar years)	60-year	0.6114	0.6823	0.2707
Paris rye (harvest years)	60-year	0.5109	0.5882	0.1830
Grenoble wheat (calendar years)	60-year	0.5700	0.7287	0.1650
Paris wheat (11-year moving average)	60-year	0.7167	0.8250	0.3924

the founding of the Banque Générale (1716). John Law himself, in the *Restablissement du Commerce,* proposed 714,285,714 livres; other estimates almost double this figure to 1,200,000,000 livres. Véron de Forbonnais arrived at a total of 1,000,000,000 livres. The last figure was also proposed by Adolphe Vuitry and, after discussion, was accepted by Earl J. Hamilton in calculating the currency expansion under Law's system.[7] The thirty-year and sixty-year cumulative series for 1716 give 949,000,000 and 1,144,000,000 livres, respectively. Although there can be no certainty about the accuracy of all these calculations, there is, nevertheless, an interesting measure of concordance with the "surface" between the thirty-year and the sixty-year series proposed here. Taken as a whole for the sixteenth and seventeenth centuries, the series of cumulative coinage offer points of comparison with the trends in development of "total incomes" and "public revenues."

[7] John Law, "Restablissement du commerce, Septembre 1715," in *Œuvres complètes,* ed. Paul Harsin (3 vols., Paris, 1934), III, pp. 67–259; Adolphe Vuitry, *Le Désordre des finances et les excès de la spéculation à la fin du règne de Louis XIV et au commencement du règne de Louis XV* (Paris, 1885); Earl J. Hamilton, "Prices and Wages at Paris under John Law's System," *Quarterly Journal of Economics,* Ll (1936–1937), p. 59; François Véron de Forbonnais, *Recherches et considérations sur les finances de la France depuis l'année 1595 jusqu'à l'année 1721* (2 vols., Basle, 1758), I, p. 297; II, pp. 330, 604. Ambroise Marie Arnould, in *De la balance du commerce et des relations commerciales extérieures de la France, dans toutes les parties du globe, particulièrement à la fin du règne de Louis XIV et au moment de la Révolution* (2 vols., Paris, 1791), II, p. 205, proposed a declining stock of money:

Year	Millions of livres tournois
1683	500
1693	548
1697	489
1715	474

In this, his conclusions are similar to those of Pierre le Pesant, sieur de Boisguillebert, who estimated a falling national income during the closing years of the reign of Louis XIV; see n. 23, below.

Second, I shall consider "income." Real per capita income during these two centuries probably changed only within restricted limits. It should be noted that there is evidence of relative changes. A vast literature exists on the question of real wage rates, which Charles Verlinden in the case of Belgium and E. H. Phelps Brown and Sheila Hopkins in the case of England have admirably reviewed.[8] The paradox in these studies — falling real wage rates in the expansion of the sixteenth century and rising real wage rates in the price recession of the seventeenth century — has not yet cleared up the other question, no less important, of the number of days worked and the level of annual employment.

The estimates of "national income" given here are, in effect, based on minimum budgets calculated in current prices. Although the estimates are highly approximate, they have some interest. The inquiry starts from the basis of a minimum average personal budget, about which, it may be said at the outset, there is little information. Is it possible to approach the problem by way of the minimum levels of subsistence? Assuming that the population of France was relatively "young," with high birth and high mortality rates — typical of many preindustrial societies — then a low daily calory consumption for a temperate climate would have been (at the subsistence level) on an average of 2,500 calories for the whole population.[9] A study of diets shows that in low-income brackets, the food intake was largely composed of farinaceous foods and drink. Ernest Labrousse has observed, in the case of France, that the prices of the main agricultural products, wheat and wine, were the chief components in the flow of incomes.[10] Wine in France, where large areas were devoted to wine growing, was volume for volume, roughly equal in price to wheat, but its caloric value was less than one-fifth.[11] Studies also show that wheat was by no means the staple diet of the low-income groups; they were obliged to rely on rye (roughly at two-thirds the cost of wheat), maslin, maize, various mixtures of grains, chestnuts, and other cheaper substitutes.[12] On the other hand, budgets surviving for people in better material circum-

---

[8] Charles Verlinden, Jan Craeybeckx, and E. Scholliers, "Mouvements des prix et des salaires en Belgique au XVIe siècle," *Annales: Économies, Sociétés, Civilisations,* [hereafter cited as *Annales*] (1955); E. H. Phelps Brown and Sheila V. Hopkins, "Seven Centuries of Building Wages," *Economica,* XXII (1955), "Seven Centuries of the Prices of Consumables, Compared with Builders' Wage-rates," *ibid.,* XXIII (1956), "Wage-rates and Prices: Evidence of Population Pressure in the Sixteenth Century," *ibid.,* XXIV (1957), "Builders' Wage-rates, Prices and Population: Some Further Evidence," *ibid.,* XXVI (1959), "Seven Centuries of Wages and Prices: Some Earlier Estimates," *ibid.,* XXVIII (1961).

[9] "Calorie Requirements," in *Report of the Second Committee of Calorie Requirements* (Rome, 1957).

[10] C.-Ernest Labrousse, *La Crise de l'économie française à la fin de l'ancien régime et au début de la Révolution* (Paris, 1944), especially p. xxxv.

[11] Braudel and Spooner," Prices in Europe from 1450 to 1750."

[12] In Udine, mixtures of wheat and rye with inferior grains appeared on the market from the 1660s. Maize was quoted officially from 1621.

stances often show a high calory intake.[13] By averaging out the cost of drink, the average expenditures for food (or implied expenditures in what was apparently a quasi-subsistence economy as far as food was concerned), the low grade and the more protective items of diet, the total expenditures may have been approaching the equivalent of a total calory intake in terms of wheat (taken at 334 calories to the 100 grams).[14] This, of course, omits the cost of preparation and distribution, which as John U. Nef has observed,[15] were not subject to the same degree of inflation as grainstuffs themselves. On the basis then of a quantity of wheat equivalent to 2,500 calories, a further computation of the value of this quantity can be made using averages from the best "central" series of wheat prices in France, those of Paris.[16] It goes without saying that over the long run the market prices in the capital probably were not the same as those in the provinces, and the differences were exceptional during the troubles of the League in the 1590s and during the Fronde. In addition, recent estimates have proposed that four-fifths of the personal expenditures were for food.[17] In more recent times, in "undeveloped" economies, in China, for example, this proportion does not appear unreasonable.[18] The value of the estimated annual food expenditures thus has been increased by a quarter to bring the yearly average budget to an equivalent of about 5⅓ (5.374) hectoliters of wheat.[19] The purpose here, in these very approximate estimates, is to attempt to establish a working minimum total income.

The next factor in estimating these total budgets is inevitably the size of the population, which is a very difficult problem indeed. Although it is relatively easy to survey the territory of France, little is known about the total number of its inhabitants.[20] There seems to be good reason to infer that the development of this population of France was similar to the general development in Europe: growth in the sixteenth century, pause and in some places recession in the second quarter and mid-seventeenth century, and probably

[13] Frank Spooner, "Régimes alimentaires d'autrefois: Proportions et calculs en calories," *Annales,* XVI (1961), pp. 568–574, and "Régimes alimentaires d'autrefois: Deux nouveaux cas espagnols," *ibid.,* XVII (1962), pp. 93–94.

[14] Charlotte Chatfield, *Food Composition Tables* (Rome, 1954).

[15] John U. Nef, "Prices and Industrial Capitalism in France and England, 1540–1640," *Economic History Review,* VII (1937).

[16] A modified eleven-year moving average of wheat prices in Paris has been used. In each set of eleven terms, the three maximums and three minimums have been discarded and an average taken of the five central terms.

[17] Phelps Brown and Hopkins, "Seven Centuries of the Prices of Consumables," p. 297, and subsequent articles in these studies; see n. 8, above.

[18] For this information, I am indebted to conversations with Peter Schran at Yale University.

[19] It should be stressed that this calculation has been made in terms of a variable value of wheat equivalent to the actual expenditure which could have been made on various grains and commodities.

[20] Roland Mousnier, "Études sur la population de la France au XVIIe siècle," *Le XVIIe siècle,* IV (1952); P. Gonnard, *Histoire des doctrines de la population* (Paris, 1923); Joseph J. Spengler, *Les doctrines françaises de Budé à Condorcet* (Paris, 1954).

gradual recovery by the closing decades of the seventeenth century. If it is assumed that the late eighteenth and early nineteenth centuries experienced a slight acceleration in the population increase, it is possible to establish an exponential curve to satisfy these requirements. This would infer a population of about 14,000,000 in 1450, 14,500,000 in 1500, 16,000,000 in 1600, 19,-000,000 in 1700 and 22,000,000 in 1750. These figures are slightly different from recent reappraisals of this difficult problem, but they offer the advantage of a measure of continuity for the estimates envisaged. J-C. Toutain has recently proposed a figure of 19,000,000 to 19,500,000 for 1700 and 21,500,-000 to 22,000,000 for 1755. Jean Marczewski, accepting France in this period as having a territory of 501,000 square kilometers, proposed figures of 20,000,000 for 1700 and 21,700,000 for 1750–1755. J. L. E. Bourgeois-Pichat has, in turn, suggested a population of 25,612,000 for 1776. It should be noted in passing that a report of 1777, which does not necessarily demand confidence, indicated that France had a population of 24,000,000, which by chance coincides with the line of the curve used in Graph 31.[21] Although there are significant variations among these different estimates, the important consideration in the present study is to retain the rate of growth. In the final assessment, the estimates must, of necessity, converge in the region of the census figures of 1801.

For the purpose of the present inquiry, the stagnation or slight recession which has been suggested for France by some authors has not been included, since there were some compensations in new territories acquired. These population estimates combined with the series of budgets are given as "income" in the series (A) of Graph 31. The curve rises from about 150,000,000 livres tournois in the second quarter of the sixteenth century to 1,000,000,000 livres at the beginning of the third quarter of the seventeenth century and falls to about 900,000,000 livres at the end of the century. The exceptional values in the 1590s at the time of the League have been adjusted.

These estimates, it must be emphasized, are very approximate. They take little account of the social differences which existed under the *ancien régime*. They could, within the scope of possibility, be increased by a factor of two or three.[22] Bearing this in mind and with the purpose of giving a possible range of estimates, I have smoothed the curve (A) in Graph 31 to give the curve (A.1). This has then been doubled to give (A.2). The surface between these two curves has been shaded on the graph; this offers a surface of com-

---

[21] J.-C. Toutain, "La population de la France de 1700 à 1959," *Cahiers de l'Institut de Science Économique Appliquée,* Suppl. No. 133 (Jan. 1963); Jean Marczewski, "Resultats provisoires d'une étude sur la croissance de l'économie française 1700–1958," typescript, Paris, 1959; J. L. E. Bourgeois-Pichat, "Évolution de la population française depuis le XVIIIe siècle," *Population* (No. 4, 1951). The report of 1777, in Archives Nationales [hereafter cited as A.N.] Affaires Étrangères, Mémoires et Documents, France 153, f° 13, gives an estimate of the population of France by provinces and parishes. The total came to a figure of 22,189,100 inhabitants, but the report went on to state "it is claimed that at present it can well be 24 millions."

[22] For this, I am grateful for the advice of Simon Kuznets.

parison against which the estimates of the national income of France, made both by contemporaries and in more recent studies, can be made. Boisguillebert in his *Détail de la France* (1697)[23] proposed a figure of 1,400,000,000 livres for 1661 and 900,000,000 livres for 1690, the decline being part of the price structures of the period. These fall within the range between the two series A.1 and A.2. Ten years later he revised these estimates to 3,000,000,-000 and 1,500,000,000 livres, respectively; the first falls outside, the second inside the surface. It should be noted in passing that Sir William Petty estimated the annual per capita income in England at £7.[24] If that of France were of the same order, then the figure of 1,500,000,000 would again be attained. Marshal Vauban in his *Project d'une dixme royale*,[25] according to Charles Dutot, proposed for 1707 a figure of 2,336,000,000 livres, which is 20 percent outside the upper limit of the range of the area A.1 to A.2. Dutot himself proposed again to raise this estimate to 2,416,000,000 livres.

In the same context can be set the estimates of J.-C. Toutain of the total agricultural product of France during the eighteenth century. He gives the following upper and lower estimates within which the total product should fall:

Period	Total agricultural product in millions of livres tournois
1701–1710	964–1,406
1751–1760	1,212–1,542

The first set of figures appears in Graph 31 in the form of a rectangle, giving the limits of both the decade and the product.[26]

For the gross public revenues more information is available. The evolution of the fiscal system depended on the authority of the monarchy. The government of Francis I and Henry II, the civil disorders during the civil wars and at the time of the League, and the great Bourbon restoration of the seventeenth century had varying effects. The collection of taxes and the multifarious expenditures made large claims on the monetary capacity of the country. It is often thought that political disturbance against the monarchy was a direct symptom of its fiscal weakness. A closer examination of the revenues of the French crown (see Graph 31) soon puts this in some perspective.[27] In 1523

---

[23] Pierre le Pesant, sieur de Boisguillebert, *Détail de la France sous le règne de Louis XIV* (n.p., 1697), and *Supplément au détail de la France* (n.p., 1707).

[24] Sir William Petty, *Political Arithmetic* (London, 1690), in *The Economic Writings of Sir William Petty,* ed. C. H. Hull (2 vols., Cambridge, Eng., 1899), I, pp. 310–311; see also Gregory King, *Natural and Political Observations and Conclusions upon the State and Condition of England* (London, 1696); and John Locke, *Some Considerations of the Lowering of the Interest and Raising the Value of Money* (London, 1692).

[25] Sébastien Le Prestre, maréchal de Vauban, *Project d'une dixme royale* (n.p., 1707–1708), ed. Émile Coornaert (Paris, 1933).

[26] J.-C. Toutain, "Le produit de l'agriculture française de 1700 à 1958," *Cahiers de l'Institut de Science Économique Appliquée,* No. 115 (July 1961), Table 63, p. 202.

[27] The estimates are taken from Jean-Jules Clamageran, *Histoire de l'impôt en France* (3 vols., Paris, 1867–1876).

the Venetian ambassador asserted that the gross revenue of Francis I was 5,165,000 livres tournois; in 1607 Henry IV claimed 31,437,671 livres from his subjects; in 1639 and in 1690 the returns showed, respectively, 82,155,000 and 121,931,000 livres. A report of 1777 proposed even higher estimates for dates close to the last two years.[28]

This indeed was remarkable. From the beginning of the reign of Francis I to the death of Louis XIII the long-term rate of increase in gross revenue was more or less constant; this has no small importance since during the period of high prices in France in the second half of the sixteenth century Nicolas Froumenteau asserted in 1581 that the royal revenues had fallen in real terms. However, the upward movement continued during the fall in prices of the early seventeenth century and especially under Richelieu. It seems that there was a fiscal restoration of the French monarchy. The centralizing successes of Richelieu brought considerable gains, although it is not yet clear whether they were new exactions or merely increases in the share of public revenue by a monarchy triumphing over feudal nobles and taking over revenues. After the death of Richelieu, indeed after the crisis of 1640, a new, slower trend emerged. Was there in France, as perhaps in many other states of Europe, a growing resistance to governmental exactions? The fiscal aspects of the Fronde must be considered in this context, along with the bad harvests of the late 1640s and the flows of inferior money already observed. However, there were means of escape from this check to the growth of public revenues: the greater efficiency of Colbert and his reforms of the tax and fiscal structures of France; and, almost *pari passu,* the expedients of the later Bourbons to sell offices, acquire debts, and mortgage future revenues. More detailed studies will no doubt clarify these important considerations in the supply of money.

What emerges from the comparison of these three series of money stock, incomes, and public revenue? If the total income series is taken as the basis of comparison, the changes in proportion to the other two series — coinage and public revenue — during the sixteenth century were not large. This takes into account the exceptional price level during the League. In the seventeenth century, however, noticeable changes took place. While the income series rose at a slower rate, the cumulative coinage declined, but the public revenue, at least until 1640, expanded at the fastest rate of all. After this date the income series tended to fall from the mid-century. Cumulative coinage in-

[28] The report of 1777 (A.N. Affaires Étrangères, Mémoires et Documents, France 153, f° 121vo) gives the following estimates of the revenues of the state:

Year	Livres tournois
1640	115,179,000
1702	191,867,791
1722	214,867,791
1739	242,747,417
1746	279,279,912
1750	250,367,206

creased spectacularly; public revenue increased but at a much slower rate compared with the period before 1640.

During the whole period the proportions changed appreciably. Public revenue ran at about 5 percent of the income series during the sixteenth century, but reached over 10 percent in the late 1630s and about 15 percent in the 1680s. In the early seventeenth century cumulative coinage fell in proportion (severely, in the instance of the thirty-year series), but, after the reforms and recoinage of the 1640s, the coinage accumulated to reach about a third or more of the income series and apparently resumed the trend of the sixteenth century. Did this imply a real increase in the proportion of cumulative money, or did it merely indicate that the total income series heavily underestimated the reality? Ferdinando Galiani in his *Della Moneta* (1751) calculated that the supply of money in Naples was one-eighth of the national income.[29] If the series of cumulative coinage in France were close to the reality of money in circulation, then the national income of France would approach the figure of 2,333,000,000 livres proposed by Vauban. In this context, the huge volume of coinage at the time of John Law must be regarded as exceptional.

In general, it is possible to suppose that, under these circumstances, the effect of the bullion from the New World over two centuries increased the proportion of money to income in France. It is clear that there were important changes from the late fifteenth to the turn of the seventeenth century. Although the speeds of the diffusion of information and of movement generally in France did not greatly alter, nevertheless there were improvements in communications. The building of roads and the attempts to liberate the internal trade by reforms of tolls and dues were signs that the material life of France was undergoing change, even though slowly. It is reasonable to suppose that, by the end of the seventeenth century, a larger part of the French economy came within the definition of a market system, which implied an increased demand for money, but about this, much more information is required before conclusions can be drawn beyond doubt.

Lastly, to return to the earlier remarks, what more can be said about the two dominant factors in the supply of money — the export sector and governmental finance? The former was by no means as simple as it at first appears. France under the *ancien régime* was above all an agrarian economy. In some respects, it had disadvantages since the economies which found fortune after the collapse of the bullion economy of the sixteenth century were notably Holland and Britain, and they had highly developed commercial sectors. Yet France also had latent strengths. The export commodities came notably from the agricultural sector, as contemporary writers such as Jean Bodin, Barthélemy de Laffemas, and Antoine de Monchrétien, among others, constantly reminded their audience: wheat and wine formed the basis of French wealth. The rich producing areas which developed exports were within access to the

---

[29] Ferdinando Galiani, *Della Moneta* (Naples, 1751), ed. Fausto Nicolini (Bari, 1915), pp. 275–276.

cheap transport of rivers and the sea, such as the grainlands of Provence and Brittany and the vineyards of Languedoc and the Bordelais. The expanding needs for food in the international economy of the sixteenth century and the increasing differentials in favor of food prices and especially grain prices offered advantageous conditions for the grain and wine producers of France. François Garrault, writing in 1578, noted the relatively recent interest of the Portuguese, Spaniards, and Flemings in the wheat of Brittany.[30] There, in the 1580s, as already observed above, the arrival of fleets carrying bullion became an important feature. After the 1590s, however, Dutch trade forged ahead. Complaints came from maritime towns, especially in Brittany, of heavy competition in the grain-exporting sectors. This competition combined with a decline in the imports of bullion from the New World and may have accounted for the drastic slump in the specie available for coinage. During the Twelve Years' Truce and the beginning of the Thirty Years' War, at least, this is one possible explanation.

The second factor concerning monetary circulation was the dominant role of the state. In the sixteenth century the gross public revenues ran at between one-third and one-half of the series of cumulative coinage; they returned more or less to these proportions in the second half of the seventeenth century. In the first four decades of the seventeenth century the cumulative coinage fell off, but governmental levies continued to rise. This concerted movement in opposite directions coincided with the pressure to use "substitute" moneys: copper billon and credit instruments. Efforts to establish public banks to facilitate the management of public finance and indebtedness in the early seventeenth century may indeed tend to show that the experience in France was symptomatic of conditions generally in Europe. More ample empirical data will again be required before these propositions can firmly be maintained. At present, according to the estimates above, the role of government in money supply, through its taxation and institutions, was apparently of prime importance. If a rate of renewal of the coinage higher than the thirty-year interval proved to be the case, then the dominant position of the public sector could only have been greater.

These aggregate problems fall outside the possibility of precise measurement, partly because the necessary empirical data are not yet available and partly because the inquiry once more faces the diversities inherent in France. The hierarchy of economic regions found unity in the administration of the state, but the basic fragility remained, both because of shifts and pressures on the domestic scene and the grandiose destiny of Spain abroad.

The particular relationship between the bullion movements of France and those of Spain, the dominant economy, the great imperial complex not only of the sixteenth but also part of the seventeenth century, remains to be seen. Spain in time became something of a "sick man" in Europe, overreaching in its efforts to control other powers, even before the long reign of Philip IV

[30] François Garrault, *Paradoxe sur le faict des monnoyes* (Paris, 1578).

(1621–1665). On the assumption of the falling marginal efficiency of bullion in international trade, a question remains for consideration: what was France's share in this activity?

In the first place, the figures published by Earl J. Hamilton indicate that there was a significant gap at the turn of the century between the movements of coinage in France and the imports of bullion into Seville. These figures show that the imports peaked in the decade of 1590–1600. Using the evidence of the total volume of the transatlantic shipping to and from Seville,[31] Huguette and Pierre Chaunu prefer to place the turning point a decade later. The differences in the case of Seville are not the important point at issue here. In France, the overall movement of coinage, taking account of the difficulties of the League, culminated in the 1580s and was prolonged until 1587–1588. The movement of exchange rates in the fairs of Lyons also underlined the significance of the year 1589 in the general history of France. In effect, there was a precocious decline in mint activity in France; the bullion entering Spain was apparently finding other outlets. It has long been assumed that the aging Philip II engaged in the bitter struggle to claim the French crown and lavished the treasure of the New World on France to rebuff the upstart Henry of Navarre, all in order to acquire the throne for his favorite daughter, Isabel Clara Eugenia. But the documents in the archives of Simancas show the geography of payments of the Spanish monarchy abroad, and the findings of Alvaro Castillo confirm that the Spanish subsidies were in reality on a much smaller scale than is customarily assumed (see Map 8).[32] A slight revival can be observed in the coinage of France between 1603 and 1605; this probably resulted from the monetary reform of 1602, more favorable terms of trade, and the inflow of specie driven from the peninsula after the excessive Spanish issues of copper vellon.

In the decade after 1588 the lag between the movement of coinage in France and the imports of bullion into Seville poses a problem of some importance. The economic explanation (by no means the only one valid in the discussion) goes beyond purely quantitative considerations. Actually attention must be given to dynamic factors. The geography of the monetary and economic development of Europe occupies a place of prime importance.

I did not set this study in the context of the international economy to avoid the obvious difficulties of reaching a convincing solution. There are basic difficulties such as population growth and its distribution and the available technology, in brief, the level of knowledge and its application. In addition to these basic forces, the monetary factor must be included in the analysis of the particular form which economic expansion assumed in the sixteenth century and of how it fared in the seventeenth. In this, the imports of bullion into

---

[31] Huguette and Pierre Chaunu, *Séville et l'Atlantique* (8 vols., Paris, 1955–1959).

[32] I appreciate having had discussions with Alvaro Castillo, whose research has greatly clarified the problems of the finances of the Spanish monarchy in the sixteenth and seventeenth centuries.

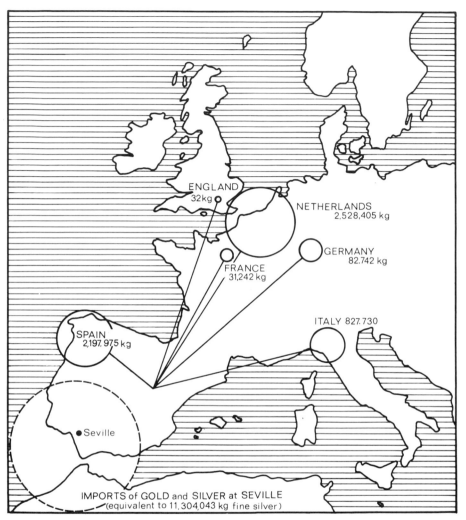

ENGLAND
32 kg

NETHERLANDS
2,528,405 kg

GERMANY
82.742 kg

FRANCE
31,242 kg

ITALY 827.730

SPAIN
2,197,975 kg

• Seville

IMPORTS of GOLD and SILVER at SEVILLE
(equivalent to 11,304,043 kg fine silver)

8. Payments of Spanish Asientos, 1580–1626, in Kilograms of Fine Silver (Reference: A. Castillo. The imports of gold and silver at Seville have been included for reference.)

Seville require close attention. Their distribution from Spain was partly a function of the political complex of the Spanish Empire and the subsidies through which the Spanish monarchy persistently strove to impose its authority. The diffusion of bullion was also in much larger measure a function of the international economy. In the analysis of the mechanism of such transfers of bullion, a fruitful line of inquiry into the comparative advantages and commercial structures would be to pursue the method proposed by Albert Hirschman and Michael Michaely. Frédéric Mauro has also investigated the interesting possibility of establishing a model for European overseas expansion.[33] Circulation of bullion followed in large measure the directions of Spanish trade, including that with its Empire in the New World and in the Pacific. For the economies dependent on Spain, export sectors were one of the means by which bullion could be acquired; the bullion then spread throughout Europe and the world. Trade to the Baltic, the Levant, and the Far East showed that debtor balances were often settled in bullion. As has already been noted, its "marginal efficiency" became a key factor in international trade. The distribution from Seville constituted a significant factor in the whole structure of relative costs and price differentials, which played their part in covering high transport costs and in easing settlements. Europe was obliged to absorb relatively large imports of bullion for its economic activity. These imports of bullion were commodities, products of investment and industrial activity, and monetary raw materials for coinage in the different economies.

What was France's place in the network of Spanish politics? It is likely that the documents will reveal that the payments were not massive, at least in Spanish currency; Alvaro Castillo has already confirmed much of this. The leaders of the League in France were bribed, it is true, but it is almost certain that foreign money did not flood the country for political purposes. The French fought among themselves, giving themselves up rather than selling out to the Spaniard. Graph 30 shows that from the end of the 1580s and more particularly from 1588 to 1589 France was short of silver from Spain. What explanation can be offered for this shortage?

Many theories, a priori, have been proposed: 1588 was, after all, the beginning of a short but violent crisis in Europe. A crisis of such proportions mortgaged the years to follow in the same way that the conquest of Portugal affected the distribution of Spanish payments. The development of the situation presented itself logically as a series of choices. The preference of Philip II for Portugal and the Atlantic Ocean in 1580 appears in the present state of our information as an event of some magnitude. It is reasonable to assume that France suffered a short-term setback in 1588, the effects of which were relatively severe. Because of a positive balance of trade, bullion flowed into France through its export sectors. The disruption of this activity through civil wars doubtless also provoked serious consequences.

All of the above is very possible. In the same way it can be supposed that the shift in Spain's interest toward the Atlantic resulted in additional expenditures in the regions associated with that ocean. Spain became involved in an open conflict on the high seas, which meant a much larger arena for hostilities. Because of this, the country found itself in a terrible war of attrition over

---

[33] Albert O. Hirschman, *The Strategy of Economic Development* (New Haven, Conn., 1958); Michael Michaely, "The Shares of Countries in World Trade," *Review of Economics and Statistics,* XLII (1960); Frédéric Mauro, "Towards an International Model: European Overseas Expansion between 1500 and 1800," *Economic History Review,* 2d Ser., XIV (1961).

long distances. Serious disadvantages resulted: wasted strength in sustaining communications, in shipbuilding, in transport networks, and in establishing ports of call, relay points, and reserves of victuals. At the same time, Spain was handing its fortune to its enemies, the predatory Dutch and English, the pirates of Protestant La Rochelle, and, indeed, the traders and chandlers from far and wide, with their cargoes of wheat, wood, sails, and tar. Did this distribution fall outside the waiting net of France, so strategically placed?

Such suggestions are plausible enough. They are not, however, the only ones allowed by the circumstances. And they do not, perhaps, go deep enough into the realities of monetary movements in an international context. A mathematical economist might be tempted to review the data of Hamilton drawn from the documents of Seville and explain the experience in France by a significant retardation in the distribution of bullion from Seville. This opens up a line of inquiry with its own implied risks: it offers the possibility of passing from the quantitative, static aspects of the problem to the more dynamic features.

The imports of bullion into Seville became significant after the mid-sixteenth century, when Spain began to take increasing control of its redistribution. For the various reasons already indicated, silver in particular was relayed from Seville; that area became a stage in a monetary network which spread its benefits into Europe and the world in varying degrees. If, however, the level of economic activity largely depended on an increasing stock of bullion under the monopoly of Spain, it can be inferred that the structures of the international economy had a propensity to converge, to return to scale, that, in order to maintain regional differences in price levels, the increases in bullion needed to follow an exponential curve. This would conform to a function of the type $y = ab^x$. Yet in actual fact this was not to be, as the simple calculation of first differences by ten-year periods of the imports of gold and silver shows (see Graph 32).

During the 1550s an equilibrium was established in the deliveries of gold and silver, but the rate of increase in silver imports rose in the decade 1561–1570 and was also significant in the boom period of the 1580s. In the decade 1591–1600, however, this rate declined, and it became negative with the first decade of the seventeenth century. As for gold, a fall in the rate of increase in the 1560s was followed by a rising trend, positive in 1581–1590 and culminating in 1591–1600. From that point, with the exception of 1641–1650, these first differences were negative.

The return to scale was a further sign that the silver inflation was diminishing. The crisis years of 1589–1593 represent an even more significant movement in the general circulation of bullion, in the position relative to gold, which silver had long maintained. If such a situation really prevailed, the crucial position of Seville is set in perspective, but this explanation must be related to the discussion of the particular conditions of France.

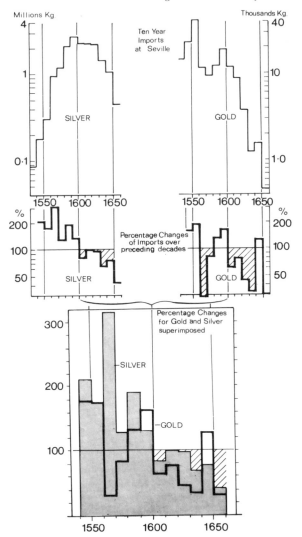

32. Differential Rates of Imports of Gold and Silver at Seville (Reference: E. J. Hamilton)

To be more precise, how did France react to bullion from Spain, sent via Seville? Undoubtedly this reflected an important aspect of the development of Spain and its empire and stressed the dominant position which the flow of silver conferred. There were three different periods of the silver phase in France: until 1575; from 1575 to 1588; and from 1589 to 1619–1620.

The severe crisis of 1575 opened a new era for France in the "strategy" of silver in Europe. Until then France had made efforts to check the gold disappearing in the direction of Spain. It was no mere chance that up to the crisis of 1575 the Spaniards regarded France as a source of supply for gold specie.

With the change to silver in the mid-sixteenth century, gold was probably drawn toward Spain, with France among the first to react to this movement. The subsequent issues of gold coinage from the mints in the 1560s acted as compensation.

The integration of France in the system of silver came during the years 1575–1588 — a great period of France, when its monetary system was adjusted to the flow of silver. France thus became part of the system of currency dominated by Spain. It is possible at this point, perhaps even after 1568–1569, that the frontier of adjustment between gold and silver currency zones passed further north in the direction of the Netherlands.

During the last phase (1589 to 1619–1620) there were increasing signs of slackening in the metallic inflation in France. In this period also Spain experienced a considerable alteration in its preeminence. Spain would have needed two or three times as much silver to sustain its acquired style of activity, but this could not be maintained. Its façade of greatness in the seventeenth century continued to deceive even astute observers, but the substance decayed.

With this change in the hierarchy of economic power in the sixteenth century, the differentials in levels and consequent activity became less pronounced. Gradually the earlier differences in Northern Europe slackened, in the sense that the silver deflation in Spain after 1600 probably was accompanied by continuing silver inflation, in the north and east, as the evidence for the cities of Poland demonstrates. The continued price rise in the countries in Northwestern Europe was also accompanied by monetary stability, which was, in itself, an indication of the way the nimble Dutch Republic was supplanting the magnificence of imperial Spain.

The reorganization in Eastern Europe, the outbreak of the Thirty Years' War, and the subsequent crisis of 1619–1620 also meant changes in the terms of trade and foreign exchanges. About 1607 Jacques Margeret had reported that in Russia "the alien merchants bring many silver reals and rixdollars there, on which they make profits." [34] This currency passed at the rate of 36 *denins*. A decade later Peer Petreieus noted their changed activity: "The aliens," he wrote, "willingly take goods against goods, and leave them the coins . . . having brought more money and *Reichsthaler* than goods, and Russian wares and goods repurchased, for that reason the currency in the land has greatly increased." [35] The growing inflation affected the terms of trade and foreign exchanges, in some places giving way to barter. In Moscow in 1619 the *rijksdaalder* quoted at 48 denins rose more than a third in less than a decade.[36] In Germany and Central Europe at the beginning of the ferocious Thirty Years' War, the *Kipper- und Wipperzeit* of the early 1620s was a brief phase of severe

[34] Jacques Margeret, *Estat de l'empire de Russie et grande duché de Moscovie* (Paris, 1607), pp. 44–45.

[35] Peer Petreiusu de Erlesunda, *Historien und Bericht von dem Grossfürstenthumb Muschkow* (Leipzig, 1620), p. 601.

[36] Stanislas de Chaudoir, *Aperçu sur les monnaies russes et sur les monnaies étrangères qui ont eu cours en Russie* (2 vols., St. Petersburg, 1836–1837), I, p. 69.

debasement and governmental manipulation of the currency.[37] In Poland the
ducat went for 60 grosz in 1601 and for 180 in the exceptional year 1622,
while the *taler* valued at 36–42 grosz in 1611 went for 120 grosz in 1622.[38] A
final view of these disturbances takes us to Danzig. On the Amsterdam exchange market, the rate of the *Vlaamsche* pound (or 6 guilders) in Danzig
rose from 106½ grosz in 1609 to 123½ in 1619, to 206 in December 1624,
and settled in 1628 at about 220.[39] There are few more striking examples than
the inflation in the Baltic and Eastern Europe, with the implied readjustment
in the terms of trade at the beginning of the Thirty Years' War. It was not the
last; Poland repeated the experience in the great devaluation of 1661–1663,
although on this occasion it was "Poland" rather than Danzig which bore the
brunt of the fall in exchange values. In brief, the expansion of the "sixteenth"
century tended to reach a peak. This crisis or turning point covered the first
half of the seventeenth century, commensurate with the long period which preceded it.[40] It was apparently no longer a question of a world economy: the
unity of a trading world, insofar as it had been achieved by the turn of the
century, was faced with disruption. The possibility of expanding credit, even
within restricted limits, and of using copper as a substitute coinage, influenced,
above all, the creation of national currencies. They did not offer the same geographical disparities in means of payment, so favorable to international trade,
which were brought about by the gold and silver from the New World. It became much more a question of national economies.

Perceptive historians have given considerable attention to the "empires" of
the sixteenth century. In the seventeenth century, national states took pride of
place; these states were of more modest proportions, but were under the strict
control of their rulers and directed to national objectives. They supervised
customs, mints, and minor monetary problems, and the results were much the
same: behind all the reorganizations, controls, or "destructurizations," the
leitmotiv of bullionist theories[41] in the early seventeenth century looked to conditions which were fast disappearing, pursuing a dream to recover, to revive the
earlier pressures of gold and silver. Mercantilism was the theme; Leviathan
called the tune.

At this point another question arises: what were these international mone-

---

[37] Moritz Elsas, *Umriss einer Geschichte der Preise und Löhne in Deutschland* (2 vols.,
Leiden, 1936–1940); Alfred Pribram, *Materialien zur Geschichte der Preise und Löhne
in Österreich* (Vienna, 1938).

[38] See, for example, Stanislas Hoszowski, *Les Prix à Lwow* (Paris, 1954), pp. 26–32.

[39] Nicolaus W. Posthumus, *Inquiry into the History of Prices in Holland* (2 vols.,
Leiden, 1946–1964), I, pp. 590–600.

[40] Frank C. Spooner, "The Economy of Europe, 1609–1650, in *The New Cambridge
Modern History*, IV, ed. J.P. Cooper (Cambridge, Eng., 1970).

[41] See, in particular, Charles Wilson, "Treasure and Trade Balances: The Mercantilist
Problem," *Economic History Review*, 2d Ser., II (1949), and "Treasure and Trade Bal-
ances: Further Evidence," *ibid.*, IV (1951); Eli Heckscher, "Multilateralism, Baltic
Trade and the Mercantilists," *ibid.*, III (1950).

tary structures? It is apparent that the situation was complicated by bimetallism, by the double problems of gold and silver. These two superior moneys were either in excess or were insufficient. And it is probable that the dominant economy must be considered in this context. From 1500 to 1550, when gold was relatively abundant, the masters of the silver mines of Central Europe held a controlling position. After the middle of the century, Augsburg, as already shown, clung to a fading glory. By this time, almost all the imports of silver and the majority of gold passed through the hands of Spain; only elsewhere did it rely on banking and financial operations, especially on the merchants of Genoa, to handle the wealth of the New World. Once again, this was a success story of a "fringe" state, endowed with drive and acumen. A little later, seemingly almost against the tide of events in the incoherent seventeenth century, the United Provinces carried off another triumph, drawing on the bullion of Spain, offering more adroit financial facilities, and using its intermediary position to serve the needs of the international economy. What more can be said? Later came the gold from Brazil under the control of the small but fortunate Portugal,[42] and, once more, as the fleets laden with gold sailed for Lisbon, the map of money and payments underwent further modification. This is not the place to review the history of the expansion of British power, linked openly since the Methuen Treaty (December 27, 1703) with its most ancient ally, Portugal. With the new phase in monetary movements, there is some reason to infer that the sequence of gold, silver, and inflation once more followed through the eighteenth century. For the moment, however, it is enough to note that the fluctuations of gold and silver constituted a large, indeed very large, part of the monetary history of the sixteenth and seventeenth centuries.

Behind the façades of state power, the complex movements of international trade flowed to the fortunes of the great commercial houses. Wealthy families, or, rather, dynasties, such as the Fuggers and Welsers, the Grimaldi and Spinola, were agents of economic expansion, with its concomitant demands on monetary resources. The preeminence of these families, it should be noted, was all too often a measure of the range of their investments and activities.

France responded on occasion to their needs and behests. Joined to the Spanish peninsula and quick to react to outside monetary pressures, France had all the natural diversities and complex structures necessary to play the role of a reservoir, to adjust to the needs of its more powerful neighbor, Spain. In a wider context, this helps perhaps to explain some of the French policies and attitudes toward precious metals and the interest of the Bourbons and later even of the two Napoleons with regard to Spain and the mines of the New World. It may be possible to speak at least for a time of a bullion "fixation" in France, which gave a particular character to mercantilist policies at the time of Richelieu and Colbert. The attachment for better or worse to the fortunes of Spain is yet another story.

[42] Frédéric Mauro, *Le Portugal et l'Atlantique au XVIIᵉ siècle, 1570–1670* (Paris, 1960).

The purpose here is to close with a few supplementary remarks on precious metals. Some of the problems were raised in Rome in 1955 at the International Congress of Historical Sciences.[43] It is clear that the supply of metallic currency was relatively inelastic, "rare," as contemporaries would have said. Every study emphasizes that crises were all the more disastrous for such conditions of metallic viscosity, in what were essentially the beginnings of credit systems. Chronic failures encouraged prudence in hoarding and the maintenance of large reserves. And, in an agrarian society, they favored the continued existence of the usurer.

The crises were of varying severity. If precious metals abounded, everything went off with relative ease. If circulation failed, the situation crumbled before unresponsive credit resources. This was the weakness of the bullion system of the mid-sixteenth and of the seventeenth centuries. An endemic hunger for gold, before the gold output of the late seventeenth century and above all of the rushes of the nineteenth century, held back the adoption of true mono-metallism based on gold. This was openly established in Britain after 1816 and accepted in Europe officially after the 1870s. In effect, only in the nineteenth century, with the extension of credit and the growth of bank deposits, did gold become king and for a time at least was apparently undisputed in a world of differential monetary systems.[44]

The constant mutual adjustment of gold and silver presented problems which, through the centuries, all too often reduced the effectiveness of bullion. The premium on silver in the gold phase and on gold in the silver phase implied endless difficulties and readjustments, giving opportunities for copper and credit to claim a larger role. Though copper was not raised to the level of a third precious metal, it played its part, largely during difficulties over the precious metals.

Money, it must be repeated, was not the only factor; there were much more important human considerations. The inhabitants of Europe and, indeed, of the world were either more or less numerous. Few will question the cumulative effects of population growth on the process of expansion in preindustrial economies. Labor, with its skills, constituted a major source of applied energy. It also represented the level of aggregate consumption. In turn, the deliveries of bullion to Europe, for many reasons, were outstripped by the demand for monetary means; hence the series of devaluations. The excess demand for bullion formed a basis for the dramatic crisis of 1589–1593 and the beginning of the breakup of the sixteenth century. In France the children of the prosperous 1580s could become the future disturbers of civil peace during the minority of Louis XIII. The upsurge in population was one of the major strengths in the expansion of the sixteenth century, while the "maturity," indeed the "crisis,"

[43] Fernand Braudel and Frank C. Spooner, "Les métaux monétaires et l'économie du XVIᵉ siècle," in *X Congresso Internazionale di Scienze Storiche, Rome,* ed. Aldo Ferrabino (8 vols., Florence, 1955–1957), IV, pp. 233–264.

[44] Michael M. Postan, "Recent Trends in the Accumulation of Capital," *Economic History Review,* VI (1935–1936).

of the early seventeenth century was also associated with a pause, if not a recession, in the growth of population in Europe.

At an even more profound level, the monetary factor was overshadowed by the significance of the level of knowledge and technology. The sixteenth century did not acquire the methods necessary to escape from the traditional framework of activity. The seventeenth century, both less fortunate and more fortunate, witnessed scientific advances which in the years ahead proved to be of revolutionary import. More knowledge about the natural world penetrated further into the uncertainties of life, to have their effect much later.

In sum, the material achievement of the sixteenth century ended in setback. For all its humanism, it still looked largely to the past for inspiration, absorbing the colors and glories of another age. There was something about it to compare with the Athens of Plato, with the Rome of Cicero and Seneca, with the Israel of the great apostles. It did not ultimately have the success enjoyed by the eighteenth century which burst through with humanism and endeavor. If a little more gold had been panned from the river sands or more silver taken from the lodes of Mexico and Peru, perhaps the story would have closed in a blaze of success. Yet history cannot allow such ifs. The reality was not so simple.

Appendixes and Index

Tables of the Main Series of Coins Issued in France, 1493–1726

These tables give a summary of the series of coins issued in France from 1493, together with the date of the introduction of the series, weight, fineness, and face value of the coins. The fineness of the gold coins is given in terms of fine gold, divided into 24 karats (k.). That of the silver coins is given in either fine silver or argent-le-roi (a.r.) at $\frac{23}{24}$ fine. Fine silver was divided into 12 deniers (d.), each denier being divided into 24 grains (g.).

The weights are given in terms of the marc of Paris (244.7529 grams); 1 marc = 8 onces = 192 deniers = 4,608 grains. The face values are given in livre tournois; 1 livre (L.) = 20 sols or sous (s.) = 240 deniers (d.).

Gold coins	Date of introduction	Fineness	Number of coins per marc	Face value at issue in sols and deniers
Ecu	(1488)	$23\frac{1}{8}$ k.	70	30 s. 3 d.
Ecu	1519 (May)	$22\frac{7}{8}$ k.	$71\frac{1}{2}$	40 s.
Ecu	1519 (July)	23 k.	$71\frac{1}{6}$	40 s.
Henri	1549	23 k.	67	50 s.
Ecu	1552	23 k.	$72\frac{1}{3}$	46 s.[a]
Ecu	1561	23 k.	$72\frac{1}{2}$	50 s.[b]
Louis	1640	22 k.	$36\frac{1}{4}$	200 s.
Lis	1655	$23\frac{1}{4}$ k.	$60\frac{1}{2}$	140 s.
Louis	1709	22 k.	30	400 s.
Louis	1716	22 k.	20	600 s.
Louis	1718	22 k.	25	720 s.
Quinzain	1719	24 k.	$65\frac{5}{11}$	300 s.[c]
Louis	1723	22 k.	$37\frac{1}{2}$	540 s.
Louis	1726 (January)	22 k.	30	400 s.

Silver coins	Date of introduction	Fineness	Number of coins per marc	Face value at issue
Teston	1514	11 d. 18 g. (a.r.)	$25\frac{1}{2}$	10 s.
Teston	1521	11 d. 6 g. (a.r.)	$25\frac{1}{2}$	10 s.
Franc	1575	10 d. (fine)	$17\frac{1}{4}$	20 s.
Quart d'écu	1577	11 d. (fine)	$25\frac{1}{5}$	15 s.
Ecu	1641	11 d. (fine)	$8\frac{11}{12}$	60 s.
Lis	1655	11 d. 12 g. (fine)	$30\frac{1}{2}$	20 s.
Ecu	1709	11 d. (fine)	8	100 s.
Ecu	1718	11 d. (fine)	10	120 s.
Livre de la Compagnie des Indes	1719	12 d. (fine)	$65\frac{5}{11}$	20 s.
Louis	1720 (March)	11 d. (fine)	30	60 s.
Ecu	1720 (September)	11 d. (fine)	10	180 s.
Ecu	1724	11 d. (fine)	$10\frac{3}{8}$	80 s.
Ecu	1726 (January)	11 d. (fine)	$8\frac{3}{10}$	100 s.

[a] Coined only in the Étuves, Paris.
[b] General coinage.
[c] In reality, it appears that no coins of this type were minted.

Silver billon	Date of introduction	Fineness		Number of coins per marc	Face value at issue
4 sous	1674	10 d.	(fine)	150	4 s.
30 deniers	1709	2 d. 12 g.	(fine)	100	2 s. 6 d.
Sols parisis	1550	4 d.	(a.r.)	82	1 s. 3 d.
"	1565	6 d. 18 g.	(a.r.)	150	1 s. 3 d.
"	1577	4 d.	(a.r.)	106	1 s. 3 d.
Sols (or douzains)	(1493)	4 d. 12 g.	(a.r.)	86	12 d.
"	1519 (May)	4 d. 6 g.	(a.r.)	$92\frac{1}{2}$	12 d.
"	1519 (July)	4 d. 6 g.	(a.r.)	92	12 d.
"	1540	4 d. 4 g.	(a.r.)	92	12 d.
"	1541	3 d. 16 g.	(a.r.)	$91\frac{1}{4}$	12 d.
"	1550	3 d. 12 g.	(a.r.)	94	12 d.
"	1550	3 d. 16 g.	(a.r.)	$93\frac{1}{2}$	12 d.
"	1551	3 d. 12 g.	(a.r.)	$93\frac{1}{2}$	12 d.
"	1572	3 d. 12 g.	(a.r.)	102	12 d.
"	1575	3 d.	(a.r.)	102	12 d.
"	1623	11 d.	(a.r.)	?	12 d.[d]
"	1640	1 d. 21 g.	(fine)	102	15 d.[e]
"	1692	2 d. 21 g.	(fine)	132	15 d.
Dixains	(1493)	4 d.	(a.r.)	$92\frac{1}{2}$	10 d.
"	1519	3 d. 18 g.	(a.r.)	98	10 d.
Liards	(1493)	3 d.	(a.r.)	234	3 d.
"	1541	2 d. 6 g.	(a.r.)	231	3 d.
"	1566	2 d. 6 g.	(a.r.)	272	3 d.
"	1572	2 d.	(a.r.)	256	3 d.[f]
"	1577	1 d. 12 g.	(a.r.)	244	3 d.
Doubles	(1493)	1 d. 12 g.	(a.r.)	186	2 d.
"	1519	1 d. 9 g.	(a.r.)	188	2 d.
"	1541	1 d. 6 g.	(a.r.)	196	2 d.
"	1572	1 d. 2 g.	(a.r.)	240	2 d.
Deniers	(1493)	1 d.	(a.r.)	252	1 d.
"	1519	21 g.	(a.r.)	250	1 d.
"	1541	18 g.	(a.r.)	252	1 d.
"	1551	18 g.	(a.r.)	306	1 d.
"	1566	18 g.	(a.r.)	352	1 d.
"	1572	16 g.	(a.r.)	336	1 d.

[d] Lettres patentes of May 2, 1623, by which the number of coins per marc was left to the discretion of the Cour des Monnaies; this detail has been omitted from the registers.

[e] Although technically these coins were sols parisis, the documents refer to them as sols douzains, and they have been included here as such.

[f] Lettres patentes of Oct. 17, 1571.

Copper coins	Date of introduction	Fineness	Number of coins per marc	Face value at issue
Deniers	1577	Pure copper	156	1 d.[g]
Doubles	1577	Pure copper	78	2 d.
Liards	1654	Pure copper	64	3 d.
Liards	1709	Pure copper	80	3 d.[h]

[g] The first issues of copper deniers and doubles were made in 1578.
[h] Coins of 6 deniers were also issued, weighing 40 to the marc.

Coinage by Zones in Each of the Four Phases (see Graph 22)

	1493–1550	(in percentages) 1551–1610	1611–1680	1681–1725	1493–1725
Zone 1	17.75	13.67	61.32	35.34	38.21
Zone 2	1.32	1.30	1.89	5.18	4.53
Zone 3	51.45	72.42	24.87	37.08	36.62
Zone 4	23.00	9.02	8.02	15.33	14.15
Zone 5	6.48	3.59	3.90	7.07	6.49
Total	100	100	100	100	100
Total in millions of livres tournois	33.2	96.0	427.3	2393.0	—

Tables of Total Coinage and Percentage of Gold Coined in France, 1493–1725 (see Graph 30A and 30B)

Year	Copper	Billon	Silver	Gold	Total	Percentage gold
1493	—	624,713	—	271,520	896,233	30.3
1494	—	810,411	—	1,869,058	2,679,469	69.8
1495	—	556,839	—	988,049	1,544,888	64.0
1496	—	339,621	—	719,643	1,059,264	67.9
1497	—	148,598	—	475,124	623,722	76.2
1498	—	150,050	—	371,179	521,229	71.2
1499	—	139,279	—	387,260	526,539	73.6
1500	—	142,779	—	446,871	589,650	75.8
1501	—	122,846	—	415,977	538,823	77.2
1502	—	124,022	—	318,664	442,686	72.0
1503	—	155,779	—	341,059	496,838	68.6
1504	—	157,114	—	351,394	508,508	69.1
1505	—	148,500	—	286,663	435,163	65.9
1506	—	83,488	—	371,279	454,767	81.6
1507	—	111,171	—	387,927	499,098	77.7
1508	—	56,005	—	169,166	225,171	75.1
1509	—	35,276	—	209,598	244,874	85.6
1510	—	20,066	—	222,377	242,443	91.7
1511	—	63,561	—	258,964	322,525	80.3
1512	—	56,984	—	262,059	319,043	82.1
1513	—	52,097	—	262,927	315,024	83.5
1514	—	53,673	80,723	262,784	397,180	66.2
1515	—	20,898	21,170	382,457	424,525	90.1
1516	—	5,684	48,423	176,868	230,975	76.5
1517	—	5,338	12,737	326,671	344,746	94.8
1518	—	4,006	—	310,713	314,719	98.7
1519	—	22,511	12,622	350,738	385,871	90.9
1520	—	12,046	—	416,177	428,223	97.2
1521	—	185,788	116,610	372,053	674,451	55.2

Year	Copper	Billon	Silver	Gold	Total	Percentage gold
1522	—	233,799	331,723	417,924	983,446	42.5
1523	—	297,414	276,520	478,645	1,052,579	45.4
1524	—	195,806	215,561	184,906	596,273	31.0
1525	—	156,105	222,479	229,051	607,635	37.7
1526	—	116,434	83,759	346,192	546,385	63.4
1527	—	112,458	52,129	300,945	465,532	64.6
1528	—	83,861	98,242	268,353	450,456	59.6
1529	—	77,627	84,790	303,470	465,887	65.1
1530	—	68,218	61,700	197,900	327,818	60.4
1531	—	62,734	52,047	234,581	349,362	67.1
1532	—	55,233	28,678	258,254	342,165	75.5
1533	—	17,654	16,122	346,172	379,948	91.2
1534	—	14,261	9,174	321,138	344,138	93.2
1535	—	21,738	9,217	237,790	268,745	88.5
1536	—	30,426	107,943	239,118	377,487	63.3
1537	—	21,354	214,576	292,834	528,764	55.4
1538	—	42,017	44,125	187,426	273,568	68.5
1539	—	358,637	212,681	254,272	825,590	30.8
1540	—	267,745	193,728	513,390	974,863	52.6
1541	—	317,305	—	279,258	596,563	46.8
1542	—	278,068	14,443	362,254	654,765	55.3
1543	—	290,932	55,080	267,605	613,617	43.6
1544	—	207,407	478,489	231,344	917,240	25.2
1545	—	222,548	77,470	101,752	401,770	25.3
1546	—	239,096	54,592	880,544	1,174,232	75.0
1547	—	206,193	20,240	24,754	251,187	9.8
1548	—	266,165	33,323	20,565	320,053	6.4
1549	—	118,710	23,959	34,378	177,047	19.5
1550	—	1,968,589	72,808	39,023	2,080,420	1.9
1551	—	2,105,961	37,916	50,788	2,194,665	2.3
1552	—	555,341	546,405	110,650	1,212,396	9.1

Year	Copper	Billon	Silver	Gold	Total	Percentage gold
1553	—	221,941	544,087	52,766	818,788	6.4
1554	—	97,618	882,408	64,906	1,044,932	6.3
1555	—	58,557	324,098	33,557	416,212	8.0
1556	—	124,242	499,231	60,274	683,747	8.8
1557	—	99,360	276,523	181,664	557,547	32.6
1558	—	57,850	364,211	241,137	663,198	36.4
1559	—	38,880	257,326	101,089	397,295	25.4
1560	—	14,028	671,816	98,197	784,041	12.5
1561	—	36,690	826,763	109,853	973,306	11.3
1562	—	4,063	1,261,565	196,696	1,462,324	13.4
1563	—	144	1,393,316	140,898	1,534,358	9.2
1564	—	261	777,096	457,473	1,234,830	37.1
1565	—	99,355	624,212	861,080	1,584,647	54.3
1566	—	103,275	476,974	1,223,796	1,804,045	67.9
1567	—	113,224	782,595	722,979	1,618,798	44.7
1568	—	82,347	505,556	586,687	1,174,596	50.0
1569	—	140,086	290,669	315,837	746,592	42.3
1570	—	91,369	194,723	213,580	499,942	42.7
1571	—	180,712	60,252	313,555	554,519	57.5
1572	—	134,102	56,333	329,718	520,153	43.4
1573	—	93,762	405,018	254,083	752,863	33.8
1574	—	182,963	320,907	164,535	668,405	24.6
1575	—	193,734	2,109,700	149,090	2,452,524	6.1
1576	—	427,227	1,396,434	79,897	1,876,558	4.2
1577	—	336,556	918,613	93,420	1,348,589	7.0
1578	9,419	358,041	4,631,344	960,102	5,958,906	16.1
1579	40,864	137,641	1,954,769	112,549	2,245,823	5.0
1580	26,320	151,004	2,168,209	108,647	2,245,180	4.4
1581	13,671	170,933	2,773,396	47,058	3,005,058	1.6
1582	10,215	211,603	3,309,730	50,142	3,581,690	1.4
1583	5,177	275,957	2,586,480	151,497	3,019,111	5.0

Year	Copper	Billon	Silver	Gold	Total	Percentage gold
1584	9,737	185,968	2,335,208	91,774	2,622,687	3.5
1585	11,475	203,576	2,029,063	56,379	2,300,493	2.5
1586	22,128	191,507	2,058,463	83,540	2,355,638	3.5
1587	18,308	86,692	4,765,213	493,980	5,364,193	9.2
1588	33,306	125,381	2,589,178	487,047	3,234,912	15.1
1589	21,668	71,424	1,830,118	335,209	2,258,419	14.8
1590	9,588	53,229	1,505,436	427,318	1,995,571	21.4
1591	38,136	155,393	1,694,987	488,869	2,377,385	20.6
1592	43,812	265,790	1,002,431	203,691	1,515,724	13.4
1593	30,739	846,691	357,817	86,960	1,322,207	6.6
1594	3,728	922,201	799,176	66,417	1,791,522	3.7
1595	2,954	426,445	547,401	42,573	1,019,373	4.2
1596	—	199,743	767,644	46,420	1,013,807	4.6
1597	—	71,177	953,999	65,119	1,090,295	6.0
1598	6,170	26,424	430,171	16,053	478,818	3.4
1599	8,415	—	752,085	32,824	793,324	4.1
1600	2,107	—	475,253	16,756	494,116	3.4
1601	—	4,247	836,766	25,098	866,111	2.9
1602	—	—	1,457,275	19,734	1,477,009	1.3
1603	11,599	11,664	3,174,291	10,442	3,207,996	0.3
1604	9,328	—	1,297,894	10,696	1,317,918	0.8
1605	8,882	—	2,506,360	9,438	2,524,680	0.4
1606	18,283	—	1,569,472	26,065	1,613,820	1.6
1607	26,306	—	1,058,212	78,975	1,163,493	6.8
1608	40,130	—	949,496	49,507	1,039,133	4.8
1609	22,256	—	569,473	43,201	634,930	6.8
1610	24,562	—	614,292	43,608	682,462	6.4
1611	44,089	—	583,859	63,256	691,204	9.1
1612	52,307	—	400,001	42,429	494,737	8.6
1613	33,663	—	304,128	42,486	380,277	11.2
1614	44,358	—	245,145	75,631	365,134	20.7

Year	Copper	Billon	Silver	Gold	Total	Percentage gold
1615	38,351	—	1,724,773	1,527,746	3,290,870	46.4
1616	27,394	—	482,616	323,464	833,474	38.8
1617	21,897	—	426,385	143,074	591,356	24.2
1618	21,047	—	282,941	51,536	355,524	14.5
1619	14,862	—	148,318	19,998	183,178	10.9
1620	19,708	—	125,724	20,353	165,785	12.3
1621	22,614	—	157,608	28,920	209,142	13.8
1622	9,245	—	115,036	38,955	163,236	23.9
1623	—	—	166,225	60,000	226,225	26.5
1624	3,934	—	272,774	56,681	333,389	17.0
1625	7,512	—	118,853	27,455	153,820	17.8
1626	22,490	—	115,215	112,792	250,497	45.0
1627	28,856	—	160,413	159,086	348,355	45.7
1628	41,805	—	153,917	206,220	401,942	51.3
1629	20,631	—	163,822	213,860	398,313	53.7
1630	17,415	—	101,442	185,053	403,910	70.6
1631	28,855	—	41,165	506,933	576,953	87.9
1632	33,635	—	58,017	629,854	721,506	87.3
1633	27,807	—	31,540	675,222	734,569	91.9
1634	27,390	—	34,993	738,775	801,158	92.2
1635	13,261	—	24,749	849,804	887,814	95.7
1636	—	—	91,446	1,674,952	1,766,398	94.8
1637	18,496	—	153,644	3,397,572	3,569,712	95.2
1638	—	—	176,197	1,749,119	1,925,316	90.8
1639	—	—	346,640	2,175,292	2,521,932	86.3
1640	—	—	199,602	16,398,744	16,598,346	98.8
1641	—	—	412,745	26,614,998	27,027,744	98.5
1642	73,648	—	6,958,272	15,137,885	22,169,805	68.3
1643	254,111	—	13,301,872	8,327,797	21,883,780	38.0
1644	—	—	11,925,240	5,107,172	17,032,412	30.0
1645	—	—	5,386,628	2,326,105	7,712,733	30.2

Year	Copper	Billon	Silver	Gold	Total	Percentage gold
1646	—	—	2,396,750	2,039,689	4,436,439	46.0
1647	—	—	2,967,033	2,324,639	5,291,672	43.9
1648	30,000	—	6,379,560	3,584,723	9,994,283	35.9
1649	30,000	—	6,632,637	4,430,405	11,093,042	39.9
1650	—	—	3,585,177	4,078,133	7,663,310	53.2
1651	—	—	12,055,768	10,681,327	22,737,095	47.0
1652	—	—	27,758,588	11,596,320	39,354,908	29.5
1653	—	—	11,892,801	10,841,291	22,734,092	47.7
1654	1,135,489	—	3,984,475	577,104	5,697,068	10.1
1655	3,502,688	—	3,445,614	351,982	7,300,284	4.8
1656	2,642,967	—	1,140,220	1,927,842	5,711,029	33.7
1657	151,830	—	371,493	493,783	1,016,106	48.5
1658	—	—	762,505	339,456	1,101,961	30.8
1659	—	—	1,848,795	1,131,137	2,979,932	38.0
1660	—	—	1,680,116	984,533	2,664,649	36.9
1661	—	—	1,018,395	1,115,315	2,133,710	52.3
1662	—	—	4,889,928	1,092,945	5,982,873	18.3
1663	—	—	1,089,110	887,998	1,977,108	44.9
1664	—	—	1,860,891	477,905	2,338,796	20.4
1665	—	—	917,341	587,703	1,505,044	39.0
1666	—	—	2,949,650	1,043,674	3,993,324	26.1
1667	—	—	3,273,251	597,572	3,870,823	15.4
1668	—	—	2,939,200	1,525,774	18,196,941	83.8
1669	—	—	1,146,640	8,145,595	9,562,235	85.2
1670	—	—	3,359,590	4,152,795	7,512,385	55.3
1671	—	—	1,419,971	3,070,451	4,490,422	68.4
1672	—	—	2,351,649	2,512,225	4,863,874	51.7
1673	—	—	6,782,344	1,815,558	8,597,902	21.1
1674	—	646,976	887,357	722,736	2,257,069	32.0
1675	—	6,108,331	429,222	811,848	7,349,401	11.1
1676	—	6,745,219	4,939,334	553,099	12,237,652	4.5

Year	Copper	Billon	Silver	Gold	Total	Percentage gold
1677	—	6,711,971	746,948	315,917	7,774,836	4.1
1678	—	—	414,078	295,374	709,452	4.6
1679	—	—	13,810,881	7,810,950	21,621,831	36.1
1680	—	—	9,494,106	8,085,261	17,579,367	46.0
1681	—	—	4,555,212	4,824,263	9,379,775	51.4
1682	—	—	4,725,322	2,896,857	7,622,179	38.0
1683	—	—	5,705,403	1,888,546	7,593,949	24.9
1684	—	—	1,483,515	1,068,105	2,551,620	41.9
1685	—	—	4,619,104	752,899	5,372,003	14.0
1686	—	—	6,905,748	3,986,341	10,892,089	36.6
1687	—	—	2,751,113	6,826,903	9,578,016	71.3
1688	—	—	793,056	2,044,912	2,837,138	72.1
1689	—	—	2,633,457	1,797,138	4,430,595	40.6
1690	—	—	14,505,701	26,512,258	41,017,959	64.6
1691	—	—	4,204,296	13,896,332	18,100,628	76.8
1692	—	—	1,862,273	3,066,630	4,928,903	62.2
1693	—	685,392	660,839	4,679,950	6,026,181	77.6
1694	—	26,401	7,094,690	7,579,160	14,700,251	51.5
1695	—	610,165	1,022,797	7,034,188	8,667,638	81.2
1696	—	356,692	787,057	4,034,188	5,177,937	77.9
1697	—	30,100	5,806,803	5,201,559	11,038,462	47.1
1698	—	58,424	3,457,440	2,278,509	5,794,373	39.3
1699	—	28,400	453,008	1,427,711	1,909,119	74.8
1700	—	87,416	230,817	5,341,512	5,659,745	94.4
1701	—	68,005	1,300,532	4,606,210	5,974,747	77.1
1702	—	48,723	5,695,322	13,961,719	19,705,764	70.9
1703	—	79,503	10,611,402	3,900,825	14,591,730	26.7
1704	—	21,832	16,497,309	1,747,459	18,266,600	9.6
1705	—	27,811	19,270,732	3,949,478	23,248,021	17.0
1706* [a]	—	26,136	20,720,430	2,594,093	23,340,659	11.1
1707*	—	19,785	35,178,368	3,088,892	38,287,045	8.0

Year	Copper	Billon	Silver	Gold	Total	Percentage gold
1708*	—	12,462	18,609,942	1,462,094	20,084,498	7.3
1709*	—	—	127,516,473	35,429,851	162,946,324	21.7
1710*	—	3,783	94,238,525	41,259,838	135,502,146	30.4
1711*	—	—	78,739,679	35,688,915	114,428,594	31.2
1712*	—	—	48,452,150	21,384,999	69,837,149	30.6
1713*	—	—	30,796,901	17,549,337	48,346,238	36.3
1714*	—	—	9,074,938	3,434,216	12,509,154	27.4
1715*	—	8,340	24,020,922	6,978,152	31,007,414	22.5
1716*	—	—	51,138,687	19,476,728	70,615,415	27.6
1717*	—	—	25,447,245	88,971,576	114,418,761	77.8
1718*	—	—	191,228,629	127,673,708	318,902,337	40.0
1719*	—	—	90,575,294	46,651,625	137,226,919	34.0
1720*	—	—	145,512,798	23,992,627	169,505,425	14.1
1721*	—	—	61,493,890	82,659,504	144,153,394	57.3
1722*	—	—	24,984,580	38,852,339	63,836,919	60.9
1723*	—	—	32,249,052	133,996,536	166,245,588	80.6
1724*	—	—	40,579,048	121,379,268	161,958,316	74.9
1725*	—	—	83,566,022	41,179,834	124,745,856	33.0

[a] For an explanation of the construction of the totals marked with an asterisk, see Chap. 4, n. 4.

Appendix D

Manuscript Sources for the Period 1681–1725

For the period 1681–1725, the statistical data have been established from three principal sources:

(a) the Departmental Archives, as listed in Chapter 4, footnotes 2 to 8.

(b) the contrôle des boîtes in the Archives Nationales [hereafter cited as A.N.], $Z^1B.297$, for the period 1681–1703, $Z^1B.298$ for the period 1704–1723, and $Z^1B.421$ for the period 1724–1725.

(c) the états des déliverances in the A.N., as follows:

Aix-en-Provence, A.N., $Z^1B.309$;
Amiens, A.N., $Z^1B.324$, 816;
Bayonne, A.N., Z^1B309, 312;
Bordeaux, A.N., $Z^1B.314$, 315, 839;
Bourges, A.N., $Z^1B.316$, 322;
Caen, A.N., $Z^1B.325$;
Grenoble, A.N., $Z^1B.318$, 879A;
Lille, A.N., $Z^1B.319$;
Limoges, A.N., $Z^1B.315$, 883;
Lyons, A.N., $Z^1B.322$;
Montpellier, A.N., $Z^1B.323$;
Nantes, A.N., $Z^1B.324$, 905, 906;
Orleans, A.N., $Z^1B.325$;
Paris, A.N., $Z^1B.329$, 330, 920;
Poitiers, A.N., $Z^1B.331$, 332;
Rennes, A.N., $Z^1B.332$, 335, 943, 944;
Rheims, A.N., $Z^1B.333$, 940, 943;
Riom, A.N., $Z^1B.318$, 949;
La Rochelle, A.N., $Z^1B.337$, 961;
Rouen, A.N., $Z^1B.338$, 974;
Strasbourg, A.N., $Z^1B.338$, 989;
Toulouse, A.N., $Z^1B.966$;
Tours, A.N., $Z^1B.316$, 1003;
Troyes, A.N., $Z^1B.316$, 333, 1006, 1007.

Index